# ISHI'S BRAIN

# ISHI'S BRAIN

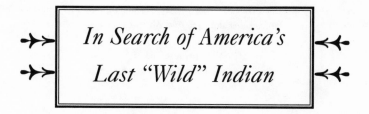

*In Search of America's*
*Last "Wild" Indian*

## Orin Starn

*W. W. Norton & Company*
*New York    London*

"When I Have Donned My Crest of Stars" from *Kiliwa Texts* by Mauricio Mixco (*University of Utah Anthropological Papers* 107 [1983]) is reprinted by permission of the University of Utah Press. "Half-Indian/Half-Mexican" by James Luna reprinted by permission of James Luna and *News from Native California*.

For information about permission to reproduce selections from this book, write to Permissions, W. W. Norton & Company, Inc., 500 Fifth Avenue, New York, NY 10110

Manufacturing by Quebecor Fairfield
Book design by BTDnyc
Production manager: Julia Druskin

Library of Congress Cataloging-in-Publication Data

Starn, Orin.
Ishi's brain : in search of America's last "wild" Indian / Orin Starn.—1st ed.
p. c.m.
Includes bibliographical references and index.
ISBN 0-393-05133-1 (hardcover)
1. Ishi, d. 1916. 2. Yana Indians—Biography. 3. Yana Indians—Anthropometry. 4. Kroeber, A. L. (Alfred Louis), 1876–1960—Relations with Yana Indians. 5. Kroeber, Theodora—Relations with Yana Indians. 6. Human remains (Archaeology)—Repatriation—United States. 7. Human remains (Archaeology)—Moral and ethical aspects—United States. 8. Cultural property—Repatriation—United States. I. Title.
E99.Y23 .I785 2004
979.4004'9757—dc22

20030201066

W. W. Norton & Company, Inc., 500 Fifth Avenue, New York, N.Y. 10110
www.wwnorton.com

W. W. Norton & Company Ltd., Castle House, 75/76 Wells Street, London W1T 3QT
1 2 3 4 5 6 7 8 9 0

TO ROBIN

and the memory of Rosalie Bertram, *wenem kuhlah*

# CONTENTS

# ISHI'S BRAIN

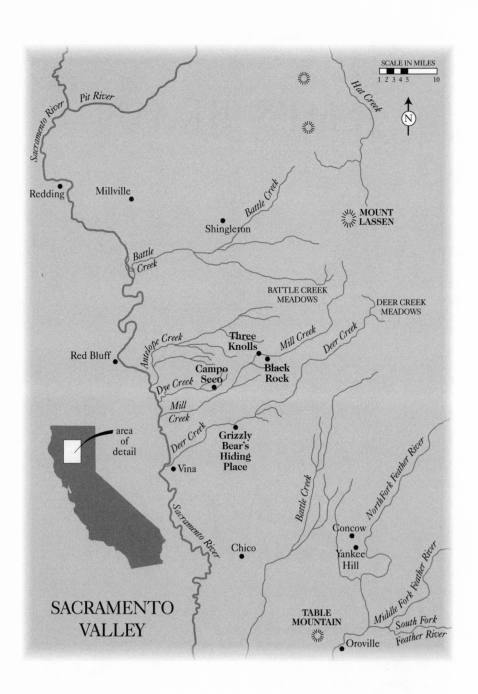

SCALE IN MILES
1 2 3 4 5          10

N

Pit River

Sacramento River

Hat Creek

Redding

Millville

Battle Creek

MOUNT
LASSEN

Shingleton

Battle
Creek

BATTLE CREEK
MEADOWS

DEER CREEK
MEADOWS

Antelope Creek

Three
Knolls

Mill Creek

Deer Creek

Red Bluff

Campo
Seco

Black
Rock

Dye Creek

Mill
Creek

Deer Creek

Grizzly
Bear's
Hiding
Place

area
of
detail

Vina

Battle Creek

North Fork Feather River

Concow

Yankee
Hill

Chico

Middle Fork Feather River

South Fork
Feather River

SACRAMENTO
VALLEY

TABLE
MOUNTAIN

Oroville

# TRAILS TO ISHI

I grew up in the sixties just across the bay from San Francisco in the university town of Berkeley. Our house was down the street from the abandoned campus parking lot that activists commandeered in 1969 for People's Park, the Elysian Fields of Berkeley's counterculture and the meeting point for protest marches against the Vietnam War. My dovish parents dragged me to the biggest rallies, but I also had to take violin lessons, even ballroom dancing class up in the Berkeley hills. Great was my adolescent relief when the tear gas drifting down from People's Park meant my mother could not drive me to the year-end luau, for which I'd been garbed in the requisite flowery Hawaiian shirt. Later that week, the riot police shot down a rock-throwing protester on nearby Telegraph Avenue.

The peace marches, tear gas, and police helicopters form part of my Berkeley memories—together with baseball cards, slingshot practice, and trolling for crawdads with hotdogs on a string at Lake Temescal. And like so many American kids, before and after that turbulent time, I was fascinated by Indians. My early interest was of a very traditional Middle American variety, fostered in a YMCA summer camp where we practiced archery, received a "secret" Indian name, and made beaded "wampum" for our parents. I was not old enough to want to try peyote or go off to live in some vegetarian commune's tepee. At this time in Berkeley, however, a young generation of hippies and radicals was enshrining Native Americans as icons of countercultural spirituality and community, even as inspirations to rebellion. One leaflet explaining the takeover of People's Park featured a picture of a resolute Geronimo with his rifle. That the protest leaders were white did not stop them from acting in the name of the Apache chief and "the spirit of the Costanoan Indians" who had once roamed the East Bay's marshlands.

I'm not sure just when I first heard about Ishi. Then, as now, every California fourth grader learns the well-known story of this last "wild" Indian in North America. Along with a few other holdouts from his tiny Yahi tribe, Ishi had hidden out in the hills above the Sacramento Valley for more than fifty years. The others died, and Ishi was captured in 1911, then brought to stay in a San Francisco museum. Since my father was a historian of the Italian Renaissance, we lived in Italy for several years and I went to fourth grade in a town near Florence. There we were taught about Garibaldi and the Risorgimento, not American Indians—the *pelle rossi*, as the Italians knew them from spaghetti Westerns. I do remember—sometime later and back in the United States—being taken to Kroeber Hall on the Berkeley campus, named after the famous anthropologist who became Ishi's main guardian in San Francisco. One corner of Kroeber Hall's exhibition space was devoted to Ishi. It included arrowheads that Ishi had made at the museum, among them one fashioned from the royal blue glass of a Phillips' Milk of Magnesia bottle. I was mesmerized by the perfect symmetry and form of these objects—and the idea of heading off to the hunt with a real bow you had made yourself.

A trip to a friend's family summer cabin took me near Ishi's country for the first time when I was in junior high. The cabin was an A-frame in a vacation development behind Mount Lassen, close to a reservoir packed with waterskiers and houseboats. It was six hours from Berkeley, and the last part of the drive wound over the mountains by Highway 32, which runs for a time next to the black boulders, powerful rapids, and deep emerald pools of Deer Creek. This stretch of road is many miles upstream from the territory once inhabited by Ishi and the last Yahi survivors. Blissfully ignorant of this fact, I was busy imagining a long-ago Ishi spearing salmon in the stream's shimmering water—or maybe even some as yet undiscovered tribesman at that very moment monitoring the slow progress of our giant fake-wood paneled station wagon from his secret lookout in the cliffs above. Ishi and his people held the same mystique for my friend as they did for me. As a tribute a few years later, he posed himself for his individual high school yearbook picture, standing next to Deer Creek clad only in an imitation Yahi breechcloth.

As a judgmental teenager, I had no interest in a professor's life. I found my parents' Berkeley faculty world of lectures and dinner parties stuffy and artificial. In 1981, I left college and headed off with a friend to the Navajo Reservation in a decrepit VW bug. The principal at Shiprock Alternative High School, a pony-tailed Navajo poet and educator, looked bemused at the sight of a pair of white nineteen-year-olds appearing out of the desert to offer themselves as volunteers in his school. After he called our parents to make sure we were not runaways, it was finally agreed that we could sleep on mattresses in an abandoned storeroom. I lived in that storeroom for the next year.

I was the quintessential young bleeding-heart idealist, of course, the latest in that wave of missionaries, aid workers, and others who'd come to "help" the Indians in the blasted-out, impoverished town of Shiprock. Still, with the modest enough purpose of making myself useful at the school, I tried to avoid coming across as a suck-up or a savior. My main duties were to assist the school's two cooks and janitor, all of whom were glad enough for an extra hand. "You better clean that toilet really good," Mary Kehane, the old Navajo janitor, liked to tell me. One of the cooks, Jeanette, was Hopi. As we prepared lunch, she and Faye, the Navajo cook, sparred over the radio tuned loud to their favorite country music station. "Hopis don't even know how to peel potatoes," Faye would taunt Jeanette. "And you neither, *bilagáana*," she'd grin in my direction, employing the Navajo word for "white man."

If drawn to Indians, I knew little about them when I went off to Navajoland. I'd gone to Berkeley's integrated schools with whites, blacks, Japanese Americans, and the children of Vietnamese boat people, but I'd never met an Indian in the flesh, at least as far as I knew. Along with the vague idea of reservation poverty, my exposure was limited to the mish-mash of myth and stereotype offered up by Hollywood and popular culture—the bloodthirsty redskins who roasted a captured soldier alive on a spit in a grisly Western I saw as a child; the slender, Pocahontas-like Indian princess on the package of the Land O'Lakes butter with which we spread our Sunday morning pancakes; and, of course, Ishi, alone in the canyon of Deer Creek as the world closed in around him. So pervasive have these images become of a vanished or vanishing people of the wigwam, the war bonnet, and the buffalo that some Americans still do not know quite what to make of the real thing. A young Creek friend of mine still laughs about her first meeting with her freshman college roommate. "Do you live in a tepee?" the wide-eyed girl had asked. Kelly, the daughter of a schoolteacher and a businessman, explained that she'd grown up in a comfortable English Tudor-style house in her hometown of Atmore, Alabama.

My sojourn in Shiprock forced me to see beyond the stereotypes for the first time. At the high school where I was volunteering, the social studies teacher was Marvin Whitehorn, a thin, thoughtful man with a wry sense of humor. One Saturday afternoon, Marvin invited me to his isolated hogan—the circular, mud-walled traditional Navajo dwelling—in the desert toward Mesa Verde and the Colorado border. It seemed strange that no one else was there, but Marvin said he lived by himself except for his old uncle, who had a trailer by the hogan and was away in Gallup. We ducked out of the late fall chill into the hogan and sat on the sheepskin and rugs that covered the dirt floor. As we chatted over cups of sugary steaming coffee, I noticed that Marvin was edging quite close to me. I assumed that he was hard of hearing or that this was some kind of Navajo custom. I'd grown up in the tolerant Bay Area with the occasional homoerotic longing, but it had never occurred to me that an Indian could be gay. Weren't Indians those manly, heterosexual warriors who made off with white women in the Westerns and dime store novels? Marvin was too much the gentleman to press any further that afternoon. Many months later, after I'd left the reservation, I received a card in the mail. It had a little puppy with a red bow. "Thinking of You," the kind, wistful Marvin had signed it.

I returned to college in 1982 at the University of Chicago and, still the weak-blooded Californian, shivered through the frozen winter by Lake Michigan. I thought about Marvin sometimes, but in the dorm for transfer students met my soulmate and future wife, Robin Kirk. After finishing school, we backpacked around South America for a year, stopping along the way to teach English and do volunteer work, hitchhiking through the tropical ruins of Paraguay's Jesuit missions, taking a boat up the Amazon River, and plunging for a swim into the impossibly cold blue waters of Lake Titicaca. I found the Andes especially moving on that first of many journeys there. It was a beautiful, outsized land of Inca ruins, jagged green mountains, and indomitable villagers who somehow kept their humor and humanity about them as they eked out a living from their tiny plots.

I decided to go on to graduate school in anthropology, and to specialize in the Andes. Although I was coming back around to an academic career just like my father, I was still enough the rebel to want nothing to do with any traditional kind of anthropology—the study of odd tribal customs in exotic places like the Kalahari Desert and the Trobriand Islands. I had already learned that anthropologists were sometimes resented by the "primitive" people they studied. One day in Shiprock, just a week or two after my friend and I had arrived, I was playing basketball with some students at the high school. I was still just a young college student, but Ervin Yazzie believed I was an anthropologist there to observe the Navajo. "What the fuck are you here for?" he suddenly asked during a break. Ervin was nineteen like me and a tough kid with dark glasses, a knife-scarred face, and a passion for Black Sabbath and ACDC. That we would later become occasional pool hall buddies did not keep him from pressing the attack on this first encounter. "You come to study the fucking savages?" he said. "Like me? Fuck you, then!" Later, an older Navajo school counselor told a gentle joke that captured the sheer oddity of anthropology's obsession back then with tribal peoples like the Navajo. "How many in a Navajo family?" she quizzed me. When I shook my head, she answered, "Five. Father, mother, brother, sister—and anthropologist."

In my youthful idealism, I was attracted to anthropology by the possibility of transforming it. Couldn't an anthropologist play a more positive part in understanding, and even changing, the world? As I entered graduate school at Stanford University, a new generation of feminist, Marxist, and other radical professors was shaking up the discipline. They demanded more attention to the harm done to beleaguered tribal peoples by Western expansion, and, more broadly, to the study of poverty, war, social inequality, and other topics often overlooked in the older, more clinical paradigm of anthropology, which involved decoding the secrets of primitive cultures. My fellow graduate students and I immersed ourselves in Marx, Gramsci, Foucault, and other new and old apostles of anti-establishment thought—and declared our commitment to a more activist anthropology. It was the era of Ronald Reagan's presidency, and we devoted our spare time to such causes as the struggle against unlawful U.S. military intervention in Central America, the campaign to force universities to divest their holdings in apartheid-era South Africa, and the demand for funding to combat AIDS, which was then killing hundreds of San Franciscans. I grew my hair long and wore a red bandana and Peruvian poncho on winter days. The secretary at the anthropology department, Craig, who moonlighted as the guitarist in a local rock band, called me "Chief" with friendly derision.

I went off to the Andes for my dissertation research and lived for a year in a village in the dusty foothills of northern Peru. There I documented an area farmers' movement for self-help and justice, and, as anthropologists often do, formed friendships with local residents that have lasted for almost two decades. After an interlude back in the Bay Area to finish my dissertation, Robin and I returned once more to Peru for several years, and Robin worked there as a freelance journalist for National Public Radio and many newspapers. When I was offered a professor's job at Duke University in 1991, we decided to return home. Robin joined Human Rights Watch as their researcher in the war-torn South American country of Colombia. She flew there often to meet with survivors and gather information about the atrocities that were only too frequent and familiar. We had our first child and bought a big old bungalow in Durham, North Carolina.


Though our home was a continent away from California, I'd never forgotten about Ishi. By now almost forty, I understood that my continuing interest in things Indian formed part of a social pattern, all the way back to my childhood and teenage fantasies. "There has been all the time in the white American soul, a dual feeling about the Indian," D. H. Lawrence once wrote. "The desire to extirpate. And the contradictory desire to glorify him." The United States came into existence by killing and relocating Indians in order to seize their land. That conquest was rationalized by strong beliefs in the moral and racial inferiority of the continent's original inhabitants. What sort of people would roast a man alive, as that old Western had it? Modern incarnations of the Evil Savage have Indians as welfare cheats, lazy drunkards—or as greedy, corrupt "bingo tribes" with giant Las Vegas–style casinos. That less than one-fifth of this country's almost one thousand tribes have a casino has not prevented some Americans from believing that Indians everywhere have become fabulous millionaires.

At the same time, paradoxically, whites have long admired and even idolized Indians. I had dreamed as a boy of snaring rabbits and living off the land just like Ishi; in high school, I gazed at a poster of Sitting Bull I'd pinned to my bedroom wall as if the existential secrets of the universe might be revealed to me in the grave brown eyes of the Lakota warrior and holy man. In the late nineteenth century, the government was already stamping the figure of an impressive, war-bonneted brave on every nickel, making the Indian a symbol of freedom and self-reliance for a nation in search of its own distinctive identity. More recently, the fantasy of the Noble Savage has been updated in the ubiquitous portrayal of Indians as the saintly guardians of nature, the spiritual wisdom of the ancients, and all things pure and good. You'd never guess that any Indian ever had an evil thought or that tribal life was anything but idyllic from children's books like *Star Boy*, *The Girl Who Ran With Horses,* and *Brother Earth, Sister Sky* or movies like *Dances with Wolves* and *Spirit.* These romantic images show us Native Americans as a people of a mythical, bygone past. The truth is that there are more than two million Indians in America today. They include waitresses and novelists, Wal-Mart clerks and army paratroopers, lawyers and truckers, and at least one well-known professional golfer (the Navajo Notah Begay III has earned more than four million dollars on the PGA tour).

For all the perils of romanticization, I was still drawn to Ishi and his story. I hadn't ever lost my little boy's curiosity about the mysteries of the Yahi. To return to Ishi would be a chance to backpack in the dark canyons and try to understand how the Yahi had eluded pursuit by armed settlers for so long so close above the Sacramento Valley. At the same time, as an anthropologist myself, I was intrigued by the role of Alfred Kroeber, the founding father of California Indian anthropology, in the saga of Ishi. What kind of care had Kroeber and his colleagues afforded this vulnerable survivor?

Lately in the Andes, too, I'd hiked for the first time into areas that were just recovering from the devastation of war and rebellion. That conflict had pitted Peru's armed forces against a band of Maoist guerrillas called *Sendero Luminoso*, the Shining Path, and left tens of thousands dead in the 1980s. In the cold mist of the high moors, I walked with a Peruvian journalist friend through the charred, abandoned ruins of farm villages torched in the fighting. We spoke with Quechua-speaking refugees who'd watched the guerrillas hack their loved ones to death (the army had killed its share in other areas)—and heard their plans for rebuilding their lives now that the war was ending with the defeat of the

Shining Path and the capture of its leader, Abimael Guzmán. Listening to these tales made me think back with a powerful new immediacy to the Yahi and the period of Indian extermination and removal in my own home state. I felt a growing kind of duty, even obligation, to attempt to learn more about those brutal years of hatred and violence in Gold Rush California a century and a half ago.

The time was ripe for another look at Ishi's life and legend. It had been almost forty years since the publication of Theodora Kroeber's *Ishi in Two Worlds*, the pioneering work by Kroeber's widow that had made this last survivor of aboriginal America into almost a household name. Those long decades had brought the end of Jim Crow and the cold war, the advent of the computer age, and the rise of pride in their heritage among Native Americans and other minority groups. By now, I knew, there was new scholarship by archaeologists, linguists, and other researchers about Ishi and his people. How well had Theodora Kroeber's once authoritative-seeming biography held up against the test of time? What major or even minor discoveries had the latest research brought about the life of California's most famous Indian?

And what did Indians now think of Ishi? That the last Yahi seemed to be happy in San Francisco and to hold no bitterness has doubtless enhanced his appeal to whites across the decades. Thomas Waterman, the anthropologist, even claimed that Ishi was "readier to make friends with whites than other Indians like himself," perhaps a residue of an older Yahi suspicion toward surrounding tribes. Here was the wildest and most Indian of Indians—and yet one who seemed to forgive the sins committed against his people. By contrast, this ostensible conformism made Ishi unappealing to many young Indian radicals of the Vietnam War years. They wanted rebels and warriors for their heroes— Geronimo, Sitting Bull, and Crazy Horse. I'd never seen Ishi's name mentioned in any of the many manifestos of the Red Power era. I learned later that some activists had viewed Ishi as an Uncle Tom, and still others had not even heard of him.

Yet there were signs of new views. Some Indians warmed now to Ishi as an icon of suffering and resilience in the face of conquest. *What Wild Indian?* the Maidu artist Frank Tuttle entitled a painting of Ishi. The real savages were the Anglo pioneers, Tuttle and other native activists believed. In 1998, Liz Dominguez described her emotion at listening for the first time to a cassette copy of Ishi's Yahi chanting, many hours of which the anthropologists had recorded at the museum back in 1911.

"It brought chills to me when I listened to the songs and stories that Ishi shared. It was as if he was trying so hard to leave something behind, to say to all that he and his people had been here, as if he was leaving a legacy in exactly the way he was taught to do, that being oral tradition." For Dominguez, a descendant of the Chumash of California's central coast, Ishi was no race traitor. He was an ancestor of whom all Indians could and should be proud.

I hoped that a return to Ishi could somehow be a point of entry for me into Native California. This was a California about which I still knew almost nothing except for a few statistics and some scattered reading. The latest figures showed a Native American population of 242,000 (although more than half were Navajo, Cherokee, and others from out of state, making Native Californians a minority within a minority). Among the dozens of rancherias—as California's small reservations were called—I knew the names of the Death Valley Timbi-Sha Shoshone Rancheria, the Hopland Rancheria just north of the Napa Valley's wine country, and the Quartz Valley Rancheria west of Mount Shasta, to name just a few. Many other Indians were still pursuing official recognition. Getting on the roll of "recognized" tribes meant eligibility for free health care and other government services—and also the right to have their own casinos, accorded to tribes by their semi-sovereign status under the law. Robin and I came out to California every August for a vacation week in my family's old cabin in the Trinity Alps. We'd noticed the new billboards for the Feather Falls and Win-River Casino along Interstate 5 in the Sacramento Valley. I wanted to get off the highway to learn more about the people so long invisible to me and to so many other inhabitants of my native state.

In 1997, Robin and I made our first expedition to Yahi country. The main road through the foothills is a winding gravel track called the Ponderosa Highway. Our old Toyota Corona kicked up an angry plume of dust under the late summer's fierce sun. We bumped along for many miles without seeing another car except for a van of sweaty prison inmates in orange jumpsuits back from clearing a fire trail somewhere out in the bush. The temperatures in this still wild and mostly unpopulated chaparral can be among the hottest in the country. On this late August day it reached 110 degrees.

It was a relief when the sun began to sink. We'd worried about our baby, Frances, if our old car broke down and stranded us. Now at day's end, however, the temperature was already dropping, and the night's cool was not far away. We pitched our tent that night by Antelope Creek, the next watershed up from Mill Creek and two up from Deer Creek. Over millions of years, these streams have slashed their own deep canyons through the badlands of scrub oak and black volcanic rock as they wound down to the Sacramento Valley. The area where we were camping had been the northernmost part of the Yahi homeland in the old days.

In the dusk's last orange-red light, I walked up the ridge above Antelope Creek to gaze across the silent hills. It was in this patch of California that Ishi's ancestors had found a way to live for thousands of years—and where his tribe had at last been hunted down and almost exterminated near the end of the Gold Rush. I dreamed that fall, back in North Carolina, about the fast green waters in the stone-walled canyons and the shadowy shapes of the Yahi who'd lived and died there. I had no idea just what I could say about Ishi's story that would be new or different. I only knew that I wanted to get back to California again as soon as I could.

It was not until the following summer that I returned. I wanted to see what else I could find out about Ishi and his legacy and, more concretely, whether I was just wasting my time with a subject that was already exhausted. A man I wanted to consult was Jim Johnston, the Forest Service's chief archaeologist for a district that included the foothills once inhabited by Ishi's Yahi. Johnston was based in the mountain town of Susanville. He agreed to meet me in his office there in the large Forest Service compound with its gated lot of road equipment and lime-green official jeeps.

A bearded man in his early forties, Jim Johnston had grown up in the mountains and earned an M.A. in archaeology at Sacramento State under the dean of northern California archaeology, Jerald Johnson. In jeans and a flannel shirt, Johnston was easygoing that day yet guarded with his information. Looting of ancient village sites was still a large problem in northern California's backcountry. There were no golden treasures to be excavated, but whites in the Sacramento Valley had long hunted arrowheads for fun and sometimes for framed wall displays—a suburban touch of the ancient and exotic. The most aggressive looters brought in backhoes and wire screens. Johnston had arranged one stake-out in Yahi country that resulted in the arrest of two men. One, a junior high teacher, had thousands of arrowheads, stone mortars, and other artifacts squirreled away in his garage.

I also knew that Jim Johnston was part of a small expedition that had rediscovered the last hideout of Ishi and his band of survivors. *Wowunupo Mu Tetna*, or Grizzly Bear's Hiding Place, held a legendary place in the lore about the Yahi. An abandoned bear den that Ishi's fugitive people had taken over for a secret camp, Grizzly Bear's Hiding Place was somewhere in the lower reaches of Deer Creek's canyon, I knew. Still, the spot was so remote, rugged, and choked by brush that no one had been able to find it until Johnston and a companion located it in 1991. Johnston was not about to give me any clues to the location of Grizzly Bear's Hiding Place. He didn't want this fabled site trampled by curious backpackers or picked over by looters.

Johnston did mention something that caught my attention. Back down in Oroville, he said, local Maidu Indians were trying to recover Ishi's ashes from the San Francisco Bay Area. The ashes were still in a black Pueblo Indian pot in the Olivet Memorial Park cemetery, where they had lain since Ishi's death in 1916. Now the Maidu wanted to bring Ishi's remains back for reburial in Yahi territory beneath Mount Lassen. And they were raising awkward questions, too—about what was and wasn't in the pot, and about what might have been done with Ishi's brain.

I was immediately curious. I'd read that the Maidu had been enemies of Ishi's Yahi. Why would the Maidu care anything now about Ishi almost a century after his death? What might their campaign reveal about Native California today? And were they right to suspect there was some undiscovered secret about the fate of Ishi's brain? Johnston flipped through his Rolodex. He found the phone number of the man he said was behind the demand for Ishi's repatriation, a Maidu by the name of Art Angle.

Back in Berkeley the next day, I picked up the phone to call Art Angle. This simple act launched me on a strange adventure involving a promise broken, lost letters unearthed, a cross-country trail of secrets shared and concealed, and a missing body part discovered. Neither Art Angle nor I had ever dreamed of the places to which the search for Ishi's brain would take us, or what would happen when the truth emerged.

It was, for me, an improbable journey of discovery. The trail to Ishi's brain forced me back into the history of my chosen profession, anthropology, and that of Indian suffering and survival in California. Then, too, it led me into the changing mixed-up world of Native California today—a world of acorn soup and family barbecues, sweat lodges and evangelical churches, powerful personalities and varied careers, and bitterness about a heartbreaking past. Again and again, however, I returned to the man at the center of it all—Ishi, the museum curiosity, the last of his tribe, the explorer of a new world unknown to him, the man whose real Indian name remains a mystery even today. Here I was surprised, even astonished, to discover just how much mythmaking and folklore have obscured the realities of Ishi's life. At the same time, I grew intrigued by the myths and the mythmakers themselves, that diverse collection of people who have found their own meanings in the story of America's last "wild" Indian. This book is my chronicle of the search for Ishi's brain and what I found out about Ishi and his legend along the way.

But enough: *git'ip'iti*, as you might say in Yahi, Ishi's tongue: "Let's hear the story."

# One

# A "COMPROMISE BETWEEN SCIENCE AND SENTIMENT"

I t's hard to write about even now, but my story begins with a death, a difficult death: Saturday, March 25, 1916, sometime in the afternoon. The body of Ishi, the last known surviving "wild" California Indian, lay on the autopsy table at a San Francisco hospital. He had died, with blood gushing from his nose and mouth, just a few hours before. "Considerably emaciated Indian 168 cm. in length," the doctor noted. In his final months the tuberculosis had wasted Ishi to skin and bone, and his long black hair was streaked with gray. The doctor, Jean V. Cooke, a well-regarded young pathologist, made a straight cut down the torso, peeling back the thin yellow layer of fat to remove and examine the liver, lungs, and heart. He sawed around the skullcap and lifted out the brain—oyster-white, furrowed, and glistening under the lights. Cooke weighed the organ and completed the rest of his measurements and note taking. Then he stitched up the cadaver for transport to a local under-taker for embalming.

The newspapers were already preparing their stories about Ishi's death for the evening editions. Ishi was famous, after all. The capture in 1911 of the "Wild Man of Deer Creek" had caused a national sensation and turned him into an early-twentieth-century American celebrity. After hiding out for decades in the hills of northern California, he'd been found hungry and half-naked near the town of Oroville. The well-known Berkeley anthropologist Alfred Kroeber brought Ishi to live in his museum above San Francisco's Golden Gate Park. Kroeber told the newspapers that this "uncontaminated and uncivilized" Indian was an unprecedented find for his young science of anthropology, then devoted to the study of primitive peoples. Thousands of San Franciscans streamed to the museum to watch this last survivor of his small Yahi tribe demonstrate how to chip stone arrowheads, or, if the weather was nice, to construct a little Indian house of branches and bark on the hill in back. Ishi lived for almost five years in San Francisco. He had fallen sick at the end of 1915, and died on March 25, 1916, in the hospital next to his museum home.

As the newspapers had it, Ishi's death was more than just the passing of a single man, or even a tribe. It ended an epoch in human history. "ISHI, LAST OF STONE AGE INDIANS, IS DEAD," reported the *San Francisco Chronicle*. Most Californians of that time assumed that their growing state's Indian tribes belonged to an earlier, inferior evolutionary stage—and were doomed to extinction. The land's first peoples would evaporate "like the dissipating mist in the presence of the morning sun of the Saxon," a San Francisco newspaperman had predicted in 1850. As if settling the West were a fact of nature and a primordial plan rather than the will of those in power, the doctrine of Manifest Destiny absolved Americans from any personal responsibility for occupying another people's land, killing those who resisted, and confining the remainder to reservations.

This conquest took more than three hundred years, from Plymouth Rock to the defeat of the last "hostile" tribes in the Great Plains and Geronimo's surrender in northern Mexico at the end of the nineteenth century. The subjugation of California's Indians was a fast and ferocious final chapter in the takeover of North America. Although decimated by an earlier Spanish colonization, an estimated 150,000 Indians still survived just before the Gold Rush of 1849 and its accompanying flood of fortune seekers arriving to the new Eden of California in covered wagons or on clipper ships around Cape Horn. These Indians—the Hupa, Miwok, Karok, Ohlone, Yuki, and Chumash, to name just a few—were scattered in as many as five hundred groups across this vast and varied land. None was anywhere near so large as the Southwest's Navajo or the Lakota of the Great Plains ("tribelets," Alfred Kroeber called California's native societies), but each had its own territory and a bundle of myths and customs passed down along the generations. Approximately ninety distinct languages were spoken by California's native peoples, many more if you counted the dialects. An Indian could walk from present-day San Jose to Santa Cruz, a distance of just twenty miles, and encounter a tongue as different from his or her own as English is from Amharic or Urdu.

By the start of the twentieth century, however, only about 20,000 Native Californians remained. In just a few catastrophic decades, more than three-quarters of the indigenous population had succumbed to disease or been hunted down by settlers anxious to make the newest American state safe for their families and their own brand of progress and civilization. Lucy Young, an old Indian who grew up inland from the coastal town of Mendocino, recalled her grandfather dreaming about the coming apocalypse. "My grandpa say: 'White Rabbit'—he mean white people—gonta devour our grass, our seed, our living. We won't have nothing more, this world."

Ishi, the last Yahi, grew up in this time of turmoil and terror for the people of Native California. Hardly a man of the Stone Age, he was probably born sometime in the 1860s as the Civil War raged back east. In those years, the Sacramento Valley just below the ancestral Yahi foothills was filling up with homesteaders who'd come across the Great Plains to claim the promised land of California as their own. Violent clashes had broken out between the Yahi and the settlers, but the whites had the numbers and carried out attacks that culminated in 1871 with the massacre of as many as thirty Indians in a place called Kingsley Cave. At about the time of Ishi's birth, the surviving Yahi went into hiding to evade capture, no longer daring the risk of open confrontation. Near the end, a half century later, only four remained. The main hideout of Ishi and his companions was the place they called *Wowunupo Mu Tetna*, or Grizzly Bear's Hiding Place. It lay concealed beneath cliffs in the brushy canyon of Deer Creek just a few short turns from valley farmland.

Ishi's wilderness life was not so "primitive" and "uncontaminated" as Kroeber and his fellow anthropologists wanted the world to believe. To avoid starvation, he and the others stole canned beans, bags of barley, and tins of biscuit from nearby cabins, even poaching the occasional sheep. It was true, however, that the secluded Yahi also preserved many of their native ways—the old traditions of Native California. They harpooned salmon in the creeks, boiled acorn mush in their finely woven baskets, and sowed blankets from the furs of coyote, wildcat, and raccoons. From his elders, Ishi learned dozens of Yahi songs and the origin myths of his people. A full twenty years after the end of the Plains Wars,

Ishi was the last living Indian in the continental United States altogether outside white society's orbit. He was the "only man in America
who doesn't know Christmas," Alfred Kroeber once said.

In the decades after Ishi's death, it was often assumed that no
Indians remained anywhere in California. The state would come instead
to conjure the images of Hollywood and Silicon Valley, hot tubs and nou-
velle cuisine, crowded freeways and overpriced real estate. Even today,
few people know more about the Indians of California than that they
have casinos. It's a little-recognized fact that there are 107 small Indian
reservations across the state, or, astonishingly, that living speakers of
some 50 different native languages can be found even now. Ishi was the
last Yahi. He wasn't the last California Indian.

For much of the twentieth century, however, the survivors of
California's first peoples lay low and forgotten. They were concealed not
in remote wilderness but in plain sight in the tiny towns of the Klamath
River Basin, tumbleweed trailers in the Mojave Desert, and similar out-
of-the-way places. Only during the sixties and seventies did Indians
begin to call loud attention to their plight everywhere across the country. Influenced by the Black Panthers, the Chicano Brown Berets, and
other radical groups, a generation of young Indian militants began to
protest reservation poverty, broken treaties, and other injustices suffered by their people. "We're the landlords of this country, the rent is
due, and we're here to collect!" announced Clyde Bellecourt, a leader of
the American Indian Movement, the best-known of several new Indian
organizations formed in this period.

A first and spectacular bit of guerrilla theater was the occupation of
Alcatraz Island, a few miles out on the bay from Ishi's one-time home in
the San Francisco museum. In 1969, a band of young Indians seized the
legendary, by then abandoned, island prison as a kind of liberated
republic; they demanded attention to the needs of their tribes, and
attracted worldwide press coverage with support from celebrities like the
comedian Jonathan Winters, the movie star Anthony Quinn, and the rock
band Creedence Clearwater Revival (the fashionability of the movements for Black and Red Power during the Vietnam War years led one
pundit to coin the term "radical chic"). The year-long occupation of
Alcatraz would be followed by protests at Plymouth Rock and Mount
Rushmore, and, finally, a standoff with the FBI at Wounded Knee, South
Dakota, the symbolically charged spot where soldiers had gunned down
three hundred Sioux refugees a century before. Many ordinary Indians

were suspicious of the long-haired, bandanna-wearing young radicals, but the activism of the sixties and seventies was a watershed for Native America. It was a daring, aggressive new cry for rights and recognition.

In these last decades, American Indians have pressed claims for land, sovereignty, and even the return of bones and sacred objects spirited off to museum collections. In California, one can speak of a people back from extinction, with new reservations and new money earned from "gaming establishments," as the tribes sometimes prefer to call their casinos—a healthy $1.5 billion dollars in 2000 alone. My uncle found a job as a security guard at the Confederated Tribes of the Grand Ronde's Spirit River Casino in Oregon. The Indians treated him well, he reported.

It was perhaps inevitable that the retribalization of California would lead back to Ishi, still the state's most famous Indian. One man in particular decided that Ishi's body should now be removed from San Francisco for burial in his native canyonlands. Art Angle was a Korean War veteran, a trucker, and a Maidu Indian. The Concow branch of the Maidu were once the southern neighbors of Ishi's Yahi and are centered today in Angle's hometown of Oroville, the valley town where Ishi had been taken prisoner almost a century before. A reporter from the *Los Angeles Times* heard about Angle and came up to Oroville to interview him in 1996. "We need to look at what we can do for him [Ishi] in the best way we can, to put him to rest in a proper way," Angle said.

The circumstances surrounding Ishi's death were complex and controversial. Alfred Kroeber was in New York as Ishi wasted away from a white man's disease against which Indians had no immunity and for which no cure existed. In his thirties then, Kroeber, the world's leading expert on Native California, had watched just a year before as tuberculosis ravaged and killed his own beautiful, young first wife, Henriette. He demanded daily bulletins on Ishi's health from his junior colleagues back on the West Coast.

Saxton Pope, Ishi's doctor, wanted to conduct an autopsy when Ishi died. Although he had befriended Ishi in San Francisco, Pope was also very much the scientist. He'd always been curious about the physiology of this last Yahi Indian, a unique and exotic specimen of humankind to the surgeon's clinical eye. On hearing of Pope's planned dissection, however, Alfred Kroeber was incensed. The majority of California's tribes had buried or sometimes cremated their dead with as little contact as possible with the cadaver. As Kroeber noted in his monumental *Handbook of the Indians of California*, it was often considered "unclean" and even dangerous to touch a dead body; in many cases, the person who handled the corpse had later to fast, pray or undergo other rituals of purification before he or she could rejoin society. Ishi, Kroeber knew, had learned that white doctors and medical students sometimes dissected cadavers and was appalled by the thought of anyone's body being sectioned up after death. Kroeber believed that an autopsy would be a gross violation of Ishi's trust.

On March 24, 1916, the day before Ishi died, Kroeber wrote Edward Gifford, the young acting director of his museum back in San Francisco, to stop Ishi's dissection. Restrained and formal by nature, Kroeber was unable to conceal his emotion on this occasion. "Please shut down on it," he said of the planned autopsy. "We propose to stand by our friends. If there is any talk of the interests of science, then say for me that science can go to hell."

That letter arrived too late to prevent the postmortem. Gifford nonetheless reassured Kroeber by return post that the cremated ashes of their Yahi friend had been laid to rest with respect at the Olivet Memorial Park cemetery just south of San Francisco. It was those ashes that Art Angle now wanted to bring back to Ishi's native Yahi country so many years later. Angle believed the cemetery could be persuaded or forced to go along with the plan.

But a major problem remained: the whereabouts of Ishi's brain. A rumor had long circulated among the Indians around Oroville that the organ was never cremated with the rest of Ishi's body. According to this story, Ishi's brain had become a gruesome trophy of white science, pickled in formaldehyde and still shelved somewhere in a laboratory or museum. Art Angle was disturbed by these tales. He couldn't imagine burying Ishi without his brain. He didn't want to proceed with his campaign for Ishi's repatriation without resolving the question once and for all.

Cooke's autopsy report had recorded the size and even weight of Ishi's brain, exactly 1,300 grams. In all of the known papers, essays, and books about Ishi, however, only a single cryptic reference existed concerning the brain once it had been removed in the dissection. This mention came in the very last pages of *Ishi in Two Worlds*, the biography of Ishi published by Theodora Kroeber in 1961. Theodora Kroeber provided a harrowing account of the hunting down of Ishi's people, but then portrayed Ishi as contented and at peace in San Francisco under the protection of her husband, Alfred, and other sympathetic whites. She very much wanted her book to be a parable of healing, reconciliation, and mutual respect across the divides of race and culture. That Ishi had been dissected in almost certain violation of his own wishes was awkward for Theodora's redemptive story line. She acknowledged that the autopsy occurred. Yet she emphasized her husband's passionate opposition to it; trusting the goodwill of Edward Gifford, the museum's deputy director, she took consolation in the fact that the body was cremated in the end. She reproduced the long, soothing letter from Gifford to Alfred Kroeber in which the younger man explained that a "compromise between science and sentiment" was achieved in the final account.

In the same letter, however, Gifford mentioned that Ishi's brain was "preserved," a "possible departure" from Alfred Kroeber's wishes. Theodora offered no comment about just what this meant. Was the "preserved" brain later also cremated and placed with the rest of Ishi's body? Without saying so, Theodora suggested as much when she wrote that Gifford had "succeeded" in laying Ishi's remains to rest with dignity. But what if the brain had been pickled, as the Indian rumor had it? And if so, where was it now? The mother of the famous science-fiction novelist Ursula K. Le Guin (the "K" stands for Kroeber), Theodora was a talented, expansive writer. Her reticence about Ishi's brain hinted inadvertently that something had gone very wrong.

And yet how much do we even really know about Ishi himself? Early reporters compared him to Robinson Crusoe, a survivor in an alien setting far from his own society. Ishi has also been called Native America's Anne Frank. Like the attic in Amsterdam, the canyon hideout of Ishi's tiny band was the last refuge for a hunted people. And like Frank, Ishi has become the human face of a people's travails. His life offers a glimpse beyond the dry, almost incomprehensible statistics that inform us that at least five million Indians perished of disease and war in this continent's conquest—together with the slave trade, the single largest human tragedy in America's history. The slaughter of Indians in California, while not always a simple matter of good and evil, victim and victimizer, or uniform pioneer cruelty, foreshadowed later episodes of genocide, from Nazi Germany to Bosnia and Rwanda. It was an age when towns

offered bounties of $5 apiece for Indian scalps and posses of armed set-
tlers carried out massacres like the one at Clear Lake in 1850 of sixty
Pomo villagers. The cry was raised for what one newspaper editorialist
called "a war of extermination until the last Redskin of these tribes has
been killed." What happened in California was a "human hunt," in the
judgment of the late-nineteenth-century historian Hubert H. Bancroft,
"and the basest and most brutal of them all."

We have no diary from Ishi, yet we do know a good deal about him
from the writings left by Alfred Kroeber, the doctor Saxton Pope, and
others. Ishi thought white men smelled like horses; he liked coconut
layer-cake; and he led expeditions with neighborhood boys to hunt quail
in Golden Gate Park with a bow and arrow. He insisted it was dangerous
to sleep with the moon shining directly in your face—and he appreciated order and neatness, keeping his coins stacked in empty film canis-
ters and making his bed every day with a soldier's precision.

In other ways, Ishi continues to be an enigma. He spoke no English
at all at the time of his capture in Oroville. How was it that he did know
a few words of Spanish? Why did Ishi's fugitive band refuse to give itself
up for so many long decades? Did Ishi ever manage to feel at home in
San Francisco? And was he really the last of his tribe—or are there
Californians even today who have at least a bit of Yahi blood? The story
of the wild man of Deer Creek is not so simple or straightforward as it
has sometimes seemed.

If he was always a curiosity and walking museum piece during his
days in San Francisco, Ishi also inspired strong attachment and loyalty
from those who knew him best. Alfred Kroeber, not one for romantic
excess, described Ishi as a person who was "industrious, kindly, obliging,
invariably even tempered, ready of smile, and thoroughly endeared
himself to all with whom he came in contact." "He liked everybody,"
the more emotional Thomas Waterman said, "and everybody liked
him." "I loved the old Indian," Waterman wrote to Kroeber just after
Ishi's death.

Even so, the anthropologists studied Ishi as a "typical" specimen of
his Yahi culture. They noted his habits and beliefs as if everyone in his
small tribe possessed an identical set. One wonders just how typical
Ishi was. Was it pure coincidence that he among all other Indians in
North America held out on his own in the wild until well into the
twentieth century? Would any other Yahi have been able to adapt with
such grace to a foreign world? It seems almost certain that Ishi had

special, maybe unique, individual qualities of vision, resourcefulness, and purpose.

Only a few very old men and women are left who met Ishi in person, and they were small children in San Francisco while he was alive. Today we have only the bare traces of his physical existence. There are the arrowheads and spearpoints that Ishi crafted—some in museums, others treasured heirlooms belonging to the descendants of those to whom Ishi gave them as presents. And there are the photographs. One shows Ishi, gaunt as a concentration camp survivor, on the day after his capture in Oroville. Still others depict Ishi in San Francisco, an urban Indian now, dressed in suit and tie behind the wheel of a Model T, or smiling with his white friends in their box at the Orpheum Theater. We can also listen to the recordings made of Ishi's songs and stories on the wax cylinders of an early phonograph. Here he chants out loudly across the ages in the ancient Yahi tongue of which he was the world's last speaker.

"You stay, I go," Saxton Pope recalled Ishi whispering to him from his deathbed. The fact is that Ishi has never left us. The odyssey of this lone survivor from the tribal culture of his Yahi people into the strange new world of San Francisco still fascinates thousands of Americans. As the subject of a pair of TV movies, five documentaries, and three plays in the last few decades alone, Ishi is an icon of popular culture. The saga of his life and death remains as remarkable and compelling as ever. It was almost a century ago that the wild man of Deer Creek materialized like a ghost out of the hills one late summer evening.

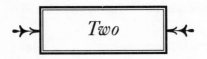

# Two

# THE WILD MAN

# OF DEER CREEK

The butchers were just finishing a long day's work at the slaughterhouse.

It was a hard, dirty job. One of the men, Adolph Kessler, was already washing up and changing his clothes. The other three were still salting the last hides and hosing the blood and urine off the cement floor. The stench was bad no matter how much they scrubbed down. That was why the slaughterhouse was out in the rolling countryside a couple of miles above the little town of Oroville. The butchers lived in town. At quitting time every evening, they drove back down the hill together in a horse-drawn wagon.

The Western Pacific Railroad was laying track back across the mountains to Nevada. Kessler and his companions slaughtered five hundred head of cattle a day to feed the crews. By dusk they were exhausted, all the more from the summer's blazing heat in these dry foothills of the Sierra Nevadas. On this day, August 28, 1911, it had reached exactly 100 degrees.

A dairy sat a quarter mile up the country road. School did not start for another week, and the owner's teenaged son, Floyd Hefner, sometimes came over to help the butchers with their work. That day about sunset, the boy was heading out to find the horses to hitch up the wagon, or so

Adolph Kessler would recall many years later to those who now and then dropped by to hear the old man's story.

All of a sudden, as Kessler told it, he had heard the boy yell from the yard.

"Ad! There's a man here."

The boy sounded frightened.

Kessler grabbed a hog gambrel, a short meat hook. He rushed outside in his long johns. Meat had disappeared in recent weeks. Kessler assumed the intruder was a thief. Just nineteen himself, his adrenaline was pumping now. The man was crouched in the dirt by an old oak tree. Kessler charged, knocking over the man, raising the hog gambrel to strike.

"I thought if he was going to fight, well then I'd fight him."

Yet the man only cowered. He whispered frightened, unintelligible words. The young butcher saw that the man was barefoot. He wore only a tattered denim shirt down to his knees. He was not only skinny and ragged, but also older, perhaps in his fifties.

Kessler relaxed. He wouldn't have to fight. But who was the intruder?

A Mexican, Kessler first thought. Only a half century before, California had belonged to Mexico as the sparsely inhabited far northern province of Alta California. Now the land belonged to the United States, but many Mexicans were coming north to work on the railroad and area ranches. The butchers suspected these "greasers" of "stripping beef" from the hanging carcasses. With his brown skin and close-cropped black hair, Kessler's captive looked as if he might be one of these men.

"At that time, I could talk fairly well in Mexican," Kessler would later recall. He had tried out a few words.

The man showed no sign of understanding.

The young butcher noticed his captive had bits of buckskin threaded through both ears. There was a small stick through the septum of his nose, too.

Could this be an Indian?

Kessler wasn't sure what to think. By then, it was already half a century since California's last free tribes had been wiped out or removed to reservations. The state now had cars, telephones, factories, and paved highways and was otherwise part of the new, modern world. There were still Indians around Oroville, but they were "friendlies" who wore

Western clothes, spoke English, and had names like Pancho, Betty, Grapevine Tom, and Shasta Frank. The "wild" Indians of frontier legend had vanished long ago, or so it was widely thought. You had to go to a motion picture show to see fierce-looking Indians dressed up in war paint and feathers.

The other three butchers stood guard. Kessler went inside to ring Oroville's sheriff, John Webber.

"John, we have something out here. We don't know what it is. He's barefooted. He's covered all right. But he ain't got any good clothes."

Webber drove out in a horse and buggy with another policeman. He had no more luck than Kessler in communicating with the suspected thief. For lack of a better plan, he decided to take the man back to the jail in Oroville. He had Kessler handcuff the prisoner for the ride.

The man appeared to take no offense.

"He had a big smile," Kessler recalled, "as much as to say, 'Are they for me? Are you giving those to me?' "

Sheriff Webber and his constable drove back to town with their prisoner seated between them. By then it was night. Still, the news of a mysterious man's capture spread quickly. Excitement was rare in Oroville, a farm town of less than a thousand people. A crowd of the curious thronged outside the jail. Further attempts at Spanish and even Chinese failed. A local Indian tried Maidu. The man gave no sign of understanding this language, the tongue of the Indians who still lived in Oroville's hills, either.

Amid the hubbub, somebody mentioned the Mill Creeks. This was the pioneer name for the little Indian tribe that the Berkeley anthropologists would soon decide should be more properly called the Yahi. For many decades, it had been assumed that the Mill Creeks were extinct, all killed by settlers in the old days of the stagecoach and the covered wagon. In 1908, however, a party of surveyors from the Oro Power and Light Company had stumbled upon a concealed Indian camp just above Deer Creek, the next stream down from Mill Creek and also part of the territory of the Mill Creeks. It was Grizzly Bear's Hiding Place, the tribe's hideout and last refuge. The power company men had glimpsed two Indians fleeing toward the cliffs; and they found an old, crippled woman in the camp itself, although she vanished later, too. The surveyors' tale made the newspapers across the Sacramento Valley. It prompted speculation that a few Mill Creeks, or Deer Creeks, as the same Indians were sometimes also known, had managed somehow to stay alive hidden away in the rugged canyons fronting the high country.

Could the man captured at the slaughterhouse be a survivor of this lost tribe? Robert Anderson came by the jail and added his opinion's weight to the identification of the man as a Mill Creek. An old man by now, Anderson was once the county sheriff and, in his youth, an Indian fighter. He'd just published his memoirs, which boasted of killing dozens of "prowling savages" in the "general clean-up" of Mount Lassen's foothills. Anderson admitted to some uncertainty after so many years, but he told a reporter that the man in the jail very much resembled a boy of about twelve he had met and spared in 1864. "I think it is extremely probable that he is the boy, grown to manhood, and now reaching the decline of life."

That the Indian was near starvation was beyond any doubt. Sheriff Webber sent out for a hot bowl of beans, bread and butter, and doughnuts. The Indian devoured the food in a flash. His only possession had been a rough canvas sack. It had contained only a few manzanita berries and a bit of jerked meat. The sheriff wondered how long the man had gone without eating a full meal.

It was getting toward midnight. Sheriff Webber wanted to go home, so he shooed away the last onlookers. He had the prisoner locked in his own cell for protection from the other inmates.

Adolph Kessler watched the man being locked down for the night. Many years later, a second butcher, Bill Kroeger, would insist that he had been the first person to find the Indian at the slaughterhouse. Kessler, who became Oroville's chief of police after World War II, stuck to his version of that night's events. By his account, he had been the last one at the jail after Sheriff Webber had gone home for the night.

"At the last look I got of him, he was still standing there. There was a little light in the cell. Still standing there, looking out."

"And I just wondered what in the world was going through his mind."


"ABORIGINAL INDIAN, THE LAST OF THE DEER CREEKS, CAPTURED NEAR OROVILLE." It was the banner headline in the next morning's *Oroville Daily Register.* The accompanying story explained that the "last surviving member" of this "proud tribe of warriors" had been found "still untouched by [the] civilization that destroyed his people." "His feet were almost as wide as they were long," the reporter noted, which showed "plainly he had never worn either moccasins or shoes." The newspapers down in the San Francisco Bay Area soon picked up the story. "He is a savage of the most primitive type," the *San Francisco Examiner* informed readers. "With gestures more eloquent and expressive than could have been the spoken word," the reporter further claimed, "he laid bare the tragedy of his people in a silence broken only by his mournful incantations chanted to the Great Spirit when his story dealt with death."

Alfred Kroeber read the stories with special interest. Already one of America's leading anthropologists, Kroeber was the founder and chair of the department at the young University of California at Berkeley. Kroeber had come to California from Columbia University and his native New York in 1900 and, with characteristic single-mindedness and energy, plunged into the back country to track down surviving Indians who could still tell him about their aboriginal language and customs. The idea of finding a "wild" Indian intrigued Kroeber. His Mojave, Yurok, Karok, and other informants knew a great deal about the old ways, but they were already what the colorful Spanish linguist and novelist Jaime de Angulo called "Indians in Overalls," who had chosen or been forced to adopt the white man's ways. When Kroeber had heard about remnants of the lost tribe of the Mill Creeks in 1908, he had dispatched his colleague, Thomas Waterman, to search the area. These Indians, Kroeber wrote, could be a "rich mine to the ethnologist and anthropologist of the future," a group still "totally wild and independent." Waterman found a scrap of a rabbit-skin blanket and other evidence of occupation, but the poison oak, crumbling lava rock, and rust red cliffs allowed the Indians to elude pursuit. Despite hiring two guides and tracking dogs, Waterman never glimpsed an Indian. Now, almost three years later, it appeared that a survivor had turned up at Oroville.

Kroeber had hired Waterman in 1907 as the third member of Berkeley's growing anthropology department. Both men had studied at New York's Columbia University under the brilliant German expatriate, Franz Boas, and they had a good working relationship, even though Kroeber was nine years Waterman's senior and always the man in charge. By temperament, Waterman was much more emotional and sometimes impetuous than his drier, always methodical departmental chair. Waterman's passionate enthusiasm made him one of Berkeley's most popular teachers, but he was also restless and sometimes impatient. He would later leave the Bay Area for other jobs in Guatemala, Arizona, and Washington, and he died young in Hawaii at the age of forty-nine.

It took Waterman eight hours by train to reach Oroville over the foothills and across California's Sacramento Valley. Lying between the Pacific Coast Range and the Sierra Nevada, the valley was a marsh when the first Spaniards appeared there in the early 1600s—and thick with waterfowl, fish, and freshwater mussels that fed the villages of the Yokut, Nomlaki, and other native peoples. By the early twentieth century, a network of canals and dikes had been built to control the flooding, and farms blanketed the plain. Waterman gazed from his window at the orchards and rice paddies that stretched out toward the blue-gray peaks of the Sierra Nevada. Initially planted to feed the many thousands of Chinese who came to California during the Gold Rush of 1849, rice had adapted well to the Sacramento Valley's heavy clay soil. This great, pancake-flat valley remains one of America's single largest rice-producing regions even today, although more and more farmland is being paved under for new housing developments.

Alfred Kroeber had advised Sheriff Webber of Waterman's arrival. When Waterman reached Oroville, he was taken to see the jailed Indian—this "last free survivor of the Red Man," as the newspapers were billing him. The man before Waterman was gaunt, but otherwise in good physical health, about 5'6" with close-cropped hair and clear dark eyes.

Mill Creek lay in the southernmost part of a stretch of hills where the Indians had once spoken a language called Yana; Waterman had brought along a list of words from Yana, which had several dialects. To the anthropologist's delight, the Indian understood many of these terms. At hearing *si'win'i*, or "yellow pine," he tapped the frame of his wood cot. That the man spoke a Yana dialect was more confirmation that he was one of the last survivors of the little band of Mill Creeks that Waterman had tried to track three years before.

"It was a picnic to see him open his eyes when he heard Yana from me," Waterman wrote Kroeber. Rudimentary communication was possible now. "We had a lot of conversation this morning about deer hunting and making acorn soup, but I got as far as my list of words would take me. If I am not mistaken, he's full of religion, bathing at sunrise, putting out pinches of tobacco where the lightning strikes, etc." There was an old man named Sam Batwi up in Redding who spoke Yana's northernmost dialect. Waterman made arrangements for Batwi to come down to Oroville as a translator as soon as possible.

What was the Indian's mood? Waterman was not quite sure what to make of it. The man had been the center of attention for his five days in captivity. Hundreds of people had stopped by the jail to stare and gawk. It may just have been fear about his fate in the hands of the people who had killed the rest of his tribe, but the Indian had been cooperative through much of his ordeal. He demonstrated animal calls and seemed to enjoy the cigars he was offered by jail visitors—and even joked in pantomime at one point about shooting Sheriff Webber with bow and arrow. A reporter had judged the man and his jailers to be on "very friendly terms."

Yet the man's own story of his wanderings, even the little that the reporters could tell of it, was harrowing. The territory of the Mill Creeks lay some thirty miles to the northeast of Oroville. On his second day of captivity, the man had pointed back up in that direction to indicate "from where he had come," the *Oroville Daily Register* had reported. "Enumerating on his fingers, he informed the officers who had him in charge that originally there had been four in the band. By the same pantomime he conveyed to the officers that two of the band had been drowned; that he and his mahala had come on alone; that the mahala had died and been partially devoured by coyotes; that he had come to the slaughter-house alone; and that there were no more of his people to be found." *Mahala* was a word for "woman" in a trading jargon shared by California's Indians. That the man's hair was short suggested that he had indeed suffered the very recent loss of a loved one, perhaps a wife, sister, or cousin. To singe off your long hair was a common ritual of bereavement in Native California.

Now with Waterman the Indian seemed to communicate a version of the same story—except that the anthropologist took him to say that his female companion and also a baby had perished in the Feather River that cut down from the mountains above Oroville. "He has a yarn to tell about his woman, who had a baby on her back and seems to have been drowned," Waterman explained to Kroeber. Yet Waterman also confessed his puzzlement at the man seeming "so cheerful" in relating this terrible story. Was he hiding his real emotions of shock and grief? Was there more to the story of his lost loved ones? Waterman didn't know.

Alfred Kroeber wanted the Indian brought to San Francisco for further study. Sheriff Webber was happy to relinquish the captive. He had grown fond of the man, but he had also worried about what to do with him. "He has committed no crime and he does not apparently want to remain in confinement," the sheriff told a reporter. "If I turn him loose he would be unable to secure a living, for he does not know how to work or to beg. . . . He is absolutely ignorant of our rules of conduct and in our midst would be almost as helpless as an animal."

At that time, Native Americans were wards of the state; they would not be granted citizenship until 1924. Jim Thorpe, "Indian Jim," the legendary athlete who dominated the 1912 Stockholm Olympics, couldn't vote. Thus the Bureau of Indian Affairs had to approve any decision about the Indian in Webber's captivity. Alfred Kroeber induced the authorities to telegraph the sheriff with the necessary permission. Only then did Webber turn over the Indian for Waterman to escort to San Francisco. The anthropologist signed a receipt for "the person of an elderly Yana Indian, name and place of residence at present unknown."

A festive crowd saw the Indian off at the train station. The first settlers of the towns at the Sacramento Valley's edge had viewed the "red devils" up in the mountains as savage killers to be exterminated by any means necessary. By now, half a century later, the Indians had long been defeated and no longer posed any threat. A few mean-spirited young Orovilleans had made sport of the captured Indian; they gave him a banana one afternoon in front of the jail and howled with laughter when he tried to eat it peel and all. Yet the lone survivor of the Mill Creeks was an object of pity and even sympathy for other townspeople. Someone had donated a light-colored jacket, pants, and suit for the Indian to wear to San Francisco. At the station, a lady pinned a rose to his lapel. Shoes had also been provided, but the man was not yet used to this convention of his new world. He stood in his suit, calm and barefoot, in the middle of the crowd that buzzed around him on another scorching summer day.

Alfred Kroeber had decided to house the still nameless Indian in his new museum in San Francisco. The University of California's anthropology department was located across the bay on Berkeley's campus but lacked the space for its growing collections of Greek statues, Peruvian pots, Egyptian mummies, and other artifacts. Kroeber had taken over a building just above Golden Gate Park, which he hoped would one day become a museum. A pair of full-time employees already lived on site, and they could see to the Indian's needs. Kroeber and Waterman had offices in the museum, too. It would be convenient to have the Indian there to study his language and culture.

The Indian was taken to his new home immediately on his arrival in San Francisco. A gaggle of waiting reporters demanded to know the wild man's real name. "We can't just go on calling him, 'Hay [sic], there!'" Thomas Waterman acknowledged to one of them. By custom in many California tribes, however, you did not share your name with strangers, and the anthropologists did not want to press the Indian for his. Sam Batwi, the bespectacled Yana octogenarian whom Waterman had recruited as a translator, suggested "John" as a working pseudonym. According to one reporter, Alfred Kroeber had rejected Batwi's proposal as "lacking in individuality." He must have felt a less generic and more Indian-sounding appellation for his new "wild" Indian was in order.

The name finally chosen was Ishi. Later, the butcher Adolph Kessler would credit the name to John Webber, the Oroville sheriff. "What is he?" dozens of visitors to the jail house had inquired of the sheriff. For lack of any better option, the story went, Webber began to call his captive "Is he" and then just "Ishi" for short, or so Kessler asserted. In the 1930s, perhaps pulling the leg of an overinquisitive white researcher, an elderly Indian from north of Mount Lassen named Albert Moody told the visiting linguist John Peabody Harrington that Ishi had been named after Isa, a "great chief" of his tribe. This story was surely apocryphal. We have no other evidence that any such figure as "Isa" ever existed. Ishi's loosely organized, largely egalitarian people did not even have a single "great chief" in the first place.

It was actually Alfred Kroeber who supplied the name. In Oroville Waterman had already begun recording the Indian's Yahi words for various things. *I'citi* meant "man," he had learned. Kroeber thus informed the reporters that the Indian would go by the anglicization, Ishi. The newspapers picked up the name right away, even if for good copy they also used more lurid designations: "cave man," "wild man," "redskin," and "primeval savage."

A tribal identity for Ishi had to be agreed upon as well. Didn't every Indian belong to a tribe? The inhabitants of the area around Mill Creek had been called by a variety of different names, which was confusing, to say the least. The pioneers had known them as the "Mill Creeks," or sometimes "Deer Creeks"; the Maidu and other neighboring Indians used "Nozo" or "Kombo." For his part, Thomas Waterman told the newspapers that Ishi was "southern Yana" because he spoke that language. Yet Sam Batwi told Waterman that Ishi's tongue did not sound exactly like the southern dialects of Yana he had heard. The anthropologists thus decided that Ishi and his band must have spoken a fourth dialect of Yana—and named it "Yahi" after *yaaxi*, Ishi's word for "the people." "Yahi" had a much more distinctive, even poetic ring than "Mill Creek" or "southern Yana"; the name added to the drama of Ishi's story by making him the last survivor of a whole tribe, not just an obscure subgroup. American readers were well acquainted with James Fenimore Cooper's *Last of the Mohicans*, the single best-known nineteenth-century book about Indians. Now they could follow in the newspapers the real-life epic of Ishi, the last of the Yahi.

It cannot have been easy for Ishi to adjust to a new world. Still in the shadow of his people's extermination, he was also now alone among the *saltu*, his word for white people. Although the killings had occurred in the mid-1800s, when he was just a child or perhaps not even born, Ishi knew that whites had massacred dozens of his people. He'd expected Adolph Kessler to kill him, too, Alfred Kroeber later understood him to explain. There was also the strange first sight of the phonograph, the electric light switch, and similar modern curiosities. City crowds were especially disconcerting for this man who'd lived his whole life in the depopulated canyons of Mount Lassen. "*Hansi saltu*," so many white people, he exclaimed on a excursion to Ocean Beach, on one of the rare days this gray, foggy strip of sand was warm enough for sunbathing.

According to Alfred Kroeber, Ishi early on was occasionally "bewildered," broke into a "high unnatural giggle," and showed "not the least initiative," simply following orders mechanically. Because victims of trauma and extended warfare sometimes exhibit similar symptoms, it's been suggested recently that Ishi may have suffered from post-traumatic stress disorder, or PTSD. Ishi's life had certainly been full of hardship and loss. By his account to Alfred Kroeber and others in San Francisco, four Indians were left when the surveyors and their cowboy guides broke into Grizzly Bear's Hiding Place in 1908, including Ishi himself and his mother—the sick, aged woman that the men had come upon in the last Yahi hideout. "A poor old squaw," one of the surveyors later described her, a tiny, shrunken woman bundled in rags and too weak even to stand. Ishi, who was probably hiding nearby, came back later to carry his mother to some other makeshift hiding place.

The other two last survivors were the Indians that the surveying party had spied fleeing across a rock pile. One was Ishi's elderly uncle; the other was probably Ishi's sister or wife, the woman he called his *mahala*. According to Ishi's jailhouse explanations to Thomas Waterman and the Oroville reporters three years later, this woman had perished just before his capture at the slaughterhouse (Waterman later came to believe he was mistaken in thinking Ishi had also mentioned a baby). Ishi's mother and uncle had died sometime earlier, probably still back in Deer Creek canyon. He was the only one left of his people, Ishi always said.

Yet Ishi also managed to adapt to and even enjoy his new life in San Francisco. As he grew more comfortable, he no longer exhibited the nervousness and apathy of his first days in the city. In a way, Ishi was used to trying to make the best of a difficult and sometimes lonely existence. He had lived with hunger and danger in his decades in hiding. The mythology of the Yahi, as recounted by Ishi, also prepared its people for life's perils. A part of their creation story said:

> Rattlesnake will bite
> Grizzly Bear will bite
> and they will kill people.
> Let it be this way.
> Man will get hurt falling off rock
> Man will fall down when gathering pine nuts,
> He'll swim in the water, drift away, die.
> They'll fall down a precipice,
> They'll be struck by arrow points,
> They'll be lost,
> He'll have wood splinters get in his eye,
> They'll be poisoned by bad men,
> They'll be blind.

On one of his first days in the museum, a cannon boomed across the city from the Presidio. A reporter described Ishi's reaction: "[He] jumped to his feet and stood for a moment with fear in every feature." The anthropologists and Batwi tried to explain that there was nothing to fear. A second blast rattled the museum's windows a few moments later. This time, the reporter said, "Ishi sat with hands demurely clasped in his lap and said nothing."

Before long, the white man's inventions ceased to astonish or even surprise him. Ishi watched pilot Robert Fowler circle Golden Gate Park in 1911 at the start of what would be a failed attempt to cross the continent. A $50,000 prize had been offered to the first to accomplish this feat by the newspaper tycoon William Randolph Hearst; the powerful Hearst was the son of Phoebe Apperson Hearst, a major patroness of Kroeber's anthropology museum, now Ishi's San Francisco home. "*Saltu?*" Ishi now inquired of the rickety biplane as it veered over the trees toward the bay. "White man up there?" He laughed and arched his eyebrows when told that the answer was yes.

Yet Ishi was never closed to his new world or its strangeness. Although proud of his skill at chipping arrowheads, he regarded steel as a superior technology and preferred machine-made knives and saws over any stone tool. He also liked pillows, beds, screened porches, and civilization's other creature comforts. Anything but the stereotype of the silent, granite-faced warrior, Ishi was also quick to joke and smile, especially after the uncertainty of his first days in San Francisco had passed. He laughed at Waterman's antics and chuckled at incongruities like a gardener pulling weeds as if he were a Yahi digging for wild lilly bulb or some other edible root.

Ishi's own upbringing had taught him to respect tradition's protocol. He had learned dozens of songs, hundreds of plant names, and a storehouse of other traditional knowledge from his elders—and insisted now on learning and following the proprieties of his new world. Conducting his own anthropology, Ishi observed the other guests during his first sit-down dinners in San Francisco. He soon managed fork, knife, and napkin with a late Victorian gentleman's decorum. "A certain member of my family," Thomas Waterman admitted only half tongue-in-cheek, "urged me to model my own behavior in such respects after the Indian's shining example."

Ishi learned how to communicate in broken English, and his vocabulary grew to about three hundred words (among them colloquialisms like "Sure, Mike," and also less benign terms like "nigger" and "Chinaman"). This was more English than Kroeber ever grasped of Yahi, the professor admitted. Ishi made up his own names for his new white acquaintances by adding the Yahi ending *–ee* as he did with many English words. There was "Popey," Saxton Pope, and "Watemany," Thomas Waterman. As much as he may have liked Kroeber, Ishi saw right away that this direct, self-confident man gave the orders at his new museum home, and was careful not to presume too much. He called Kroeber "Chiep"—the *f* sound did not exist in his native tongue—or sometimes "Majaupa," the Yahi word for headman.

Even so, Ishi's flexibility had its limits. He never lost a sense of his own identity. Shaking hands was unknown in Native California, and Ishi never liked the practice. He complained about the city water's bad taste, so unlike the "sweet water" of his mountain creeks, even though it did not take him long to develop a liking for tea and coffee. Ishi would take aspirin and other white medicine, but also insisted on the value of many traditional Yahi remedies. His preferred cure for a cold was to thread a twig of bay or juniper through a hole in his septum.

The matter of Ishi's hair was also revealing. The Indians in Mount Lassen's foothills had kept their hair long, sometimes pulled up in a top knot. Ishi arrived to San Francisco with his hair still close-cropped in mourning, but he grew it back out in the city. It mattered not that short hair was then the current men's fashion—or that other Native American men were keeping their hair above their ears in accordance with assimilation's demands. Ishi followed Yahi tradition. The neighbors in Parnassus Heights soon grew accustomed to the sight of the last Yahi going down to buy groceries with his long black hair tied in a pony-tail to keep it from whipping around his face in the salty breeze that came off the Pacific.

The museum became Ishi's permanent home. Kroeber had the university appoint him to a part-time job as janitor so he would have spending money and to keep him occupied. On Sundays, too, Ishi offered his demonstrations of arrowhead making and other Yahi arts to curious visitors. That Kroeber had Ishi as a clean-up man and a living exhibit became a matter of controversy much later. When he was not occupied at the museum, however, Ishi would stop to visit with neighbors, even carving wood dolls for a pair of delighted little girls who liked to accompany him to the grocery store on Hugo Street. With the anthropologists, Ishi was willing and even eager to share Yahi myth and custom. He never liked to discuss the destruction of his people or the details of his decades in hiding, events perhaps too painful to remember. Any mention of his old life left Ishi "in a fit of depression, from which it took him some time to recover," Thomas Waterman noted.

In the summer of 1915, Edward Sapir came out to California to work with Ishi. Still in his twenties then, Sapir was already acknowledged as one of the greatest linguists of his time, with a perfect ear for language. He'd worked in 1907 with Betty Brown and Sam Batwi, Ishi's aged translator, who were among the last living speakers of the Yana language's northern dialect. As Sapir took them down phonetically, Ishi dictated six traditional Yahi tales, mostly about the exploits of Coyote, Lizard, and other mythical animal deities. The trouble lay in the translation: Sapir's Yahi was still rudimentary, and Ishi's English only marginally better. The two men had to agree on translations of the tales in what Sapir later recalled as a "crude jargon composed of English, quasi-English, and Yahi." Ishi was sometimes weak with what his doctors would later realize had been the first symptoms of tuberculosis, and Sapir left the stories partially or completely untranslated into English. Only toward the end of the twentieth century would modern linguists manage to finish translating the bulk of the tales for the first time, a body of Yahi tradition in Ishi's own words.

The University of California's hospital was one of Ishi's favorite haunts throughout his five years in San Francisco. It was next to the museum and part of the cluster of university buildings on Parnassus Heights then known as the Affiliated Colleges, including a dental and veterinary school. At the hospital, Ishi met Saxton Pope, the handsome and enthusiastic chief of surgery who was the doctor to the movie star Jean Harlow and many San Francisco socialites. By later accounts, Pope and Ishi had taken to one another right away. They spent hours practicing archery together in Golden Gate Park and once took a week-long tour down the coast to Santa Cruz and Monterey Bay.

Saxton Pope would later recall Ishi's visits to the hospital. "He quietly helped the nurses clean instruments or amused the interns and nurses by singing his Indian songs, or carried on primitive conversation by means of a very complex mixture of gesture, Yana dialect, and the few scraps of English he had acquired in his contact with us. His affability and pleasant disposition made him a universal favorite. He visited the sick in the wards with a gentle and sympathetic look which spoke more clearly than words. He came to the women's ward quite regularly, and with his hands folded before him, he would go from bed to bed like a visiting physician, looking at each patient with quiet concern or with a fleeting smile that was very kindly received and understood." The idea of Ishi as a healer would later become one of the legends that clung to the last Yahi.

Ishi himself was hospitalized with chills and fever soon after his arrival to San Francisco, but he recovered and put on weight. Besides coconut layer cake, he also liked doughnuts, ice cream sodas, and other sweets. One newspaper reported that the "famous redskin" was "fat and pudgy," and a cruel columnist joked about the "survival of the fattest." It did not take Ishi long to recognize the dangers of San Francisco's fatty temptations, and he restricted his diet. In the winter of 1915, however, he again became weak and feverish, this time with a wheezing cough. Saxton Pope began to suspect tuberculosis, even though Ishi still tested negative for the disease. Tuberculosis was the single largest cause of death in the United States at that time. Given their lack of resistance and the conditions of hunger and poverty on the reservations, it had taken an especially devastating toll on Native Americans.

Kroeber was away in New York that year finishing his *Handbook of the Indians of California*. Even so, he received regular reports about Ishi's condition and treatment from Edward Gifford, the San Francisco's museum's acting director, a personable, conscientious young protégé of Kroeber's. "It's our responsibility, and we ought to live up to it fully," Kroeber wrote Gifford about ensuring that the weakening Ishi received the best possible care. At that time, however, the standard and only treatment was to send the patient to a drier, high-altitude climate, the proverbial magic mountain. Kroeber and Pope corresponded about moving Ishi to some Sacramento Valley ranch, or even Arizona, once the weather warmed again.

It became apparent by the winter's end that Ishi would not last that long. A week before his death, he entered the hospital for the last time, his bed in the very same wards where he had come by to sing for patients. He could not eat and had wasted away to skin and bone. His urine had turned the color of coffee. Saxton Pope described the end: "I was with him at the time, directed his medication, and gently stroked his hand as a small sign of fellowship and sympathy. He did not care for marked demonstrations of any sort. He was a stoic, unafraid, and died in the faith of his people."

It was in that last week that Kroeber had been informed of Pope's plan to dissect Ishi as soon as he died. "He wants to make a cast of his face and hands after death; also to perform an autopsy," Edward Gifford wrote. When he was still healthy, the curious Ishi had sometimes watched Pope cut open living patients from behind the glass-paneled window in the operating room. The art of surgery was in a way familiar to Ishi from his own experience at eviscerating rabbit, bear, deer, and other game. Once Ishi watched Pope remove a man's diseased kidney. When the patient went under anesthesia, Ishi thought Pope had killed him; he was impressed when the man awoke and later recovered. Ishi told others that Pope had the makings of a great *kuwi*, a Yahi medicine man.

In her biography, however, Theodora Kroeber elaborated upon Ishi's special horror of dissection. The University of California's hospital, then as now, was a teaching facility. One day Ishi wandered alone into a dissection room when the class was out on break and saw the cadavers lying cut up on marble slabs. According to Theodora, this was "a revolting and a terrifying experience" for Ishi. Theodora, who married Alfred Kroeber a decade after Ishi's death, never knew the subject of her biography in person. Alfred was in all likelihood her source for the incident in the dissection room. Since he knew that Ishi's Yahi and most other California tribes believed a corpse should be buried whole and without delay, Alfred must not have been surprised by Ishi's horrified reaction to the sectioned dead bodies in the hospital. Ishi had also related a story to the anthropologists about his people's belief that a person made his or her way to the upper world after their death. The dead shinnied up through the sky on a rope, according to this Yahi myth. Ishi may have believed that dissection would interfere with or make this journey impossible.

For Alfred Kroeber, then, it was a matter of duty to Ishi's wishes to block the autopsy. As Kroeber also explained to Gifford, "We have hundreds of Indian skeletons [already] that nobody ever comes near to study. The prime interest in this case would be of a morbid romantic nature." Such was Kroeber's concern that he not only wrote Gifford to "shut down" the autopsy but also sent a telegram on the day before Ishi's death: "URGE COMPLETE ADHERENCE ORIGINAL PLANS POPE WILL HONOR MY WISHES." Pope also knew that Ishi would not want his body dissected, but the doctor assumed his right to override his unschooled primitive friend for what he believed were the greater interests of science and knowledge. The autopsy would leave for posterity a record of every last physical detail of the Wild Man of Deer Creek, or so Pope justified his position in the matter.

Whether or not Gifford showed the telegram to Pope, the doctor still insisted on an autopsy and somehow had his way. He didn't do the dissection himself, leaving it to Jean Cooke, the pathologist on duty, who had sometimes joined Ishi and Pope for archery target practice. After the autopsy was completed, Ishi's sewn-together body was stored at the funeral home for two days. Then his white friends accompanied the body to the Olivet Memorial Park cemetery just a few miles down Highway One from San Francisco. The funeral was attended by Pope, Waterman,

Gifford, and two other museum staffers, Robert Warburton and Llewellyn Loud, a Welshman. "We cremated his [Ishi's] body," Pope later wrote. "This was his tribal custom. With him we placed his trusty bow, a quiver of arrows, his fire sticks, some obsidian, ten pieces of Indian money, some acorn meal, some jerky and a pouch of tobacco." Everyone there knew that Ishi had been dissected, but this did not stop Thomas Waterman from assuring inquiring reporters that every propriety had been observed. The remains of the fabled Yahi had been "disposed of according to the customs of the California tribes," the anthropologist told the *San Francisco Examiner*.

The newspapers accepted these declarations at face value. If reporters knew about the dissection, they didn't say so in their stories. Nothing at all was mentioned about the fate of Ishi's brain. "Modern Life Kills Ancient Indian," one story concluded. It explained that the "noted aborigine" had "passed on to his happy hunting grounds" from tuberculosis, a "white plague of the palefaces." A regretful last poem "To the Late Mr. Ishi" appeared in another newspaper:

> *You did not fit. Your ways were other.*
> *This madhouse life was all too strange.*
> *It was a shame they found you, brother.*

*Three*

# ISHI, ALFRED, AND THEODORA

No name has been more closely linked to Ishi than that of Kroeber. It was Alfred Kroeber who brought Ishi to San Francisco with so much fanfare, and it was Alfred's second wife, Theodora Kroeber, who would make Ishi famous a second time. In a first photograph of Ishi in the Bay Area he and Alfred are standing side by side—both unsmiling, about the same height, as they stare at the camera. Ishi, less than a month removed from his life in the wilderness, is still shoeless.

My family's first Berkeley apartment was just down the street from the Kroebers. Alfred had died in 1960, but Theodora still lived there. As a boy, I recall my father telling me that the big old redwood house belonged to the widow of a famous professor, a woman who'd written a book about the story of Ishi. I only remember being impressed by the size of the house in comparison with our little apartment, regulation starter housing for an untenured Berkeley professor and his family.

Only when I became an anthropologist myself did I learn more about Alfred, Theodora, and their role in the story of Ishi. In his time, Alfred was one of Berkeley's most prominent intellectuals, acclaimed by an admiring peer as the "dean of American anthropology." Born in 1876 as the eldest of four children, he grew up in the New York City of the Gilded

Age. His father, Florence, was an immigrant from Bavaria, an importer of specialty clocks with a shop on Broadway and another at Union Square; his mother, Mimi, a small woman with large gray eyes and a ready smile, was also of German ancestry. There was money for servants and tutors, and Alfred had piano lessons; he also mastered Greek and Latin along with German, the home's first language. The Kroebers were Protestant, but they mixed with Jewish families; an interest in the arts, literature, and science was a common denominator of these affluent or at least middle-class New Yorkers. One of Alfred's cousins won a Nobel Prize for genetics. Many of his boyhood playmates also went on to be leaders in their fields. One invented the typhoid fever vaccine; another became a speechwriter for F.D.R. There was also a co-drafter of the Universal Declaration of Human Rights; a well-known modernist painter; and the designer of the spectacular stained-glass windows in Fifth Avenue's Church of the Ascension. This talented, ambitious generation imagined a more modern, secular America for the twentieth century, a country in which progress was founded on a belief in science, democracy, and freedom from the dogmas of religion and hierarchy.

Alfred displayed an early interest in science. The future anthropologist's room in the family's Manhattan brownstone was a miniature laboratory. He had a microscope, a collection of beetles and butterflies, an aquarium, a terrarium, test tubes, Bunsen burners, and other chemical equipment. Mimi encouraged her son's pursuits, even though she disapproved of the acid burns on the carpets and feared the house might blow up in a failed experiment. Though many years later Kroeber would object to Ishi's dissection for personal reasons, anatomy was very much part of his boyhood experimentation. A wish list the thirteen-year-old made in 1889 included a "sharp knife for dissecting." He and his friends once sliced open a dead skunk to study its spray mechanism. They had to take an extra bath and change clothes before being allowed at the dinner table.

Kroeber entered Columbia University in 1892. There he met the man whom he'd later call his lifelong "guru," Franz Boas. A muscular German-born scholar with piercing eyes, a droopy moustache, and a thick accent, Boas was the first curator of anthropology at the Upper West Side's American Museum of Natural History and founded Columbia's anthropology department. There his students included Margaret Mead, Ruth Benedict, Melville Herskovits, Edward Sapir, Paul Radin, and others, many of whom went on to begin departments in other American universities. The black novelist and folklorist Zora Neale Hurston also studied with Boas, who in 1908 was elected to the presidency of the American Anthropological Association. Boas—"Papa Franz" to his legion of students as his hair and moustache whitened in his later years—was anthropology's most famous figure, the person who turned it into a full-fledged profession in the United States.

More broadly, Franz Boas was an intellectual who stood with the likes of John Dewey, Jane Addams, Louis Brandeis, and Ida B. Wells in the front ranks of great reformers. Anthropology—literally, the acquisition of knowledge (*logos*) about humankind (*anthropos*)—had come into existence as a discipline during the rise of the other sciences, natural and social, in nineteenth-century Europe and North America. The new field was to study the human species—both its biology and its culture and society. Until Boas, however, anthropology had been mired in the prejudices of the times, especially the assumptions of white superiority and Social Darwinism so prevalent in the Victorian age. Nineteenth-century anthropologists ranked the world's people from savage to civilized, placing "Caucasians" at humanity's apex. The "darker races" were assumed to be inferior in intelligence and thus handicapped in the climb up the ladder of human evolution. Anthropology's "scientific" racism justified Europe's aggressive expansion—and both the enslavement of Africans and the extermination and confinement to reservations of Native Americans. The French anthropologist Claude Lévi-Strauss would concede that the field had been a "handmaiden of colonialism" in those first decades.

Boas, who had grown up Jewish in Kaiser Wilhelm's Germany, had experienced prejudice and hatred as a schoolboy there. Once in the United States and ensconced at Columbia University, he attacked the established mythology of the inferiority of the "lesser races." Although still too cautious to declare the absolute equality of peoples everywhere, Boas insisted that "the differences between the races are so small that they lie within the limits of the narrow range in which all forms may function equally well." He believed that it was impossible and arbitrary to divide the human continuum into demarcated "types" with fixed "racial characteristics." His own landmark 1911 study of the changing head size of immigrants and their children showed that the body's form could change in just a generation with an improved standard of living. At that time, lynching was common in the Jim Crow South and Midwest, and xenophobia was rampant everywhere, along with fears of a "national degeneration" brought about by the flood of "uncivilized" and "swarthy" immigrants from the poorest parts of Eastern Europe and southern Italy. Boas spoke out against the "complacent yielding to prejudice" in defending the rights of blacks and immigrants. An early opponent of Nazism, Boas also derided the "Nordic nonsense" of Hitler's doctrine of Aryan supremacy. His books were burned at one Nazi rally a few years before World War II.

Importantly, too, Boas advocated a new relativist conception of culture. The Victorians had taught that Europeans were superior in biology as well as culture, but Boas's early fieldwork among the Eskimos led him to see that non-Western and Western cultures were systems of habit and belief that made sense in their own terms. If American lovers kissed on the lips, for example, Eskimos rubbed noses. "Our ideas and conceptions are true only so far as our civilization goes," Boas explained in 1925. "What is considered good by one [culture] is considered bad by another." The challenge for the anthropologist was "to succeed in entering into each culture on its own bases," be it the Kwiakutl of the Pacific Northwest or the Andaman Islanders in the Indian Ocean. That most Americans now pay at least lip service to the ideals of diversity and respect or at least tolerance for other cultures traces back in part to the revolution in thought led by Boas among other early twentieth-century thinkers.

Franz Boas's thinking and his personal example exerted a profound influence on Alfred Kroeber and the other leading anthropologists of his generation. Kroeber was among Boas's first Ph.D. students at Columbia and one of Papa Franz's favorite sons. Boas helped Kroeber get his first job at San Francisco's California Academy of Sciences and then the very first anthropology professorship at the young University of California at Berkeley across the bay in 1901. Boas wanted Kroeber to succeed him at Columbia, but the Bay Area had gotten into Kroeber's blood. With its growing young cities, sun-drenched hills, and vistas of the bay and the blue Pacific beyond, it was a kind of Arcadia at the continent's end. Alfred and Theodora would eventually have both a country retreat in Napa and their beautiful Berkeley home, which was designed by the pioneering California architect Bernard Maybeck. Although Alfred returned to the East throughout his life as a lecturer and visiting professor at Harvard, Yale, and other prestigious universities, he declined many offers to return for good and remained a professor at Berkeley for the entire span of his sixty-odd-year professional career. Under his steward-ship, Berkeley's department became one of the best and biggest programs in the country, even the world.

When Ishi came under his care, Alfred was in his mid-thirties, at the height of his physical and intellectual powers. Slight, with thick black hair, a sensitive mouth, and the well-trimmed beard that he kept throughout his life, the good-looking Kroeber was a formidable pres-ence. A talented, tireless administrator who never lacked for confidence in his professional life, he was equally sure of himself arranging for a uni-versity expedition to excavate a ruin in Peru, acquiring a carved Kwiakutl totem pole for the museum, and hiring a temporary professor to teach a course on Native American languages. Kroeber had an old-school professional formality and could be impatient and sometimes sar-castic. He was also serious about his duty as an educator beyond the classroom and the lecture hall. Even the most naive inquiry often received a reply from Kroeber in his clear, direct hand. "Would like," one San Francisco man wrote in 1913, "to learn the Indian jargon that is spo-ken by almost all Indians . . . would also like to get a book that gives Indian methods of fishing, hunting, trapping and that gives their 'tricks' of making fire with sticks, catching trout with soaproot, etc." Kroeber answered that there were "nearly a thousand [Indian languages] in the United States originally" and suggested that his correspondent go to "any larger public or private library" to read more about Native American life.

The range of Kroeber's skills as a scholar was enormous. His "guru," Franz Boas, still envisioned anthropology as the comprehensive study of humankind that its name suggested. To this end, Boas wanted his stu-dents to be capable in each of the discipline's four subfields—cultural anthropology (the study of culture), biological or physical anthropology (the study of human evolution and anatomy), linguistics (the study of language), and archaeology (the study of vanished ancient societies). Kroeber had the preternatural memory and intelligence to master the very different skills required in each. He could decode the grammar of the Arapaho language, analyze the symbolism of the Hupa White Deerskin Dance, dig up a Nazca tomb in Peru, or measure the heads of the natives on a trip to a remote island in Mexico. He was an "anthro-pologist's anthropologist," in the words of an admiring colleague, and his aura was still considerable in his emeritus years after World War II, when his trademark beard had turned snowy white. "I thought he was a genius," recalls a student who interacted with Kroeber in the 1950s. "It was like Moses when he talked—and he looked like Moses, too, with that beard." The proportions of Kroeber's scholarship were surely biblical enough: ten books and nearly 600 published articles.

Kroeber and a few others of his generation would be the last members of the tribe of generalists. Today anthropology is so sprawling and specialized a discipline that few have much expertise outside their own subfield. As a cultural anthropologist, I know very little about, say, the methods for DNA-testing the bone fragments found in an ancient ruin. By the same token, not many physical anthropologists keep abreast of the latest currents in cultural anthropology. Anthropology at Duke, Stanford, and several more major universities is now divided into separate departments of cultural and biological anthropology in recognition of the reality of the more humanistic, interpretive drift of former—and the very different laboratory-based, hard science flavor of the latter.

Kroeber's career divides into two broad, overlapping phases. In his first two decades in the Bay Area, he concentrated especially on the collection of information about the language and culture of vanishing tribal societies—and also their baskets, pots, and other material objects for the museum. He did fieldwork in the Southwest and Mexico, but he was focused on the Indians of California. In later years, when the rigors of fieldwork in out-of-the-way places were no longer so appealing, Kroeber wrote more abstract, theoretical books such as *The Nature of Culture* and *Style and Civilization*, variously inspired by his interests in philosophy, history, and psychoanalysis (he'd corresponded with Freud and even tried his hand as an analyst for an interlude in 1918 at the Stanford Clinic).

There was nonetheless a striking measure of consistency to Kroeber's thought across the decades. He was even more unambiguous than Boas when he insisted in 1915 on the "absolute equality and identity of all human races" in their moral and intellectual capacity. Kroeber lived long enough to see the principles of racial equality and justice begin to gain wider currency with the birth of the civil rights movement and the end of Third World colonialism. He also adhered to the relativist Boasian credo that other ways of life deserved the respect of study and understanding. "Anthropologists now agree," Kroeber wrote in 1952, "that each culture must be examined in terms of its own structures and values, instead of being rated by the standards of some other civilization exalted as absolute—which in practice of course is always our own civilization."

In his own way, however, Kroeber was also a determinist. The great Boas had emphasized culture's role in shaping the behavior of its members, but Kroeber pressed this argument to such an extreme as to leave almost no room for personal choice or action. Our actions, he believed, are always unconsciously determined by our cultural upbringing. As he had it in a famous 1917 essay, culture was "superorganic"—an entity above and beyond any single person and yet nonetheless guiding each of our behaviors like some internalized computer shareware. The anthropologist was to delineate the "pattern" or "configuration" of each culture, and each culture was presumed to be shared, unitary, and static. In Kroeber's view, the individual was a mere product of his or her socialization, possessing "no historical value save as illustrations" and "shrinking to insignificance." These ideas would lead the eminent anthropologist Eric Wolf to complain that Kroeber's writing had "no people" in it. And his unitary view of culture would be supplanted by one that asserted that culture is always contested, fragmented, and constantly in flux.

It was another, more unlikely Kroeber who was most responsible for the survival of the legend of Ishi into our own times. After his death, the Wild Man of Deer Creek faded somewhat from the public memory. Ishi seemed to be turning into just another footnote in northern California's folklore, like Sir Francis Drake's mythical landing near Point Reyes or the fabled bandit Joaquin Murieta. The second half of the twentieth century, however, brought surging interest in the last Yahi Indian, thanks to the efforts of Alfred Kroeber's second wife, Theodora.

In 1961, the University of California Press published Theodora's *Ishi in Two Worlds: A Biography of the Last Wild Indian in North America*, and it became a surprise bestseller (today, more than forty years later, there are almost a million copies in print). The book was excerpted in *Reader's Digest*, serialized on the radio, and translated into Japanese, Hungarian, Italian, and several additional foreign languages. The University of California Press also issued a "deluxe" edition of *Ishi in Two Worlds* on fancier paper with more illustrations—and an anthology of source materials about Ishi co-edited by Theodora and Robert Heizer, a close family friend and the leading archaeologist of Native California of his time. Theodora later published a children's book called *Last of His Tribe*, also a great commercial success. Her work introduced Ishi to a new generation of Americans and made him as well known or perhaps even better known than he'd been in his own lifetime. One of the two subsequent made-for-TV movies about Ishi's life featured Jon Voight as Alfred Kroeber, Anne Archer as Kroeber's first wife, Henriette, and, as Ishi, Graham Greene, the Oneida Indian actor and star of *Dances with Wolves*. In 1984, the U.S. Congress set aside the heartland of Yahi country for protection as the Ishi Wilderness Area.

As a housewife who only late in life became a bestselling author, Theodora was an intriguing story herself. She grew up in the Rockies, the child of a small-town portrait photographer in Telluride who taught his only daughter to love Shakespeare and the outdoors. Her Western childhood exposed Theodora early on to things Indian. "My brothers and I took Indians for granted," she wrote much later. "Our horses came from Ute Indians who trained them to take the steep trails at an easy gait which did not jolt and tire horse or rider. We rode on horseback to visit various cliff dwellings before the road was put into Mesa Verde Park; and the floors of our home were covered with rugs from the looms of Navajo women who wove them." Like many liberal-minded twentieth-century white Americans, Theodora developed a powerful romantic attraction to and even identification with Indians as emblems of wisdom and dignity—and her very first book was a collection of California Indian tales. "When I write, I turn most often to something Indian. This is not because I am an Indian "specialist," or feel that I have anything novel to say about Indians, but because I find their stories beautiful and true and their way of telling a story to be also my way."

In 1915, Theodora's family moved to Sacramento, and Theodora enrolled in college at the University of California at Berkeley. A bit shy, yet full of curiosity and talent, she was, if not beautiful, a handsome young woman with short hair and clear brown eyes. At that time there were still relatively few women attending the university, yet Theodora excelled, graduating with honors in 1919. A year later, "Krakie," as she was nicknamed after her maiden name, married an aspiring San Francisco lawyer, Clifton Brown, but his health was frail from his time in the trenches during World War I. The young couple moved to Santa Fe, New Mexico, in hopes that the desert air would heal Clifton's weak lungs. It did no good, and he died there in 1923. Theodora was widowed, with two small children, at the age of twenty-six. She brought her husband's body back to California for burial and moved in with her mother-in-law in north Berkeley.

In 1918, when she had been a student at Berkeley, Theodora had taken a class from Alfred Kroeber. They met once again in 1925, this time at a campus reception for the visiting Margaret Mead, who was just back from the fieldwork in Samoa that would make her America's most famous twentieth-century anthropologist. Alfred was twenty years older than Theodora, yet both had been widowed. A decade before, Alfred had lost his first wife, Henriette, with whom he had been very much in love, to tuberculosis. As Theodora later put it, she and Alfred had in common a recognition "of the fragility of human expectations, of the ruthlessness with which such expectations can be brought to nothing."

Alfred invited Theodora for dinner and dancing in San Francisco, a lover's city with its fog and hills. Theodora later recalled noticing Alfred's "smoothly brushed back hair, and closely trimmed beard, both streaked with gray; the sensitive and elegant hands; the quick but undramatized motions and gestures." Still and always a bit the worshipful student, Theodora was also impressed by Alfred's stature as a leading intellectual, even if she was not so starry-eyed to overlook his occasional burst of imperiousness, which became less frequent as he mellowed in his later years. Any such impatience was for Theodora more than compensated for by Alfred's large curiosity and enthusiasm about the world. Alfred was a world-class talker who could discourse about anything from Napa Valley wine to Greek mythology. Unlike most academics, however, he was also a good listener. He had that rare quality Theodora once described as "unboreability."

The more reserved Alfred does not seem to have shared his impressions of Theodora in any such detail. When his mother, Mimi, wrote to ask him to describe his new wife, he hid behind the mask of a dry, half-witty sarcasm as he sometimes did instead of expressing his real emotions. "You ask me what Theodora is like. Well, she has pink hair and is left-handed. And she is amiable." Alfred must nonetheless have been very much attracted to his bright, fresh-faced former student, for they were married within a year of their reacquaintance. The Kroebers raised Theodora's two children by her first husband, Clifton and Theodore, and also had two of their own, Ursula and Karl. By all accounts it was a happy marriage and a happy family.

During the first decades of her marriage, Theodora was the prototypical faculty wife of a certain generation. She tended to the house and children, did the shopping, bought the birthday and Christmas presents for friends and family, and cooked dinners for such local and visiting luminaries as the physicist Robert Oppenheimer, the philosopher Pierre Teilhard de Chardin, and the psychologist Erik Erikson. There were sometimes Indian house guests, too, Alfred's informants who'd also become friends. The Kroeber children would remember Robert Spott, a Yurok wise man and World War I veteran, and Juan Dolores, a Papago museum helper who had also befriended Ishi, as their "Indian Uncles." Only in her fifties, during the Eisenhower years and with her children grown, did Theodora find time to write her first book, *The Inland Whale*, a collection of California Indian tales. She once joked about taking up the craft at an age when she was "old enough to know better," and never admitted to any regret for her late start. "I think if I had tried to write 30 years ago," she insisted toward the end of her life, "I would have made a mess of both my family and my writing."

Theodora completed *Ishi in Two Worlds* in 1960. The book took her two years to write, and she described the work of bringing Ishi's story to life as a "hand-to-hand struggle." It was all the harder since she herself had never met the man her biography would once again make famous. The Wild Man of Oroville was captured before Theodora's family moved to California, and he had died when Theodora was still a Berkeley undergraduate. With a novelist's instinct, however, Theodora perceived the power of the story—and its archetypal, dramatic theme of a man marooned away from the world, and ostensibly a Stone Age man at that. According to her son Clifton, Theodora had sometimes prodded and teased Alfred and their friend Robert Heizer, the archaeologist and also a Berkeley professor. "When are you two lugs ever going to do something about Ishi?" she'd ask the two men, over a late glass of red wine. "Why don't you do it yourself?" they'd joust back, eventually inspiring Theodora to take up the challenge. Albert Elsasser, another Berkeley professor and friend of the Kroebers, has another version of the story. He believes that Alfred always knew that a book about Ishi would be a money-maker—and left it to Theodora so that she'd have a source of income once he died. In any event, once she decided to write *Ishi in Two Worlds*, Alfred became Theodora's single most important source. He was in his eighties by then and the only man still alive who had known Ishi well. Alfred commented on the final draft but died just before the book, dedicated to him, hit the bookstores.

*Ishi in Two Worlds* became an instant classic. A convict at Folsom State Prison was just one of Theodora's legion of admiring readers. "I've read an average of 700 books per year during the past 15 years which I've spent in prison," he wrote her, "and your book brought me more reading enjoyment than any others." Theodora was writing after Auschwitz, Hiroshima, and Stalin's gulags, and she portrayed the hunting down of the Yahi as another episode of hatred and the planned extermination of whole peoples and cultures. By this time, a hundred years later, the ugly history of Indian extermination in California had been largely forgotten, at least by most whites. Though she was not an articulate public speaker ("I am a worse uh-uh-uher than most," she admitted to an interviewer in her later years), Theodora was a highly gifted writer. The details of her account would later come into question, but she reconstructed the massacres of Yahi by whites at Three Knolls, Kingsley Cave, and Campo Seco in a straightforward, almost understated way that made the tale of the destruction of Ishi's people all the more terrible. Perhaps because she was growing old herself by then, Theodora never traveled to see rugged Yahi country in researching *Ishi in Two Worlds*. It was a tribute to her compassion and skill that she could create so believable a portrait of Ishi's homeland and the killing that had occurred there a century before. That she wrote with such immediacy about a land she'd never seen recalled William Prescott, a blind Bostonian historian and lawyer of the nineteenth century. Prescott penned his famous *The Conquest of Mexico* without ever leaving his study.

Theodora's portrait of Ishi was warm and admiring, sometimes to the point of condescension. Although she once criticized those "to whom Ishi was Rousseau's unspoiled savage," Theodora herself tended to fall into this trap. Her Ishi was "gentle," "cheerful," and "willing" with a personality that was "affectionate and uncorrupt." To her credit, however, she avoided the worst excesses of romanticism. Like Ishi's preference for day-old bread to save money or his interest in purchasing a horse and wagon, she layered in enough idiosyncratic, humanizing detail to allow her readers to feel that they were being introduced to a real, flesh-and-blood human being.

If unflinching about the horrors suffered by California Indians, Theodora also wanted very much to make Ishi's biography into a story of eventual healing and the triumph of the human spirit. She wrote when Martin Luther King Jr. was just rising to prominence and the much angrier, more militant voices of Malcolm X, Stokeley Carmichael, and the Red Power radicals had not yet been heard. According to Theodora, Ishi came through his people's destruction because of his

own wherewithal, but also thanks to the kindness of her husband Alfred
and Ishi's other white protectors. The happy conclusion to her telling of
Ishi's story modeled an innocent white liberalism that wanted to
acknowledge this country's crimes against blacks and Indians—and yet
also to find newly liberated peoples grateful and eager to grasp well-
meaning white hands outstretched now in friendship and reconciliation.
Once settled at the museum, Ishi was contented with his new life and
embraced Alfred, Thomas Waterman, and the surgeon Saxton Pope as
his "intimate friends," Theodora insisted.

Timing is everything in the reception of art and literature. The success of *Ishi in Two Worlds* had very much to do with the changing times
in America of the 1960s and 1970s. As a chronicle of violence and terror,
the book came out amid the war's escalation in Vietnam and a new
round of massacres committed by armed Americans, this time halfway
around the world. Another of that era's bestsellers was Dee Brown's
*Bury My Heart at Wounded Knee*, a hard-hitting and unrelenting chronicle
of atrocities against Indians in the westward expansion of the United
States. Both books invited readers to mourn the victims of their own
country's progress—and reinforced the impression of Indians as a vanishing race. "Dear Mrs. Kroeber," read one of Theodora's many fan letters, "What a beautiful, beautiful thing you have done about Ishi.
Moved to the depths I wept." Stirred in some readers was that guilty,
heartfelt, and sometimes paternalistic wish to "save" any surviving
tribesman from poverty and mistreatment by other whites. After finishing the book, one Rhode Island woman wrote to Theodora on behalf of
herself and her husband: "We both feel deeply about the Indian and
would like to do something to help. However, we do not know where to
begin. Could you possibly send us information and suggestions toward
this end?"

Theodora also tapped into the enchantment with Native Americans
so much on the rise in those years. Still another bestseller of the
Vietnam War years was Carlos Castaneda's *Teachings of Don Juan*, about a
wise, peyote-taking Yaqui Indian shaman (probably a made-up character, as it turned out). The Indians of northern California did not have
hallucinogens or vision quests, but Theodora offered an attractive, glowing portrait of the traditional Yahi way of life—"A Copper-Colored
People on a Golden Land," as the title to her book's first chapter had it.
Her vision of Yahi beauty and harmony appealed to the kind of
Americans who went on to embrace the tenets of New Age spirituality

later in the twentieth century, especially its fascination with shamans, sweat lodges, dream-catchers, and things Indian. "The peace of the bay tree you taught me, the soft leaflight of hope," went one poem in a collection called *Ishi Country*. Ishi's story also appealed to the growing environmental movement with its enshrinement of Indians as symbols of a stewardship of the land lost in the West's voracious version of progress. A Sacramento Valley Sierra Club named itself after Ishi and the town of Chico installed the Ishi Nature Trail through a city park.

Theodora's tale stirred an intense, almost religious identification with Ishi himself. This man's saga of loneliness, survival, and life at death's edge was often especially moving for the sick and the old. Like a saint's devotee, one elderly Atlanta woman wrote the Berkeley anthropology museum to request a keepsake, an arrowhead by Ishi's hand or at least his photograph. "I hope I can get across to you what the story meant to me," this woman wrote after reading the excerpt of *Ishi in Two Worlds* in *Reader's Digest*. "I would have loved to have known Ishi. I feel very close to the person he was. I would have been content just to have been around him." Theodora became a Bay Area celebrity, the high priestess of the new cult of Ishi and the wise old grandmother of liberal northern California. She received fan letters from as far away as Norway and Germany, and when California's governor, Jerry Brown, appointed her to the Board of Regents of the University of California, she became the oldest member in the history of this powerful oversight committee.

Even in retirement, Alfred Kroeber was pulling strings in the Berkeley department and churning out books—*The Nature of Culture, Style and Civilizations, A Roster of Civilizations and Culture*. One graduate student then recalls the legendary old man coming to seminars, nodding off in his chair, and then suddenly waking to interject some astute comment into the discussion. Kroeber never wrote his own memoirs, or about his personal relationship with Ishi. According to Ursula K. Le Guin, his author daughter, whose science fiction is laced with Indian legend and lore, he "was too interested in the present to want to spend much time reminiscing."

As I would find out as I learned more, Alfred Kroeber's scholarship about Native California had gaping holes. Nor was his treatment of "his" wild man, Ishi, always so magnanimous as Theodora wanted her readers to believe. But long after Ishi was gone and Kroeber had become the dean and, some complained, the pontiff of American anthropology, the old anthropologist kept his connections to Native California. He maintained close friendships with Juan Dolores and other Indians. And he testified for California's tribes in 1953 before the Indian Claims Commission (although the government only made token payments of $800 then to each surviving man, woman, and child). The "salvage" anthropology conducted by Alfred and his Berkeley anthropologists is still our single best record of pre-contact Native California. Now modern-day Indians will sometimes consult Kroeber's *Handbook of the Indians of California* to learn more about the culture and traditions of their ancestors. "I am grateful," one older Yurok wrote not long ago, that a "few of the best Anthropologists of the late eighteen hundreds and early nineteen hundreds were in California and took an interest in our tribe." The information available in the books of both Kroeber and Thomas Waterman, this man added, "has been invaluable to me and will be passed on to our children and grandchildren."

Theodora outlived Alfred by almost twenty years. After his death in 1960, she married once more, this time to a man twenty years her junior, her editor, John Quinn. In her last years, Theodora grew evermore insistent that Ishi was a talisman, a good luck charm, and a symbol of reconciliation and healing. She probably didn't know his work, but Frank Day, a Maidu artist, had recently completed his *Ishi at Iamin Mool*, with its depiction of Ishi as a shaman ministering in the wilderness to a mysterious wounded companion. In their own ways, Indians and non-Indians alike have believed Ishi was a life-giver, a figure of power and protection.

Theodora's last book was a biography of Alfred. After the success of *Ishi in Two Worlds*, Theodora and the University of California Press had high hopes for *Alfred Kroeber: A Personal Configuration*. Not only did Theodora love Alfred, but she had always thought of him as one of the twentieth century's major intellectuals. In the early 1970s, however, Alfred's star was already fading. Sales of *Alfred Kroeber* were poor, even though the book was favorably reviewed and evocatively written, as was Theodora's way.

In *Alfred Kroeber*, as historian James Clifford has noted, Theodora attributed therapeutic powers to Ishi. After his wife Henriette's death from tuberculosis, Alfred had felt his own life "torn, disordered, without design or meaning," according to Theodora. On returning to the museum after the funeral, he'd found Ishi working peacefully alone to finish an arrowhead with a deer antler chipper. Alfred sat nearby in companionable silence. In that calm, wrote Theodora, "he felt Ishi trying to comfort him, to transmit something of the strength and wisdom of his own Yana faith." Alfred had been rescued from the "grief, worry, and the agony of living [that] threatened to engulf and overwhelm him."

We'll never know whether Ishi really was a shaman in his life in the wild. That Theodora insisted on Ishi's capacity to heal had to do with her own wish to find truth and even magic beyond the visible limits of her own Berkeley world. Neither Alfred nor Theodora was a churchgoer or follower of any organized faith. "Anthropology is my religion," Alfred declared, the modern man committed only to the creed of reason and science. He liked Ishi but saw no special powers in him. By contrast, Theodora had always looked to native cosmology for beauty and even guidance. She was not so starry-eyed as those modern pilgrims who nowadays journey to New Age meccas like Sedona and Mount Shasta City to stock up on crystals and be cured by real and pretend "native" shamans. She was enough the believer to want her readers to learn from, if not be healed, from the example of Ishi's life and "the strength and wisdom of his Yana faith."

Such was the magic of Theodora's storytelling that *Ishi in Two Worlds* became the general public's bible of Ishi studies. As the twentieth century drew to a close, few people knew that fresh academic research was opening up new views of the last Yahi's life—or that Indians in northern California had their own, quite different understanding of Ishi and his life's meaning. Theodora had written in the prologue to *Ishi in Two Worlds* that she believed she had recovered the "bone beads" of Ishi's story and threaded them "onto a single strand." The necklace so skillfully strung was about to loosen and let the beads slip off the string.

# Four

# ISHI'S ANCESTORS

Like so many small-town museums across the West, Oregon's Klamath County Museum, near the border with California, boasts the usual potpourri of expected and sometimes unlikely objects—a gold miner's pan, a collection of bird nests, a stuffed coyote, a stagecoach, spiked lumberman's boots, and a framed picture of local hero Dan O'Brien, the 1996 Olympic decathlon champion. It also has several of those old-style dioramas you no longer see in modern museums with their track-lighting and interactive computer stations. One, of considerable artistry, depicts the Modoc and Klamath Indians who'd inhabited the marshlands in California's far northeast. The diorama shows its little brown model Indians repairing a fish net, smoking a quartered deer, and canoeing on a clear epoxy lake against a painted backdrop of Mount Shasta's snowy peak. Viewers are invited to imagine that life was just like this in precontact times, right down to the tiniest little painted and shellacked clay water lily.

In truth, however, the sum of our knowledge about ancient California is far from complete. Unlike the Mayans in Central America, the Indians of California developed no writing system, leaving no parchment codices for us to decipher. We do have the chronicles of the early Spaniards, albeit not so detailed as those they provided for the empires of Peru's Incas or Mexico's Aztecs. The first Spanish settlers never even contacted the most remote inland tribes; much of the information they and the later Americans had about these "upstream" Indians, as they were called, came from the secondhand and sometimes unreliable accounts of peoples who lived downstream. Alfred Kroeber and his Berkeley colleagues began their more systematic research in the early twentieth century, but by then many of California's tribes and their cultures had already been destroyed forever, a "Praxitelean marble . . . broken and turned to dust," as Theodora Kroeber once lamented. Even the elderly from surviving groups like the Hupa and Karok had grown up during and after the Gold Rush. They could provide the anthropologists only a distant glimpse of what Native California was like before the saloons and the saw mills, the roads and the churches, the ranches and the towns.

We have also the work of the archaeologists. Without the lure of gigantic pyramids, intricate canal systems, or fabulous golden treasures, California has never been a magnet for archaeology like ancient Egypt, Greece, or China. Still, a U.C. Berkeley researcher, Martin Baumhoff, conducted excavations in the 1950s in Ishi's Yahi homeland. In those days, archaeologists didn't hesitate to claim whatever Indians goods and bones they found for their own institutional collections. Baumhoff's team brought various projectile points and thirty Yahi skeletons, nine children among them, back to the Berkeley museum, where they remain to this day. The leading archaeologist of the Yahi would later be Jerald Johnson, a former student of Baumhoff's and now an emeritus professor at Sacramento State. As I would discover when I met him in person, Johnson devoted much of his long professional career to reconstructing the ways of Ishi's ancestors. He'd even celebrated his wedding under an old oak tree above the silent canyon of Dye Creek in the northern part of the Yahi homeland.

What is certain is that Indians occupied the land we now call California for many millennia. The first people arrived about twelve thousand years ago, probably from the north and gravitating in the beginning to the valley wetlands with their abundant fish, freshwater mussels, and waterfowl. By first contact with the Spanish explorer Juan Rodríguez Cabrillo in 1542, the Indians numbered about 300,000, the highest native population density anywhere north of Mexico. By that time, tribes were distributed from the northern redwood coast to King's Canyon in the Sierra

Nevada and the southern Mojave desert. They spoke between seventy-five and one hundred mutually unintelligible languages. Among regions anywhere else in the world, only Central Asia and Papua New Guinea could compare with Native California in their linguistic diversity. In contrast to the grander empires of ancient Mexico and Peru, however, the Indians of California lived in little villages, and their Stone Age technology was more akin to that of Australia's aborigines or the tribes of Africa's interior. The first step out of savagery and "primitive life," in the opinion of the Spaniards, was farming, and it was already highly advanced among those peoples they found in Central, South, and parts of North America. Those societies gave the world the potato, tomato, corn, avocado, and squash, among many other cultivated crops. Yet the peoples of California subsisted principally by hunting and gathering, which further lowered their standing in the eyes of the Euro-American newcomers, Spanish and Anglo. In the early nineteenth century, Fray Gerónimo Boscana, a Mallorcan priest, wrote that the "Indians of California may be compared to a species of monkey." The German physician Georg Heinrich von Langsdorff marveled at California's "moderate and equitable climate" and "abundance of roots, seeds, fruits, and products of the sea"; he dismissed the Indians as "small, ugly, and of bad proportion in their persons, and heavy and dull in mind."

Among other prejudices, those early visitors failed to understand that Indians managed the land in their own ways. Down the mountains from Ishi's Yahi, for example, the Miwok in Yosemite Valley weeded patches of sedge to encourage this grass used for basketweaving. Farther south in Death Valley oases, the desert Cahuilla planted fan palms for shade and fruit. Many other such forms of pruning, irrigating, sowing, transplanting, and selective harvesting were practiced throughout Native California. In these ways, the very distinction between "hunting and gathering" and "farming" was an illusory one. Intervening to ensure nature's bounty was an integral part of the aboriginal way of life. That these tribes survived for hundreds and even thousands of years was a tribute to the sustainability of their land use practices.

Fire was a tool almost everywhere. Many villages burned off brush to promote the right seeds—and to ease travel and hunting. Sometimes these fires—or ones caused by lightning strikes—could rage out of control, blanketing a region with smoke until the first rains. Yet the pattern of deliberate burning explains why the early American traveler James Borthwick found the countryside near Placerville had "all the beauty of an English park"—that is, grassy hills free of underbrush under canopies of tall oaks. Borthwick was closer to the truth than he imagined. He and the other Westerners had not wandered into a wilderness; they had happened into a garden tended by human hands.

The archaeologist Jerald Johnson has traced the story of Ishi's tribe back about four thousand years. His research suggests that Yahi roamed from the hills down into the flatlands of the Sacramento River in those very early times. The Yahi language belonged to the larger Hokan family, among the oldest stocks anywhere in Native North America. About 2,500 years ago, however, new tribes arrived from the north—the so-called Penutian intrusion, after the family of languages spoken by the new arrivals. The Yahi and speakers of related Yana dialects in the older Hokan family chose or were forced to withdraw from the Sacramento Valley back into the hills. Over the ensuing centuries, these Yana speakers maintained uneasy and periodically hostile relations with the Wintu, Maidu, and other valley Penutians—or "Peanuts," as the archaeologists sometimes call them.

The Yana, Ishi's Yahi among them, were short even among California's Indians (all of whom were small by modern standards). The average man stood about 5'4", the average woman 5'2". One tribal creation story told to nineteenth-century folklorist Jeremiah Curtin had it that Penutians were created first from long, straight sticks, whereas Yana were made from stumpy, gnarled pieces of bark. Jerald Johnson estimates that the Yahi and other Yana subgroups numbered about 1,900 people just before first contact with whites. That population was spread across an area of the foothills about the size of the state of Delaware.

It must have been a challenge to survive shut out of the Sacramento Valley's plenitude in the barren hills. Acorns were a staple across Native California, and there were oaks even in the rocky Yahi canyons, but the harvest was not always dependable. During droughts, the deer stayed down by the wetlands of the Sacramento River. Salmon rushed up the canyon creeks to spawn several times a year, but the valley Indians caught many of the silver fish in weirs before they got that far. The foothills lacked lakes that would draw waterfowl. From their lonely position in the hills, Ishi's Yahi could watch the sky fill with geese that touched down only in the Sacramento Valley's marshes on their flyway between Canada and Mexico.

Yet the Yahi endured for centuries, even if this Yana subgroup probably never numbered more than a few hundred people at any one time. Their population density was less than one person per square mile, much lower than the tribes down in the Sacramento Valley. These broken foothills, with soil far too thin and rocky for farming even today, could sustain no larger numbers. Though it was no land of plenty, Yahi territory did possess tremendous diversity in plant and animal life—more than a hundred species of native shrubs and grasses alone. Besides spearing salmon and hunting deer, bear, and bobcat, the Yahi snared rabbits and quail, trapped doves, scooped up trout they stunned by crushing soaproot into the creeks, and roasted grasshoppers. Acorns were a mainstay, but Ishi's ancestors also ate honeysuckle, manzanita berries, and the seeds of doveweed, wild buckwheat, and other native grasses. They knew how to make the most of what this unwelcoming volcanic land offered.

Of course, pieties about Native Americans and their "harmony" with nature can become tiresome. What the anthropologist Shepard Krech has called the stereotype of the "ecological Indian"—a kind of latter-day concept of the Noble Savage—has been a mainstay of Anglo romanticism. Recall, if you are old enough, the famous TV commercials of a lone proud Indian warrior shedding a tear at the sight of a lake polluted by discarded trash. The Yahi have often been represented as prototypical children of nature; in this vein, the cover of one edition of Theodora Kroeber's children's book shows a boyish, kneeling Ishi reaching out gently with two hands to a rabbit like an Indian St. Francis. In general, as Krech and other researchers have shown, Indians were not always simple guardians of the environment. The Iroquois, for example, broke off whole branches of cherry trees rather than simply picking the fruit. Although the case is still debated, the late Pleistocene Indians have been accused of being "blitzkrieg" hunters who drove the megafauna of their time to extinction. Meanwhile, the ancient Anasazi have been charged not only with cannibalism but also with deforesting parts of the American Southwest. More recently, tribes have leased lands for strip mining and even nuclear waste dumps, proving themselves as capable as whites of sacrificing the environment for needed cash. The Campo Indians in southern California run a garbage landfill with a contract worth several million dollars from the city of San Diego. "It's our land," the tribal chairman told an interviewer in 1992. "We'll do what we want to do with it."

At the same time, it's true enough that the Yahi had developed their own special, intimate knowledge of the natural world. Every grown Yahi had a mental map detailing hundreds, even thousands, of sites that boasted the best deer runs, berry brambles, fishing pools, and patches of wild tobacco. There was *hanmawi madu*, a salt lick by Pine Creek; *matowi*, a mineral spring below Cohasset Ridge; and *kulu*, a crossing place at the junction of Big and Little Mill Creeks. The wild grape had small sweet fruit, Ishi knew, and his Yahi boiled the nuts of the bay tree to make a fragrant mush that was rubbed on the body after a sweat bath. When Ishi returned in 1914 to Deer Creek in the company of the Berkeley anthropologists, he named more than two hundred plants and their uses. Ishi also knew how to call quail, deer, and even, as in the cover of the children's book, rabbits. To draw a rabbit from the brush, he'd purse his forefingers to his lips and make an unusual cork-popping sound. These calls were meant to attract the animals for purposes of the stewpot, not interspecies communion.

The Yahi moved their camps with the changing seasons and in this way were very much in touch with nature's cycles. They wintered lower down in the foothills closest to the Sacramento Valley. Although this area fell beneath the snow line, winter was still a cold, lean time with little to forage and deer scarce, staying down in the warmer valley. By winter's end, however, the foothills turned a velvet green, as they still do everywhere in California that has been spared the bulldozers. The wild grasses rushed up heavy with spring seed, and the first salmon came back up the creeks on their thousand-mile journey from the Pacific. When the summer's heavy heat again parched the foothills, the Yahi headed to the high country. There beneath Mount Lassen they hunted the deer that had also drifted up to the mountain meadows in the summer. They dug lily roots and stripped bark from redbud trees to border their baskets. Only with the autumn chill did Ishi's ancestors loop back down to the foothills, completing their year's large circle.

The ways of the Yahi were well suited to this peripatetic life style. They lived in flexible, mobile bands of a few dozen people or less that could take to the trail without elaborate preparations. Their baskets, bows and arrows, and fur capes were easy to transport, and their small, conical brush houses could be put up in just a few hours for a new camp. Like the languages of other hunting and gathering peoples in North America, the Yahi tongue was precise about place and direction. The name assigned to a place often provided its coordinates in relation to other landmarks—*puniwi* was "a cave west of Spring Hill," *wansk'ana* "a camp west of Twenty Mile Hollow." There was no simple verb to indicate that a group of people had "departed." You had to say *"hancinji'"* ("left west away from camp"), or some even more exact specification.

As far as we know, the Yahi had no hereditary chiefs or much else in the way of social hierarchy. Whether men exercised more power than women is also unclear, but the distinction between the sexes was a definite organizing principle in Yahi society. There was the classic division of labor: women gathered acorns, men hunted deer and other game. Taboos also differed by gender, at least according to what Ishi told the anthropologists. A woman could eat a salmon's head, for example, but doing this would cause a man to lose his balance. Men could gorge on deer brains; women had to avoid this same food for fear of going bald. Ishi told the anthropologists that a Yahi man had to avoid contact with his mother-in-law at all times—and with any woman during her period or childbirth. In his excavations Jerald Johnson has found that a standard Yahi village feature was a hut presumably for women's use at those times, always a hundred yards or so removed from the main camp. That we have direct testimony only from a man, Ishi, leaves us to wonder how Yahi women viewed these restrictions and their lot in society.

It's also uncertain whether men or women ever thought of themselves as members of a larger "Yahi" tribe. Insofar as *Yahi*, the name coined by Alfred Kroeber, derives from Ishi's own word for "people," this label may be more appropriate than "Mill Creeks," "Deer Creeks," or other names concocted by outsiders. Yet the band of a few interrelated families was the foundation of Yahi society—and the band itself was a flexible design for living that changed in size and composition as people joined or split off for a time or for good. We can only speculate about whether any larger, more overarching structure of governance or even cooperation existed in Yahi territory.

At another level, the Yahi were one people. The several hundred souls who made their homes in the thirty or so miles of foothills from Battle Creek to Deer Creek had language in common. Their Yahi dialect was as different from more northerly Yana-speaking people as Spanish is from Italian. Sam Batwi, the translator who spoke a northern Yana dialect, could not understand everything Ishi said. The language divide was even more pronounced between Ishi's Yahi and the Maidu, Wintu, and other valley tribes, whose Penutian languages were altogether unrelated to Yahi and the other Yana dialects. The silent record of archaeology also shows many other distinctions between the Yahi and adjoining peoples, however small. The Maidu down toward the Feather River mashed acorns for stew in bedrock mortars, depressions that they chipped into solid rock formations. By contrast, the Yahi ground food on flat river rocks, or *metates*, that were portable enough to bring to camp. In these ways, the collection of little bands that Kroeber and the other anthropologists decided to call the Yahi had much in common, whether they chose to recognize it or not.

Certainly, Ishi's ancestors interacted with other tribes. When they summered in the high country, they shared the meadows there with the Atsugewi and Achumawi among and other groups. The Yahi also evidently scraped together enough extra deer meat or other items for occasional barter with their neighbors. Baumhoff's crew unearthed bleached white clam shell beads near Mill Creek, probably obtained by trade from the distant Pacific Coast. Far from being self-sufficient or oblivious to the advantages of trade, the peoples of Native California established far-reaching networks of exchange that reached into the Great Basin and as far south as Mexico, bartering goods such as soapstone pipes, obsidian, and dentalium shells. There were systems for conveying information, too. Runners sometimes carried news between allied villages in the northern Sacramento Valley as far north as Mount Shasta. Some Indians were multilingual, facilitating communication. Ishi himself knew a few words of Maidu, Wintu, and Atsugewi.

Yet the Yahi were also an ingrown community, set in their ways. They may have intermarried with neighboring tribes (and sometimes kidnaped women in the mid-nineteenth century), but outsiders were absorbed into the Yahi way. Elsewhere in Native America before Columbus there was volatility and change—disease, war, migration, cultural invention, and adaptation. In the Southwest, for example, the legendary Anasazi cliff dwellers suddenly vanished in the twelfth century, for reasons still debated. Over time, however, the Yahi showed more continuity and stability than these other groups. Relatively little modification occurred in fashioning spear points, laying out a camp, pounding acorns, or other routines of the Yahi existence. By all appearances, Ishi's ancestors followed more or less the same way of life for many centuries.

During my years of fieldwork in the Andes, I'd visited Chan Chan, Sechín, Machu Picchu, and the other great ruins of the pre-Columbian civilizations. ("Towering reef of the human dawn," the Chilean poet Pablo Neruda had declared of Machu Picchu, the lost citadel of the

Incas perched just above the Amazon jungle.) The surviving artifacts of the Yahi are much more inconspicuous, even more so than the shell-mounds left by the Ohlone along San Francisco Bay. Instead of temples, we have only the faint outline of a housepit, a broken spear point, a boulder scratched with a small petroglyph no one now can read. Yet Ishi's people inhabited these hills for so many centuries that they left these traces everywhere, for those with the eyes to see them. That the chaparral looks so wild and empty now of any sign of early human occupation is yet another illusion. In the northernmost Yahi country Jerald Johnson and his students have mapped more than three hundred camps around Dye Creek alone.

The stones and bones excavated by archaeologists give us precious clues about the organization of Yahi society. They tell us less about religion and belief, about how the Yahi understood their world. Here we must rely on Ishi, the only Yahi from whom any information was ever recorded. What can be learned about a people's worldview from a single individual is partial at best, of course—almost like trying to save a record of Judaism from the testimony of a lone survivor of the Nazi Holocaust. At least, however, Ishi shared much of the Yahi tradition with the anthropologists, among them the six stories he dictated to Edward Sapir in the last year before his own death. In the 1980s, a team of linguists at U.C. Berkeley—Victor Golla, Leanne Hinton, Herbert Luthin, Jean Perry, and Ken Whistler—formed to finish translating Sapir's notebooks. Even with a special computer program, progress was slow and the team split up as they were drawn away to other important work. Recently, however, Herbert Luthin and Leanne Hinton have finished the translations of three of Ishi's stories. We also have Jean Perry's translation of a fourth story that contains part of the Yahi creation myth.

These stories give us our best view yet of Yahi mythology. As Ishi told it, the world was once populated by mythical animal divinities that included Coyote, Rabbit, Duck, Lizard, and Grizzly Bear. These legendary figures traveled underground, swung between mountains on ropes, and whirled with the wind. The Promethean Grizzly Bear had retrieved fire from the upper world sometime very long ago, and others of his kind also did good for humankind. Yet the animal beings were also imperfect, and in this way they were more like the Greek gods than the

Christian one. As in other storytelling across Native America, Coyote was an especially untrustworthy trickster, sometimes funny, sometimes dangerous. In one of Ishi's stories Coyote rapes his sister, then almost burns down the world. When he spied some villagers, Ishi chanted:

> *Coyote came up to meet them.*
> *He begged for fire.*
> *"You can't have it."*
> *"You'll burn your hand," they told him.*
> *He took the fire into his hand.*
> *My hands are all burnt!," said Coyote.*
> *So, in secret, he threw the fire down on the ground.*
> *It broke into pieces.*
> *He let it fall,*
> *he let it fall to the ground and break into pieces.*
> *The fire made a burning sound.*
> *It burned to the west, to the east, back to the south.*
> *It burned to the north:*

Coyote burns his toes in the forest fire, then munches on them for a snack. "They are better than grasshoppers!" he declares, referring to the crunchy insects that the Yahi roasted for snacks.

The Yahi cosmology marked no single originary moment of creation. It took Rabbit to raise the sun into the sky sometime back in the early days. "It was really dark in the mornings then," as Ishi recounted it, until:

> *Rabbit took the sun on his back*
> *He went along with the sun to the east*
> *The sun appeared*
> *Coming to the east over the earth*
> *It was no longer dark.*

Even humans had been made only in stages. One of Ishi's tales explained that men and women had been indistinguishable in early times. It took Gray Squirrel to give women vaginas—and, culture following nature, tasseled deerskin aprons to further distinguish themselves from their men. While we sometimes like to imagine Native Americans as grave and humorless, the tales of Coyote and the other animal beings abound in laughter, sex, violence, and absurdity. These myths explained the world but also entertained around the campfire.

The first whites did not set foot in Yahi country until very late in the West's conquest of the Americas, probably the early nineteenth century. As the farthest frontier of three great powers, California was one of the last places on the continent to be fully colonized. For the Spaniards, it was the far north. When they established their first mission near modern-day San Diego in 1769, the Mother Lode was still undiscovered and only a thousand or so Spaniards ever occupied California at one time. The Russians saw California as their exotic east; only in 1812 did Tsar Paul's men establish a beachhead a hundred miles north of San Francisco at Fort Ross, mostly to hunt the sea otter for its treasured pelt. Anglo Americans came last to California. For the pioneers who began to cross the Great Plains in 1849, it was the far West, the fertile valleys and oceans of a New Arcadia, the last and most beautiful frontier. The arrival of the Chinese, Slavs, Latin Americans, and freed blacks to labor in the Gold Country would add still more diversity and potential conflict to the mix. We sometimes wrongly imagine today's multicultural California to be a recent development; by the nineteenth century, the land was already a crossroads for peoples from Native America, Europe, and Asia.

The Spaniards established a string of twenty-one missions in the region they called Alta California. The missions were built for evangel-izing purposes, spearheaded by the indomitable Franciscan Junipero Serra, who in penance for mankind's sins practiced self-flagellation, scarred his chest with candles, and wore habits with sharp spines pointed inwards. The friars encouraged and often succeeded in luring, or forcing, Indians into the missions. There they were given Spanish names like Pedro and Maria, instructed in the gospel, and put to work as farmhands and herders. Confinement to the barracks at the missions hastened the spread of measles, smallpox, influenza, and other infec-tious diseases among the Indians. In the first decade of the nineteenth century alone, an average of more than one hundred Juaneños a year perished at one of the largest missions, San Juan Capistrano, abode of the famous swallows.

Yet the Yahi were insulated from any early contact with the Europeans. The nearest mission, San Francisco Solano de Sonoma, located in today's wine country in the Sonoma Valley, was a full two hundred miles to the southwest. Just as great a distance protected Ishi's people from the Russians at Fort Ross, although a party of the tsar's men supposedly passed through Clear Creek north toward Mount Shasta as early as 1815. The Yahi may not have seen their first white men until sometime in the 1840s. These might have been trappers from the Hudson Bay Company making their way down from Canada—or perhaps an expeditionary force of Spanish troops (*saltu*, the Yahi word for "white people," perhaps derived from *soldado*, the Spanish for soldier).

What did the Yahi make of the pale new people? The folklore of today's living descendants of the Yurok along California's far northern coast offers one account of first contact. According to this story, a Spanish galleon had anchored near the Bay of Trinidad. The Yurok concealed themselves in the rocks to watch the sailors come aboard in rowboats, but they were not too shy to come down to the beach and snatch a couple of axes when the Europeans were not looking. The size of the great sailing ship was not what had most astonished the Yurok, or so the legend has it. It was the white men's many varieties of hair color—blonde, red, and so many shades of brown. No Yurok had seen anything except black hair ever before.

One suspects that Ishi's Yahi wondered at the hair color of their first white arrivals—and also at much else. Whether trappers or Spaniards, those early expeditionaries probably came on horseback. The sight of horses was a novelty for the Yahi, who had no domestic animals of any kind. The largest farm animal anywhere in pre-Columbian North America was the turkey, although the Sioux and other Plains tribes soon became expert riders and made the horse an integral part of their cultures. The composition of the first parties of hunters and explorers must have also puzzled Ishi's people. Did the strangers have no women? There were none among the earliest whites to explore the foothills of the Sacramento Valley.

Only in the 1840s did whites begin to settle this northern part of California. By then, Mexico was independent of Spain. Worried about losing California to the Russians, French, Americans, or even the British, the authorities in Mexico City decided to hand out large tracts of land to promote settlement in its northernmost province. Under the new law, even non-Mexicans could receive a land grant if they swore allegiance to Mexico's government. There were a couple of Mexicans among those procuring titles in the northern Sacramento valley just beneath the Yahi homeland, but no one claimed the parched foothills themselves. The settlers of this region were mostly of northern European extraction—the Dane Peter Lassen, the Americans John Bidwell, Albert Toomes, and Pierson Reading.

Many years later, John Bidwell recalled his first reconnaissance of the area in 1843, among the earliest by any white man. This future member of Congress and larger-than-life figure of the Sacramento Valley was joined by Peter Lassen and an Indian named François, perhaps a French Canadian. The three pushed north along the valley's edge in this territory still lacking a single white homestead. They came upon stream after stream tumbling out of their canyons onto the floor of the giant valley. The Yahi already had their own names for these creeks, but Bidwell did not know or care anything about this. California's Indians, he thought, were too backward to have any real claim to ownership; the land was a wilderness that whites had the right and duty to civilize. Like a Yankee Adam, the young Bidwell assigned his own spare stock of predictable names to each creek his party forded. The first was "beautiful and clear. On its banks appeared deer in great numbers; they seemed to be in droves; so we named it Deer Creek. The next flowing stream having still more fall where we crossed it, suggested its value as fine water power, so we named it Mill Creek."

Bidwell's companion Peter Lassen decided to settle just where Deer Creek spilled onto the plain. His ranch was the terminus for an early wagon trail across the Great Basin over into California—and the snow-capped volcanic peak that rose up behind the foothills would later be named after the Danish blacksmith. Bidwell's ranch a bit farther to the south grew into the largest settlement in that part of the Sacramento River Valley, the modestly named town of Chico, Spanish for "small."

When it came to Indians, the Mexican settlers of Alta California had followed the old template of Spanish colonialism. The Spaniards had looked on the Incas and Aztecs, no matter what their cultural and architectural achievements, as inferiors. At the same time, they sought to convert their new subjects to Christianity and incorporate them into their society. Having no other workforce available, they wanted to exploit the labor of Indians, not to exterminate or remove them. At first the Americans followed their colonial predecessors' example. An offshoot of the Maidu called the Mechoopda had inhabited the land that the young Bidwell claimed with his Mexican title. He put the Indians to work clearing land for wheat, erecting barns, and pasturing his sheep and cattle. Bidwell, who later in life became a teetotaler and a Methodist, always considered himself a friend and protector of the indigenous Californians. He found the aborigines "as wild as a deer and wholly unclad," one admiring contemporary wrote, and he left them in "happy homes," instructed in civilization's ways. Yet this was a medieval system of peonage at heart. Paid only with trinkets, the Indians received no wages and depended on their master for protection against hostile settlers or being sent to a reservation. For many years, the Mechoopda went by their master's name and were known simply as the Bidwell Indians.

But what of the Yahi? The latter-day mythology about Ishi and his people has represented them as untouched by history and the modern world. Ishi's role is that of California's Tarzan, a child of the forest primeval. On any closer look, however, the Yahi were by no means a legendary lost tribe existing in a state of nature. They spent the final half century of their existence as refugees in their own land, pilfering canned food, sacks of flour, and even livestock from settlers in order to survive. As a boy, Ishi would never know what it had been like to roam the hills without fear of being gunned down.

One small, interesting fact, however, is that the Yahi had somehow learned a few Spanish words, a clue that suggests an earlier and perhaps more peaceful history of contact in the years before Ishi's birth. In 1850, a prospector's diary mentioned coming across Indians on Deer Creek who spoke some Spanish. This "party of squaws with large conical baskets on their backs, 2 men with them" had used that language to direct the lost, starving man down to Lassen's ranch. When the surveyors broke into the Yahi hideout above Deer Creek in 1908, they found the crippled old woman who was Ishi's mother. This woman spoke no English at all, but after overcoming her fear she had begged for water in a few words of broken Spanish. *Malo, malo,* Ishi's mother had repeated to describe the painful condition of her legs. Later in San Francisco, Ishi's doctor Saxton Pope noted that Ishi himself knew several Spanish words—*camisa* for shirt, *paka* for cow, and *papelo* for paper, among others.

The Yahi may have picked up words like *malo* and *paka* from neighboring Indians. Elsewhere in California, linguists have discovered that Spanish words could pass from group to group into areas not yet visited by any outsider, sometimes incorporated into a kind of pidgin used in contact with other tribes. Language resembled disease in this capacity to fan out in advance of the physical arrival of any white man. Ishi's people could have acquired *malo* and the rest of their Spanish vocabulary from the Maidu down the hills toward Oroville. These Indians were closer than the Yahi to areas visited early on by Spanish explorers, and more than thirty Spanish words had entered into their standard vocabulary.

Possibly, however, the Yahi had direct contact with Mexicans or some other native Spanish speakers. Ishi's people lived just a few miles above the ranches that began to fill the Sacramento Valley in the 1840s. Lassen, John Bidwell, and the area's earliest farmers were of northern European extraction, but California still belonged to Mexico and Spanish was everywhere the lingua franca for the Anglos, Mexicans, and Indians. The Yahi may have traded or had other casual dealings with Spanish speakers from one of the nearby valley ranches. A few might even have been in Lassen's employ, learning Spanish that way. An 1849 visitor noted that Lassen had "from fifteen to twenty Mexicans and Indians to take care of his cattle and horses." Many California Indians had already become expert cowboys.

Lassen's property actually extended up into the lower reaches of Deer Creek. If any Yahi had once worked for a rancher (and only later gone into hiding when trouble began after the Gold Rush), this could explain how Ishi knew some Spanish terms but none at all in English. When his mother gave birth to him sometime about 1860, the Yahi were already fugitives, avoiding any direct contact with the settlers trying to hunt them down. The fragments of Spanish in Ishi's speech could have come down from his mother or other older Yahi who'd worked on the ranches two decades before—a vestige of a chapter in Yahi history just before the United States admitted California to the Union, in 1850, as the thirty-first state.

At the very least, the Spanish words in the Yahi vocabulary prove that Ishi's people had contact with other nineteenth-century peoples, even if these were only adjacent Indian tribes. We can assume as well that the Yahi understood early on that their world was changing. If only from the bluffs above the valley, the Yahi of Ishi's grandparents' generation must have noted the arrival of more cattle, sheep, wagons, and a people who stuck to farming unlike their own peripatetic traditional society. Now there were women among the settlers, too, who looked after the cooking and laundry, sometimes with the help of their Indian servants. The Yahi also grew accustomed to the sound of a rifle's crack. The settlers sometimes ranged into the foothills after antelope, deer, and even the grizzlies that still menaced people and livestock. The retorts of Hawken and Winchester rifles echoed across the stone walls of the canyons.

By that time, too, the Yahi must have heard about the strange deadly plagues down in the flatlands, even if they were not yet affected themselves. An epidemic of smallpox had swept up the Sacramento Valley in 1833. It killed hundreds of Indians while leaving the survivors blind, scarred, and maimed for life. In a way, however, the worst of the storm was still yet to come. The relatively isolated northern interiors of California had still been spared the worst ravages of contact. As late as 1840, Indians still outnumbered whites in the state by nearly ten to one. Farms remained few in the Sacramento Valley. The less hardy Americans gave up to return East or to other, more hospitable parts. With the area's ranchers still reliant on Indian labor, posses were not yet scouring the chaparral for scalps. At this relatively peaceful moment in time, no one guessed that the Gold Rush was about to begin. Almost overnight thousands of new settlers would arrive—bringing with them unimaginable consequences for California's already decimated indigenous peoples.

A famous myth of Mexico's Aztecs foretold the arrival of the plumed serpent-god Quetzalcoatl from across the shining sea—and the ensuing destruction of the native world. Ishi's Yahi tales warned of the unexpected, too; in one story Coyote almost burned down the world by accident. Still, no explicit prophecies of doom appeared in Yahi mythology, or at least in what Ishi recounted of it to the anthropologists. The expectation of survival infused even small routines. On breaking camp for the high country or some other spot, the Yahi always flipped over their metates, the flat river rocks they used to grind acorns, to protect the stones' polished grinding surfaces from the elements until their return the following year.

Even today you can still find the Yahi's metates lying face down in the grass scattered across these barren foothills. By the end of the nineteenth century, there was no one left—except for Ishi and a few other last fugitives—to come back and turn them over.

# Five

# OROVILLE

I was nervous about the call.

It was the winter of 1997, and I was in Berkeley, about to dial Art Angle's number up in Oroville. I'd learned about this Maidu activist from the Forest Service archaeologist Jim Johnston, who had told me about Angle's interest in bringing Ishi's remains back for burial in the ancestral Yahi homeland below Mount Lassen.

I've never much liked talking on the telephone, and especially having to call someone out of the blue. That I was both white and an anthropologist added to my unease now. Like millions of Americans who label themselves black or white, I have a tiny bit of Indian blood myself. One of my nineteenth-century ancestors was Mary Steele, the "Indian Mary" of my grandfather's stories, a woman with dark, aquiline features in a faded photograph in an old family album. For all practical purposes, however, I am white, and I knew from the Navajo Reservation about the estrangement still between whites and Indians in many parts of the country. I'd made friends there, but I was also a *bilagáana*, a white man. Besides Marvin, only a few people ever invited me to their hogans or houses, although it might have been different if I'd stayed for more than just a year.

It wasn't much of a calling card to be an anthropologist, either. This made me a member of a profession that had been a favorite whipping boy for advocates of Red Power in the 1960s and 1970s. The well-known Lakota writer Vine Deloria Jr. had denounced "anthros" for invading privacy, revealing tribal secrets, careerism, and a general lack of commitment to Native America's welfare. Into every life, Deloria only half-joked, "some rain must fall. But Indians have been cursed above all other people. Indians have anthropologists."

I'd seen dislike for "anthros" first-hand in Shiprock. Those encounters were still fresh in my mind when I began graduate school at Stanford a few years later. By then, the early 1980s, most of us younger, would-be anthropologists would have been the first to agree about our own field's past sins. Plenty of self-flagellating books had already appeared about anthropology's failure to speak out against poverty and oppression, obsession with the exotic, and other real and imagined crimes. It was true enough that colonialism had enabled whites to study natives in the first place and also that nineteenth-century anthropology had justified slavery and the subjugation of the Third World by painting the West as the zenith of human achievement. The hope for a radically reformed and more socially responsible anthropology was the bait that drew me and many of my graduate school friends to the field in the first place.

As I was returning to Ishi now almost two decades later, anthropology had succeeded in reinventing itself in important ways. Although there had been prominent female anthropologists like Margaret Mead and Ruth Benedict early in the twentieth century, women now comprised more than half of tenure-track anthropologists nationwide. My graduate students at Duke, the future's professors, were not only mostly women, but also very often African-American, Chinese-American, Colombian, Turkish, and Taiwanese. Now peoples once just the objects of what the writer Zora Neale Thurston called "the spyglass of anthropology" were entering into the field themselves.

The stereotypical view of the anthropologist as the scientist of the customs of half-naked savages was also outdated. By the end of the twentieth century, the field was no longer restricted mainly to the study of native and "primitive" peoples. I was almost an oddity myself for having worked in the Andes of Peru, in the once conventional setting of the Third World village. More common now was research in the United States—and this research focused on strip clubs, campus fraternities, farmworkers, waitressing, television shows, and an assortment of other contemporary phenomena. Our new buzzwords were "hybridity," "hegemony," and "globalization," and many of us preached the need for attention to the politics of race and identity, sex and gender, and poverty and violence across the world. Anthropology had not become the kind of front-line, activist profession I'd hoped for as a young graduate student. Even so, a fair number of anthropologists stepped out of their now-questioned roles as "objective observers" to involve themselves in the lives of their subjects and related real-life causes of various kinds. A colleague at Duke, for example, had donated the royalties from his prize-winning book on Togo to a village health clinic—and testified as an expert witness in political asylum cases of refugees fleeing West African dictatorships.

I wondered if Art Angle had views about anthropology in one way or another. Would he even want to talk to me? I called five or six times over several days, since nobody was home or picking up the phone and there was no voice mail. When Angle answered at last, I couldn't tell much from our brief conversation. I introduced myself as an anthropology professor from North Carolina and explained that the Forest Service's Jim Johnston had given me his name and number. Angle sounded a bit wary but not averse to meeting. We set a date for later that week at Oroville's Cornucopia Restaurant. "It's by Highway 99," Angle said. "Right there next to the Shell Station."


I knew that Art Angle was a Maidu, or, more properly, a Concow Maidu, since his people were only one of the group's several surviving branches. In pre-European times, Angle's Maidu, the southern neighbors of Ishi's smaller Yahi tribe, numbered several thousand people. Their territory lay just above the Sacramento Valley's clinging tule fog, but it was low enough to escape the winter snowfall in the Sierra Nevadas rising up in the east under the big Western sky. Although their villages were larger and more permanent than those of the Yahi, the Maidu also hunted rabbit, deer, squirrel, elk, duck, and geese, fished for salmon, trout, and eels, and gathered acorn, roots, and seeds of many kinds. Like many northern California Indians, the Maidu had turned basket-making into a high art incorporating brilliant geometric designs. They were skilled featherworkers, too, and possessed elaborate tales of their own about Lizard, Coyote, Grizzly Bear, and the other great personalities of mythical times. In Maidu myth, the world was covered with water until Turtle dove down to bring up the gobs of mud that dried into the earth.

First contact came in the early 1800s, probably some years earlier than it did for the more northerly Yahi. One old Maidu man recalled his grandparents' account of that time to an interviewer in 1973. "Little things precede great changes," he remembered his elders saying: "Before the White Men came, Swarms of Honey Bees and Wild Cattle appeared, Wild Hogs and Turkeys settled in the foothills." By this account, the first Spaniards had not bothered the Maidu—and some even came to be cured by Indian doctors in their roundhouses. Any such harmonious relations only lasted a couple of decades, however. In 1848, James Marshall spied flecks of gold in the American River. Nuggets were found soon afterward in the Feather River, the heart of Maidu country. Thousands of miners with dreams of a big strike rushed into the great canyon in 1849 and after. Oroville, or "gold town," sprang up in 1850 as a miner's camp at the gateway to the hills.

We've grown accustomed to thinking about the Gold Rush as a quaint time of white-bearded prospectors with their pick axes, gold pans, and special sourdough recipes. From the Indian standpoint, however, it was a disaster of unimaginable proportions, the shattering of their world. Almost overnight, the Sierra Nevada was overrun with fortune seekers not only from the east coast of the United States but as far away as Chile and Poland, Italy and China, Turkey and Hawaii. The Gold Rush was the single largest movement of people since the Crusades; an estimated 90,000 prospectors pressed into California in 1849 alone and 300,000 had arrived by 1854. Their mining turned the hills into a wasteland of tree stumps, piles of boulders, and mud-clogged streams, and Indians found themselves uprooted from their native land. Even before the Gold Rush, the Maidu had suffered horribly from infectious diseases introduced by Europeans into the region. John Work, a fur trapper from the Hudson Bay Company, found the local Indian villages "populous and swarming with inhabitants" in early 1833. On his return a few months later, he found the area devastated by a foreign epidemic, probably the smallpox that ravaged the Sacramento Valley that year. The villages were "now almost deserted and have a desolate appearance. The few wretched Indians who remain . . . are lying apparently scarcely able to move." Hundreds more Maidu would perish with the malaria, cholera, syphilis, and other infectious diseases that the forty-niners spread everywhere in Feather River country.

Many forty-niners viewed the Indians as little more than animals—

"a naked, filthy, degraded set," according to one prospector. In the backcountry, the rape and prostitution of Indian women were common practices, and in 1850 the state approved the so-called Act for the Government and Protection of Indians authorizing the indenture of Indian children as virtual slaves. According to one Sacramento Valley newspaper, the unofficial price in 1861 for an Indian boy was sixty dollars; a girl could cost as much as one hundred dollars because she could be made to serve the "purposes of labor and of lust." Dealers in Indian women classified their "merchandise" as "fair, middling, inferior, [or] refuse," and set their prices accordingly. Although some concerned whites denounced the mistreatment of Indians, the abuses reached unconscionable extremes. One pioneer in northern California's Trinity County would recall a "Kentuck" buying an Indian girl of just eight or nine years old as his "seraglio."

If Indians suffered at the hands of the settlers, they made no common cause with the other largest group at the bottom of the racial pyramid, the Chinese. The two groups seldom intermarried, and the newspapers sometimes reported "bucks" shooting or robbing "Chinamen" in the Mother Lode, or vice-versa. In 1854 north of Oroville, Chinese laborers set with sticks and stones upon an Indian trying to make off with a bag of flour. The newspaper related that the Chinese "succeeded in sending master Indian to the Heavenly hunting grounds," this enmity between the despised a source of amusement to the white reporter.

In those years, Ishi's Yahi had retreated into protective isolation. Because the canyons of their traditional territory were cut from volcanic rock and thus bore no gold, this region was spared from mining and remained a refuge in the changing times. By contrast, the Maidu had nowhere to hide from the outsiders who were picking and blasting their way through their canyons. Art Angle's people had tried to make the best of their situation. Eventually they earned something of a reputation as "friendlies" for converting to Christianity, learning English, wearing Western clothes, and taking up the pick axe themselves. Ultimately, however, many Maidu were forced off their land. After rounding up 461 Maidu and other Indians, the U.S. Army marched them across the Sacramento River to the remote reservation at Round Valley, inland from present-day Mendocino. An outbreak of malaria had left many Indians—and some soldiers—weak with what a local rancher called a "bilious intermittent fever." Yet there were only fifteen carts for the sick, the old, and the very young; most of the Indians had to make the two-week, 150-mile walk on their own. Thirty-two perished in this forced exodus reminiscent of the Cherokee "Trail of Tears" four decades before.

Over the next decades, many Maidu trickled back over to their old territory. By then, fear and the desire to blend in was so ingrained that new babies received all-American names like "George Washington," "Benjamin Franklin," and "Thomas Jefferson." Many parents stopped speaking Maidu before their children and refrained from instructing them in the old ways. Sometimes they sent their kids to the government's Indian boarding schools in Oregon and Nevada. These schools sought to strip a young generation of Indians of their tribal traditions by obliging them to speak English, receive vocational training, and learn how to become "Americans." Back in the vicinity of Oroville, meanwhile, many Maidu married whites, further weakening lines of culture and continuity. Unlike the Yahi, the Maidu managed to survive. Yet many of their old ways were lost, and in the process they had become invisible and ignored as a people. Only three fluent speakers of Oroville's dialect of Maidu were left by the end of the twentieth century.

I'd learned about the unhappy history of the Maidu from a few stray articles and books. Not much was yet in print about Oroville's Maidu in more recent times, but the Internet carried hints of a burgeoning tribal revival. There were now three small reservations, or rancherias, in the area: Berry Creek, Enterprise, and Mooretown. Under the assimilationist policy of the Eisenhower years, the government had tried to legislate California's tribes out of existence and force Indians into the mainstream. A successful 1978 lawsuit overturned this unhappily named "termination" program. Many tribes regained the stamp of official recognition and accompanying rights to partial self-government and eligibility for special federal health and social funding.

Then in 1988 the Indian Gaming Regulatory Act cleared the way for casinos. The four rancherias in Oroville had won back their recognition in the early 1990s, and three of the four already had casinos of their own. Mooretown Rancheria's Feather Falls Casino had a stage, too, offering shows with performers like Sister Sledge, Tower of Power, and Frankie Valli. According to Mooretown's Web home page, the tribe wanted to encourage its members to feel a "renewed sense of community and, with time, an appreciation for their cultural identity." It had used its growing casino profits to build a library, day care center, low-cost housing, and even to start Maidu language classes taught by one of the last fluent speakers.

I drove into Oroville in the early evening of the appointed day. One hundred and fifty years after the Gold Rush, it was a valley town of thirteen thousand with a gritty, working-class look. Even here you could get a drive-in latte, but it was another world from the shiny New Economy of Silicon Valley and the Bay Area. When the last gold was dredged from the Feather River in the early twentieth century, the town's economy was reduced to logging and a couple of canneries. When the biggest cannery closed, the area had been one of California's few counties to shrink in population as the unemployed headed elsewhere. Although the Chamber of Commerce had tried to cash in on the town's Gold Rush heritage, Oroville lacked the cutesy appeal that drew tourists to Nevada City and Sonora farther south in the Mother Lode Country. A few subdivisions had spacious ranch houses with shiny motorboats and SUVs in the driveway. In general, however, Oroville was low Middle America: there were plenty of gun and liquor stores, gas stations, trailer parks, and strip malls.

The Cornucopia Restaurant, a diner in the mold of a Denny's or International House of Pancakes, was open twenty-four hours a day, served breakfast anytime, and had orange plastic booths and a March of Dimes card by the cash register. The teenaged hostess showed me to a table. I ordered an iced tea and waited for Art Angle to arrive.

Art had said he'd wear a black Western shirt so that I could recognize him. He had on a light-colored striped shirt instead, but the restaurant was almost empty and it was easy enough to see that the man who came in a few minutes after I'd sat down was looking for someone. I got up to introduce myself, and we went back to my table to talk. Jim Johnston had told me Art was a trucker by profession, and I guessed that he was in his late fifties. He had thick black hair streaked with gray, watchful brown eyes, and an aging cowboy's air of toughness and durability. It was easy to picture Art behind the wheel of his big rig as it rumbled down a twisting mountain highway with a load of logs for the sawmill.

Art said little about himself at our first meeting, but I learned much more as we came to know each other better. Like just about every

California Indian at the end of the twentieth century, Art had mixed blood—his mother was a Maidu, his father a white lumberman who came from Arizona to work in the Feather Falls mill above Oroville during the Great Depression. Yet Art was his Indian mother's son in appearance. He had the broad brown face of the Maidu I'd seen photographed in old anthropology books.

Art's mother had died when he was just ten. Art and three of his nine brothers and sister had spent part of their childhood in a foster home. Still, this youngest of the Angles had graduated in Paradise High School's Class of 1960. Although not tall, Art was strong and athletic— an offensive lineman on the football team and the school's best wrestler in the 147-pound class. He'd enlisted in the Army straight out of high school and drove a jeep in Korea. "It was better than just freezing your butt off every night on the DMZ," he said.

Back then, many Indians were leaving their reservations for the cities. As part of pushing Indians into the mainstream, the government relocated willing families to the Bay Area, Los Angeles, and other metropolitan areas, sometimes with promises of good housing and jobs that never materialized. Yet Art had not liked it away from home in the army and returned to Oroville after his stint was over. Now he owned his own truck and hauled logs or sometimes hatchery fingerlings, olives, and peaches; he also performed other seasonal jobs. He was married with two daughters and lived outside town. Art's wife, Lindy, was white. A friendly, no-nonsense blonde, she worked the night shift at a photo processing lab.

Art was suspicious of me at the start. He turned out not to harbor any special dislike of anthropology or anthropologists, but I was an outsider and a university professor from the other side of the country. "What's this for?" Art demanded, motioning to my notebook with some antagonism. I repeated what I had said earlier on the phone: I was looking into writing a book about Ishi. This explanation sufficed for the moment. Art could be prickly, intense, and guarded about his privacy and things Indian. At the same time, he was also a social man who loved a laugh and human company. As I would learn, he seemed to be on a first-name basis with just about everybody in his hometown. The waitresses at the local coffee shops gave him the "Hey, hon," greeting they reserved for favorite customers.

That night, Art and I talked for several hours over the faint rattle of trucks and RVs rumbling by on the highway. He had much to say about Ishi, Oroville, and Native California. He also wanted something from me.

I asked Art first about his plan to bring Ishi's ashes back from San Francisco. It had originated, he explained, in his efforts to recover bones of his Maidu ancestors. In the early 1960s, the state of California had erected a gargantuan earth-filled dam across the Feather River and flooded the canyon to create a reservoir. Lake Oroville was designed to attract boaters, fishermen, and weekend picnickers—and, more importantly, to generate electricity and supply water to valley agribusiness and the growing suburbs of southern California. Before the canyon was flooded, state archaeologists salvaged about thirty skeletons from a Maidu graveyard. According to Art, his people's remains had just been dumped into cardboard boxes and filed away in the Sacramento warehouse of California's Department of Parks and Recreation. "There was a white cemetery in the part they flooded, too," Art asserted. "They took the white people's bones away to another cemetery with a hearse and a priest." Art had filed paperwork requesting that the Maidu remains be turned over to him and other descendants for reburial back in Oroville.

In larger context, Art's actions measured the growing nationwide concern among Native Americans for rescuing their people's archived bones from museums and storage centers across the country, or "repatriation" as the cause had come to be known. In an older time, it was common for curious whites to dig up tribal burial grounds, seeking clues about the ancient inhabitants of the continent they'd now seized for themselves. Thomas Jefferson, an amateur archaeologist, had his black slaves unearth hundreds of skeletons of Virginia's Monacan Indians in 1764 to learn more about their mortuary rituals. In the following century, scientists wanted Indian bones to prove their spurious theories about the inferiority of Indians and other "primitive" races. Thus the celebrated Victorian doctor Samuel Morton measured Pawnee, Cheyenne, and other skulls to demonstrate the smallness of non-white brains (much later, the Harvard biologist Stephen Jay Gould would show how Morton, consciously or not, rigged his study to achieve the desired outcome). Morton concluded that "the American savage" was by nature "averse to cultivation, slow in acquiring knowledge; restless, revengeful, and fond of war."

The procedures for obtaining bones were sometimes macabre and were tied to the atrocities of Manifest Destiny. At the urging of several prominent nineteenth-century scientists, the U.S. Surgeon General William A. Hammond ordered army medical officers in the West to "diligently collect, and to forward to the office of the Surgeon General, all specimens of morbid anatomy, surgical or medical, which may be regarded as valuable." Sometimes field commanders had the warm bodies of slaughtered Indians gathered up so their bones could be shipped back to Washington in fulfillment of this order. That occurred in 1869 with the corpses of six Pawnee Indians shot down in a firefight with federal troops near Mulberry Creek, South Dakota. The massacre itself was a horrendous mix-up: the murdered Pawnees were actually former scouts for the U.S. Army, and one even carried his discharge papers. That discovery did not stop the post surgeon at Fort Harker from boiling down the bodies and sending the skulls to Washington. They were stored in the Army Medical Museum, then transferred to the Smithsonian Institution, which eventually assembled a collection of about 18,000 Indian skeletons.

By the 1980s, however, there was a loud and rising Native American outcry about the hoarded bones. In some cases, tribal beliefs about the sanctity of the dead stoked the demand for repatriation. According to historian James Riding In, for instance, the Pawnee still believe that "if the body is disturbed, the spirit is restless and cannot be in peace." To dig up bones is to commit an act of sacrilege and desecration from this standpoint. Yet repatriation was just as much a political as a religious cause, and many of its early champions were veterans of or at least influenced by the Red Power struggle in the 1960s and 1970s. It stated a refusal to accede any longer to the dictates of white scientists or white society—and to allow the dismembered and plundered bodies of ancestors to remain in museums any longer. The archaeologists who'd dug up Indians were no more than "grave robbers with a Ph.D.," insisted the Pawnee lawyer Walter Echohawk, a leading repatriation activist.

Archaeologists countered that relinquishing bones would cripple their field's advancement. The hateful skull science of the Victorian age had long since been discredited, but these scientists believed Indian remains held precious clues about the early human history of the Americas. Especially with advances in DNA testing, they wanted to test new theories that the first Americans had not walked across the Bering Land Bridge during the Ice Age, as once believed—and perhaps had instead come by boat from northern Japan, or even Western Europe, in a more complex series of successive migrations. The conflict between archaeologists and Indians crescendoed with the discovery of Kennewick Man. On preliminary examination, this 9,000-year-old skeleton unearthed in 1996 by Washington's Columbia River intrigued archaeologists because it did not seem to resemble more modern-day Native Americans. By contrast, local Umatilla Indians insisted that Kennewick Man was their ancestor and demanded that he be reburied as soon as possible. The story ended up on *Sixty Minutes* and *Nova*, and in *Time, Newsweek,* and *U.S. News & World Report*—and a coalition of archaeologists sued for possession of the skeleton.

When I asked Art about archaeology and the rights of scientists, he expressed his admiration for a "lot of the things that science has accomplished." Like many Indians, however, he was unmoved and even insulted by the proposition that studying old bones was for humanity's greater good, or even necessary to advance knowledge about the early Americas. "We already know who we are," he insisted. The origin myth of the Maidu asserted that they'd occupied the gob of mud that became the earth from its first creation. Art didn't want Indian bones analyzed any longer. "They've had us under the microscope long enough," he grimaced. "Enough is enough."

Art also felt a deeply personal stake in repatriation. Although a leader at his small Enterprise Rancheria, he earned no salary, and made his living from his truck. He was a loyal San Francisco 49ers fan, and, in his youth, was by his own admission too busy with sports, work, and family to pay much attention to the Red Power protests of the Vietnam War years. Yet Art had grown up hearing stories from his older relatives about the nineteenth-century Indian hunters who smashed the heads of babies on rocks in the Feather River canyon. Art's grandmother had still instructed her grandchildren to run away and hide from white men in uniform. In his own lifetime, Art had seen the last old people who knew about the traditional ways pass away and his own Enterprise Rancheria flooded to make way for Lake Oroville. His childhood house was under a hundred feet of water. Art couldn't make whole again the broken cup of Native California. But he could at least try to bring back the bones of his Maidu forbears from their storage drawers in Sacramento to a proper graveyard in their own homeland.

Then, one spring day in 1996, a big downtown mural of Ishi was unveiled for Feather Fiesta Days, Oroville's annual fair and parade. Orovilleans didn't have much to brag about, and the discovery of what a local columnist called "our Ishi" was still the town's biggest claim to fame. Like everyone else in town, Art had always known the story of the Wild Man of Deer Creek, but the mural reminded him of it once again. He was already working to bring Maidu bones back home. The mural prompted Art to think that Ishi's ashes should also be repatriated to ancestral Yahi land.

An expedition to the Olivet cemetery had converted that thought into action. Art and Lindy had piled their two girls into the car and made the drive down to the Bay Area to see for themselves the pot with Ishi's ashes at the cemetery. "He's in a jar behind some glass with a bunch of funeral music playing," Art said. Ishi had lived his last years in San Francisco. By Art's way of thinking, however, the last Yahi's real home and rightful resting place could only be by Deer Creek, his native land. Art stared into his cup, searching for the right words. "It's not right," he said. "We need to get him back home."

One immediate obstacle lay in the path to any plan for Ishi's repatriation. Under the Native American Graves Protection and Repatriation Act and other new laws, museum bones had to be restored to the closest living tribal descendants. Yet the Yahi had been completely exterminated and Ishi was the very last of his tribe, or so it was always assumed. Who had the rights to his remains? Of California's surviving tribes, the Maidu did not seem the right proxies, since they and the Yahi were supposed to have been enemies. According to Marie Potts, a Maidu basketmaker and elder who died in 1984, the Yahi were feared more than any other group. "They would sneak in our camps when the men were gone and kill or carry off the helpless," Potts wrote. She said that the Yahi had kidnaped and raped her own grandmother in 1863. This grandmother, Mariah, had only managed to escape Deer Creek several months later.

I asked Art about this. He shrugged. "There was a lot of fighting back then," he said. But relations between the Maidu and Yahi were not entirely unfriendly, he added. "My grandmother told me stories. She used to leave out food for the wild Indians on Table Mountain." Table Mountain, which rises just to the northwest of Oroville, is sparsely settled wilderness even today. "That was right before they found Ishi there in town. There were several wild ones up there on the mountain, my grandmother said. Ishi was one of them. My grandmother never talked to them, but she knew they were there. The food was always gone."

This tale established a precedent in Art's family for reaching out to needy Yahi. In general, though, Art felt no need to justify his concern for Ishi's repatriation to Deer Creek. Ishi was Indian. So was Art. The Yahi and the Maidu had shared the world-shattering experience of the nineteenth century's storm of blood and terror. As Art saw it, it was silly to dwell any longer on the past's enmities or other divisions. If anything, that there were no more Yahi only confirmed his own feeling of obligation. "They killed all his people," Art said. "Who's going to do the job if we don't?

Art had brought his nine-year-old daughter, Sadie, along to the Cornucopia. Sadie, who had her mother's blonde hair and light complexion, had grown visibly bored at so much adult talk and was drawing geometric designs on her arm with a ballpoint pen.

"Pay attention," Art scowled at his daughter. "I brought you here to learn something." Sadie nodded now, as if she knew her father was more bark than bite yet still wanting to indulge him by a show of obedience. She sat with us for a few more minutes and then drifted away on a long trip to the bathroom and a thorough inspection of the gumball machine by the door.

I asked Art about the current state of his Maidu. The Indians of California would soon be wiped out by the "sure onward march of the white man," *Hutchings' California Magazine* guessed in 1857. As an Indian himself, Art knew that the fortune tellers of Manifest Destiny had been mistaken. The Maidu and many other tribes had survived, albeit with bloodlines like his daughter's and his own now crossed with those of whites. Art spoke only a few words of Maidu, but he had also learned bits and pieces of the old ways—a story about Lizard, the knowledge of a few medicinal plants, the art of making a hunting bow. He gathered with other Maidu on weekends to play the traditional stick gambling games in a roundhouse concealed in the forest above Oroville. At the same time, he had no illusions about just how much had been lost. "They wanted to destroy our culture," he said. "And they did a damn good job of it."

The casinos had been an unexpected windfall. At Mooretown, the largest of the four area rancherias, the Feather Falls Casino had not only paid for a variety of social programs but also dispensed payments of a few thousand dollars a year to tribal members. As I learned, however, the casinos here were nothing like the giant Vegas-style Foxwoods and Mohegan Sun of the Indians back east, which made millions of dollars a year for the small tribes that ran them. Oroville was too far from the nearest big city to attract huge numbers of gamblers. The Berry Creek Rancheria's Gold Country Casino was nothing more than a large plastic tent with a dirt parking lot. Even at Mooretown, the Maidu kept their jobs as schoolteachers, loggers, Kmart clerks, and social workers. Art's Enterprise Rancheria did not have a casino at all. Art made most of his money hauling logs to the sawmill during the summer and fall. Despite Lindy's job, the family had a hard time making their mortgage when logging shut down for the mountain winter. "I'm sure not getting rich off any casino," Art smiled.

Art and I also talked a bit more about Ishi. It struck me just how much Art's understanding of the last Yahi's life diverged from the classic account, Theodora's *Ishi in Two Worlds*. As Theodora described it, the rescue of the desperate, starving Ishi by her husband Alfred and other whites had reaffirmed humanity's essential goodness, expiating the sins of the Indian hunters. Here was a vision of America healing itself from the wounds of genocide and slavery through the powers of goodwill, tolerance, and mutual respect and understanding.

Art had never read Theodora's book, but he came at Ishi from a very different point of view. He refused to believe that Ishi had ever been helpless or disoriented even in his last years in the wild. To the contrary, Art was convinced that the last Yahi was a man of power, a healer, and always very much in control of himself. A Maidu conception of Ishi as a shaman was expressed in the well-known painting by the self-taught Oroville artist Frank Day, a distant cousin of Art's. As a boy with his father, Day claimed to have come across Ishi near the Feather River just a few days before his capture in Oroville, and he painted the scene in 1973 from this childhood recollection. Though ragged, Day's Ishi looks big and strong, even oversized, in the manner of a character in a Diego Rivera mural. He does not appear in an "abulia induced by starvation and grief," as Theodora depicted him in his final fugitive days, but as a figure of will and action, a shaman ministering to an unidentified wounded companion with a complex traditional system of stones, water, and reflected sunlight. Art had seen the painting. He shared Day's belief that Ishi was not some sort of helpless, almost childlike victim in need of rescuing by Alfred Kroeber and other kind-hearted whites.

Art also questioned the motivations of the anthropologists. "The man was a prisoner all his life," was Art's pithy evaluation. The settlers had first confined Ishi and his people to a warren of brush in Deer Creek. Then he'd been a captive in the museum, or so Art believed, skeptical that Ishi would have stayed in San Francisco if he had had any real choice. That an autopsy had been performed against Ishi's wishes was Art's confirmation that Alfred Kroeber had never viewed the wild man of Oroville as anything more than a specimen. According to several Maidu old-timers, Art added, Ishi's brain had also been removed and pickled after the dissection: "It was a freak thing and people paid to see it."

Could this Maidu rumor be true, I wondered? If so, it would not be the first case of preserved organs and even entire bodies displayed as a "freak thing." That people in Europe and the United States so often regarded the native peoples they subjugated as almost subhuman curiosities licensed these kinds of exhibitions. Perhaps the most infamous example was Saartije Baartman, a Khoi Khoi from South Africa, exhibited in England and France as the "Hottentot Venus" as an object of voyeurism, derision, and pseudoscientific speculation about her large breasts and buttocks. After her death in 1815, Baartman's genitals and brain were displayed in jars next to a plaster cast of her body in Paris's Musée de l'Homme as late as 1985. Then there was the tribesman from Botswana whose body was snatched fresh from his grave in the nineteenth century, stuffed by a French taxidermist, and purchased by the Francisco Nader Natural History Museum near Barcelona in 1910. This stuffed man came to be known simply as "El Negro" ("The black man"); holding a harpoon in one hand and a little leather shield in the other, he stood for decades in a hall of monstrosities close by a two-headed calf and a five-legged pig. What was billed as the pickled head of the legendary California bandit Joaquin Murieta was carted around the West as a featured attraction at local fairs in the Gold Rush era.

There was also the precedent of the dismemberment of the single best-known California Indian besides Ishi. Captain Jack—Kintapush was his Indian name—headed the last real armed uprising of any tribe in the far West against Anglo conquest. In the several decades after first contact, the Modoc had more or less gotten along with whites, working as hired hands and cowboys and gaining colorful frontier names: Bogus Charley, Curly-Headed Doctor, One-Eyed Dixie, Hooker Jim, Shaknasty Jim, and Captain Jack himself. By 1870, however, a series of tensions escalated into war, and the army laid siege to some two hundred Modoc warriors in an extinct lava bed east of Mount Shasta. The Indians held out for almost two years in this nearly impregnable retreat and killed thirty soldiers, but in the end Captain Jack was betrayed by a faction of his own tribe. The army tried and hanged the captured Modoc chief and three of his lieutenants at Oregon's Fort Klamath despite pleas for mercy sent to President Ulysses Grant by humanitarians back east.

The bodies of Captain Jack, Boston Charley, Black Jim, and Schonchin were allowed to hang for thirty minutes before being lowered down. In a tent near the gallows, an army surgeon removed the black canvas hoods in which the four men had been hanged—and then cut off the heads from each corpse, one at a time, on a table covered with a rubber sheet. The headless bodies were buried in coffins at Fort Klamath, and the heads were mailed to Washington, where they also ended up in the Smithsonian's bone collection along with those of the murdered Pawnee scouts.

Art believed the rumor he'd heard from the old-timers about the exhibition of Ishi's brain. He felt most whites in Oroville and beyond didn't fully respect the rights of Indians even now—and cited as an example a local school principal's decision not to allow a Maidu girl a day off from school to gather acorns with her parents, a rite of early fall. "A lot of people still don't get it," he complained.

It was getting late. A new crew of waitresses arrived for the graveyard shift. Sadie wanted to go home. I asked how things stood now with Ishi's repatriation.

A couple of years before, Art replied, he had begun an organization called the Butte County Native American Cultural Committee. The committee had no budget or office. Because he was on the road so much, Art had little time to spare. Still, he proposed Ishi's repatriation at a meeting in the spring of 1997 in addition to pursuing the return of the Maidu bones. The other members liked the idea. They would try to recover the body of California's most famous Native American, and an Oroville legend at that.

Art, his sister Rosalie, and a few others had rounded up endorsements for the plan from the Forest Service, the Butte County Board of Supervisors, state assemblymen, and the chairs of the four rancherias. A far cry from the liberal Bay Area, the hardscrabble, bass-fishing, deer-hunting town of Oroville was no cradle of multiculturalism and political correctness. Even so, Art found a sympathetic local lawyer who drew up a formal resolution announcing the Butte County Native American Cultural Committee's intent to "bring Ishi back home" to his Yahi homeland. The lawyer believed that the Olivet Memorial Park cemetery could be encouraged, or forced, to hand over Ishi's ashes to the Maidu in the absence of any surviving Yahi.

There was one remaining problem: Ishi's brain.

According to the rumor Art had related to me, it had been shelved somewhere in a museum or hospital after it was exhibited. Art wrote California's governor at the time, Pete Wilson, who in turn asked Berkeley's University of California to look into the matter. A Berkeley vice-president had sent a letter to Art in 1997. It summarized an investigation into the whereabouts of the brain conducted by the university's anthropology museum, supervised by director Rosemary Joyce. The report's conclusion was unambiguous: Alfred Kroeber and the other anthropologists "would under no circumstances have preserved the brain." They were "opposed to treating Ishi as a specimen and wanted him cremated or buried." Joyce and her staff had good reason for this conclusion based on the information available to them at that time. No one yet knew about a small yet significant cache of Alfred Kroeber's correspondence, letters confirming that Art had been correct in being so suspicious about what had really happened to Ishi's brain.

The Berkeley official's cover letter explained to Art that the university considered the case closed. "The brain of Ishi," it insisted, "was removed for purposes of autopsy only, and then placed back with the rest of his remains to be cremated at the Laurel Hill cemetery near San Francisco shortly after his death on March 25, 1916."

Art remained skeptical. That the university vice-president misidentified the Olivet cemetery as the nearby Laurel Hill did not heighten his confidence. The Butte County Native American Cultural Committee had decided not to proceed as long as any doubt remained about Ishi's brain.

Yet Art did not have time for further investigation.

"Maybe you can help us," he told me now.

To avoid sounding unhelpful or uncooperative, I did not say that I doubted I was going to turn up anything new. Nothing I'd read held any clue to the mystery of the final disposition of Ishi's brain. We walked out to the parking lot. At ten o'clock in the evening, the blacktop still burned from the day's summer heat. I promised Art I would let him know if I came across anything, and we said goodbye.

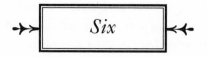

# Six

# THE DESTRUCTION
# OF THE YAHI

I found a room that night at Oroville's Travelodge, by a strip of fast food joints just off Highway 99. I watched a bit of ESPN, then fell asleep at midnight with the motel swimming pool's blue floodlights glowing through the curtains like the beams of an alien spaceship. The next morning I rose early to make a pilgrimage to the famous slaughterhouse—the place where almost ninety years before the butchers had discovered a fearful and hungry Ishi, the "Wild Man" of the next day's banner headlines. I was able to locate the spot with the help of a map in a Chamber of Commerce brochure called "101 Things to Do in Butte County." Along with Oroville Dam ("the nation's tallest earthen dam"), Kelly Ridge Golf Course ("a rolling, parklike setting with lovely foothills views), and Palermo Park ("home of the Feather River Horseshoe Club"), the slaughterhouse was advertised as a regional attraction.

In Ishi's day, the slaughterhouse was situated in the countryside a mile to the east of town. Now the scrub oak slope was an Oroville suburb full of well-kept tract houses with garden gnomes and manicured lawns. The slaughterhouse itself had fallen down long ago; all that remained was a vacant lot enclosed by a wood fence with a roadside marker in front. In 1966, after Theodora Kroeber's biography had made

Ishi famous once again, Orovilleans put up a marker with stones brought down from Deer Creek, the red and brown rock of Ishi's country. The plaque informs the visitor that the last Yahi Indian was discovered in this place, California Registered Historical Landmark No. 809.

It was a chilly dawn, quiet except for a first few cheerful birds. The valley spreading back to the west burned hot in the summer, but temperatures dropped at night. Out across the Feather River the bluffs of Table Mountain caught the first rays of light coming over the Sierra Nevada. The day was breaking beautiful and fair, with the clean scent of the mountains in the air. I parked my rented Hyundai, got out, and stared over the fence at the spot where the slaughterhouse had once stood. With a pile of rotting wood, some scraps of old barbed wire, and rusted beer cans strewn among the weeds, it looked like any other vacant lot.

In truth, however, this unprepossessing site was a major landmark in the grim story of one people's seizure of a continent from another. Here, almost three centuries after the Pilgrims landed at Plymouth Rock, the last fugitive of the conquest of North America had been brought in from the hills. Yet did Ishi's capture really mark an ending, a people vanquished? Or was it more accurately only one chapter in a story still being actively written? Although the Yahi were gone, the Maidu and thousands of other Indians were very much around, or so I'd begun to learn. It was only a few miles down Foothill Boulevard to Art Angle's ranch house. Beyond Angle's house lay the Mooretown Rancheria's Feather Falls Casino. Later that day, the blackjack dealers, waitresses, and security guards, many of them Maidu, would be arriving to serve the blue-haired retirees and other gamblers coming in from around the valley.

I'd spent considerable time reading about the last years of Ishi's Yahi, and now, in California, I sought out anyone who might tell me more. In an older, triumphant view of the winning of the West, the cowboys were the good guys, and the Indians the bloodthirsty brutes. Theodora flipped the story upside down in *Ishi in Two Worlds*. She depicted the destruction of the Yahi as an archetypal story of hatred and genocide—the progressive hunting down of Indians by ignorant heartless whites, the unprovoked murder of a Native American tribe pure and simple. After the upheavals of the late 1960s and early 1970s and the debacle in Vietnam, it would become far more common for Americans to accept that atrocities had been committed against Indians. Hollywood films like *Little Big Man* and *Dances with Wolves* drove home the point that the West has been lost as much as it was won. Theodora's version of Yahi history would go unchallenged in the late twentieth century because it seemed to confirm the new politically correct common sense about white guilt and Indian innocence in frontier history.

There is no doubt that Ishi's people had suffered death and terror beyond measure. And yet I'd already begun to question the reliability of Theodora and her bible of Ishi studies. In reading old newspapers, diaries, and other primary sources, I'd noticed a string of small errors, a pattern that included careless research and made-up dramatic effects. Tracking down microfilm of the original Chico and Oroville newspapers established that Ishi was captured on the evening of August 28, 1911— not the morning of August 29, as Theodora for some reason had it. Theodora also stated that Ishi "would eat and drink nothing during his first days of captivity," a pathos-sharpening yet false embellishment. Multiple eyewitness and newspaper accounts from the time agree that from the start Ishi wolfed down the beans, doughnuts, and other food offered to him in the jail.

As small as many of them were, the list of Theodora's mistakes was long: she misspelled the last name of a farm wife murdered by Indians as "Dirsch," when it was actually "Dersch." She wrote that Ishi and the other last few Indians in their hideout at Grizzly Bear's Hiding Place dug a pit that they kept "packed full of snow" in the winter as a source of drinking water. Yet Grizzly Bear's Hiding Place is barely 1,000 feet above sea level and it hardly ever snowed there—certainly never enough for any kind of reservoir. In her children's book about the Yahi, Theodora depicted the young Ishi watching the train wind through the Sacramento Valley from Black Rock above Mill Creek. The truth is that you can't see the valley at all from Black Rock because hills block the view. Theodora had Alfred Kroeber, the last man alive who knew Ishi well, as her main informant, and *Ishi in Two Worlds* was still a fountainhead of useful detail and information. But her lack of meticulousness and her willingness to take poetic license with the truth meant one had to be careful about taking anything she wrote at face value

What, then, about the destruction of Ishi's people? I knew that the so-called New Western historians were warning against making frontier history into a morality play in the way Theodora and almost everyone since imagined the hunting down of the Yahi. Skeptical of black-and-white views of white beastliness and Indian saintliness or the other way around, these revisionists demanded attention to the role of African Americans, Chinese, Russians, Spaniards, Hawaiians, and Mexicans in the West's tapestry of migration and settlement. They also pointed out that whites and Indians were seldom even united among themselves. Hundreds of Cherokee warriors joined Andrew Jackson and his troops to crush Creek rebels at the Battle of Horseshoe Bend in 1812. In the West, tribes like Oregon's Warm Springs and Kansas's Pawnee employed as U.S. Army scouts to fight "hostiles" (often a chance for these Indians to settle old scores with other tribes). No one in the West had a monopoly on moral virtue and humanitarianism, many scholars also noted. Patricia Nelson Limerick, the most influential of the New Western historians, observed that Indians as well as whites had employed a "full vocabulary of terror": fire, kidnaping, rape, murder, and mutilation.

Could the story of Ishi's people also be more complicated than it appeared on the surface? Here I was pulled back once again to early California and the era of the Gold Rush, the great cataclysm for the Yahi and other tribes in northern California's mountains. Prospectors never panned "colors" out of the Yahi creeks, but the discovery of the Mother Lode not far south had speeded California's 1850 takeover by the United States. Tens of thousands of Americans headed for the Far West's promised bonanza. A famous Gold Rush route, the Lassen Trail, zig-zagged down between Mill and Deer Creeks through the heart of Yahi country—and many more homesteads sprang up in the Sacramento Valley. There was already trouble by 1851, when settlers had burned an Indian village on Mill Creek, supposedly retaliating for the theft of a cow. The conflict grew more vicious over the next two decades, with many killings by both sides. By 1870, Ishi and the last other survivors had gone into hiding, too outnumbered and overmatched to offer any further open resistance.

A small band of settlers spearheaded the extermination of the Indians. They were not faceless killers, nor were they particularly concerned to hide their role. Two, Robert Anderson and Sim Moak, later wrote their memoirs, though probably with a ghostwriter; Moak, in particular, could barely read and write. A third man, Hiram "Hi" Good, was a legend in his own time. According to a traveling journalist's description, Good, a dead shot and more than six feet tall, towered "like a lone, but trusty sentinel" over the Sacramento Valley. Anderson and Moak, younger than Good, were neither one even twenty years old when they began to hunt the Indians up in the chaparral. Anderson later became Butte County's sheriff. He was the one to identify Ishi in the jail in 1911 as the boy he'd run across near Mill Creek half a century before.

Sometimes alone, sometimes with others, Good, Anderson, and Moak tracked Indians in the hills, and certainly fit the worst stereotypes about heartless pioneer death squads. On one chase above Deer Creek, Robert Anderson described his human prey as "dodging and ducking through the thickets like frightened deer. I brought down one with a shot from my double-barrel, but he was up and streaking it [*sic*] through the brush before I could lay hands upon him. Several of us followed him for a half-mile or more down the slope towards Little Dry Creek before we finished him." Anderson took the man's scalp and tied it to his saddle for the ride back home. Hiram Good decorated his homestead's yard with dozens of scalps. "We . . . [sent] a good many Indians to the happy hunting ground," Moak boasted.

What motivated such acts? Moak and the others saw the killing as self-defense. Even Robert Anderson would later admit that whites had probably been responsible for the "first act of injustice, the first spilling of blood." However, he believed that action was necessary once Indians began to raid and burn farms in the 1850s. In 1859, state militiamen circled across Mill Creek and behind Mount Lassen to the country of the Pit River Indians. This campaign left as many as a hundred Indians dead; about a thousand more were rounded up and marched to the Nome Lackee and Round Valley reservations far across the Sacramento Valley. At least some Indians in the Yahi foothills evaded the sweep, however. Sometimes they murdered homesteaders on their raids. Exhausted from all-night vigils and the alarms of barking dogs, poor farmers demanded new measures to protect their families. "It was decided to retaliate by carrying the war into the Indians' own territory," explained Robert Anderson.

The time's prejudices also underwrote and even justified the dispossession of Indians, of course. If the Spaniards and Mexicans had scorned Native Californians, the Americans brought an even more extreme contempt for these "lower" races. "The Indians lived like Swine," wrote one forty-niner. "They ate raw tripe and their filth and gluttony were beyond description." The Indians looked more "like orang-outangs than human beings," another commented. In one diarist's opinion, the peoples of California were not even "redskins": "their true color is closer to chocolate brown." Granted, there were more sympathetic observers, like an early San Francisco merchant who described the Indians as "ready and eager to adopt the habits of civilized life." Commonly, however, the pioneers considered California's Indians more akin to scorned blacks than to the romantic Indian warriors of the Great Plains and the Eastern Woodlands. These "Diggers," so named for their consumption of wild roots and bulbs, lay at the "very foot in the scale of humanity," another American concluded just after the Gold Rush.

Many pioneers also found California's Mexican settlers "miserable people" content to "sleep and smoke and hum some tune of Castilian laziness." In the twentieth century ruined Spanish missions would be reconstructed as tourist attractions, and the days of Mexican California would sometimes be recalled as a sleepy, romantic period of flower-trellised haciendas, silver-bridled black horses, and "dusky" señoritas with red roses in their hair. Little such nostalgia had yet developed in the days of the Gold Rush. As many settlers saw it, seizing beautiful California from the Indians and the Mexicans was not just self-interest but a moral duty and a boon to humanity's progress. The arrival of still more Anglos would turn California into a place of "unbounded happiness and prosperity, of civilized and enlightened man," declared Lansford W. Hastings, an early publicist who urged Americans to migrate to this potential Eden.

Robert Anderson and his companions were contemptuous of Indians, a very "filthy lot" in the opinion of Sim Moak. Yet they distinguished between "good" and "bad" tribes. It was the "bad" mountain Indians of Mill Creek canyon who had to be hunted down; spared would be the "good" valley Indians employed by ranchers. At the start, the Indian hunters also operated by a frontier code of male honor, not killing women and children. Once, in 1859, Indian women made themselves into human shields to save their men. Anderson explained, "The squaws . . . perceived that we were seeking to spare their lives, so they clung to the bucks." Subsequently, a few men managed to escape by disguising themselves as women. "A warrior would wrap himself in a blanket, throw a blanket or a basket over his head, with a rifle concealed next to his body, seize a child by the hand, or hoist one upon his back, and go shuffling past us." Even so, Anderson boasted in his memoir about slaughtering forty Indians that day.

A Chico researcher, Steve Schoonover, questions the large casualty numbers. He points out that Anderson published *Fighting the Mill Creeks* in 1909, almost fifty years after the fact—and the elderly Anderson, in the time-honored tradition of the frontier tall tale–teller, almost certainly exaggerated his prowess. In *Ishi in Two Worlds*, though, Theodora cited Anderson's uncorroborated body counts as if they were established fact. She wanted to highlight white guilt, and it suited her to give the most awful numbers possible for atrocities against Indians. Others would inflate the figures still further, completely without evidence. Schoonover observes that many recent published and filmed accounts—for example, a History Channel documentary in 1996—give a death toll of forty Indians for the 1865 ambush at Three Knolls by Mill Creek. How could a party of sixteen whites with Civil War–era weaponry kill almost forty Indians running for their lives, Schoonover asks? More tellingly, Schoonover tracked down two contemporary newspaper accounts about the Three Knolls killing. In one published story, Hi Good told the *Red Bluff Record Searchlight* that nine Indians were killed; in the other, another in the party of whites put the death toll at five, with several others mortally wounded. Yet the much bigger mythical death toll at Three Knolls would be repeated again and again—as if it were somehow not enough for just eight or ten Indians to have been killed.

The routines of killing and the gun did become second nature for Good and the other Indian hunters. On one occasion, with their human quarry still many miles ahead, Robert Anderson proposed having "some fun with the bears." The animals, especially grizzlies, had actually multiplied in Mexico's California, numbering as many as ten thousand. The so-called monarchs of the mountains found a diet of sheep and cattle to their liking; they also had less to worry from humans at that point with the numbers of Indians in the backcountry already declining. Now Anderson sneaked up on a bear family by Deer Creek, or at least so his story went in his memoir. "I waited until the largest one turned full side toward me, when I raised my rifle and let her have it." The wounded animal rushed Anderson with a "fierce bellow" and only collapsed when he "threw a second ball into her." Anderson also killed the three smaller bears, crippling still another that managed to get away. Except for cutting out the gall bladders for later sale to "Chinamen," who prized the organs for medicine, the party of whites left the carcasses to rot. In the pioneer worldview, the bears, just like wild Indians, belonged to a primordial, uncivilized California that had to be tamed or exterminated in America's westward progress. Not surprisingly, grizzlies were extinct in the area by the century's end.

When he detailed his youthful exploits in *Fighting the Mill Creeks* almost fifty years later, Robert Anderson styled himself a mountain man in the mold of Daniel Boone, Kit Carson, and the other great tamers of the wilderness. Even in his own time, Hi Good, the most famous of the Indian hunters, enjoyed the sobriquet the "Boone of the Sierras." Part of the legend of frontiersmen like Boone and Carson was that they knew the Indian enemy so well that they could turn his own weapons against him. In fact, Good prided himself on speaking several Indian dialects (the tongues of California's Indians were not dignified with the label of "languages")—and Anderson used poultices of tobacco to cure gunshot wounds just as the natives did. These men were convinced no regular soldiers could ever defeat the Mill Creeks in their inaccessible canyons. It would take their own more intimate, Indian-style expertise to carry out the "general clean-up," as Anderson once called it.

Especially at the start, however, the fighting did not always go the way of the whites. A bullet grazed Robert Anderson's head in one firefight; in a later ambush he almost drowned. If the whites knew something of Indian ways, then the reverse was also true. One day, a band of Indians burned down Anderson's barn, killing his cattle and driving his horses back up into the hills packed with vegetables and corn. The raiders also took a seventy-five-dollar suit that Anderson's brother Jack had just purchased in town. Anderson had his revenge a few months later. In Deer Creek's ravine, he gunned down an Indian wearing the vest and trousers of his brother's suit.

It should be pointed out that the line between whites and Indians was not always clear cut, even in these years of killing and confrontation. For a start, at least a few non–Native Americans, whether running from the law or for other reasons, had joined the Indians in the canyons. Robert Anderson told of killing a "Spaniard"—probably a Mexican who was living with the Indians—in one ambush south of Deer Creek. A victim of the Three Knolls massacre was Billy Sill, a mixed blood, or "halfbreed," in the era's argot. Sill grew up on his pioneer uncle's farm but later switched over to the renegades in the hills. Valley farmers often complained about "squaw men," those of their own race, usually miners, who took up with Indian women in the backcountry. Robert Anderson suspected that the "bad" Indians in the canyons "procured arms and ammunition" from such compromised white men.

Conversely, many Indians crossed, or were more often forced, into the white world. Among those then laboring in the valley's kitchens and fields were John Bidwell's Mechoopda. They feared the attacks of the "bad Indians" in the hills as much as the pioneers did (one Mechoopda was murdered in a dawn raid in 1850). Commonly, too, Hi Good and other Indian hunters seized babies on their sorties, sometimes after killing their parents. Farm families routinely brought up the infants for laborers. The indenture of Indians was legalized in California in 1850, and this policy contributed to a business in the kidnapping and sale of native children. Even poor settlers sometimes kept an Indian servant for cooking and chores.

Richard Burrill, a Sacramento researcher, has reconstructed the biography of Mary Hoag, who perhaps was a Yahi. A valley farmer, George Hoag, rescued Mary from drowning when she was a little girl. That she later became the children's nanny suggests that Mary was hardly an equal in her new family, but she kept the last name and stayed with the Hoags for seventy years until her death in 1932. Mary's story was typical of the entanglements across the lines of blood, culture, and place in the fluid, violent world of early California. There were the "squaw men" with the Indians up in the badlands; the Indians like Mary Hoag who'd joined the valley life of rough-planked homesteads, starched dresses, and Sundays in church; and "half-breeds," Billy Sill and perhaps others, who went back and forth between fugitive canyon life and white farm society, restless in both worlds.

The eventual murder of Hi Good, the "Boone of the Sierras," demonstrated the frontier world's mixed genealogies and uncertain allegiances. A story had it that Sioux had killed Good's fiancée on the trail to California, making Good the most pitiless of the pioneers when it came to Indians. Even so, Good had a mixed blood farmhand, Indian Ned, who became his drinking buddy along with Robert Anderson and the others. One day in 1870, Good received four thousand dollars for a land sale and buried it for safekeeping. Indian Ned found out about the money, shot Good dead, dragged the corpse into a ravine, and dug up the cash for his own. When a search turned up the body, Indian Ned confessed to the crime. Good's friends strung the young man from a tree limb, then shot him in the head. They left the body to rot under the tree, where it lay unburied for years.

But exactly who were those Indians in the canyons? Good and the others always called their human quarry the "Mill Creeks." As Theodora

Kroeber portrayed it, the Mill Creeks were simply Ishi's people, the Yahi by an earlier pioneer name and victims of a campaign of extermination. Once more, however, the real story was not so simple as this. In fact, the Mill Creeks were not entirely or even mostly Yahi at all, but an amalgam of mountain Maidu, Wintu, and other Indians who'd taken refuge in the canyons of Deer and Mill Creeks by the mid-nineteenth century. Recall that hundreds and perhaps thousands of northern California Indians had been uprooted from their homelands during the Gold Rush and the years afterward. They'd either been sent to one of the three reservations established in the 1850s or had become homeless refugees and sometimes criminals, rustling livestock or robbing miners.

During this time Yahi country became a region of refuge for Indians of many tribes, some fleeing the law, others probably just homeless—men with names like Malo Joe and Old Captain. At least some of the Indians were reservation veterans who spoke English, wore stovepipe hats and trousers they stole or purchased in the valley, and were handy with a gun. "Goddam you American sonsabitches," Sim Moak recalled one man screaming from his cliff's safety, fleeing the latest white attack. The Mill Creeks were "composed of renegades of all other tribes in this section of country," U.S. Army Captain J. C. Doughty said in an 1864 report.

I was reminded of Florida's Seminole Indians. Like the Mill Creeks, they were a "tribe" that came into existence only after contact, refugees from various other Indian groups and escaped slaves. The Seminoles—the word is Creek for "runaway"—made the Florida Everglades into their stronghold much in the same way that the Mill Creeks used the northern California canyons. Yet it made for a morally far starker drama to imagine that canyons held only a single small Stone Age Yahi tribe that was systemically hunted down by heartless pioneers—not a mixed lot, at least some of whom were English-speaking and gun-wielding. Whether consciously or not, Theodora again molded the story to her own agenda, leaving out the fuller, more complex truth. Again, too, her version would be embraced without question in later years because it meshed so well with well-meaning yet sometimes simplistic post–Vietnam War orthodoxy that wanted to see the injustices suffered by Native Americans in the most unambiguous way possible.

What about the Yahi, then? Did they keep their distance from the new arrivals to their canyons? Or did they mingle and perhaps intermarry with the Mill Creeks, those "renegades" from other tribes? Here I recalled a theory posed by Steven Shackley, a U.C. Berkeley archaeologist, that Ishi was the child of a mixed union. Shackley's theory went like this: You learned to make projectile points from a close male relative in Native California. The surviving examples of Ishi's workmanship generally look more Wintu, Nomlaki, or perhaps Maidu than Yahi; therefore, Ishi's father or perhaps an uncle may have belonged to one of these neighboring tribes. A few other clues also hinted that one of Ishi's parents may have been an outsider who'd come to the Yahi canyons from other parts. Jerald Johnson, the Sacramento State archaeologist, noted that Ishi, taller and more thick-boned than the average Yahi he'd found in his excavations, looked more like individuals from the somewhat physically larger Maidu and other valley tribes. In addition, two baskets in the coiled Maidu style were found and carried off from Grizzly Bear's Hiding Place in 1908 by the surveyors from the Oro Power and Light Company. Women wove the baskets in Native California. Could Ishi's mother have been Maidu? The Indians from Mill Creek had raided the Oroville area for women in the nineteenth century. Maybe Ishi's mother was one of the young Maidu kidnaped in those years.

It's hard to say now, more than a century later, and with such spotty information. The Yahi may have merged with other Indians in the 1850s and 1860s—and Ishi may have been conceived in a mixed union and grown up in a mixed band. That Ishi knew a few words and songs in Maidu, Wintu, and Atsugewi would also point to such a possibility. On the other hand, Ishi's first language was Yahi; his tales and the majority of his songs were different from those of neighboring tribes and so they were presumably Yahi, too. Perhaps Ishi belonged to a band still exclusively Yahi that kept apart from any others in the quiet canyons. I didn't realize it, standing in front of that vacant lot in Oroville in the cool dawn air, but the repatriation of Ishi's remains to the Yahi foothills would later turn on the unresolved and perhaps irresolvable question of Ishi's ancestry.

How to handle the "Indian problem" was a matter of controversy across the United States in the nineteenth century. By the 1820s, Quakers and other humanitarians in the East were already denouncing corrupt government agents, the massacre of innocents, and the theft of Indian land. Newspapers in San Francisco and even Sacramento also sometimes reproached northern California's Indian hunters. The Indians would "succumb before the advance of civilized races," predicted San Francisco's

*Alta California*. Yet there was no "justification of the slaughter of women and children in [a] cold-blooded and heartless manner." Bret Harte, who became famous for his short stories about the Old West and the Gold Rush, was a young newspaper editor with Arcata's *Northern California Union* in 1860. That year, whites wielding knives murdered more than fifty local Wiyot Indians who were gathered for a dance on an island in Humboldt Bay. Harte denounced the perpetrators of the massacre in his column and, amid white backlash, left his job less than a month later.

Calls for restraint carried less weight in California's interior valleys, which are, even today, more hard-edged and politically conservative than the liberal Bay Area. The fight against the Indians should "go on towards extermination, as there is no safety in trusting such treacherous devils anywhere," editorialized the *Yreka Herald* in 1854. At the same time, a fight over Indian policy broke out between the northern Sacramento Valley's single wealthiest and most powerful man, John Bidwell, and less prosperous, newly arrived settlers. Since first reconnoitering the creeks a decade before, Bidwell had established a small empire for himself, including the town of Chico, which he located by Butte Creek, on his Mexican land grant. The bearded Ohioan had political clout and more than twenty thousand acres of prime farmland as well as a saloon, hotel, and general store.

Armed Indian rebels had to be crushed, Bidwell agreed; yet he also insisted that the natives would be loyal and even docile if fairly treated, like the proverbial children under the guidance of good parents. Bidwell had made his own great ranch with the labor of Chico's own Mechoopda Indians, who numbered 250 as of 1863 and constituted the majority of his workforce. Fearing the settlers and also the "wild" Indians in the hills, the Mechoopda had nowhere else to go, but Bidwell took their adaptation to ranch life as a sign of their gratitude to and even love for him. He believed he had an "intuitive insight" into the "aboriginal races" and protected them from the "malicious and brutal vagabonds" who'd shoot an Indian for no reason.

Many smaller farmers regarded Bidwell as dangerously soft about Indians. As raiding became more serious in the 1850s, opinion mounted that the Mechoopda were not so "tame" as Bidwell believed—and that some of his "pet Indians" provided succor for the "boys in the hills," sometimes even vanishing from the valley to join in their attacks. Whether any such collaboration actually occurred is hard to say, but poorer pioneers on their isolated farms were much more exposed than Bidwell in his comfortable Chico quarters. And unlike Bidwell, these families did not depend on Indian labor except for the occasional servant or ranch hand. Taking the brunt of the raids out of the canyons, they were easily persuaded that all of northern California's Indians, friendly or not, should be exterminated—or at the very least marched to some faraway reservation.

As the political scientist and historian Michele Shover has shown, Civil War passions also intruded. John Bidwell was a Union man, but the region also had many Confederate sympathizers. With the war between the states imminent after Abraham Lincoln's election in 1860, Chico fell into what one contemporary observer called a Little Civil War. Soldiers beat up local "Secesh" even as Bidwell and other Unionists raised money for northern troops. Local Confederates, many Southern-born, killed a Union sympathizer in a bar—and later fired off guns to cheer Lincoln's assassination. Some local small farmers backed the Confederacy, their resentment at Bidwell for his "softness" on Indians now fueled by anger at his Union sympathies. Bidwell was a hypocrite, they claimed, a "black abolitionist" who opposed slaveholding Southern plantation owners while keeping his own Indians in bondage.

Tensions boiled over in 1862, the year of the bloodbaths at Shiloh and Antietam back east. A party of Indians murdered a mule driver, Thomas Allen, and, later that day, the three children of Frank and Elvira Hickok, a farm couple from Vermont. The killings may have been carried out in retaliation for the lynching of five Indians a few months before. White settlers gathered above Bidwell's store to discuss what to do. Since California remained in the Union, Confederates could not publicly express their sympathies, and yet now they seized control of the meeting to attack Bidwell. Bidwell himself was there, and emotions ran high: Hi Good had just discovered the mutilated body of the youngest Hickok child at a Mill Creek camp. One man now repeated the charge that Bidwell's Mechoopda were aiding the Indians in the hills. Rancho Chico's owner bore responsibility for the latest killings, this man claimed. Applause arose from the packed room.

John Bidwell later attributed the accusations to envy of his prosperity, dismissing them as the ravings of "infuriated drunken men." A year after the Hickok killings, however, the Indians struck again. This time, they shot one child and kidnaped his two siblings. Two of the men had their hair cut short and darkened with pitch, a sign that they may have been in mourning for murdered kin and out once more for revenge. The Indians killed the little boy when he slowed their escape. Yet the girl, Thankful Lewis, managed to get away. This latest attack pitched the settlers into a frenzy of rage and anger (although, to his credit, the father of the Hickok children urged against any wholesale slaughter of Indians). "It is becoming evident," the *Red Bluff Independent* reported, "that extermination of the red devils will have to be resorted to before the people . . . will be safe."

Posses of whites went on the rampage. They hanged four Indians at Dogtown—and descended upon Bidwell's ranch to shoot two more. Bidwell used his connections to have the army send infantrymen to Chico under orders to guard "friendly Indians, particularly those residing on the ranches of citizens, against the brutish assaults of bad white men." The troops protected Bidwell's Mechoopda, but they were too few to ensure the safety of all valley Indians. The army decided instead to march these others—among them the Concow Maidu, Art Angle's people—away to Round Valley.

Yet the removal of the valley Indians did not end the raiding from the hills, and even Bidwell now agreed on the need for decisive action. In the summer of 1865, a party of Indians ranged down the hills to rob and murder a farm wife, a Mrs. Workman, together with her hired man, "Scotch John" Banks, and her sister, Rosanna Smith, newly arrived from England. Now the white reprisals reached their greatest violence and fury. Days after the killing, relatives and neighbors of the murdered Mrs. Workman, who had lived in the Concow area near Oroville, joined Hi Good and the other regular hunters. Daniel Klauberg, a local rancher, was one of the sixteen armed whites who tracked the Indians to Mill Creek. He later described the final ambush of the sleeping camp at Three Knolls:

> As soon as the sky in the east began to show day was coming, we took our line of march—Anderson taking the left and Goode [sic] the right of the ridge,—and crawled down within shot gun shot of the Indians, and laid 10 minute longer, when Goode fires his rifle and shot an Indian 'buck' through. This was the signal for us to commence. The Indians were completely surprised and broke for a ford in great confusion. We ran up within 25 yards and all of our guns were brought into action, and just as they came up on the other side, the Indians began to fall thick and fast, some rolling down into the creek and floating off; others crawling into the brush, their trails plainly marked with blood.

In the camp, the men found a dress belonging to Mrs. Workman, and some skeins of silk that had also been hers, although it is hard to see how this justified the attempted wholesale slaughter of everyone in the camp, among them many women and children.

Like so much of Ishi's story, it's impossible to be sure of the details of the Three Knolls massacre. Theodora Kroeber believed that the Indian hunters had raided the Yahi village called Tuliyani—and that Ishi's father may have been among those murdered that day. She guessed that Ishi's mother escaped by grabbing the toddler Ishi, perhaps jumping into icy Mill Creek and floating downstream, as it would later be asserted in the History Channel documentary. "Ishi," Theodora wrote, "remembered the morning attack, but he did not talk about it in after years." Yet how could Theodora know that Ishi remembered the massacre if he "did not talk about it"? And if he had been only two or three years old, could he have recalled much or anything about that morning at all? It's even more improbable that any escape could have been made by floating down the creek. The water there is only knee-high in mid-August, when the attack took place. Placing Ishi's mother and Ishi at Three Knolls was still another of Theodora's uncorroborated or invented writerly touches—a possibility, but little more than a guess in the end. It's certain that the camp was not composed only of Yahi, as Theodora wrote, since the "half-breed" Billy Sill was among the seven or so people shot down that dawn.

Yet Theodora was right about the savagery of the ambush. By the frontier code of male honor, it was always the killing of women and children that most enraged the pioneers; the men from Concow who came along on the ambush had just had two of their women murdered. The ferocity of the grieving, enraged Concow men surprised even the Indian hunters. Sim Moak, the companion of Good and Anderson, wrote, "I saw one [of the Concow men], after an Indian was killed and scalped, cut his throat and twist his head half off." Women were not spared at Three Knolls, except one that Hi Good wanted to have to carry a baby back to the valley. This infant had caught Good's fancy as a curiosity because it had six toes. When the woman refused to go, Good fired a bullet into her and left her dead on the trail.

Not even the young escaped a last massacre at Kingsley Cave six years later. The Indians had stolen a cow. Only a few were left by this time and they were most likely desperate and hungry. Settlers tracked the thieves with dogs and cornered them in a cave. There were children among the trapped, but the settlers were determined to exterminate the Indians once and for all, not caring whether they were Yahi, runaways from others tribes, or some combination thereof. Norman Kingsley, the rancher for whom this cave would later be named, began to shoot down the Indians. He "could not bear to kill these children with his 56-calibre Spencer rifle" because "it tore them up so bad," another pioneer later recalled: "So he did it instead with his 38-calibre Smith and Wesson Revolver."

After Kingsley Cave, there would be no more raids in the valley, and the last surviving Indians went into hiding. As I sought to reckon with those extremes of human cruelty in early California, I had to agree with Patricia Nelson Limerick and the other New Western historians that it was not just a matter of bad whites and good Indians, no matter how tempting this version of the story. With violence escalating in the northern Sacramento Valley in the 1850s and 1860s, there was brutality from both sides, fueling a willingness to justify virtually any measure to avenge the latest atrocity. Norman Kingsley murdered children in that cave above Mill Creek, but Indians had kidnaped and then smashed out the brains of eleven-year-old Jimmy Lewis a few years before. At the same time that Indians were perishing of the white man's diseases and their old world was crashing apart, pioneers had endured every manner of hardship on the trail to the promised land of California—punishing desert heat and mountain cold, ambushes by hostile Indians, hunger and a hardtack diet, dozens of children dying of scurvy. In the winter of 1846, thirty-seven people died trapped in a blizzard in the Sierra Nevadas; the survivors of the Donner Party had to cannibalize the frozen bodies of dead friends and relatives to avoid starvation. Most pioneers were poor people. Those who made it to California labored hard to make a living from farming.

At another level, of course, the final outcome of the confrontation between the Indians and the pioneers was never in doubt. A few hundred "bad" Indians in the foothills above the Sacramento Valley, however fearless, could not hold out forever against the advance of a nation of forty million. Their land was lost to the invading Americans. And while the settlers also suffered adversity, the Indians paid by far the greater price in human life. Historian Sherburne Cook estimated that 4,267 Native Californians were gunned down by Robert Anderson, Hi Good, and men like them between 1847 and 1865; by contrast, the poorly armed, less numerous Indians managed to kill fewer than three hundred settlers. The U.S. Army sometimes protected Indians (in several places, refugees camped next to stockades to save themselves from settlers), but this aid was limited. The newspapers of Chico, Red Bluff, Yreka, and other valley towns continued to issue the call for an end to any "temporizing" with the natives. In 1866, the *Chico Courant* explained, "It is a mercy to the red devils to exterminate them, and a saving of many white lives. Treaties are played out—there is only one kind of treaty that is effective—cold lead." Bounties offered by town and county officials encouraged a policy of extermination. For example, the citizens of Honey Lake near the Nevada border paid 25 cents for Indian scalps. One resident of Shasta City in 1855 reported seeing men bring in mules laden with ten heads to collect the reward of five dollars for every dead Indian offered by that town. The state of California reimbursed Indian hunters for more than one million dollars in expenses in 1850. Insofar as it aimed to wipe out a whole race of people, the hunting down of Indians in the 1850s and 1860s deserves that big and sometimes overused twentieth-century word, genocide.

The terror of those times brings us back once more to Theodora and her version of Yahi history. Theodora's account oversimplified and sometimes overdramatized the actual history of Indian extermination in Yahi country. At the same time, *Ishi in Two Worlds* did more than any other book to call attention to the crimes committed in California and to force some kind of reckoning with the human costs at which the Far West had been settled. The irony is that Theodora did not need to take any writerly liberties. The unembellished history of Native California was gripping and poignant enough as it was.

The Indians of California had only limited options toward the end of the nineteenth century. Like the Modoc fighters led by Captain Jack upstate near Oregon, some fought it out to the end. Yet the only hope for survival was to adjust in some measure to the new realities of defeat. Among the survivors were Bidwell's Mechoopda, who sacrificed their independence to a white master and in return were protected from the worst of the violence of the Gold Rush years. Today, the descendants of the Mechoopda run the Chico Rancheria, trying to revive their traditional dance society and making plans for a casino.

East of Mount Lassen in the Great Basin, the Paiute prophet Jack Wilson, or Wovoka, sparked the famous Ghost Dance Movement that spread all the way back to the Dakotas during the 1880s. Wilson prophesied that the Indian dead would soon return to life, with "no more sickness" and everyone "young again." Yet popular as it was, the Ghost Dance was a cult of the defeated. The prospect for salvation had shrunk to a fantasy of resurrection linked to the expectation that the white man would vanish by some unexplained magic. The truth was that Indians everywhere in the West now had to make their way in a world of which they were no longer the masters.

Everywhere, that is, except in the deep canyons above Chico, where Ishi and a few others still lived in hiding. Homesteaders in Deer Creek and the surrounding area knew about and sometimes saw the "wild" Indians. Later, they would take exception to the idea that the Yahi were ever a "lost tribe." Angry about a series of thefts, the old bachelor Elijah Graham left out a bottle of poisoned whiskey in his cabin about 1902, hoping that the Indians would steal it while he was away and poison themselves. Interestingly, however, relations were not always so hostile, and a frontier reciprocity could sometimes prevail. In 1885, a cowboy, Frank Norvell, came upon four ragged Indians carrying off discarded clothes from his line cabin, a supply shack that the cowboys used as temporary shelters on their trips into the backcountry to round up the sheep. One of the Indians was a young woman. She gestured toward Mill Creek and, using the Spanish pidgin that Ishi's people had picked up, said *dos chiquitos papooses*," as if to explain that she had small children to provide for. Norvell allowed the Indians to take the clothes and they melted back into the chaparral. A few months later, when Norvell returned to the cabin, he found two small, lovely baskets that the Indians had left for him in gratitude for his kindness.

The Speegle homestead was located by Deer Creek, a mere two miles upstream from the last Indian hideout at Grizzly Bear's Hiding Place. Marse and Della Speegle and their six children did not intrude downstream, especially during the salmon run when the Indians might be by the water. For their part, the Indians limited their pilfering from the Speegle cabin to occasional basic supplies; they never broke dishes or otherwise ransacked the cabin as they sometimes did in their other forays. There are still Speegle descendants in the Chico area, and one perhaps wishful family legend even has it that nine-year-old Clyde Speegle met, swam, and learned deer calls from Ishi about 1910. We do know from various accounts that Ishi recognized and was cordial to Clyde's father Marse on his way back to Deer Creek in 1914.

An early anthropologist, Stephen Powers, had heard stories of "wild" Indians on a visit to the Sacramento Valley in 1874. He was told that only five were left, although there may have still been more at that time:

*No human eye ever beholds them, except now and then some lonely hunter, perhaps, prowling and crouching for days over the volcanic wastes and scraggy forests which they inhabit. Just at nightfall he may catch a glimpse of a faint camp-fire, with figures flitting about it; but before he can creep within rifle-range of it the figures have disappeared, the flame wastes slowly out, and he arrives only to find that the objects of his search have indeed been there before him, but are gone.*

Powers reported "the bloody and hellish treacheries" of these people at an earlier time. Yet nostalgia and even sympathy for Indians was rising in late-nineteenth-century America. In the "unconquering and undying determination" of the final fugitives, Powers saw "something sublime." One of those fugitives was Ishi, perhaps ten years old at that point. Although he'd later be portrayed as the purest and most untouched of primitives, the truth is that Ishi was born at a time when his people had already been decimated, white homesteads dotted the canyons, and the nearby valley was filling up with roads and towns. Ishi grew up in hiding without ever knowing what it had been like in the old days, when the Yahi had the hills mostly to themselves.

At least once, the Indians tried to surrender. In 1870, a party of fifteen or so appeared at a homesteader's cabin, Ishi among them; there they handed over five staunch wooden bows and allowed themselves to be taken down to Hi Good's cabin for transport to a reservation. While waiting for Good to return, the Indians saw a rope tied to a steel bar suspended over a tree limb, a system for weighing livestock or other heavy objects. Apparently believing they were about to be hanged, the Indians fled back into the hills. They made no more attempts to give up after this so-called Incident of the Five Bows, which the anthropologist Thomas Waterman reconstructed from interviews with settlers much later.

The massacre at Kingsley Cave occurred the following year. After that, the young Ishi and the other last survivors may have felt that hiding was their only option, that they'd be killed if they gave themselves up. Possibly, too, their decision to keep to the wild had other motivations. In their new translation of Ishi's tales as recorded by Edward Sapir in 1915, Herbert Luthin and Leanne Hinton, two leading scholars of

Native American languages, have discovered that Ishi devoted extraordinary attention to the details of daily life. His tale "Coyote and His Sister," for example, was interspersed with four lengthy descriptions of arrow-making, four about gathering firewood, and still others about dressing rabbit and boiling buckeye nuts. In one passage, Ishi described Coyote's sister cooking acorn mush in the Yahi manner, placing red-hot rocks in the basket to boil the water and meal into a thick, oily stew:

> *She took up her acorn mush*
> *Put hot stones in with them to cook—*
> *finished.*
> *She took the rocks out of the food.*
> *She stooped pouring water on the cooked acorns.*
> *Now she sat,*
> *She sat at her roasting.*
> *She took and removed it from the fire.*

These were just the last lines of a lengthy, step-by-step description of acorn mush-making. In the Yahi original, Ishi made liberal use of the suffix *-andi*, a kind of exclamation point employed for emphasis by storytellers of Yahi and related Yana dialects. That Ishi was here so detailed and enthusiastic, Luthin and Hinton insist, evinced his "clear reverence and love" for traditional Yahi ways, however difficult life was for the last survivors in the confines of the most inaccessible parts of the foothills. Besides their fear of being hanged or shot, the decision made by Ishi and his little band not to surrender may also have measured an attachment to their own way of life—a steaming bowl of acorn stew on a chilly morning, the gorgeous starry nights, and the reassuring rhythms of the seasons.

A few reported sightings of "wild" Indians made it into the newspapers in the late nineteenth century. By 1900, however, it seemed improbable that a lost tribe of natives could still be secluded just above the town of Chico—as fanciful as Bigfoot, that tall, hairy hominid of modern myth. At the turn of the twentieth century Chico had electric lights, a public swimming pool, two department stores, and a growing population of five thousand. There'd been a few freed blacks among the town's early settlers; their descendants, excluded from other jobs by Jim Crow practices, earned a living now as bootblacks, drivers, and hotel porters. The Sacramento Valley was becoming part of Middle America, California's

Kansas, with a Lion's Club, a baseball diamond, and a coffee shop in every town. For everyone in the valley, the days of the stagecoach, the Gold Rush, and the Indians were fast fading into myth and memory. These times were known to the young only through the tales of youthful exploits related by old-timers like Robert Anderson and Sim Moak.

Even so, a dwindling band was still concealed in the canyons as the twentieth century began. As far as Alfred Kroeber and the Berkeley anthropologists later reconstructed it, the Indians numbered just four by then: Ishi, his elderly mother and uncle, and the woman who was his wife, sister, or cousin. These last fugitives had their main hideout at Grizzly Bear's Hiding Place, the little village just above Deer Creek that was concealed by the brush and protected by cliffs. In that secret place they escaped detection for many years until they were discovered by the surveyors in 1908. Just three years later, the hungry, haggard Ishi arrived alone at Oroville's slaughterhouse. He had walked at last into the strange new world of those whose forefathers had destroyed his own people.

# Seven

# NICHE 601

My summer in California was almost over, but I wanted to visit the cemetery that held Ishi's ashes before returning to North Carolina to teach my fall classes. Olivet cemetery lies off Highway 280 just down the peninsula from San Francisco on the way to San Jose and Silicon Valley. Once farmland, the hills of Colma together with adjoining Daly City and San Bruno have long been San Francisco's unofficial necropolis; the many local cemeteries include Woodlawn, Avalon, Cypress Lawn, and the Greek Orthodox Memorial Park. Although still dotted with graveyards, the area has by now been built up with gas stations, strip malls, and modest stucco houses occupied by immigrant families from Cambodia, El Salvador, Vietnam, and everywhere else in Asia and Latin America. The Olivet cemetery occupies several acres below San Bruno Mountain, a lone protuberance covered with radio towers and patchy stands of eucalyptus. You can look from the cemetery towards the old Candlestick Park (whose name was changed to 3Com Park in the heady days of the dotcom 1990s), the home of the San Francisco 49ers, the San Francisco International Airport, and the gray-green waters of the bay.

A young receptionist with the sly smile, black nail polish, and black lipstick of Morticia from the Addams Family greeted me at the cemetery's office. She was new at Olivet and had never heard of Ishi. "Is that a burial today?" she puzzled. Only after consulting an administrator in the back office did she find the entry in the burial registry. Apparently, if only for purposes of alphabetizing, you could not be buried at Olivet without a first and last name. The little card containing Ishi's information, it turned out, was filed under "Indian Ishi." The card indicated that Ishi's remains were in Niche 601 in the Columbarium, the building reserved for the ashes of the cremated dead.

With the aid of a little map, I struck out for the Columbarium. Even though a uniformed attendant was herding a few leaves across the parking lot with a backpack blower louder than a Harley, Olivet still had the charm of an older, well-kept cemetery that advertised itself as "for all faiths." The Garment Workers, Merchant Marines, and other old-time trade unions had their own plots here. So, oddly, did a group called the "Improved Order of Red Men." An early example of Euro-American fascination with things Indians, this Victorian social club had elected "chiefs," traded "wampum," met in "wigwams" for their "tribal councils," and boasted more than five thousand members at the time of Ishi's death. From outside, the Columbarium looked like a venerable neighborhood bank. Fluted columns lined its thick whitewashed walls. Inside, a high row of windows gave the interior the mild tropical light of an old greenhouse. I stood alone in this quiet space, looking around me. Every wall was filled with niches almost up to the ceiling; an amphora sat behind glass in each niche. The amphoras were mostly in the shape of Greek vases or bibles: a few, including a bronze sailing ship containing the ashes of an old sea captain, were more whimsical.

I soon located Niche 601. The black Pueblo Indian pot I'd read about in Theodora Kroeber's *Ishi in Two Worlds* was a simple, graceful container about the size of a flower vase; its top was plugged with a smooth plaster. This pot had probably come from the village of Santa Clara in New Mexico, whose potters were famous for an ebony glaze so perfect and gleaming that you could see your reflection in it like the polished black granite of Washington's Vietnam Veterans Memorial. As far as we know, Edward Gifford, the young anthropologist who supervised Ishi's funeral in Alfred Kroeber's absence, chose the vessel from the anthropology museum's large collection of Pueblo pottery. He'd had "Ishi, the last Yahi Indian, 1916" inscribed across the pot's belly.

A pot: there was some irony in this choice. Like many northern California Indians, the Yahi had a genius for basketmaking. They were never potters and had no ceramics of any kind in precontact days. Yet the selection of the pot, and of cremation, had not been haphazard. Gifford and the other anthropologists were under the impression that cremation was the Yahi custom and thus had Ishi's body reduced to ashes in Olivet's crematorium after it had been brought down from a San Francisco undertaker two days after his death. According to Theodora, Gifford and Kroeber had decided beforehand that a "cemetery urn" would be "the closest equivalent to the basket and rock cairn" they believed the Yahi used for their dead's ashes. The pot was not Yahi or even Californian. It was, however, at least Indian, and thus it must have seemed more culturally appropriate than a bible-shaped urn.

I stared at the shiny black pot. Were the ashes of Ishi's brain in there along with the rest of his cremated body? Or had the brain ended up instead in some still undetermined place? That Kroeber and Gifford had taken such care and even pride in adhering to what they believed was Yahi tradition made it hard to imagine that they would have permitted the brain to be bottled as a specimen or curiosity. But what about that fleeting, uncomfortable mention in Theodora's *Ishi in Two Worlds* about the organ being "preserved"—and also Art Angle's rumor up in Oroville that it had been pickled and put on show? Art had asked me to keep an eye out for any new information. I'd found almost nothing yet to shed any further light on the mystery of Ishi's brain—except for a single clue, a lead so slim I'd not bothered to tell Art until I learned more.

One day I had gone to the Bancroft Library, an archive at U.C. Berkeley containing one of the world's most important collections related to California and the West. Lauren Lassleben, the archivist for anthropology, was not surprised when I introduced myself as someone researching Ishi. "It's like a cult," she said. "We get at least two people a month coming in for Ishi." With admirable patience, however, Lassleben pointed me to useful sources, among them Alfred Kroeber's papers. She also mentioned that a historian of science named Nancy Rockafellar had come recently to the Bancroft in search of clues about Ishi's brain. Lassleben thought that Rockafellar was conducting some sort of an investigation for U.C. San Francisco, which ran the hospital where Ishi had died.

I had called Rockafellar several times that summer, but she hadn't returned my messages. A few days after visiting Olivet, I had to fly back to North Carolina without ever making contact with the elusive U.C.

San Francisco researcher. Once the semester ended, though, I returned to the Bay Area over Christmas break. Now I phoned and e-mailed again, and this time Rockafellar e-mailed back, agreeing to meet at her office at U.C. San Francisco's medical complex on Parnassus Heights.

I parked in the medical center's garage and found my way through a maze of elevators and walkways over to her office. Although much changed today, the hilly city neighborhood of Parnassus Heights had been Ishi's San Francisco home, the streets he'd often walked. Various branches of what were then called the University of California's Affiliated Colleges once shared this prime land, elevated above Golden Gate Park, which boasted a view out toward Ocean Beach. On a clear day you could see the Farallon Islands, a patch of rocks far off the coast where a great-uncle of mine had once captained a pilot boat. The Victorian buildings of Ishi's day had long ago been demolished, and the anthropology museum had moved in 1964 to its new facility at Kroeber Hall on the campus of U.C. Berkeley. Meanwhile, what had been a single building in Ishi's day was now a massive glass and concrete modern medical complex that dominated Parnassus Heights. With three Nobel Prize winners on its faculty, U.C. San Francisco had an annual budget of $850 million and was one of the nation's leading centers for medical research.

Nancy Rockafellar's office was in an old hospital building slated for demolition. It had been built in 1915 as a replacement for the university's original nineteenth-century wards. At that time, Ishi was already sick with tuberculosis and been hospitalized several times. Edward Gifford and Thomas Waterman, the anthropologist who'd brought Ishi back from Oroville, felt they could give Ishi more personal care back in the museum. Earlier, Ishi had shared a bedroom with one of the museum watchmen, but now Gifford had a special exhibition room cleared out for Ishi's convalescence. "This is the sunniest room in the house," Gifford wrote that fall to Kroeber, who was already in New York: "Waterman and I feel that the Indian must come first, even though we will not get as much of the other work done in caring for him. At the museum he will be treated as Ishi. At the hospital I fear that the nurses were so busy that he was treated simply as a hospital patient, without regards for his personality."

Now the bedridden Ishi watched the high-wire act of the construction crew at work on the new hospital building right next door to the museum. The men maneuvering like acrobats on the steel girders reminded him of an animal he had only seen for the first time on coming to San Francisco. "All a same monkey-tee," he supposedly laughed. *Tee* was the Yahi suffix that Ishi added to many English nouns, and "all a same" a classic expression in Chinese-Pacific pidgin, which Ishi may have picked up in his wanderings in San Francisco, with its large Asian population. Sun Yat-Sen, the hero of Chinese nationalism, was fundraising in San Francisco in 1911 just as Ishi arrived there. An editor from one of Chinatown's several newspapers once visited Ishi in the museum for a story about him.

That the anthropologists felt Ishi's well-being should "come first" reflected the affection and protectiveness they had developed for the man one newspaper described as a "likeable old Indian." It was also paradoxical, given the fact that the anthropologists had exposed Ishi to great risk by bringing him to the city in the first place. Kroeber and the others may have rationalized their actions by asserting that Ishi would starve or be killed if he were left in the hills, but their own self-interest in having Ishi handy for study doubtless also entered into their decision to bring him to San Francisco. In fact, the anthropologists were fully aware of the city's dangers, tuberculosis included. Although no cure yet existed, it was common knowledge that tuberculosis spread through human contact. Hundreds of sanatoriums had been constructed in the late nineteenth and early twentieth centuries to isolate those suffering from this disease that counted Henry David Thoreau, D. H. Lawrence, and Anton Chekhov among its many famous victims. The rate of infection from this imported Old World plague among the already decimated Indian population was more than twice as high as for other Americans. In 1908, a survey showed that more than two hundred Oglala Lakota had perished from tuberculosis in the past year alone, many of them children.

Ishi, after his isolated life in the wild, was especially defenseless against infection of all kinds. At the museum, however, he was placed in contact with thousands of potentially germ-carrying visitors. That Ishi was allowed to visit the nearby U.C. San Francisco hospital further increased his exposure to peril. A full third of the patients in the hospital had the disease, but, as we have seen, it became one of Ishi's favorite haunts after he befriended Saxton Pope, the chief of surgery there. Pope did nothing to discourage these visits, although, as a trained epidemiologist, he must have understood the risk of contagion even better than the anthropologists did. It is a small miracle that Ishi did not fall sick and die much sooner in San Francisco.

No one among Ishi's immediate circle of friends ever acknowledged any irresponsibility about his health. The emotional Thomas Waterman came the closest. As Ishi's condition worsened, Waterman wrote to Kroeber, admitting what they both well knew already—that "a museum is a hell of a place for a fragile Indian." Later, Waterman would blame himself for "killing Ishi" by letting the linguist Edward Sapir "ride him too hard" in their work together in the summer of 1915, although by other accounts Ishi enjoyed relating his stories and Sapir was the exhausted one at the day's end. It is likely that Ishi had contracted tuberculosis from contact with someone at the museum or hospital—or maybe even from dining at the Kroeber house with Kroeber and Henriette Rothschild, Kroeber's beautiful young wife, who was still alive yet already gravely ill with the disease. In the medical history of Ishi he published in 1920, Saxton Pope suggested without explanation that food must have been the infection's source. It was an explanation, whether consciously or not, that allowed the doctor and others to insulate themselves from any personal blame for their friend's death.

Alfred Kroeber was never one to dwell in the past, and, as far as we know, he never expressed any regrets for having brought Ishi to San Francisco. As Ishi's condition worsened, though, the famous anthropologist wanted to know every detail. When Gifford wrote to say that Ishi had "dropped somewhat in weight," Kroeber replied immediately, insisting on knowing the exact figure. "How about his temperature?" he added. "Wish you would tell me what you know." From then on, Gifford mailed off regular reports of Ishi's morning and afternoon temperatures (an elevated afternoon temperature was a recognized tuberculosis symptom). That Kroeber cared so much measured the meticulous, sometimes compulsive, streak in his own character, frustration at being so far away, and a real concern for a man he liked and wanted to protect. I wondered if it was also guilt for not having been more careful with Ishi from the beginning.

I found Nancy Rockafellar's office on the fourth floor. Only offices and labs remained in the condemned building now, since patients had long since been moved to facilities with heart monitors, piped-in oxygen, cable TV, and other expected modern amenities. Yet the corridors still had that old-time hospital look, like a ward out of some World War II movie. It was not hard to imagine the smell of ether, the steel beds, the nurses in starched white caps. My grandmother, Frances, had been a secretary for a time in this hospital while her husband was away fighting in the South Pacific. Now an assistant opened the office door at my knock. A pleasant, no-nonsense blonde woman of about fifty, Nancy Rockafellar rose from her computer to introduce herself, then led me to a little conference room next door. From the big window there, the tops of the twin towers of the Golden Gate Bridge were just visible out beyond the low green hills of the Presidio, the one-time army garrison at the entry to the bay.

Nancy Rockafellar had a bad cold that day and sipped tea for her raspy throat. We made polite conversation about health and the holiday for a few minutes, but Rockafellar knew I wanted to hear about her investigation. Her sister lived in southern California, she began, and had sent her a *Los Angeles Times* feature story about Art Angle and his Butte County Native American Cultural Committee—their campaign for Ishi's repatriation and their search for information about the fate of Ishi's brain. Rockafellar knew that Ishi had been treated at U.C. San Francisco and had also been dissected there. She wondered if her university might have some old record of the brain, or even have it stashed away somewhere, perhaps at a warehouse at Oyster Point that contained other body parts preserved for research.

Rockafellar, an anti-war protester in her younger days at the University of Minnesota, sympathized with Native American causes and the idea of Ishi's repatriation. If U.C. San Francisco still had it, she wanted Ishi's brain returned to Art Angle's Butte County Native American Cultural Committee for a proper burial with the rest of his remains. It would also look bad if U.C. San Francisco were discovered to have the famous Yahi's brain squirreled away somewhere without having informed the Indians who were searching for it. Thinking that her university needed to learn the truth, Rockafellar went to a vice-chancellor, Dorothy Bainton, who agreed. Bainton asked Rockafellar to begin an investigation. Although they lie across the bay from one another and belong to the same state university system, U.C. San Francisco and U.C. Berkeley do not have close ties. Bainton and Rockafellar did not know that the Berkeley anthropology museum was conducting its own search—and that Berkeley officials would soon inform Art Angle that Alfred Kroeber and the others "would under no circumstances have preserved Ishi's brain" and that after the autopsy it must have been placed with the rest of Ishi's remains for cremation.

The U.C. San Francisco search had already lasted almost two years, conducted mostly in secrecy because the matter was sensitive. What had happened at the autopsy? What was done with Ishi's brain? A one-time lab technician with a doctorate in the history of science, Nancy Rockafellar was the director of U.C. San Francisco's oral history office. This post gave her familiarity with the medical center's early years and made her well qualified to search for answers. An obvious first step was digging up Ishi's medical records; Rockafellar hoped these charts might contain clues about the handling of his body. The U.C. San Francisco archives contain thousands of bound volumes, including charts of every patient from the early twentieth century. Now that the seventy-five-year confidentiality period had expired, these records were available for public scrutiny. The chief archivist helped Rockafellar locate Ishi's records in the stacks. Here, too, because a full name had been needed for the exigencies of filing, the doctors had filled out their unusual patient's charts under "Ishi Indian," the reverse of the cemetery's order.

Rockafellar learned that Ishi was first hospitalized on November 11, 1911, less than three months after arriving in San Francisco. He had chills and his bones ached, which perhaps signaled only bronchitis at that early point. When he returned to the hospital in 1914, Ishi now displayed the violent, sometimes bloody, cough that was one of tuberculosis's classic and most terrifying symptoms. The usual test at that time was to inject a bit of the patient's saliva into a guinea pig. This method often gave a false negative, however; an animal injected with the infected fluid did not always sicken itself. Not until just a month before his death did Ishi at last test positive, not that it much mattered in the final account since there was as yet no effective cure; streptomycin would not be invented for almost another thirty years (by now, in another turn of the cycle, many strains of tuberculosis are resistant to this drug and the disease is on the rise again, and cases are reported on both the White Mountain Apache and Navajo Reservations). The end came in the spring of 1916. As San Francisco prepared for the visit of controversial labor leader Samuel Gompers and the Battle of Verdun was beginning across the Atlantic in the fields of Belgium, Ishi entered the hospital for the last time. He was given codeine and then morphine. Still, the ugly brutality of the tuberculosis comes through in the chart's dry clinical annotations—vomiting, retching, blinding fever, and the final flood of blood through the nose and mouth. Ishi's suffering must have been great, even though his friend Saxton Pope said he never complained. It was Pope who injected Ishi with morphine to relieve the pain and stroked his friend's hand in the final moments.

A central figure in Ishi's San Francisco life, Saxton Pope was a strong, likeable, good-looking man, already the hospital's chief of surgery by his mid-thirties. Pope was a man of many talents and enthusiasms—a world-class surgeon, an adept magician, a maker of fine violins, and a skilled writer. Though they knew Pope by reputation, the two anthropologists Kroeber and Waterman met him for the first time only in connection with Ishi. Kroeber later invited Pope on their 1914 return expedition to Deer Creek, knowing it would please Ishi to have his doctor friend along. Later, Kroeber wrote a warm obituary for Pope, who died suddenly of pneumonia in 1926 at the age of fifty-one: "He was energetic, original, self-reliant, unwaveringly loyal, and modest. He left no enemies and only the warmest of friends."

Why did Pope befriend Ishi? There was much of a little boy's fascination and even obsession about Indians in this well-known surgeon's attraction to the "wild" Indian. The Yahi ate wild roots and bulbs just like other Native Californians. Even so, the starry-eyed Pope was not content to put Ishi and his people in the same league with other tribes in the state, even then still often dismissed as "diggers" at humanity's lowest rung. "Instead of being diggers of roots they lived by the salmon spear and the bow," Pope wrote several years after Ishi's death. The Yahi were not "yellow in color, fat, and inclined to be peaceable" like "the usual California natives," or so the doctor also wanted to believe. They were "hunters and warriors," they were "lithe, of reddish bronze complexion"—in other words, the more glamorous "redskins" of the Indian head nickels and pulp novels.

Pope and Ishi found a shared passion in archery. An expert shot, a contributor to *Field and Stream* magazine, and the author of a popular 1925 book called *Hunting with Bow and Arrow* (which he dedicated to Robin Hood), Pope has been credited with reviving the sport of archery in early-twentieth-century North America. In his exuberant view, the "glory and romance" of bow hunting allowed modern men to reconnect to earlier, less technologically encumbered times, when heroes from Hiawatha to Little John showed their masculine prowess with the straight shot of a feathered shaft. Together, Pope and Ishi experimented with ancient bows from Japan and other exotic places that were part of the museum collection, breaking several in their enthusiasm. Ishi taught Pope how to make bows, and the two men made a special hunting expedition to a ranch in the Pacheco Pass above the San Joaquin Valley. Pope once noted that he could outshoot Ishi, who, like "all savages," failed to "understand the optics and ballistics of archery." Yet he praised his new friend's skill at calling deer, wildcat, and rabbit and his "perfect" eye in stone tool making. When Ishi died, Pope wrote that he had gone to "hunt[s] with his people" but "left us the heritage of the bow." One of Ishi's lesser-known personae nowadays is as a totem for contemporary archers, especially the "traditionalists" who make their own wood bows instead of hunting with the high-powered manufactured graphite weapons. A popular archery club in California's San Joaquin Valley town of Riverbank is called "Yahi Bowmen." And a recent feature in *Bowhunter* magazine details the quest of Roger Rea, a hunting guide and the owner of "Roger's Screaming Eagle Archery Store" outside Pittsburgh, to bring down a deer with a wood bow and stone arrowheads copied exactly from museum pieces made by Ishi.

Despite his romanticism and condescension, Pope found in Ishi a "wonderful companion" who "loved to joke" and had a knack for putting others at ease. Ishi considered the man he called Popey to be "the most fascinating person in the world," according to Theodora Kroeber. In an unpublished reminiscence, Pope claimed that Ishi had trusted him alone with his real Indian name: a Yahi word that the doctor reported meant "strong, straight, and stalwart." This may be true, given the many hours they spent together and their real human connection. Pope was probably Ishi's closest friend in San Francisco.

Yet Pope was also the man who later insisted on dissecting Ishi. He'd always considered his friend a "rare find," a "Stone Age Man," the "last of his tribe"—and with a scientist's curiosity made measurements of Ishi's body, noted down his every like and dislike, and been the one to have casts made of Ishi's feet and teeth. An autopsy was simply the extension of Pope's wish to complete the record. He and other men of science didn't regard dissection as violating the dignity of the dead; in fact, such famous nineteenth-century scientists as the great German mathematician Karl Friedrich Gauss and the American explorer and geologist John Wesley Powell had already donated their bodies for study, granting permission also for their brains to be pickled as specimens. The cutting apart of a corpse was antithetical to Ishi's own Yahi mortuary customs, and yet the fact that Pope saw his friend as "primitive man," and thus a kind of child, allowed the doctor to press forward without any apparent second thoughts. Despite its violation of the wishes of a man he'd claimed to love, and probably really did, Pope wanted an autopsy.

Pope made his views known sometime just in advance of Ishi's death. The acting museum director, Edward Gifford, had objected that a dissection would contravene the wishes of both Ishi and Kroeber, who was away in New York but wanted Ishi's own feelings in the matter respected. In Gifford's self-described "compromise between science and sentiment," the autopsy had been performed, but the body was then cremated according to what the anthropologists believed was Yahi custom. Pope must have had no hard feelings about this outcome, for he joined Gifford and Thomas Waterman at Olivet for Ishi's cremation and the depositing of the ashes in the pot and then the niche. In the moments before the embalmed body went into the oven, the little party of Ishi's white friends laid beside it Ishi's favorite bow, his quiver, and the few other things that Pope later explained were for Ishi's "long journey to the land of the shadows." Pope slipped an arrow he'd made himself into the quiver in a last token of affection for the dead man.

That the dissection had taken place was no secret, however, and it was the more specific question of Ishi's brain that U.C. San Francisco's Nancy Rockafellar was charged to investigate. Although Pope had his own special interest in Ishi's dissection, an autopsy was standard for anyone who died at the hospital on Parnassus Heights. The founder, Hugh Toland, a pioneer who came west in the Gold Rush and later trained in France as a surgeon, was an early advocate of the importance of dissection in the education of medical students, and U.C. San Francisco was a teaching hospital from the start. In theory, then as now, an autopsy entails examining each of the body's vital organs: brain, lungs, heart, liver, kidneys. In practice, the doctors often skipped the brain. Because it required sawing off the skullcap, a laborious task in those days before the electric circular saw, the habit was to avoid this part of the job except in cases when it was suspected that something important about the patient's death could be learned by examining the brain.

Rockafellar knew that Ishi's brain had been removed because the autopsy report listed its weight. But why had Jean Cooke gone to the trouble of taking it out in this specific case? Cooke, the pathologist who'd supervised the autopsy, was a friend of Pope's, a sometime archery companion of Pope's and Ishi's, and a later president of the American Pediatric Society. One possible reason to remove the brain might have been to see whether Ishi had died of tubercular meningitis, a disease that attacks the spinal cord. To check for meningitis required a microscopic examination of tissue from the top of the spine—a procedure that required taking out the brain. If Ishi's brain was removed for this reason, the results should have been noted down. Nowhere at U.C. San Francisco could Rockafellar find any such records.

A puzzled Rockafellar asked an expert to reexamine Ishi's medical history and do a "dry autopsy," in the argot of pathology. Robert Fishman, a former chair of U.C. San Francisco's Department of Neurology, reported back in early 1998. According to the charts, Ishi's skin had progressively darkened with his illness. This is a symptom of Addison's disease, a glandular infection poorly understood in the early twentieth century. Fishman thought that Ishi might have died from this disease in conjunction with tuberculosis. Ishi's neck was not especially painful or crooked prior to his death, a fact that led the neurologist to doubt the theory that the doctors would have bothered removing the brain just to check for tubercular meningitis. He guessed that Ishi's brain was taken out not for medical assessment but for "anthropological" interest—curiosity to know every last detail about weight, size, and structure of the brain of a man assumed to be the very last of his kind. As far as the organ's whereabouts, Fishman reached the same conclusion as the U.C. Berkeley investigators who'd been conducting their own search for Ishi's brain unbeknown to anyone at U.C. San Francisco. "I assume," Fishman wrote, "that it was included with the body when cremated."


Only halfway into our conversation did Nancy Rockafellar let on that there was more to the story. I was asking some question or another when it came out quite suddenly. Fishman and U.C. Berkeley had it wrong, Rockafellar said. The brain was never put back with the ashes. "They sent it to the Smithsonian," she announced. "And," she added with a suspenseful flourish, "the Smithsonian destroyed it."

How did Rockafellar know this? In the hope of turning up any new leads, she'd phoned a retired curator at Berkeley's anthropology museum. This man had told her he knew the truth about Ishi's brain. According to his story, a former student of his now directed the American Indian Program at the National Museum of Natural History, a part of the Smithsonian Institution. This woman had sometimes called to fill in her former mentor on the gossip from Washington. One time in the 1980s she had mentioned that the Smithsonian had destroyed Ishi's brain. The woman was Sioux, but she believed that archaeologists should be able to study the bones of Indians and opposed the new laws ordering repatriation. She feared the Smithsonian would soon have to disclose that it had kept the brain of California's most famous Indian for many decades without telling anyone. It had thus been decided, in secret, to incinerate the missing organ to avoid a scandal, or so the woman's old mentor had told Nancy Rockafellar he remembered her saying.

The tenacious Rockafellar had called the woman at the Smithsonian. According to Rockafellar, the woman had denied everything. Any story about Ishi's brain ever being in the Smithsonian was a "myth," Rockafellar recalled the woman saying before hanging up in anger. Rockafellar was convinced that this defensiveness meant guilt. Still, it was just a story at that point, and a secondhand one at that. Rockafellar wanted hard evidence before going any further. After several more months of searching, however, she had found nothing. As we became friends in later months, Rockafellar told me she had decided at last to share information with me in hopes that I might find a lead. "I felt as if I had hit a wall," she said.

I was astonished. Could the Smithsonian really have incinerated Ishi's brain? The nation's largest museum had run into trouble just a few years before over its exhibition of the Enola Gay, the plane that dropped the bomb on Hiroshima. Several veterans' groups were outraged; complaining that the Smithsonian was making the United States look bad, they forced the removal of text about the suffering of the bomb victims. This episode had underscored the touchiness of curating America's past, but it did not involve obstruction, lying, or a cover-up. If the Smithsonian had tried to keep the truth from Native Americans by destroying the missing body part of a legendary Indian, there might well be an embarrassing scandal. Nancy Rockafellar later told me that a higher-up at U.C. San Francisco knew people who were fundraising for the Smithsonian's Museum of the American Indian, a new museum planned for the Washington Mall. He had wondered aloud to Rockafellar whether bad publicity about Ishi's brain would harm the $199 million project.

Rockafellar understood the stakes and the potential repercussions of the information she seemed now to possess about the incineration of Ishi's brain. Later, she admitted having been ambivalent about letting me in on the secret story that had taken her so many months of research to uncover. This was why Rockafellar did not share the full details that afternoon, and in particular the name of the retired Berkeley curator or his Sioux protégé. Although hoping I might find some way to verify the story about the incineration of Ishi's brain, Rockafellar wanted me to earn anything I found by picking up the trail on my own. At one point, however, she mentioned that her retired curator lived in the East Bay—and had for a number of years been the anthropology museum's acting director at Kroeber Hall. This description fit a man named Frank Norick. "I wonder if it's Frank Norick," I said almost as if to myself, embarrassed to be pressing for more details. "Yes," Rockafellar had smiled. She took another sip of herb tea, then rose to get on with her other work: "I'd definitely follow up on your East Bay contacts."

On my way back to the parking lot, I noticed a new mural, dated 1976, in the lobby of a clinic. It was a cavalcade of San Francisco's history from the Beat poets to the Chinese New Year parade, a black woman tending a garden, a Chicano activist leafleting a street corner—and Ishi. In this iconography of diversity and multicultural correctness, he was no longer portrayed as the savage, the child, or the victim in need of rescue. The Ishi of this mural is serene and strong, a bit larger than anyone else, a man of nature in his breechcloth, showing the others how to whittle a hunting bow with a trusting quail and squirrel at his feet. Kroeber, Waterman, and Pope figure among the circle of respectful onlookers, but only as peripheral characters. Ishi, the assumed personification of the greater morality and natural wisdom of the Yahi and Native America, dominates the tableau.

That Ishi was the star of this medical center mural reflected his special place in the history of U.C. San Francisco and Parnassus Heights. Even so, I knew Ishi was not the first Indian to have been brought to San Francisco, and earlier it had sometimes been by force. Just over Twin Peaks from Parnassus Heights lay Mission San Francisco, these days a stop for tourists who want a quaint taste of Spanish California. In the early 1800s, hundreds of the Bay Area's Ohlone Indians had died of overwork and infectious diseases in the mission's dank, overcrowded barracks. Later, in the 1870s, another present-day tourist stop, the prison at Alcatraz Island, held two Modocs, Sloluck and Barncho, who were serving life sentences for their part in Captain Jack's famous rebellion. A researcher from the Smithsonian's Bureau of American Ethnology, Washington Matthews, visited the imprisoned Sloluck to take down a vocabulary of the Modoc language; the absolute privileges of the scientist to record the cultures and dissect the bodies of conquered Native Americans was still unquestioned in those Victorian times (later, Sloluck was released and found his way to Oklahoma; Barncho died in Alcatraz, and like Ishi from tuberculosis). Ishi may have been more refugee than prisoner, although I knew Art Angle would dispute even this characterization. Either way, Ishi had also ended up in San Francisco because of the forces of death and dispossession set in motion by the nineteenth-century white conquest of California.

It is possible that Ishi was not even the first Yahi in San Francisco. In 1859, in an effort to put an end to raiding from the hills, the state militia had swept through Yahi country burning camps, killing those who resisted, and marching survivors away to reservations. One confrontation on Deer Creek apparently ended with the capture of about twenty people. Could Yahi people—perhaps even relatives of Ishi—have been among those detained? It is impossible to say for sure, especially since the militia commander was later suspected of inflating his campaign's achievements. One newspaper did report that the Indians seized included "representatives of all the tribes that roam between Red Bluffs and Pyramid Lake."

On December 22, 1859, the soldiers paraded their prisoners through downtown San Francisco. Next to the bay, at the foot of Powell Street in what is today the tourist mecca of Fisherman's Wharf, they set up a prison camp for the 480 Indians. Among the prisoners was "Hat Creek Liz." This young Indian woman had spent some time on John Bidwell's Chico ranch in the 1850s, but local settlers later believed she had led or at least organized raids in the northern Sacramento Valley. Hat Creek Liz had been seized by state militiamen and brought to San Francisco along with her brother, "Shavehead," supposedly the chief of the Hat Creeks, or the Atsugewi, as they are now more often known. Shavehead had been shot in a confrontation with the settlers and his shattered arm was still in a sling.

A San Francisco reporter visited the captives just before Christmas. When he arrived, the Indians were circled around fires against the bay's damp cold, mixing flour and water together into gruel. "Their skins are as dusky as an unwashed negro's," the reporter related, falling back again on the view of California's natives as closer to blacks than other Indians, and thus at the very bottom of the totem pole of human evolution. "For clothes, the men wore grey shawls, old trousers that might have been stolen from the first miners that ever penetrated the region.

The women wore the cast-off men's clothes—or, except a shawl, noth-ing . . . The tattooing that some of them displayed did not enhance the little [beauty] they may have had." There were dozens of "little sav-ages" amid the "dirt, squalor, poverty, and homelessness," the reporter added, noting that eight babies had been born in captivity. By the next morning, the camp had vanished. After their short time on display, the Indians had been shipped up the coast to Mendocino and from there marched to the Round Valley reservation. The trophies of Manifest Destiny had been returned to their shelf.

Or had they? Like the sheer improbability of a "wild" Indian hiding in the hills until 1911 or the striking turn of tribal fortunes brought by casinos, the history of Native California has not always gone according to script. Many Indians slipped away from the Round Valley reservation in the nineteenth century, some never to return, others later coming back for a time or for good. Of the eventual fate of Hat Creek Liz, we know nothing, but Shavehead escaped in 1863. He made his way back to his native hill country beyond the town of Redding in the northern Sacramento Valley, according to some accounts traveling by night and hiding in the daytime, climbing to hilltops to orient himself by a glimpse of Mount Shasta's snowy peak.

Back home, Shavehead killed a cowhand and was captured once more. He was something of a local legend by that point, the man "who has doubtless murdered more whites than any other Indian in the state," according to one newspaper report. Somehow, this last "bad" Indian, like Ishi a survivor in his own way, escaped the gallows. By 1877, Shavehead was free again and had his own little farm and adjoining dancehouse in the Fall River valley southeast of Mount Shasta. There the old man lived out the remainder of his life in the company of his wife, their dogs, and a few relatives.

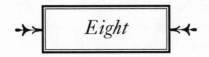

# Eight

# "DR. KROEBER'S
# PET BUFFALO"

I had it now from Nancy Rockafellar, albeit thirdhand, that the Smithsonian Institution had tossed Ishi's brain into the incinerator. Although Rockafellar was credible and smart, I still found her story almost too fantastic—too *X-Files*, with a purloined body part and a conspiracy of bureaucrats—to be true. Could such things occur in real life inside the world's largest public museum? It also puzzled me just how the Smithsonian could have obtained the last Yahi Indian's brain in the first place. Among more than a million objects, I knew this museum that served as the nation's unofficial attic had baseball cards, stuffed elephants, an antique John Deere tractor, Big Daddy Don Garlits's Swamp Rat XXX dragster, and Dorothy's ruby slippers from *The Wizard of Oz*. No doubt pickled brains were part of the collections, too. Yet Alfred Kroeber had been in charge at Berkeley. His letter from New York may have been too late to prevent a dissection, but Kroeber had been passionate about respecting Ishi's wishes for a proper burial. It seemed improbable that the anthropologist would ever have permitted Ishi's brain to be sent to the Smithsonian.

I'd learned much more about Kroeber by this time. When he'd come West from New York at the close of the nineteenth century, anthropology still took the study of "primitive peoples" as its primary mission; in the academic division of labor of that time, study of the Western industrial countries was left to sociology. Franz Boas, Kroeber's mentor, wanted his students to record everything they could about native customs—language, music, myths, rituals, religions, even toilet training. What would later be called "salvage anthropology" was predicated on the assumption that tribal cultures were destined for imminent destruction in the forward march of modernity. This project held both a scientific and educational dimension. While they were documenting vanishing cultures for posterity, anthropologists would also show that even "primitive" societies had their own sometimes admirable rules of conduct and custom. Her idyllic picture would later be challenged, but Margaret Mead, for example, argued that Americans could learn from the relaxed mores related to sex and adolescence in tropical Samoa. For his part, Kroeber refused to accept the dismissal of California's Indians as "diggers" unworthy of study. As soon as he took up his post at Berkeley in 1901, he threw himself into the job of gathering every scrap of information about the languages, habits, and beliefs of Native California.

The century's turn was a time of expansion and promise for many Californians, as indeed it was for the young Kroeber, with a long and distinguished career ahead of him. For the land's first peoples, it was just the opposite. As Hollywood was becoming the center of the new film industry, Los Angeles and San Francisco were growing into major cities, and Stanford and Berkeley ascended into the ranks of the world's great universities, the Indians of California were at a low point in their history. The march of conquest had unspooled in fast-forward here at the end of the continent, triggered by the Gold Rush. In 1874, the visiting Victorian anthropologist Stephen Powers wrote that California's Indians were plagued by "indolence" and "mental weakness," speculating that the problem was somehow "the excessive amounts of fish they consumed." Yet Powers was also aghast at the atrocities committed by whites against the Yahi, Wiyot, Pomo, and the state's other tribes: "They were, one might almost say, blown into their air by the suddenness and fierceness of the explosion. Never before has a people been swept away with such terrible swiftness."

By the turn of the century, only some twenty thousand indigenous people remained in California. These survivors had watched the ranches and towns cover the valleys that once belonged to them and had to seek handouts and menial jobs from the descendants of the settlers who'd taken their land. The new realities for many Indians were extreme poverty, dirty shanties, rotgut liquor, despair, and a sense of loss and fear conditioned by the memory of the massacres and lynchings of the mid-nineteenth century. To be an Indian was still very often to be an object of scorn and derision in California's backcountry. The survivors tried to hide away or even abandon their culture to blend into the new world as best they could—as, for example, Art Angle's Maidu had.

A frontier mentality that held the threat of violence was still prevalent even in the early twentieth century. In 1911, the year that Ishi was apprehended in Oroville, an Indian named Shoshone Mike and a few others were accused of killing a cowhand near Alturas, in the state's desolate far northeastern corner. A posse was formed to hunt what a local newspaper described as "a band of human monsters." They tracked the Indians to Nevada and gunned down Shoshone Mike and nine others, among them a toddler and a baby, at Little Rock Canyon, a brand of cowboy justice that recalled the slaughter of Indians in the Gold Rush years. Like the skull of Captain Jack, and possibly the brain of Ishi, the skeleton of Shoshone Mike was eventually obtained by the Smithsonian for its collections, macabre spoils of the conquest of the West.

Into this devastation strode Alfred Kroeber, pencil and notebook in hand. In the century that had just ended, the Victorians had practiced "armchair anthropology," penning treatises about the habits of the "savage races" from the comfort of their London studies. At Columbia, however, Franz Boas wanted anthropology to follow the lead of the natural sciences by placing a premium on careful observation—and insisted that Mead, Kroeber, Benedict, and his other students carry out "fieldwork" among the natives. Kroeber believed that aboriginal Indian tradition was already torn "to pieces" in California, but he managed to find a scattered handful of Indians who'd grown up with minimal contact with whites and could speak the language and tell the stories they'd learned from their elders. It was to the homesteads of these men and women who still had the knowledge of the life of the roundhouse, the shaman, and the tales of Coyote and Rabbit that Kroeber journeyed during his first decade in California. He wanted to collect as much information as possible before it was too late. When a house is on fire, as the linguist John Peabody Harrington put it, you have to rescue whatever you can.

Kroeber recalled meeting with a Mojave elder in 1902. Inyokutavere lived outside the desert town of Needles close to the Arizona border. With another Mojave, Jack Jones, as interpreter, the old man took almost a week to tell Kroeber one of his people's origin stories. Inyo-kutavere was "stone blind," Kroeber later recalled: "He was below the average of Mohave tallness [this was the older spelling of Mojave], slight in figure, spare, almost frail with age. His gray hair was long and unkempt, his features sharp, delicate, sensitive. . . . He sat indoors, on the loose sand floor of his house, for the whole of the six days I was with him, in the frequent posture of Mohave men, his feet beneath him or to the side, not with legs crossed. He sat still whether reciting or awaiting his turn, but drank in all the Sweet Caporal cigarettes I provided. His housemates sat about and listened, or went and came as they had things to do."

Others besides Kroeber were also fanning out to gather information, among them such amateur anthropologists as Frank Latta, known as "Mr. Pencils," a schoolteacher who spent his weekends recording the myths of the Yokuts in the San Joaquin Valley. The more eccentric fieldworker John Peabody Harrington was a brilliant student of languages who worked on contract for the Smithsonian's Bureau of American Ethnology. He was also notorious as a misogynist and anti-Semite forever jealous of the star trajectory of the "Jew Kroeber," whom he must have mistakenly believed to be such because of the latter's connection to Franz Boas and perhaps his beard and marriage to Henriette Rothschild, who like Boas was Jewish. Harrington would do almost any anything to obtain material. Upon hearing that an old Costanoan Indian, the last speaker of his language, lay on his death bed outside Santa Barbara, Harrington desperately telegrammed an acquaintance: "DO YOU SUPPOSE WE CAN PEP HIM UP BY GIVING HIM A SHOT OF MORPHINE TO GET HIM SO HE CAN TALK BEFORE HE DIES????" Although this poor man died before Harrington could put his plan into action, an elderly Luiseño, member of another of southern California's tribes, passed away in the intrepid researcher's arms as the latter tried to shake out a few last words of the man's mother tongue. Harrington, who had difficulty writing articles, left behind more than six hundred cardboard boxes of notes on the languages of Native California. They are the only record we now possess of many vanished tongues such as Chumash and Costanoan.

Justified or not, the intrusiveness of men like Harrington would later be cited by tribes banning anthropologists from their reservations. But in the less politicized early twentieth century, even the more polite

Kroeber and his Berkeley colleagues did not always have their way. To be sure, many older Indians were pleased, even honored, to describe their ancient traditions for visiting researchers from the big city. The noted linguist Victor Golla recalls an old Hupa woman, Ada Masteen, telling him that her trip to Berkeley to speak to anthropology classes about her language and culture was one of the best moments in her life. Other Indians were not so enthusiastic. Edward Sapir, who later worked with Ishi, complained to Kroeber that an Indian up near Redding named Canyon Bill demanded a dollar for every word he provided in his native Wintu. Sapir recommended to Kroeber another Indian, Stonewall Jackson, "a hunchback" who was "very fidgety and talks rapidly." Even the hunchback, griped Sapir, was "generally too busy telling you how busy he is" to be an ideal informant. Indians had been massacred, lynched, enslaved, and confined to reservations. They weren't always ready to accede to the new breed of scientists who appeared in the wreckage's rubble to document their ways.

There remains much to admire in what Kroeber accomplished in California. Others had a greater knack for penetrating the tight-knit world of native society. Jaime de Angulo rolled around drunk in the ditches with Achumawi informants like Old Blind Hall and Sumkit in the steppes beyond Mount Lassen. What the more guarded and proper Kroeber possessed was a keen intelligence and a powerful professional commitment to leaving a record of Native California's varied ways of life. He seldom spent more than a few weeks in any single place, even though Boas urged him in 1902 to "take up one group by itself and work it out thoroughly." Yet Kroeber's more peripatetic style allowed him to assemble an enormous amount of information from every corner of California—and to collect hundreds of baskets, feathered headdresses, wooden masks, and other objects for his museum, which would come to possess more than 5,000 artifacts from Native California alone. Kroeber spent the most time with the Yurok in Klamath River country along the Redwood Coast, but he also traveled to dozens of other spots in the vast and still rough backcountry. There he met, interviewed, and sometimes befriended Patwin, Nomlaki, Yuki, and many other surviving Indians. Thomas Waterman, Edward Gifford, and Kroeber's other Berkeley hires did research of their own, publishing over thirty books and eight hundred articles between them about everything from Maidu storytelling to Pomo basketmaking and the Yurok Brush Dance. Their dogged, even heroic efforts left behind what amounts to the single most complete record we have today of Native California's traditional ways.

No one questioned Kroeber's expertise about Native California during his own time. In hindsight, however, profound blind spots in his work became apparent. The largest and most disturbing was Kroeber's silence about the costs of white conquest, the atrocities committed against Native Californians, or the present-day condition of the Indians. The wounds of the Gold Rush years, still relatively fresh, were the reason Kroeber found Native California "torn to pieces." Yet one searches in vain through thousands of pages of Kroeber's writing for anything about that history of murder and extermination, much less of the poverty and misery among the Indians who'd grown up in its shadow. As anthropologist Thomas Buckley has noted, Kroeber wrote about the Indians as if their world had never been shattered and he himself "had never come among the survivors."

It was a conscious choice. Kroeber knew about the slaughter of the Indians, of course, and mentioned in passing conquest's "heartless forces." At the same time, his almost exclusive interest lay in the pre-contact period, and not in what he called the "bastard cultures" of living Indians, an amalgam of traditional and Western influences. As he stated in his *Handbook of the Indians of California*, "I have omitted all directly historical treatment in the ordinary sense; that is, accounts of the relations of the natives with the whites and of the events befalling them after such contact was established." Kroeber described the subjugation of Native California as "the little history of pitiful events," as though it were worth little consideration.

That Kroeber took this view was a matter of temperament, at least in part. He opposed what he called the "delusion" of racial superiority and even came out of retirement to direct an army language training program in the war effort against the Axis. In general, though, politics never much interested Kroeber; his voracious intellectual curiosity was not paired with active involvement in social causes. Kroeber's colleague, Thomas Waterman, wrote with feeling about pioneer brutality and the "white invasion." Another Berkeley anthropologist, Llewellyn Loud, denounced "barbarity and inhumanity on the part of . . . vicious whites." The drier, more controlled Kroeber eschewed the language of moral and political judgment. He did not even like to talk with Indians about what they had suffered, whether because he found their stories uninteresting or because—at some deeper, more repressed psychological level—he could not bear them. When a friend asked Kroeber why he didn't ask Yurok villagers about the white conquest, he replied only that he "could not stand all of the tears."

The larger explanation lies in the anthropology of that time. The reform-minded Franz Boas allowed his writings to be excerpted in *The Nation* and other leftist magazines, but he also advocated a "value-free" discipline in the tradition of the physical sciences. His own university degree was in physics and he declared his own allegiance to "the ice cold flame of the passion of truth for truth's sake." Above all, Boas objected to Jim Crow laws, Nazism, and xenophobia as "unscientific" and based upon spurious "folklore" about the inferiority of non-white peoples. The ideal of objectivity prevailed in anthropology for much of the twentieth century. With exceptions like Waterman and Loud, few anthropologists spoke up about injustices inflicted on the West's colonized peoples, as if doing so would undercut their credibility. Only during the turmoil of the 1960s and 1970s would a new generation of scholars call for a more activist and even "militant" anthropology. In the 1980s, the influence of postmodern theory introduced new doubts that anthropology could ever be more than a partial, subjective enterprise. It is still being debated even today whether anthropologists ought to embrace the ideal of neutrality or advocacy and, for that matter, whether the study of other cultures should be conceived of as art, science, or something in between.

As was true of Kroeber and Native California, the commitment to "salvage anthropology" came at the expense of studying Indians as they were in the present day. Everywhere from the outback of Australia to the Amazonian rainforest and the highlands of New Guinea, the arrival of Westerners was transforming and sometimes destroying native societies. Not until the last few decades have anthropologists finally turned their attention at last to conquest and colonialism, the varied responses of native peoples to Western rule, and the more sympathetic study of those new, crossfertilized, "bastard" cultures that Kroeber and his generation had dismissed as unworthy of study. Early-twentieth-century anthropology more often than not left the comforting yet also false impression that countless "untouched," "unspoiled" tribes around the world still flourished in their full exotic glory.

I recall those photographs that Alfred Kroeber took of Ishi on their 1914 return trip to Deer Creek. Although Ishi preferred a shirt, tie, and shoes by then, Kroeber photographed him wearing a primitive's loin-cloth in his old haunts. He had Ishi pose tying a forked wood spearpoint to a harpoon, flaking an obsidian arrowhead, and other quintessential traditional activities. The images, like Kroeber's extensive writing, give us a glimpse of what it might have been like in Native California long ago (although the loincloth was a dubious touch, since the aboriginal Yahi probably wore skins or went naked). In another way, however, the images were deceptive. One recalls how the famed photographer Edward Curtis dressed his subjects in "traditional" regalia, sometimes not even of their own tribe, and carefully tinted out tin cans and any other signs of modernity to manufacture his photographs of Indians in a romantic, "savage" state. Curtis photographed his Indians as he and other Americans wanted to imagine them and not as they any longer were or perhaps ever had been. Historian Fatimah Rony Tobing has coined the term "taxidermy" for these images that gave the illusion of life to cultures that had already been destroyed.

What about Kroeber and his photographs of Ishi? The truth was that Ishi's Yahi band had tipped harpoons with iron nails recovered from pioneer garbage dumps, wore scavenged old settler clothes, and made their arrowheads from broken window glass. Ishi had always to worry about being shot down by some wandering cowhand—and only by poaching the occasional hog or bag of flour from white cabins were his people even able to survive. Kroeber's photographs give us no hint of the mixed, traumatic conditions of Indian survival in the canyon. The more "natural," picturesque, and primordial Yahi existence Kroeber had Ishi reenact for the camera was a life Ishi himself had never fully known.

Taking stock of our ancestors, familial or professional, is always a tricky proposition. A first temptation will perhaps always be to make them out as heroes—or disown them as backward and more unenlight-ened than ourselves. It's surely a mistake to make any such black-and-white judgments in Kroeber's case, since the fact that the dismaying and the praiseworthy were so intertwined in his life's work is something we can only see now, in retrospect. Kroeber himself professed his indiffer-ence to posthumous judgment. "As to posterity," he wrote in his later years, "I'm not much concerned. I still have too many things to do."

A train from Oroville to Oakland, a ferry across the Bay, and then a San Francisco streetcar brought Ishi to his new home in San Francisco on

September 6, 1911. The last Yahi had been accompanied on the trip by
Thomas Waterman and Sam Batwi, the old Indian brought down from
Redding as a translator. Alfred Kroeber was there to welcome Ishi—or
Mr. Ishi, as he soon became more politely known. Although very much
the man of learning, Kroeber also had a nose for public relations, for
promoting himself and the young field of anthropology. On that first
day he invited reporters from San Francisco's main newspapers to meet
Ishi and held forth in his precise, professorial manner. "Even in the
interior of Africa, or in Australia, it is doubtful such a specimen of man
could be found," Kroeber announced. The reporters took the cue. The
next day's *San Francisco Call* informed its readers that Ishi was "the
greatest anthropological treasure they [the anthropologists] have ever
captured."

Kroeber must have been well contented that day. His interest in the
Yahi had already led him to dispatch Thomas Waterman to Deer Creek
canyon in 1908 in a failed attempt to open communication with the
rumored lost tribe there. Now the last survivor of those Indians had
become Kroeber's ward in San Francisco, an arrangement soon to be
approved officially by the Bureau of Indian Affairs. Kroeber knew that
Ishi had grown up while his people were already being pursued by the
Indian hunters, but he still saw him as a kind of living fossil, a man more
connected to his ancestral language and culture than any of California's
more assimilated surviving Indians. The anthropologists had almost no
information about the small, elusive Yahi. Even during Ishi's first days
in San Francisco, they took down some of his tales and what other
information about Yahi custom he was willing to share with them. On
the basis of that work with Ishi, Kroeber added a chapter on the Yahi in
his forthcoming *Handbook of the Indians of California*.

From the start, too, Kroeber knew that the public was curious about
the "Wild Man of Deer Creek" of the newspaper reports. Vaudeville
troupes and circuses had already asked to "borrow" Ishi as a sideshow.
This was the heyday of Buffalo Bill's Traveling Wild West Show, when
such icons as Geronimo and Sitting Bull had become "show Indians" for
hire, enthralling crowds by reenacting their exploits at Little Bighorn
and even the massacre at Wounded Knee. When Cody's act visited
Europe to perform for the Pope and the Prince of Wales, the Indians
took the opportunity of a show in Venice to tour the Grand Canal in a
gondola. Kroeber preferred opera and the theater to this kind of enter-
tainment, but nonetheless the Berkeley professor planned to have Ishi

as an attraction in his anthropology museum, very soon to be inaugurated in a borrowed building on San Francisco's Parnassus Heights.

The museum was bankrolled by Phoebe Apperson Hearst, a former Rocky Mountain schoolteacher who had married one of the West's richest mine owners and inherited his fortune. Her son, William Randolph Hearst, was the newspaper tycoon, inventor of yellow journalism, builder of San Simeon, and subject of Orson Welles's famous film *Citizen Kane*. Phoebe Apperson Hearst loved to travel and collect. On her expeditions to Egypt, she shipped back crates of mummies, carved wooden dogs, and painted marble jars. Hearst's Egyptian treasures would be a draw, Kroeber knew. But a live wild Indian would bring many more curious San Franciscans to the new museum above Golden Gate Park.

The museum opened in October, just a few weeks after Ishi's arrival. A giant Haidu totem pole stood directly in front of the big Victorian building. There was a formal reception for a thousand people in evening gowns and tails and top hats. Phoebe Apperson Hearst joined Benjamin Ide Wheeler, the University of California's president, at the head of the receiving line. Kroeber knew Ishi was still nervous about crowds, so he arranged that curious guests could come to a back room to meet the Indian in suit and tie, sitting in Kroeber's company. It was announced that evening that Ishi would be at the museum on Sundays to greet visitors and show his mastery of fire making, animal calls, and the other arts of his people. Over the next six months, more than 23,000 people came to visit the museum. As Kroeber had hoped, Ishi brought more visitors on Sundays than all other days combined. "We have become a distinctly Sunday institution," he informed Phoebe Apperson Hearst.

The reception Ishi received was not all enthusiastic, however. A residue of the old-fashioned frontier hatred lingered in the farm country of the Sacramento Valley. A few days after Ishi's capture at the slaughterhouse, the *Oroville Daily Register* published a long story about Indians murdering local white children a half century before. It was a cautionary tale about the treachery of Ishi's kind. Later the same newspaper derided Ishi as "Dr. Kroeber's Pet Buffalo." "In the wild, he was slender, graceful, pussy-footed, and hard as a nut. After two years in captivity he is fat, pudgy, shuffling of gait, and inglorious. He smokes cigarettes, chews tobacco, wears shoes, admires himself in the mirror and takes liver pills." There was more than a hint of sour grapes in these diatribes. As Ishi became a celebrity, many Orovilleans grew bitter about having lost him to San Francisco and its professors. The Chamber of Commerce wrote university officials demanding that Ishi's name be changed to "Oroville" so "the city may be given the publicity that belongs to it as a result of his capture."

The newspapers in San Francisco had published Kroeber's declarations about Ishi's value for science, and the best of the reporters wrote careful stories. Yet those were also the days of a journalism that played down to the worst prejudices of the age. The papers reveled in suggesting a mutual attraction between the "saddle-colored cave man" and white women, and the fearful, thrilling thought of miscegenation. The *San Francisco Examiner* had Ishi flirting with a French movie starlet on a promotional tour in the city. "Ess he wild?" the gorgeous Gaby Deslys was supposed to have inquired. Ishi had "made eyes" at the actress, the newspaper said, and Deslys pronounced "Ishi Très Drôle." When Kroeber took Ishi to the Orpheum Theater, the *Call* weighed in with the vaudeville singer Lily Lena as the putative object of Ishi's adulation. "Slowly Ishi rose to his feet," the reporter said. "He fixed on the lady an unwinking gaze of such intensity as to draw her attention away from a row of Johnnies to whom she had been warbling. Her eyes met those of the wild man. She faced him bravely and with dazzling white arms held up toward the thunderstruck worshiper, sang to him the words of 'Have You Ever Loved Another Little Girl?'"

For all the sensationalism, Ishi may have been attracted to some white women, and vice versa. With his strong features and appealing smile, the last Yahi was a good-looking man in middle age. Yet the newspapers had probably fabricated the incidents with Gaby Deslys and Lily Lena. According to those who knew him best, Ishi was reserved around women. A dental student, Esther Watson, later recalled that Ishi was "not very comfortable" playing his gambling game with her in front of the museum. Men and women did not gamble together in Yahi society. The protocol on relationships between the sexes restricted face-to-face contact between a man and his mother-in-law, and secluded women during menstruation and childbirth. Alfred Kroeber, who was seated next to Ishi at the Orpheum Theater, insisted that the reporter fabricated his entire story of the Yahi's enchantment with Lily Lena. At the time of this performance Ishi had been in San Francisco only a month, and Kroeber said that he "did not even seem conscious of the stage or the players." What truly captured the attention of the man accustomed to the company of just a few other souls, the professor noted, was the size of the crowd.

There was much good will toward Ishi in spite of these bursts of mean-spiritedness. Museum visitors addressed the Yahi not as the Wild Man of Oroville but as Ishi, if not Mr. Ishi. A Mrs. Van Den Burgh sent a package on behalf of the California Indian Association with an explanatory note for Kroeber. "I have knit a scarf of scarlet wool—which I ask you to give to Ishi—if you see no objection and it is convenient." A delegation from the Women's Christian Temperance Union came to warn Ishi about the dangers of drink, but they were preaching to the converted. Ishi did not like wine or liquor and only mixed small amounts of beer diluted with sugar and water for medicine. The only alcoholic beverage in Native California before the whites came was a weak, fermented brew of manzanita berries. "Whiskey-tee . . . die man," Saxton Pope reported Ishi replying to a query about whiskey, once more adding his customary Yahi suffix -*tee* to an English noun.

The appeal of this "primitive man" was also a barometer of new discontents, and in particular of the disenchantment some Westerners felt with what they saw as the artificiality and regimentation of their own modern ways. Picasso and the avant garde across the Atlantic were finding inspiration in Africa's primitive masks; D. H. Lawrence and other writers went to Taos, New Mexico, to celebrate things Indian in counterpoint to the West's fall into civilization. Many Americans were heading outdoors to escape the city. John Muir had just founded the Sierra Club, and, indeed, the San Francisco chapter invited Kroeber and Ishi to one of their meetings. A schoolteacher, Ernest Darling, "the Nature Boy," who had become a celebrity by declaring the superiority of primitive ways and going to live naked in the forests of New Hampshire, saw Ishi as a model and visited him in San Francisco. According to a reporter, Ishi taught Darling a few birdcalls, but he refused to join the "Nature Boy" for an overnight on the hill above the museum.

Now that Indians no longer posed a military threat anywhere in the United States, they were becoming objects of special solemnity and even veneration. On a trip to California, Robert Louis Stevenson, author of *Treasure Island*, lamented the destruction of "redwoods and redskins, the two noblest indigenous living things." At work was what the cultural critic Renato Rosaldo has called the "imperialist nostalgia" of whites who come retrospectively to admire the native peoples and the wilderness they had obliterated equally to make way for themselves. Many San Franciscans were ready, even eager, to believe in Ishi's "dignity" and "nobility." It was assumed that Native America would soon vanish altogether in modernity's progress, as good or bad as that progress might be. By this reckoning, Ishi was the last real Indian of any kind. He became the object of much mournful pathos and a sometimes soupy sentimentalism. "Ishi, the Lonely," a reporter for *Sunset* magazine entitled his story about this "remnant of a Vanished Race of Western Aborigines."

A Berkeley undergraduate would remember Alfred Kroeber bringing Ishi to class one day. On this occasion, Ishi demonstrated his ancient Yahi method for fire making. He took a hardwood stick between his palms and began to twirl it into a socket of softer wood. It was no easy trick: too much force would snap the stick; too little would fail to spark the bit of dried moss or thistledown used for tinder. The Berkeley students maintained a respectful, even reverent, silence until Ishi conjured a wisp of smoke and then flames from his tinder. "You could hear a pin drop," Genieve Chamberlain, Kroeber's student, said. "When the fire began I supposed everyone felt a sort of relief. But everyone felt the dignity of Ishi."

What, then, of Alfred Kroeber's treatment of Ishi? A number of critics have lately taken the anthropologist to task for keeping the last Yahi in his museum. According to the Pueblo poet Edgar Silex, Ishi was nothing more than an object for exhibition and study. Silex's "Postcard" describes the poet's relief on visiting New York's American Museum of Natural History with his son—and not having to see Ishi's bones exhibited there or find the last Yahi "weaving/baskets or chipping arrowheads." And Art Angle had described Ishi as a "prisoner" in San Francisco, a captive of the scientists.

That Alfred Kroeber's motives were mixed is beyond doubt. In his day, anthropologists did not doubt their right to study Indians and considered their research essential to knowledge, science, and human progress. Kroeber and his colleagues often spoke about Ishi as a kind of mother lode from whom they were "extracting" and "mining" material for the advancement of anthropology. Linguist Leanne Hinton has also noted how Ishi became a kind of "intellectual property" for the Berkeley professors. In 1915, for example, Edward Gifford wrote Kroeber to explain his decision not to "lend" Ishi with a group of traveling Plains Indians for a performance at the San Francisco Marina.

"The affair was more or less a commercial one," Gifford related, "and furthermore might endanger our hold on Ishi." As far as the Sunday demonstrations at his museum, Kroeber apparently never sought Ishi's permission in the first place—or ever reflected on the ethics of having a survivor of genocide on exhibit. That Ishi's contact with thousands of museum visitors imperiled his health made Kroeber's decision irresponsible at still another level.

Yet contemplating the circumstances, I was also wary of being too hard on Kroeber. After all, at a time when many white Americans would never think of socializing with people of other races, the Berkeley anthropologists had demonstrated their generosity and sensitivity towards Ishi in many ways. To make the Yahi feel at home, they took him sightseeing, had him to their houses for dinner or overnight, and introduced him to families and friends. "Can you pick up enough acorn meal to fill a baking powder can?" Kroeber wrote in 1915 to his younger Berkeley colleague Edward Gifford, who was away in the Sierra Nevada: "I think Ishi would appreciate it." These small acts of kindness reflected an affection for Ishi that grew through the years as the professors came to know him better.

Ishi lived in the museum. He was not a captive there, not at least in any simple sense. "He has been free to return to his old home and manner of living ever since being with us," Kroeber wrote the Bureau of Indian Affairs in 1914, "but [he] much prefers his present condition." In his first weeks, Ishi may not have felt at liberty to say he wanted to go back to Deer Creek, let alone a reservation. Once accustomed to the city, he was seldom shy about speaking his mind—and would probably have declared his desire to return had he felt that way. Yet Ishi never expressed any interest in leaving Parnassus Heights. With his own world destroyed, he may have seen San Francisco as preferable to the lonely canyons of his homeland, much less some unknown Oklahoma reservation. He came to use the word "*wowi*" for the museum, Yahi for home.

Ishi's only regular duties were as a Sunday performer and part-time janitor's assistant in the museum, earning some spending money. The anthropologists could have recompensed Ishi simply for drawing so many people to their museum, but at least his janitorial duties were not onerous and took up just a few hours a week. Ishi was placed on the official payroll to receive his salary of $25 a month; this, as Berkeley Native American Studies professor Gerald Vizenor has observed, made the last Yahi the University of California's first-ever Indian employee.

With plenty of free time, Ishi walked the streets of San Francisco unaccompanied and at will; he roamed Golden Gate Park and chatted up his neighbors on Parnassus Heights with hand signs and, before long, broken English. "I can recall him," one San Franciscan woman remembered much later, "seated on the front steps of our little home in the 1400 block of Fifth Avenue—a broad smile on his face—surrounded by a group of small children. And not infrequently, my old grandmother would come ambling down the steps to talk—as much as they could make themselves understood."

Ishi also had contact with other Indians in San Francisco. There was Sam Batwi at the start. A diminutive elderly man who wore a suit, wire-rimmed glasses, and a wispy gray beard, Batwi was of mixed Yana and Maidu blood and had grown up in the backcountry north of Mount Lassen. He ended up on the outskirts of the town of Redding in the Sacramento Valley, where he became a ranch hand on a farm owned by a settler from Vermont. As one of the last living speakers of the northern dialect of the Yana tongue, he'd worked in the 1880s with an early folklorist in California, Jeremiah Curtin, telling him Yana myths. Twenty years later, Batwi was also an informant to Edward Sapir. In his memoirs, Curtin wrote that Batwi "knew a great deal of Yana mythology," although he also complained that Batwi's wife Anna was "constantly interrupting Sam with criticism and corrections."

Batwi understood enough of the Yahi dialect of Yana to build a bridge between Ishi and the anthropologists during Ishi's first days in San Francisco, when Ishi knew no English at all and had to adjust to his new life in the museum. Apparently, however, the two men took a dislike to one another. According to Theodora Kroeber, Batwi was condescending toward the "primitive" Ishi with his ignorance of white ways. Theodora thought Ishi believed Batwi was a pretentious "phony white man," especially objecting to his beard, which more traditional Native Californians had always plucked. Like Ishi, Batwi was a survivor, and his northern Yana tribe had been almost completely wiped out early on by smallpox, measles, and the attacks of whites, many of whom in that area would kill an Indian "on slight provocation," according to the nineteenth-century folklorist Jeremiah Curtin. Batwi was a masterful, ribald traditional storyteller, but he'd learned English, kept his hair short, grown the beard, and labored for a pittance in the valley just as "good" Indians were expected to do in the nineteenth century. That made the old man seem "inauthentic" and of little interest to a new generation of whites now so fascinated by and even admiring of "primitive life." It was the "wild," "untouched" Ishi who seemed to them the glamorous and exotic Indian. Batwi must have been puzzled and was perhaps resentful at the fuss made over a bumpkin who was so ignorant of modern ways. In any event, he was sent home after just a few weeks in San Francisco and died a few years later in complete anonymity.

Later Ishi went with Saxton Pope to see Buffalo Bill's Wild West Show when it came to San Francisco, and both of them enjoyed the carnival of cowboys, Indians, sharpshooters, and daredevil riders. There Ishi met a Sioux chief, doubtless decked out in his war-bonnet and face paint for the performance. The chief examined Ishi from head to toe and fingered a strand of his long hair. Whether in jest or not, he announced that Ishi was "a very high grade of Indian." Ishi took no offense. He enjoyed the show and later described the Sioux to Pope as a "big chiep." Ishi was adept enough himself at playing the role of the stoic, chiefly Indian. When another of the day's many traveling revues came to San Francisco, Ishi posed next to two Blackfoot performers. There was no smiling here. A solemn, self-possessed Ishi stands tall in his dark suit, with a bow and a bundle of arrows, a gift to the oldest Blackfoot warrior from one Indian to another.

Ishi's one close Indian friend in San Francisco was Juan Dolores. A Papago from southern California's deserts, the likeable Dolores was a part-time employee of the anthropology museum, fluent in Spanish and several indigenous languages, and a friend of Kroeber and his family. Ishi and Dolores sometimes rode San Francisco's trolley cars together. A favorite destination was the marina, with its smell of the sea and the Italian fishermen docking with ling cod and crab just pulled from the Pacific—a body of water Ishi had only heard about in Yahi myths before coming to San Francisco. The two friends shared the experience of being Indian in the city. We can only wonder what they spoke about in their many hours together.

It's true that Kroeber had Ishi on display at the museum. A grotesque tradition of Westerners putting their human trophies of conquest on exhibition goes back a very long way. Christopher Columbus brought six captured Indians back from his first voyage to show off at the Spanish court along with gold, emeralds, exotic parrots, and other New World novelties. An early-twentieth-century contemporary of Ishi's was Ota Benga, a young Pygmy brought from the Congo and exhibited for a time in the Monkey House at the Bronx Zoo. There he was taunted and gawked at as a "missing link" between apes and humans. "The pygmy was not much taller than the orangoutang," reported the *New York Times*, "and one had a good opportunity to study their points of resemblance. Their heads are much alike, and both grin in the same way when pleased." A group of outraged African-American ministers forced the zoo to release Ota Benga to a black bible school in Lynchburg, Virginia. He committed suicide there on March 20, 1916, just five days before Ishi's death on the other coast.

Ishi was also a curiosity, and yet it would be wrong to make too much of the comparison between the way he and Ota Benga were treated. Unlike the Pygmy, Ishi was never behind bars or glass (although a partition might have been better for his health). There was no carnival barking connected to Ishi's museum appearances, and the anthropologists expected the audience to be quiet and respectful. Typically, Kroeber or one of the others accompanied Ishi onto the dais in the main hall, and related the outlines of his life story. Then Ishi would chip an arrowhead or spear point with his percussion stone and a deer antler for flaking. "Occasionally," remembered Nels Nelson, a younger anthropologist who often did duty on those Sundays, "men or boys were invited to the platform to compete with him [Ishi] in his favorite guessing game, which consisted simply in taking turns at guessing in which closed fist a small section of bird bone was held." Nelson, at least, believed Ishi himself enjoyed the chance to demonstrate his mastery of the Yahi way of life. He often made gifts of his work to delighted museum goers, usually children.

The intended message of Ishi's appearances was also very different from the exhibition of Ota Benga, which was managed by impresarios who presented the young Pygmy as a freak of nature and an example of the "stunted" development of the "lower" races. In contrast, Kroeber believed in Franz Boas's credo of the essential equality of humankind— and the need to understand each culture as a system of behavior deserving study in its own terms. There was some residual Victorian snobbery in Kroeber's 1914 description of Ishi's Yahi as a "puny native civilization." Even so, Kroeber wanted visitors to leave the museum with an appreciation of Ishi and the skills of his people. The suggestion that Ishi was somehow less than human—a "missing link," as some reporters wanted to cast both him and Ota Benga—infuriated Kroeber. He dashed off an immediate reply to one newspaper's report that the "wild man" was "mentally a mere child." "There is nothing underdeveloped about him," Kroeber declared. "He has the mind of a man and is a man in every sense."

In the final account, too, I do not think Ishi was a helpless victim any more than Kroeber was the evil scientist. It must have demanded great force of character to survive for so many years in hiding, and even in San Francisco Ishi often exercised his own will when it mattered to him. At the press conference on his first day at the museum, the newspapermen wanted Ishi to remove his shirt and pose for a picture as the naked or at least topless child of the forest. Old Sam Batwi translated the request and Ishi's reply. No, Ishi said, he wouldn't strip down. Although he was still going barefoot then, his new clothes must have felt fine and clean by comparison with the filthy canvas miner's apron he'd worn in the wilds above Oroville. Plainly, too, it was nobody's custom to go naked in the city. Ishi agreed to be photographed showing off his archery skills, but only fully clothed. The next day's front page of the *San Francisco Chronicle* showed the "aboriginal Indian" in a dress shirt and tie, perhaps disappointing readers who'd expected something more exotic.

Even when cooperating, Ishi sometimes had his own reasons, as Kroeber and Waterman soon learned. As part of their salvage anthropology, the Berkeley professors had been recording the native songs of visiting Indians, not to mention collecting thousands of baskets, canoe paddles, feather blankets, and other artifacts for the museum collection. Kroeber had authorized the purchase of a phonograph, Thomas Edison's recent invention, to make the sound recordings. Only a few days after Ishi's arrival, Kroeber and Waterman sat him down in front of the "talking machine" with its wax cylinders, hand-crank, and large gilded trumpet that served as the speaker and microphone. Because a wax cylinder lasted just two minutes, Ishi had to pause and wait many times along the way for the anthropologists to change the record. He also had to speak very loudly, since the phonograph's recording mechanism was not yet electrical. It took sheer force of sound to scratch a song into the black wax.

None of these challenges fazed Ishi in the least, and the anthropologists got more than they had planned for or even wanted. On the first day Ishi went on for seven hours chanting the tale of Wood Duck and his wives. This one session filled more than a hundred cylinders, which were stored in tins about the size of a baking powder can. The tale of Wood Duck was the longest single performance ever made at that time, more than everything even Caruso had recorded. One reporter who'd been present confessed to nodding off during the "interminable droning" (the three-note scale of Yahi music can sound like "droning" to Western ears, which cannot recognize the modulations in tone and the phrasing that is akin to jazz improvisation). A distracted Waterman left to take a telephone call. On the anthropologist's return, Ishi had delivered a "lengthy harangue" in Yahi, the same reporter noted. "Better work all time, no leave, go away" was Sam Batwi's pithy translation. The chastened Waterman had to stow away the telephone in his desk.

Exactly why, or for whom, Ishi felt the imperative to leave a record will never be known. As the historian of anthropology and museum specialist Ira Jacknis writes, however, Ishi's knowledge that he was the last Yahi survivor "may have motivated his excitement and commitment to the project." Later, Ishi spent many long days dictating his traditional tales of Lizard, Rabbit, and the First People to Edward Sapir. That Ishi was so willing to convey Yahi traditions was not just a matter of pleasing his patrons but measured his own interest and enthusiasm for the culture passed down to him. Ishi's purposefulness still comes through in his museum recordings, later transferred to reel-to-reel tapes. As we hear Ishi singing into the phonograph's trumpet without pausing, we cannot know what these stories meant as a living legacy within the surroundings of his tribe. But it is hard not to hear in the lone Indian's forceful "droning" a last testament—a desire to preserve his Yahi songs and stories for posterity.

After the uncertainty of his first weeks, too, Ishi noted deficits in the white way of doing things. If Kroeber noted his "cheerfulness" and "good humor," he also heard Ishi's complaints about the bitter taste of San Francisco's treated water and, like many a latter-day visitor, the chilling ocean fog. Always serious about his craftsmanship, too, Ishi was also demanding, even fastidious, about his materials. His Papago friend Juan Dolores described him grousing one afternoon that a nail for chipping an arrowhead was too small. "You know he always finds fault with the things he have [sic] to use," Dolores reported to Kroeber. That Ishi felt comfortable enough to complain was hardly the behavior of a prisoner afraid of his captors.

I could see why Art Angle had such a negative slant on Alfred Kroeber's treatment of Ishi. A view of Ishi as an exploited victim was surely understandable given the brutalization of Native Americans through this nation's history—and the degradation and humiliation to which other human exhibitions like Ota Benga were subjected. From my perspective, however, a view of Kroeber's heartlessness toward the last Yahi was just as incomplete as Theodora's portrait of a perfect friendship between them. The truth was more paradoxical. Kroeber and the other Berkeley anthropologists had viewed Ishi as a specimen of another culture—yet also as a beloved friend. Almost a century later Thomas Waterman's words after Ishi's death still sound heartfelt: "I loved the old Indian." But Ishi's brain had still been cut out, and the question now was just what had become of it.

# Nine

# THE PAPER TRAIL

I was eager now to investigate Nancy Rockafellar's tale about Ishi's brain. Had the Smithsonian Institution once really possessed the missing organ—and then destroyed it to preempt bad publicity for having kept it in a jar for eighty years without telling anyone? I could already see the newspapers: "BRAIN OF LEGENDARY INDIAN INCINERATED: SMITHSONIAN CHARGED IN COVER-UP." An unpleasant, bizarre scandal, surely.

I located the name of the retired curator of Berkeley's anthropology museum in the local phone book. Frank Norick was guarded yet cordial enough when I called and explained I was writing a book about Ishi. His house in Kensington, just north of Berkeley, was torn up for renovations, he said. He proposed that we meet instead for a drink the next day at Brennan's.

Brennan's, a venerable Berkeley landmark, is a cavernous bar and cafeteria down by the train tracks featuring cold beer and giant TV screens—and a buffet line with macaroni and cheese, corned beef, and other old-time specialties not for the faint of appetite. A throwback to a Bay Area before the traffic, yoga studios, and outrageous real estate prices, Brennan's today remains a favorite watering hole for firefighters, plumbers, policemen, retirees, and university types tired or pretending to be tired of being in a college town.

Frank Norick was very much at home at Brennan's. A genial, salty Korean War veteran, he'd grown up in a working-class family in San Francisco's Mission District, then a stronghold of Irish immigrants and today of Latinos. As a student at Berkeley in the 1950s, Norick explained over his bourbon and soda, he knew Alfred Kroeber, Edward Gifford, Theodora Kroeber, and other principals in Ishi's story. Norick himself had done research on Native California, but the topic had already fallen from fashion by the mid-twentieth century. Anthropologists assumed that no more "real," untouched Indians remained in the state and that the "bastard cultures" of the survivors were not exotic enough to be worth studying. "You weren't really considered an anthropologist if you just drove across the Bay Bridge to do your fieldwork," Norick laughed.

The assumptions of anthropologists were also very different now. A hallmark of influential postmodern and postcolonial theory was its challenge to the calculus of purity and authenticity that once led Alfred Kroeber and his generation to dismiss some cultures as more "legitimate" than others. All cultures are hybrid and changing, it would be noted, since "primitive" societies before contact with the West had already always borrowed and incorporated influences from their neighbors and beyond. As their adoption of the bow and arrow about 1,500 years ago showed, even a relatively self-contained tribe like Ishi's Yahi sometimes took up outsider ways (in this case, a technology that was spreading down from the Canadian Arctic across California). By the time I went to graduate school in the mid-1980s, many anthropologists were interested in the new, crossbred cultures that have taken shape at the crossroads of the old and the new, the non-Western and the Western, the traditional and the modern. Yet few of these scholars returned to Native California, or for that matter to the study of Native Americans. A promising graduate student had the option now of doing his or her dissertation on the German biotech industry, Japanese and American sex tourism in Thailand, Cuban youth culture, or any number of new topics. It could also be a bit forbidding to encounter the skepticism and suspicion of more politicized late-twentieth-century tribes toward prying visitors. Eighty years after the heyday of Native American anthropology, only a handful of well-known researchers nationwide were writing about Indians. Not a single one of the thirty-five cultural anthropologists in the department Kroeber founded at U.C. Berkeley was a Native America specialist.

Frank Norick had taken a job at Berkeley's anthropology museum, and, like many museum men, became a kind of jack-of-all-trades, with expertise in everything from Eskimo snowshoes and Roman coins to the techniques of mummification in ancient Egypt. He'd retired after twenty years in the museum and now held a part-time job as the director of San Francisco International Airport's aviation archive. Flying was Norick's first love; the silver-haired, mustachioed anthropologist still had a pilot's license and sported an airman's brown leather bomber jacket.

I was unsure just how to broach the topic of Ishi's brain. After we had chatted for a half hour about Ishi and Native California, however, I finally asked Norick if he knew anything about the organ's fate from his years at the museum. "Yes, I know about the brain," he said: "I'm the only one who does." The affable Norick was not so much boasting as pleased to help. He went on to relate the tale just as I'd heard it from Nancy Rockafellar. Now and then, Norick said, JoAllyn Archambault called to chat, to "tell me about things she thought would interest me." Archambault was a Smithsonian official, a Sioux woman who had done a doctorate in Berkeley's anthropology department and studied with Norick there. Her dissertation, titled "The Gallup Inter-Tribal Ceremonial," had examined the annual pow-wow in that tough New Mexican town near the Navajo Reservation.

The topic of Ishi's brain had arisen in a conversation with Archambault sometime in the late 1980s, Norick recalled. At that time Indian activists and their supporters had been pressing new legislation to force museums to return bones and artifacts to the tribes from which they'd been taken. Soon to be supplemented by the more sweeping Native American Graves Protection and Repatriation Act, or NAGPRA, the National Museum of the American Indian Act became law in 1989. It required the Smithsonian Institution to repatriate the thousands of Indian bones and sacred objects in its collection to tribal descendants who wanted them back. Norick told me he had spoken with JoAllyn Archambault sometime just before President George H. Bush signed the National Museum of the American Indian Act. My heart raced a bit as Norick was telling me his improbable story. "JoAllyn called and said she thought I'd be interested to know that she had destroyed Ishi's brain," he told me. "She said they didn't want a bunch of protests about it."

It didn't bother Norick that Ishi's brain had been destroyed. "I told JoAllyn I thought she did the right thing," he said. "There'd just be a lot of talk about how anthropologists mistreat Indians and keep their heads in jars and all that balderdash." I saw that repatriation was a hot button with the retired curator. Like many archaeologists, Norick felt that the imperatives of science should take precedence over the feelings of Native Americans or any other particular group. He considered Indian bones as an invaluable data bank about the early human history of this continent, one that would be lost forever if they were buried back in the ground. Norick's face flushed with anger for a moment. "It's a book burning," he said.

That Frank Norick had not objected to the incineration of Ishi's brain was understandable in light of his opposition to repatriation. What puzzled me was his willingness to share his information. Norick seemed to bear no ill will against his former student, JoAllyn Archambault, and said he admired her for opposing repatriation even though she had Indian blood herself. If this story of the destruction of Ishi's brain were revealed, however, it could get Archambault into big trouble, and she would have some explaining to do. I was confounded as to why Norick was so ready to share the tale with me, much less Nancy Rockafellar, who was carrying out an official investigation for U.C. San Francisco. At this point, too, the evidence for the incineration of Ishi's brain was no more than one man's recollection of a phone call almost ten years before. Getting to the truth of the matter was going to require much more effort.

I did not have much more time in Berkeley. We'd flown out for the holidays to visit my parents, but it was almost Christmas and then it would be time to return to North Carolina. If Frank Norick's story were true, I was guessing there might be some paper trail to the Smithsonian. The next morning I went over to U.C. San Francisco's medical library on Parnassus Heights but found nothing there. On the train back to Berkeley, I decided to take one more look in the Bancroft Library. The Bancroft closed at three, which only left me forty-five minutes before the doors shut for good until after the New Year. As was the case for many university archives, thieves had struck at the Bancroft in recent years, sometimes even razor-blading out lithographs from rare books. The library had taken new security precautions as a result. I checked my bag, signed the register, and showed my ID as now required to enter the library's oak-paneled reading room.

There were only two or three other researchers in the Bancroft that day. I had little expectation of finding anything new. Plenty of other researchers had combed the Bancroft for anything related to Ishi and the Yahi; I myself had already spent many hours there. Now, at least, I had a fresh lead: the possible Smithsonian connection. The thousands of pages of letters archived from Berkeley's anthropology department went back to 1901. No computerized catalogue existed for these 59 boxes stuffed with correspondence that had been filed in manila folders. There was only a dog-eared finding guide, labeled "Department of Anthropology Paper." This booklet alphabetized the people and institutions from whom letters existed in this vast collection, specifying the box number where their particular correspondence could be found. I was disappointed to see nothing under "Smithsonian." Yet a bit more leafing through the finding guide showed a category for "Museums," and there a subheading for "Smithsonian." I gave a card requesting the carton with these letters to the work-study student manning the desk. It took only a few minutes for the box to be brought up for me from the bowels of the archive.

I found the thick Smithsonian file in the middle of the box. The first letters dated to 1908. I leafed forward to 1916, the year of Ishi's death, to search for anything relating to his brain, and I did not have to look far. Suddenly the word "Ishi" caught my eye. It appeared in a letter to Alfred Kroeber from R. Rathbun, the assistant secretary at the Smithsonian's National Museum, which would later subdivide into the present-day National Museum of Natural History, National Museum of American History, National Air and Space Museum, and other big buildings along Washington's mall. The date was December 30, 1916:

*Referring to your letter of October 27 addressed to Dr. Hrdlička, I beg to say that the National Museum will be very glad to receive the brain of Ishi, which you offer to present, and I will ask that you forward it by express, collect, addressed "U.S. National Museum, Washington, D.C."*

With a gasp of surprise I stood up at the table and even backed away a few steps. The other few people still in the reading room cast sideways glances at this departure from library protocol. When I pulled myself together enough to sit back down at the reading table, I found still more papers. A Wells Fargo and Company Express receipt from January 5, 1917, verified the shipment to the Smithsonian of the brown paper package containing the preserved organ. Then there was an ornate certificate of "grateful acknowledgment" for the receipt and "gift of the object mentioned in the accompanying list." The attached "List of Specimens Received" had only one entry: "Brain of Ishi (California Indian)."

I went back to the reference desk. This time I paged the box with letters from Aleš Hrdlička, whose name was mentioned in the letter I'd just found. Hrdlička, a very prominent physical anthropologist back in the early twentieth century, had been the founder and head of the physical anthropology department at the Smithsonian's National Museum. The contents of the manila folder under "Hrdlička" filled in still more details. Alfred Kroeber had first written Hrdlička about Ishi's brain on October 27, 1916. By this time, Kroeber was back from New York in San Francisco. The file also held a carbon copy of his letter to Hrdlička:

> *I find that at Ishi's death last spring his brain was removed and preserved. There is no one here who can put it to scientific use. If you wish it, I shall be glad to deposit it in the National Museum collection.*

"I hardly need say," Hrdlička answered ten days later, "that we shall be very glad to receive and take care of Ishi's brain, and if a suitable opportunity occurs to have it properly worked up." An exchange had followed about the packing and shipping. "The brain should be packed in plenty of absorbent cotton saturated with the liquid in which it is preserved," Hrdlička instructed. "The whole should be enclosed in a piece of oiled cloth or oiled paper. The package should then be laid in a moderate sized box with a good layer of soft excelsior all around it. In that way it will doubtless reach us in good condition."

The Bancroft would make Xerox copies, although it would take a week or so. Since I had to return that weekend, I brought the documents I'd found to the desk and arranged for copies to be sent to me in North Carolina. I retrieved my backpack from the locker, then walked back to my parents' house. As I passed by People's Park, a homeless old woman was already getting into her damp, mildewy sleeping bag in a stand of pyracantha and rhododendron close by the sidewalk. She muttered what sounded like a Buddhist prayer to ward off the cold in the winter afternoon's gathering darkness.

My astonishment at the Bancroft did not have so much to do with the actions of Alfred Kroeber—or with Theodora's account of them. As I now imagined the chain of events that had unfolded almost a century before, Alfred Kroeber had indeed been very much upset at the thought of his friend's being dissected against his wishes in the first place. The best indicator of these emotions lay in the vehemence of his "science can go to hell" letter from New York that ordered the autopsy to be "shut down." I'd read hundreds of Kroeber's letters by then; nowhere else could I recall the dry, correct professor expressing himself with any such unrestrained passion. That Kroeber would damn science further signaled his agitation, for such a declaration was also very much out of character. By October, however, it had already been more than six months since Ishi's death. Kroeber must have come back to find the brain already in a jar. Apparently he had cooled down by then and probably felt that nothing more could be done. Although not much interested himself in physical anthropology, Kroeber was always an assiduous cultivator of professional contacts. He had met Aleš Hrdlička in San Francisco in 1908 and watched his ascension at the Smithsonian. He knew Hrdlička had a brain collection and decided to offer him Ishi's brain.

That Theodora said only that the brain was "preserved" was not altogether surprising. Besides her inaccuracies about Yahi history, Theodora had also taken liberties with facts large and small to protect her husband and his friends. "It was white of you," Alfred had written in his thank you to the hospital for its care of Ishi before his death. Theodora replaced "white" with "good" in quoting this letter in *Ishi in Two Worlds* to avoid exposing that her husband had used this common yet racist early-twentieth-century colloquialism. She took more liberties to play up just how hard Kroeber and also Waterman had taken Ishi's death. *Ishi in Two Worlds* reproduces part of Thomas Waterman's letter to Kroeber, the one taking blame for having "killed Ishi" and lamenting the loss of the "best friend I had in the world." Yet Theodora had left out this letter's very next line, which indicated that pragmatism and even satisfaction had tempered Waterman's grief. "I feel like congratulating you and asking for your congratulations all the same," Waterman had continued: "He [Ishi] was bound to go this way sooner or later, and we were certainly none too soon in obtaining the material from him." Only days after Ishi's burial, the Indian disappeared altogether from the correspondence of Kroeber, Waterman, and the other anthropologists. "The most important New York news I know is that Kroeber has removed his whiskers," joked Pliny Goddard, another Berkeley anthropologist then in New York, less than a week after Ishi's death. There is no mention of Ishi in this letter to Waterman about what was to be Kroeber's short-lived experiment with beardlessness.

Theodora also exaggerated how much Kroeber had grieved at Ishi's

Ishi in the Oroville jail, August 29, 1911. He had been captured at the town's slaughterhouse the night before. (*Jed Riffe/Rattlesnake Productions*)

Thomas T. Waterman, about 1908.
Waterman brought Ishi to San
Francisco from the Oroville jail.
(*Richard Burrill Ishi Photograph
Collection*)

Ishi and Alfred Kroeber, 1911.
Kroeber called Ishi the "most
uncontaminated and uncivilized
man in the world today."
(*Jed Riffe/Rattlesnake Productions*)

Ishi and Sam Batwi, 1911. Batwi was Ishi's translator in his first weeks in San Francisco. (*Jed Riffe/Rattlesnake Productions*)

Ishi, 1912. (*Jed Riffe/Rattlesnake Productions*)

Franz Boas, 1912.
"Papa Franz" was
a mentor to Alfred
Kroeber, Margaret
Mead, Ruth Benedict,
and other well-known
anthropologists.
*(American Philosophical
Society)*

Saxton T. Pope, Ishi's
doctor and friend, wanted an
autopsy of Ishi conducted
after his death.
*(Special Collections, The Library
and Center for Knowledge
Management, University of
California, San Francisco)*

Alfred and Theodora
Kroeber at their cabin
in Sigonoy, 1931.
(*The Bancroft Library,
University of California
at Berkeley*)

Theodora Kroeber in her
Berkeley home, 1970.
(*G. Paul Bishop*)

"Ishi and Companion at Iamin Mool," by Frank Day, 1973. This spot on the Feather River was later flooded when the river was dammed. (*Courtesy of Herb Puffer*)

Attack on a California Indian village, *Harper's New Monthly Magazine*, 1861.

Sandy Young, Hiram "Hi" Good, unidentified man, and Indian Ned. Good was a well-known Indian hunter. Indian Ned later murdered Good, and then was killed by Young. (*Butte County Pioneer Memorial Museum*)

*Below:* Alfred Kroeber photographing Ishi by Deer Creek. (*Jed Riffe/Rattlesnake Productions*)

Ishi poses for Alfred Kroeber making wood harpoon, Deer Creek, 1914.

Ishi demonstrating his
technique with bow and arrow
near Deer Creek, 1914.
(*Jed Riffe/Rattlesnake
Productions*)

Ishi with Blackfeet Indians at the Panama-Pacific International Exposition, 1915.
*(Jed Riffe/Rattlesnake Productions)*

Niche 601 with the pot containing Ishi's ashes, Olivet Memorial Park, 1999.

The Smithsonian Institution.

The Smithsonian Institution, in behalf of the United States National Museum, returns a grateful acknowledgment to
University of California
Department of Anthropology,
San Francisco
California.
for the gift of the object mentioned in the accompanying list

R. Rathbun

Assistant Secretary,
in charge of National Museum.

Washington, D. C., U. S. A. March 7, 1917.

Certificate acknowledging the donation of Ishi's brain, Smithsonian Institution, 1917. (*The Bancroft Library, University of California at Berkeley*)

Aleš Hrdlička, a founder of American physical anthropology and the man who assembled the Smithsonian Institution's brain collection.

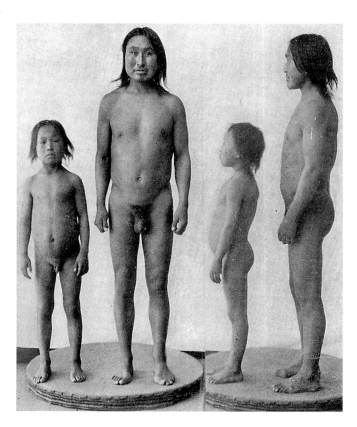

Qissuk and son, Minik, on their admission to Bellevue Hospital, 1897. Qissuk died three months later; his body was boiled down to the bones for the collection of the American Museum of Natural History.

The Maidu delegation to Washington: *from left,* the author, Rosalie Bertram, Joe Marine, Art Angle, Lorraine Frazier, Gus Martin, Sharon Guzman-Mix, Bruce Steidl.

Thomas Killion (*right*) and Art Angle with TV crew in front of Washington's National Museum of Natural History, 1999.

This is the brain of Ishi, the last Yahi Indian in California, stored in a Washington, D.C. warehouse since 1916.

This is the brain of the Smithsonian Institution official who refused to return Ishi's brain for burial in 1999.

Property of the U.S. Gov't

Property of the U.S. Gov't

The Sacramento Bee

It's a No-Brainer

Editorial cartoon in *Sacramento Bee*, 1999. (*Dennis Renault*)

Deer Creek near Grizzly Bear's
Hiding Place.

Ishi and Jack Apperson, 1914.
Apperson was one of the men who
looted Ishi's camp in 1908.

*Above:* Ishi with Saxton Pope Jr., Thomas Waterman, and Saxton Pope, Deer Creek, 1914. (*Jed Riffe/Rattlesnake Productions*)

Ishi, Deer Creek, 1914. (*Jed Riffe/Rattlesnake Productions*)

Ishi and a demonstration Yana hut he built, San Francisco, probably 1912. (*Jed Riffe/Rattlesnake Productions*)

Mickey Gemmill (*far left*), Floyd Buckskin (*second from left*), and Nancy Rockafellar (*at microphone*) at the Ishi Memorial at Dersch Meadow, 2000. (*Nancy Scheper-Hughes*)

Ishi, probably 1914. (*Jed Riffe/Rattlesnake Productions*)

death. He never liked to talk about his friend in later years because this "was too much the stuff of human agony from whose immediacy he could not distance itself," she claimed. I did not doubt Kroeber's sadness, but it was simply false that he had taken it so hard as to be unable even to talk about it. Just a year after Ishi's death, Kroeber gave a lecture at the Sacramento Valley's Chico State Normal School entitled "Ishi and His Fellow Aborigines." In a 1936 radio interview he said "Nothing gives me greater pleasure than to recall the story of Ishi"—and went on to talk about his dead friend with affectionate gusto. Theodora attributed Alfred's decision never to write Ishi's biography to his "Indian-like reserve" and the "old sense of pain and hurt." In truth, however, Kroeber was not much interested in biography in the first place. He believed, after all, that individuals were "mere illustrations" of the culture to which they belonged. As Kroeber saw it, the anthropologist's duty was to catalogue what his friend and contemporary Ruth Benedict called the "patterns of culture"—namely, the systems of behavior and belief in any society. He left the telling of Ishi's personal story to his more writerly wife as if this were not really his kind of job.

Theodora must have known that Ishi's brain had been sent to the Smithsonian. Alfred was her book's chief source of information, and, insofar as *Ishi in Two Worlds* noted that the brain was preserved, it is hard to imagine that Alfred had not also told her what had happened to it in the end. That Theodora withheld or at the very least did not pursue the details about the brain was very much of a piece with her other protective editing of the relationship between Ishi and the anthropologists. To show Kroeber and his friends as the model of kindness toward Ishi was part of Theodora's wifely love and loyalty. Acknowledging that her husband had sent off Ishi's brain by Wells Fargo Express "packed in plenty of absorbent cotton" would have detracted from her portrait of Alfred's absolute commitment to respect his Yahi friend's wishes. It would also have undermined Theodora's wish to fashion Ishi's story into an allegory of racial reconciliation and respect, tolerance, and healing in a world haunted by violence and hatred.

I recalled Walter Benjamin's famous dictum. "Traces of the storyteller cling to the story like the handprints of a potter cling to the clay vessel," the great German critic wrote four years before his suicide while fleeing the Nazis. We can see Theodora's "handprints" in the omission or revision of those parts of the story that complicated her personal and social agendas. Theodora wasn't altogether wrong about her dead husband's generosity toward and concern for Ishi, even if their friendship was not as deep as she wanted to represent it. Kroeber had tried to stop the autopsy out of his concern for Ishi and the proprieties of his Yahi culture. That concern was not sufficiently great to prevent the anthropologist from later mailing Ishi's pickled brain to the Smithsonian instead of having it cremated and combined with the other ashes at Olivet.

My own surprise, even shock, was thus not so much at learning about Kroeber's actions back in 1916; it had to do with Frank Norick and far more recent events. Norick had been correct about the brain's having been sent to Washington. I now assumed that the other part of Norick's tale might also very well be true—namely, that people at the Smithsonian had destroyed Ishi's brain in secret. The mere revelation that the brain had gone off to Washington would surely create a buzz in anthropology's small world—along with accusations of betrayal leveled against Kroeber and in all likelihood a new round of self-recrimination about our field's past abuses of native peoples. Yet the story would be far more scandalous if Norick's tale about the brain's incineration were also true. The Smithsonian would have a public relations fiasco on its hands.

I flew back to North Carolina after Christmas. There I decided that, before proceeding any further, I should contact the Smithsonian, and in particular the National Museum of Natural History's Native American Repatriation Office. In the old days it had been common practice to exhibit baskets, pots, papooses, and other things Indian under the rubric of "natural history"—as if Indians were not also part of the modern world but belonged only to a vanished and prehuman time, like fossilized dinosaur eggs or the fangs of a saber-toothed tiger. The National Museum of Natural History held the Smithsonian's collection of more than 15,000 Native American skeletons and hundreds more objects now deemed sacred to tribes, among them several Lakota Ghost Dance shirts stripped from warriors slaughtered at Wounded Knee a century before. Now the museum had to inventory these bones and artifacts and make them available for repatriation to their rightful tribal claimants. A special unit, the Native American Repatriation Office, had been created within the museum to handle this big job.

I e-mailed Thomas Killion, the director of this office, and we spoke on the phone. I explained that I had found letters showing Ishi's brain had been in the Smithsonian in 1917 and that I had been told it had been destroyed. Killion was reserved, but he sounded more puzzled than surprised. Yes, he said, he thought the National Museum of Natural History had Ishi's brain in the collection. Yet Killion told me he had never heard anything about its being destroyed; for that matter, he said, he had never known that Indians in California were looking for it. Killion promised to investigate and we agreed that I would come up to Washington to meet with him in person.

I also phoned JoAllyn Archambault. It seemed only fair to get the Smithsonian official's side of the story. As the director of the American Indian Program at the National Museum of Natural History's anthropology department, Archambault oversaw an internship program and the museum's research related to the history and cultures of Native America. I tried to reach the Sioux anthropologist in her office, but a secretary told me that she was working at home that day.

I anticipated an unpleasant call. By Nancy Rockafellar's account, Archambault had been unhelpful and curt and denied knowing anything at all about Ishi's brain. That the organ was even in the Smithsonian was a "myth," or so Rockafellar told me Archambault had said. When I reached Archambault, I explained that I was an anthropology professor at Duke, and that I had heard from Frank Norick a story about the Smithsonian and the destruction of Ishi's brain. There was silence for a moment at the other end of the line. Then Archambault fired back. "Frank is suffering from senile dementia," she said. "I don't know what he's talking about." I could call David Hunt if I wanted to pursue the matter, Archambault told me.

Hunt was the curator of the National Museum of Natural History's anthropology collection, which included its bones and preserved body parts (besides brains, there were also hearts, kidneys, and lungs, as well as stillborn fetuses). I wanted to make sure that Archambault had every chance to have her say. I asked if she had anything to add. "No," she replied, bringing our conversation to a fast close. Much later, Archambault would insist to *Science News* that she'd never known that Ishi's brain was ever at the Smithsonian in the first place. She also said she did not recall ever speaking to Nancy Rockafellar.

When I phoned David Hunt, he was hesitant. It was evident that Thomas Killion had already told him that someone had been inquiring about Ishi's brain. He tried to refer me back to the Repatriation Office's director, but I was not in the mood for a runaround. I told Hunt I'd already spoken with Killion. After a pause, Hunt spoke with a diplomat's cautious formality: "I can confirm that we've found it," he said, the "it" being the brain of Ishi. Did Hunt mean to say that the brain was never destroyed? "Perhaps there was a misunderstanding," Hunt said. "A number of other brains were destroyed in the 1980s. They had dried out, and decomposed, and were of no scientific or cultural value." Yet Ishi's brain was not among those destroyed, Hunt said; he had himself just gone to the warehouse to verify that it was still there. Hunt had also found records documenting the brain's storage in the Smithsonian for the last eighty years. "I imagine," he said, "Tom Killion will provide you with those when you come up to Washington."

I would have to speak again with Frank Norick to see if he stuck to his story about Ishi's brain having been destroyed. As far as I could make out the chain of events, Alfred Kroeber had sent the brain to the Smithsonian, and it was intact there in the museum's collection almost three thousand miles from Ishi's ashes in San Francisco and his natal land in the California foothills. The trip to Washington would clarify matters, I hoped. Then it would be time to pass on to Art Angle and the Oroville Maidu with whatever information I had gained, and they could act as they saw fit.

# Ten

# THE WET COLLECTION

I had plenty of time for reflection on the drive up to meet Thomas Killion at the Smithsonian's Repatriation Office. Taking Interstate 85 from Durham under a gray winter sky, I followed the highway north through the red clay hills and loblolly pines and across a string of muddy reservoirs into more populated southern Virginia. An exit just south of Richmond leads over to Jamestown, the first permanent British colony in the New World, now a tourist attraction. The area had been inhabited by several tribes under the chieftaincy of Powhatan, father of the legendary Pocahontas. In one of my daughter's favorite movies, Disney's *Pocahontas*, the young native woman saves a captured English soldier from execution. Here Pocahontas is the stereotypical slim and "enchanting" Indian maiden updated as a protector of the environment, a budding feminist who thinks for herself, and a defender of the ways of her people. She teaches the handsome, young, blond Englishman to care for the forest and the animals—and then they fall in love in what Disney makes into a parable of happy multiculturalism for new times.

The real history was less sunny. It is true that Pocahontas married an Englishman, but he was a wealthy tobacco farmer. John Rolfe took his new Indian bride to London in 1614 to advertise American tobacco, a crop that was then becoming the new colonies' chief export. Like Ishi,

Pocahontas was regarded as a curiosity. She was introduced as a "savage princess" at Queen Elizabeth's court. Shortly afterward, Pocahontas contracted and died of a white man's disease, smallpox, and was buried in Gravesend's St. George Church. Back in Virginia, the tribes of Powhatan's confederacy were decimated by disease and futile wars against the colonists. The surviving remnants were focibly exiled to the mountains in 1659, inhabiting the first Indian reservation in what was to become the United States.

I thought about Ishi, too, on the way to Washington. It felt strange, not to say surreal, to be searching for the pickled brain of a man I'd idolized since my own Berkeley childhood. At the same time, I was absorbed by the hunt and the dash of excitement in what had been my uneventful professor's life since Robin and I had settled in North Carolina. I'd decided not to call Art Angle until after this trip to the Smithsonian in order to be able to provide more definite information on the whereabouts of Ishi's brain. I had little idea just what I'd have to report when the time came, or how Art would react.

The Smithsonian's National Museum of Natural History has all the trappings of an old-fashioned museum of natural history—the frayed collection of stuffed birds, the hall of geodes and other mineral marvels, and the shellacked skeletons of a wooly mammoth and a brontosaurus. And like other such museums, it has exhibition space for only a fraction of its countless artifacts. The wings, closed to visitors, hold offices for museum staff and stored objects, among them the tall green metal filing drawers containing the Smithsonian's collection of 30,000 human skeletons, about half Native American, with many others from China, Latin America, and elsewhere. After spending the night in Washington, I arrived just as the museum was opening for the day. Packs of school children, flushed with the prospect of a field trip and a day away from the classroom, streamed through the big bronze doors. Tom Killion came down to meet me in the lobby. The director of the Native American Repatriation Office was a man in his forties with sandy blonde hair and the look of a clean-cut Ivy League professor, in khaki pants and wire-rimmed glasses. As we walked through a labyrinth of empty hallways to his office, Killion told me that he had trained as an archaeologist. He held a doctorate from the University of New Mexico, with a specialty in the pre-Columbian civilizations of Mexico, and was hired by the Repatriation Office on its creation in 1991. He'd become the director in 1994, and had headed the office ever since.

Tom Killion had the pleasant yet cautious manner of a man accustomed to controversy, and his was not an easy job. Among the staff scholars at Killion's own National Museum of Natural History were some of the most prominent physical anthropologists in the world. These scientists were opposed to or at the very least uneasy about NAGPRA and other repatriation laws, especially when it came to very old bones. Douglas Owsley, an expert in the ancient Americas and head of the physical anthropology division at the National Museum of History, had joined seven other leading scholars in the lawsuit for the right to study the 9,000-year-old bones of Kennewick Man. "If a pattern of returning [such] remains without study develops, the loss to science will be incalculable," wrote Owsley with his colleague Richard L. Jantz. They believed that ancient skeletons belonged to humanity as a whole, and not any single group. Unless Kennewick Man and other old bones were studied, Owsley explained to an interviewer, "the story of America . . . will forever be unclear and inaccurate."

A number of archaeologists and physical anthropologists, in fact, complained that lawmakers were sacrificing the advancement of science to the expediencies of white liberal guilt, political correctness, and Indian lobbying. That mitochondrial DNA and other techniques were allowing new and exciting information to be gleaned from bones added still another layer of frustration to the anger of these researchers about taking skeletons from museum collections and burying them in the ground forever. Archaeology was being "sold down the pike" by "ignorant legislators" in cahoots with Indian activists, wrote Desmond Clark, a professor at the University of Arizona. Frank Norick, I recalled, had called repatriation a "book burning."

The physical anthropologists at the Smithsonian's National Museum of History were more circumspect, at least in public. Still, Tom Killion knew that they shared misgivings about the repatriation laws his office was mandated to execute and, at least at the start, looked upon the Repatriation Office as a kind of internal enemy at the museum. Ironically, though, Killion and his staff had to rely upon Douglas Owsley and the museum's other house experts to update bone inventories, track misplaced specimens, and handle other mechanics of repatriation. They'd managed to maintain a working relationship with these reluctant collaborators in the process of returning bones to tribes.

At the same time, Killion had to deal with emotional and sometimes angry Indians. Some tribes—like the Navajo, who didn't want to further disturb the *chindi*, the potentially malevolent spirits of the deceased—didn't want their people's bones back at all. Many other Indians regarded repatriation as a crusade of high importance. That the Smithsonian had the dismembered bodies of Captain Jack, Shoshone Mike, and the Pawnee scouts stirred intense emotions of grief and anger among these Indians, and so did the excavation of tribal burial grounds and transport of bones to the Smithsonian. Like Art Angle, many activists were also indifferent to the research of the physical anthropologists, preferring to believe their own creation stories. The most suspicious Indians believed that theories about their ancestors as immigrants to the Americas were somehow intended to undermine their own moral and spiritual claim to the land. For others, anxious about their identities, repatriation made possible a feeling of connection to their ancestors that was impossible to achieve otherwise. "I feel like an Indian [today]," one Indian remarked at the repatriation of a lock of hair of Chief Bigfoot. The hair had been snipped off and kept in a library display case after the famous Lakota leader was killed in the 1890 massacre at Wounded Knee, South Dakota.

Tom Killion was there to assist with these acts of repatriation. Yet he was also a white and a representative of the Smithsonian, and inevitably faced mistrust of Indians. Sometimes there were even language barriers when delegations came to the Smithsonian, as with a group of Hopi that included several elders who spoke little English. As I'd soon see for myself, Killion brought considerable sensitivity and diplomacy to his work with tribes over the past decades. He'd earned a good reputation with many native activists and scholars. The Pawnee had invited him out as a guest of honor at the reburial of the six murdered scouts in a Nebraska cemetery.

In the larger view, repatriation was a novel and tricky experiment in atonement and reconciliation. Historian Elazar Barkan calls the late twentieth century the "age of apology." Whether Queen Elizabeth apologizing to Australian Aborigines for the sins of the British Empire, or Pope John Paul II to Jews for pro-Nazi priests, or the United States to the Japanese Americans interned in World War II, it became common for governments to express contrition, sometime with monetary payments, to atone for past acts of injustice. Repatriation allowed whites to assuage their guilt about the mistreatment of Indians—yet without any costly or personal sacrifice of their own, such as giving up land once seized from tribes. Since archaeologists and physical anthropologists were not an especially powerful constituency, their protests could be overridden in order to do what seemed to be the right thing by Indians. Permitting Indians to operate casinos was another kind of reparation and, though lucrative for some tribes, equally came at no direct cost to taxpayers.

Frankly, I was on the fence myself as far as Kennewick Man and other extremely ancient skeletons were concerned. Wasn't it a stretch for Indians to insist that they alone owned the right to determine the fate of a 9,000-year-old skeleton? Why shouldn't scientists be allowed to study Kennewick Man, Spirit Cave Man, or other contested bones to learn more about the human history of this continent? Or, on the other hand, should even the remains of these first Americans be left undisturbed? It seemed to me much more clear-cut that museums should repatriate the thousands of Indian skeletons excavated from more recent nineteenth- and twentieth-century burials. These were the remains of the grandparents and great-grandparents of living people dug up without anyone's permission. And only an extreme archaeologist—living down to the stereotype of "vulture culture"—could maintain that even bones like the skulls of the executed Captain Jack or the massacred Pawnee should be kept for study. All of the publicity about Kennewick Man, in fact, concealed lesser-known stories of new collaborations between archaeologists and Indians. On one hand, some archaeologists, sympathetic to tribal concerns, assisted Indians in going through museum inventories to locate bones and secure their return. On the other, a few tribes, such as Nebraska's Omaha and California's Campo, permitted DNA testing on ancestral bones. The growing, if still relatively small, number of Indian-born archaeologists also blurred and sometimes softened the lines of conflict. These native archaeologists had ties both to their tribes and to the halls of science and the university, and sometimes acted as go-betweens.

So the job of repatriation had gone forward in the midst of controversy and occasional cooperation. Even before the laws had been passed and Killion had been hired, the National Museum of Natural History had returned the skulls of Captain Jack and his three executed lieutenants to Modoc survivors. In 1985, the Indians reinterred the skulls of the four men with the rest of their remains in a private ceremony at Fort Klamath, Oregon. Although the Repatriation Office had a staff of just fifteen and an annual budget of less than $1 million, it had pressed forward under Killion's leadership. The office had returned the bones of more than 5,000 Indians to their descendants from groups like Oregon's Confederated Tribes of the Grand Ronde and Oklahoma's Ponca Tribe. Besides the skulls of the Pawnee scouts, the repatriated remains included the skeleton of Shoshone Mike, and the 758 skeletons excavated in Alaska by the Smithsonian's own Aleš Hrdlička early in the twentieth century. Now Killion and his staff would be dealing with what was to become their single most high-profile case and the first one involving an Indian from California: the repatriation of Ishi, or, more specifically, the repatriation of Ishi's brain.

The Repatriation Office was a warren of worn cubicles. Killion ushered me into a little conference area and introduced me to Karen Mudar and Stuart Speaker, two of his deputies, both cultural anthropologists. We made small talk about the traffic and weather and then got down to the matter at hand. My own most pressing concern was to establish whether the Smithsonian still had Ishi's brain or whether it had been incinerated, as I'd been told by Frank Norick. I asked Killion if he'd learned anything more since our first phone conversation a few weeks before.

Killion replied that he'd looked into the matter in greater detail and was convinced that Norick's story was false. He explained that it would have been very difficult for anyone at the Smithsonian to get at the brain in the first place. It was in the so-called Wet Collection of preserved specimens in the Smithsonian's new high-tech storage facility in the nearby suburb of Suitland, Maryland. The facility was closed to the public—and access to the collection, which was housed in an area called Pod 3, was highly restricted, even to museum employees, for safety reasons. The fumes from the ethyl alcohol used to preserve the thousands of specimens made Pod 3 a potential giant Molotov cocktail and thus a fire hazard of the first order. The area was equipped with precautionary features that included light switches engineered not to produce even the tiniest spark. The only key to Pod 3, Killion said, was in the possession of the longtime collections manager, David Hunt. Killion said that Hunt was a trustworthy professional who would never allow tampering of any kind. Ishi's brain was right there in Tank 6 of the Wet Collection—so Hunt had verified. There were thirty-two other brains floating in this stainless steel tank, each in a cheesecloth sack tied with a plastic accession tag.

Killion gave me xeroxes of the storage records that David Hunt had mentioned in our earlier phone conversation. Included was a copy of the entry in the museum's catalogue, dated 1917, for the accession of Ishi's brain. When I looked at the other entries on the same page of the ledger, the oft-noted resemblance of nineteenth- and early-twentieth-century museums to the jumble of Renaissance "curiosity cabinets" seemed entirely apt. Ishi's brain had been catalogued as Item 60884, just below "Ivory charms (Elephant tusks)" from Abyssinia and a "Set of Current Postage Stamps of the Philippine Islands."

At the same time, I knew it was much more than happenstance that Ishi's brain had ended up in the Smithsonian. Alfred Kroeber had sent the brain there knowing that Aleš Hrdlička was amassing brains for scientific study. Here Killion's deputy Karen Mudar had some information to contribute. Mudar, a pleasant, quiet woman, oversaw repatriation to Alaska and the Pacific Northwest, but she was also knowledgeable about "Hrdlička's baby," as she called it. The Wet Collection contained about 1,300 animal brains, from gorillas, chimpanzees, and baboons as well as assorted marsupials, ungulates, and reptiles. Many of these specimens came from the National Zoo; Hrdlička had an arrangement with the zookeepers to send over the brains of unusual animals that happened to die. There were also 226 human brains from around the world, including those of other notables. Ishi's brain floated in Tank 6 side by side with the brain of John Wesley Powell. The one-armed hero of Shiloh and founder of the Smithsonian's Bureau of American Ethnology had bequeathed his brain to his home museum for future study.

There were ten other Indians' brains besides Ishi's in Hrdlička's collection. So far only one, belonging to a Cheyenne River Sioux named Leon Pretty Voice Eagle, had been repatriated. Upon his death in 1928, a reservation doctor had removed Pretty Voice Eagle's brain and sent it to Hrdlička without his relatives' knowledge. A staffer from the Repatriation Office had flown to South Dakota in 1994 with the carefully packaged brain stowed gently under the seat in front of her. She returned the brain to Pretty Voice Eagle's surviving relatives, stayed for the burial, and then flew back to Washington. The other nine brains were still in their tanks at Suitland, among them Item 60844, the specimen listed in the old catalogue as "Brain of Ishi, California Indian."

I knew that Killion and his staff had every reason to be helpful. Naturally they didn't want me to spread the story about Ishi's brain having been incinerated, a tale they seemed convinced was false and sure to stir up trouble for the Smithsonian. Even so, I found these Smithsonian functionaries likeable and credible, and I admired the work they were doing. If Ishi's brain was intact, then the matter at hand would be its return. Killion explained that the Repatriation Office had to follow guidelines laid out in its regulations. Direct family descendants had first rights. When no kin existed or a skeleton was unidentified except by tribe, it went to that tribal group as a whole. But the lack of any Yahi survivors was the reason that Art Angle, a Maidu, had taken on Ishi's repatriation in the first place. I wondered whether the Repatriation Office could or would give the brain to Angle and his Butte County Native American Cultural Committee.

For now, Killion said only that his office would meet with Indians, scholars, and other concerned parties about the right way to proceed with Ishi's repatriation. A more immediate matter was how to break the news that the Smithsonian had the missing organ. Even though the possibility of the brain's having been incinerated now seemed unlikely, it was still going to look bad that the Smithsonian had kept it for so many years. Killion asked me for Art Angle's phone number so that he could inform him that the museum had Ishi's brain. For the Indians to hear the news first from a Smithsonian official would put the museum in a more desirable light than if Angle read it in the newspaper or somewhere else—or so I imagined Tom Killion's reasoning.

I gave Killion Art Angle's number, but I asked him to wait a couple of days so that I could call Oroville first. My reasons also admittedly involved self-interest. Along with the initial information from U.C. San Francisco's Nancy Rockafellar, it had been my detective work that traced Ishi's brain to the Smithsonian. I wanted to report our discovery to Art myself because I thought it would raise my standing in his eyes—and perhaps even provide me with an entree into the world of the Oroville Maidu. I did promise Killion I'd communicate the Smithsonian's wish to cooperate with the Butte County Native American Cultural Committee and willingness to work toward the brain's return to northern California. Killion asked me to tell Art to get in touch with him as soon as possible to set the process in motion.

In the afternoon I sped back down to North Carolina to teach a seminar that evening. After class was over, I walked down the department's empty late-night halls to my office to call Oroville. Art answered, sounding a bit standoffish when I told him who I was and reminded him of our meeting a few months earlier at the Cornucopia Restaurant. The toughness melted when I reported that I'd located Ishi's brain in the Smithsonian. I'd thought outrage might be Art's first reaction, but to the contrary he was relieved, even elated. His Butte County Native American Cultural Committee had suspended its campaign for the return of Ishi's ashes until the matter of the brain was resolved. "It's a wonderful thing that we can proceed now," he repeated several times. I told Art that Thomas Killion wanted to consult with him as soon as possible about the next steps. I also promised to Fed Ex the correspondence between Alfred Kroeber and the Smithsonian proving that Ishi's brain had been sent to Washington in the first place.

That call was a turning point in my relationship with Art. In the following months we talked often and became friends. Perhaps I'd exaggerated in my mind the Indians' suspicion toward anthropologists, yet the world of Oroville's Maidu was not especially easy for any outsider to enter. I was white and Art was Indian, of course; that we were a trucker and a college professor made for even more difference between us. There'd still be many things that Art would never talk to me about, and, in fact, he sometimes took a kind of wicked pleasure in whetting and frustrating my curiosity by mentioning some private Maidu ceremony to which I and other non-Indians were not invited. Art and I found plenty to talk about anyway, sometimes just about conventional male passions like football and the latest standings. That I'd been able to do something for Art had created the trust or at least communication that was the kernel of our friendship.

A newspaper up in Oroville broke the story about the discovery of Ishi's brain. The *Oroville Opportunity Bulletin* was a free weekly, published by a lawyer named Don Blake from his office in a mobile home next to Oroville's Waffle House. One of Art Angle's sisters had gone to school with Blake's wife, Marion, and Art had decided to show Blake the copies I had sent of Kroeber's letters and seek the lawyer's advice about dealing with the Smithsonian. Blake asked Art if he could publish the news about the brain, and Art had agreed. A "Special Feature Edition" of the *Oroville Opportunity Bulletin* soon came out devoted to Art's "quest to find the truth about Ishi's desecration," and it contained the full text of Kroeber and Hrdlička's letters. "It's Time to Bring All of Ishi Home," the headline announced—and so the wild ride began.

# Eleven

# ALEŠ HRDLIČKA AND
# THE GREAT BRAIN HUNT

I did not travel again until later that spring. Our second child had just been born, and it was a busy time. Ishi's brain was still floating in preserving solution at the Smithsonian, or so it now seemed likely. Even before the *Oroville Opportunity Bulletin* reported the news of this discovery, Art had called to tell me he was arranging with Tom Killion for his Butte County Native American Cultural Committee to visit Washington as soon as possible. I think Art assumed that the museum would hand over Ishi's brain to him on that trip.

I wondered how the saga was going to play out. In those weeks I puzzled as well over the chain of past events and in particular just how Ishi's brain ended up in the Smithsonian. I understood something of Alfred Kroeber's complex relationship with Ishi, how he'd come to mail the brain to Washington, and why Theodora had concealed or at least failed to investigate what had happened. But what about the Smithsonian's Aleš Hrdlička? I knew very little about Hrdlička's brain collection besides the number of brains he'd amassed and the vague, morbid image in my mind's eye of the pickled organs floating in their stainless steel vats. I decided to read everything I could to understand why this well-known early-twentieth-century scientist would have wanted the brain of the last Yahi Indian as a specimen for his museum.

Hrdlička's biography proved straightforward enough. Like Kroeber's mentor Franz Boas, he had been a child of immigrants from the Old World. Hrdlička was born in Bohemia in 1869, the son of a master cabinetmaker who had brought his family on a steamship to New York when Aleš was thirteen. The teenaged Aleš worked at a tobacco factory but later won a scholarship to medical school, graduating first in his class. He interned at a New York mental hospital, then joined scientific expeditions to the American Southwest and Mexico. On these trips Hrdlička measured and made casts of the faces of Apaches and Pimas. One wonders what the Indians made of this young man with his calipers and plaster of Paris. The trip led Hrdlička into physical anthropology, that branch of the field concerned with the study of the anatomy and evolution of the human species. The Smithsonian later named Hrdlička to head its new physical anthropology division, where he presided for almost forty years as perhaps the single most influential physical anthropologist of his day. He started the subfield's flagship journal, the *American Journal of Physical Anthropology*, whose masthead still reads "Founded by Aleš Hrdlička, 1918."

A formal portrait of Hrdlička shows him with the moustache and buttoned-up collar of an Old World man of science. Always the hard-working and talented immigrant's child, Hrdlička was also by turns misogynistic, kindly, and full of himself. He was enough the Victorian to complain that women did not belong in anthropology but was devoted to his French wife, Marie Strickler, who died young in 1918. Years later, younger anthropologists poked fun at the aging Hrdlička's pomposity— and the prudishness that once led him to walk out in protest of a lecture about the sex life of monkeys. Others found the old man, with his white hair and thick Czech accent, friendly enough, if a bit awkward and shy. He'd warm to the pleasures of banter and storytelling and sometimes giggled "like a little boy," as one colleague would later recall.

Foremost among Hrdlička's professional duties was the task of collecting. Under his direction, the Smithsonian became the world's largest ossuary, collecting bones from around the world. There were more than three thousand skulls alone, about half from American Indians, each catalogued with the breadth of the nasal cavity, the diameter of the eye orbits, and other precise measurements carefully noted. In the interests of completeness, however, Hrdlička also wanted soft tissue. The establishment of a "first-class human and comparative brain collection" was a special concern, Hrdlička wrote to William Abbot in 1903. He hoped this wealthy traveler and collector would procure a tribesman's brain from Borneo or the Andaman Islands—or, failing that, the brain of an orangutang, since Hrdlička, with his interest in the relation between brain size and body length and weight, was also gathering animal brains. As Hrdlička explained, a "reference brain collection" would permit "well-qualified scientific workers" to "elucidate the still very many dark points concerning this most important of the organs of the body."

The earliest research into human anatomy had been carried out by the Egyptians, who believed that the heart was the essence of life and the touchstone of good and evil. As early as 450 B.C., the Greek philosopher Alcmeaon had mounted the counterargument for the brain as the body's most vital organ. Yet Aristotle still insisted that the heart controlled thought and feeling; the brain, he stated, served merely as a cooling radiator. Only with the scientific revolution and an improved understanding of the human body after the seventeenth century did the brain's importance come to be widely appreciated. By the nineteenth century, the study of the brain had become a thriving enterprise. The likes of Samuel Morton, Cesare Lombroso, and Paul Broca ascended with Charles Darwin and Alfred Wallace into the pantheon of famous Victorian scientists.

Not all these men were polygenists like Morton, the Philadelphia doctor who used his skull collection to argue that the "Caucasian race" was the fruit of a separate and superior act of creation. Even among those nineteenth-century scientists who accepted that we all belong to one species, however, it was generally agreed that the "lesser races" were less evolved or, alternatively, had "degenerated" from the white standard. Cesare Lombroso, the Italian physician and social philosopher, promoted his theory that the "apish" skulls of criminals, prostitutes, the insane, and the "savages" of Africa and the New World limited their development as humans. Paul Broca in Paris was more hopeful about the eventual "improvement" of the human stock, but he believed the brain to be "larger in men than in women, in eminent men than in men of mediocre talent, in superior races than in inferior races." That a lesser native intelligence impaired "lower" groups explained colonialism, slavery, and patriarchy, according to Broca's brand of Social Darwinism. This widespread Victorian ideology justified the existing social order as the outcome of "natural selection" and the survival of the strongest and the fittest. A corollary of Social Darwinism was that the arrival of more evolved, powerful white "races" doomed Native Americans to extinction.

In a parable of the worst and best in the jagged progress of science, there was also a positive side to that nineteenth-century research. The rising interest in the brain was even then producing revolutionary discoveries. In 1812, for example, James Parkinson, who also believed in the "natural" limitations of women and the "lesser races," published "An Essay on the Shaking Palsy." This study established for the first time the symptoms—involuntary tremors without loss of mental acuity—of the disease that would later be named for the British doctor. Later, Paul Broca became the first researcher to identify the part of the brain linked to speech, a patch of cortex still known as Broca's Area in anatomy textbooks. Now physicians can often treat epilepsy, depression, schizophrenia, and other disorders of the central nervous system because the foundation for these advances was laid by the very same nineteenth-century scientists who were also apologists for white male supremacy.

Today, we know that brain size bears no relation to race or intelligence. It correlates more closely to body weight than any other factor: a smart, small woman will almost always have a smaller brain than a dumb, big man. The biggest brain of any warm-blooded animal belongs not to humans at all but the whale. Cutting-edge work in the neurosciences is no longer even much concerned with the gross anatomy of the brain. Current researchers use the more precise language of biochemistry, genetics, and molecular biology to explore the mechanisms of learning, emotion, and memory—and also use new technologies of imaging and scanning to track the brain's metabolism down to the subcellular level. Almost any neuroscientist today would agree that the field's former obsession with brain size was a dead end. Like Lamarckian or flat earth theory, it had to be discarded for science to truly advance.

The idea that at least the shape of a brain may be important survives even today, although this research is often controversial. At just 1,250 grams, Albert Einstein's brain weighed well below the male adult average, but a recent study found that it was 15 percent wider than normal and very heavily grooved in the parietal lobes. This led the researchers to speculate that these two particular brain attributes may be tied to special gifts at mathematical and spatial reasoning—a conclusion that other pathologists criticized as premature at best. Another small firefight broke out in the 1990s about new research that purported to show that sexual orientation can be predicted by the structure of the brain's hypothalamus. Meanwhile, it was revealed that scientists had secretly cut out the brains of the dead leaders of Germany's notorious Red Army Faction terrorists—Ulrike Meinhof, Andreas Baader, and others—after they committed suicide in the late 1970s. One doctor later claimed he had linked Ulrike Meinhof's anti-social behavior to "neurological abnormalities" caused by a childhood operation to remove a brain tumor, but he was forced to turn the pickled organ back to Meinhof's daughter in 2002. A bit like Art Angle had done with Ishi, Bettina Rohl had mounted a campaign to recover her mother's brain for burial.

Even now, too, the crudest and most discredited brands of skull science still sometimes return to haunt us. Matthew Hale, the leader of the Aryan supremacist World Church of the Creator, explained to a 1999 National Public Radio interviewer that "the size and shape of the brain" accounts for the "lesser capacity of the non-white races." On the Fourth of July of that year, Benjamin Smith, a follower acting upon Hale's message, gunned down a Korean student and a black basketball coach and wounded eight other Asians, blacks, and Jews in a rampage across Illinois and Indiana.

The Smithsonian's Aleš Hrdlička had spent the year 1895 in Paris studying anatomy at the famous Institute of Anthropology founded by Paul Broca. By then, though, the tenets of nineteenth-century scientific racism were already being disproved. Broca himself admitted that his measurements showed that "Eskimos, Lapps, Malays, Tartars and several other peoples of the Mongolian type" had bigger heads than "the most civilized people of Europe." A study of robbers, rapists, and murderers showed them to have brains as large as those of honest citizens— if anything, the criminals' brains were a bit bigger. By contrast, autopsies of Walt Whitman and Anatole France revealed that their brains did not reach even the average adult male weight of about 1,400 grams. That Whitman could have penned *Leaves of Grass* at just 1,282 grams and that France won the Nobel Prize for Literature at 1,017 grams was another blow to the sinking theory that the brains of "eminent men" outweighed those of "men of mediocre talent" or the "savage races."

At this time, too, the battle had been joined against the dogmas of Social Darwinism and assumptions of race and gender supremacy. Leading the way, as we have already seen, was Columbia University's Franz Boas, the most influential of early-twentieth-century anthropologists. Boas had been convinced by his own research that the craniometry of Morton, Broca, and the others was a futile endeavor. Culture, not biology, mattered most; and there was no way to "differentiate between the brains of a Swede and a Negro." There was no doubt in Boas's mind that African Americans, Eastern Europeans, and other groups were fully human and deserved equal rights and opportunity in modern life. That Alfred Kroeber so angrily rejected the suggestion that Ishi was some kind of "missing link" between apes and humans measured the great Boas's influence on his star pupil.

Aleš Hrdlička was more ambivalent about racial matters. At times jealous and suspicious of Boas, Hrdlička was still committed enough to racial classification to offer up pages of measurements of the "full-blooded American Negro" and his "very thick lips" and "coconut-shaped" head. The titles of Hrdlička's publications reflect all too clearly the stereotypes of nineteenth-century scientific racism—"Physical Differences Between White and Colored Children," "New Examples of American Indian Skulls with Low Forehead," and "Race Deterioration and Destruction with Special Reference to the American People." Hardly egalitarian by nature, Hrdlička sniffed about the Smithsonian's "lazy" and "unreliable" black porters in a letter to a colleague (although he later elevated one of these men to the position of trusted museum assistant). In contrast to the nineteenth-century craniometricians, however, Hrdlička refused to rank the races in order of merit. He was too much the scientist to ignore the lack of factual support for white superiority. He came to oppose eugenics and also signed a 1936 statement against Nazism and the creed of Aryan supremacy, albeit in the most cautious terms. "No definite relation between any physical criterion of race and mental capacity" had yet been found to justify any policy of "racial hygiene," that statement read.

Hrdlička avoided any more definitive avowal of equality by calling instead for more research and data collection. It would require years more of "assiduous excavation and collecting" to "correct the imperfect state of anatomical knowledge" and clear the way for the "definite progress of our science." As his biographer Frank Spencer puts it, Hrdlička seemed to think that the "reality of the human condition would be miraculously revealed after an undetermined amount of data collection." Collecting also gave a reserved man a great deal of boyish pleasure. Hrdlička confessed in his memoirs to a youthful "bliss" at once discovering a diamond in a plowed field (even when it turned out to be only quartz). There was an "indescribable flush" to stripping away the soil to unearth some antediluvian skull or other fossil. Hrdlička arranged to have his own cremated ashes interred with the calipers for measuring bones that were the beloved tools of his trade.

The formulas for preserving specimens of human material, especially brains, became one of Hrdlička's obsessions. In the Soviet Union, scientists cut up Lenin's brain into thirty-thousand prosciutto-thin slices that they placed on individual slides, and then stored away for future study in Moscow's Institute of the Brain. Hrdlička, who wanted to keep his brains whole, published a whole treatise on the merits of various pickling solutions for "fresh adult specimens." Formalin, diluted formaldehyde, was declared best for a "good hardening" with "little alteration in the form of the organ and preserving much of its color." Just as he had admonished Alfred Kroeber to pack Ishi's brain in "plenty of absorbent cotton," Hrdlička provided detailed instructions to anyone mailing him a specimen for the first time. His 1906 checklist of proper methods included removing "the brain as fresh as possible and with the least injury," pickling it in 4 cubic centimeters of formalin per gram of brain weight, and then closing the jar "as nearly air-tight as possible" for storage "on a shelf out of direct light of the sun."

Controversy abounded in the small world of anthropology during the teens of the last century. While Aleš Hrdlička remained noncommittal, Franz Boas had to contend with a backlash from the champions of nativism, eugenics, and the tenets of Social Darwinism and was even stripped of his presidency of the Anthropological Association during World War I. Across the line, however, anthropologists were unanimous about their prerogative to dig up Indian burials or study any dead body whatsoever. In the 1920s and 1930s, Hrdlička excavated more than seven hundred skeletons of Native Alaskan peoples just south of Anchorage, packing them in crates for shipment back to the Smithsonian. The Aleut called Hrdlička *ashaalixnamamaatax*, "the dead man's daddy," and he knew that many of them were upset and resentful about these digs: "Religious beliefs, sentimentality, and superstition, as well as love, nearly everywhere invest the bodies of the dead with sacredness or awe which no stranger is willingly permitted to disturb." Yet the uneducated failed to appreciate that "remains would be dealt with and guarded with the utmost care, and be used only for the most worthy ends, including the benefit of the living." Hrdlička and other men of learning of that time assumed that the imperatives of science trumped any other considerations. The surgeon Saxton Pope had insisted on Ishi's dissection using just this reasoning.

In the case of Osceola, the legendary nineteenth-century Seminole chief, a doctor had retained the Indian's whole head in formaldehyde for future study. Was it heartless for this "child of the forest" to have been put in his grave "a headless corpse"? the doctor asked rhetorically. No, he explained, "the scientific and intelligent" understood that "in the preservation of the dead we do not do violence to the feelings of humanity or even the strongest attachments of love."

Even Franz Boas had robbed graves in his younger days. On an expedition to British Columbia in the 1880s, he purchased skulls for five dollars apiece for the British Association for the Advancement of Science and the Canadian government. One afternoon, Boas went so far as to have his photographer distract the local Indians so he could dig in their cemetery. "Someone had stolen all the skulls, but we found a complete skeleton without head. I hope to get another one either today or tomorrow. . . . It is most unpleasant work to steal bones from a grave, but what is the use, someone has to do it."

Collecting in that era was not restricted to the bones of Indians. Boas and the other researchers also found ways to obtain the skeletons and even brains of whites—whether from prisons, the black market, or men like John Wesley Powell, who willed their bodies to science. But no anthropologist would have dared to shovel up white graveyards as they did Indian ones. In 1788, New Yorkers rioted for three days on learning that medical students had unearthed cadavers from a city cemetery to practice dissection on. That Indians remained among the poorest and most disenfranchised of Americans meant they could do little to stop the depredation. British Columbia's Cowichan Indians contracted a lawyer in 1888 to prosecute a man who plundered their graveyard, but such organized opposition was unusual. Sometimes Indians even guided the grave robbers to their people's cemeteries for a few coins.

Ishi's own dissection had had a direct and disturbing antecedent in 1897, one that also directly involved Alfred Kroeber and Aleš Hrdlička. In that year, a triumphant Admiral Robert Peary returned to a New York ticker tape parade celebrating his discovery of the North Pole (his African-American companion, Matthew Henson, would not be acknowledged until many decades later). Peary had brought back six Eskimos for Franz Boas, who wanted to learn more about their culture. Boas was also a curator at New York's American Museum of Natural History, and he found a room for the Eskimos there. Too busy himself, Boas assigned the task of working with the Eskimos to his talented twenty-one-year-old student Alfred Kroeber, who would leave for Berkeley just four years later. Kroeber spent many hours with the Eskimos; according to historian Kenn Harper, they found him a sensitive, likeable young man. Just like Ishi, however, the Eskimos were highly susceptible to the white man's diseases. Four of the six perished of tuberculosis within eight months of coming to New York. The first to die was Qissuk, a shaman and the leader of his band. Qissuk had brought his small son Minik from Greenland. The eight-year-old was devastated by his father's death. Boas wanted the dead Qissuk's skeleton for his museum collection, but to console the bereaved son he staged a phony Eskimo-style funeral in Central Park. The museum men substituted a shrouded log for the corpse so that Minik would think that his father's body was being buried under a pile of stones according to Eskimo custom.

Qissuk's body was duly boiled down, and the bleached white bones were stored at the American Museum of Natural History. When Minik discovered the truth as a teenager, he campaigned to recover his father's remains, accusing Boas and the others of betrayal. Boas was unapologetic. Scientists, he told the *Evening Mail*, had the right to study the body; the trickery had only been to "appease" Minik and to spare the little boy "any shock or uneasiness." Only in 1993 were the bones of Qissuk and the other three Eskimos who died in New York repatriated to Greenland, more than eighty years after Minik's own death at the age of thirty-one.

Aleš Hrdlička had had a role in this unhappy story. In 1898 he was still in New York, and the doctors at Bellevue Hospital invited the young brain specialist to help with a dissection of Qissuk before the body was boiled down for the bones. Subsequently, Hrdlička published an illustrated scholarly article called an "An Eskimo Brain" with the measurements he made that day. A plate on the first page shows Qissuk and Minik on admission to Bellevue Hospital (Minik also contracted tuberculosis but recovered). Weary and expressionless, father and son stand stripped naked on a dais in front and profile shots. A few pages later comes a close-up of Qissuk's dissected brain with the severed spinal cord like an eye in the middle of the convoluted cerebrum. "Weight of brain, denuded of dura matter, after a few minutes' exposure, for drain, 1503 grammes," Hrdlička noted. He thanked the "authorities of Bellevue hospital and the American Museum of Natural History for the privilege of examining the specimen."

A good deal of what Aleš Hrdlička and others once did in the name of science would be illegal today. A body of state and federal laws now forbids disturbing any Indian burial without tribal permission, with violators subject to fines and even prison time. Still other statutes now require the next-of-kin's written permission for any autopsy, except in cases of suspicious or violent death (and then the coroner must examine the body). By present-day standards, Qissuk's wife back in Greenland would have had to consent to his dissection. Ishi had no known living kin, but few doctors would today conduct an autopsy in express violation of a dead man's wishes. In reaction to the universal revulsion toward Nazi medical experiments in the death camps, a concern for medical ethics began to mount after World War II and at least some legal mechanisms were developed to ensure their enforcement. Further spurring reform were the later revelations about the Tuskegee Syphilis Study, in which government researchers beginning in the 1940s withheld penicillin from sick black sharecroppers in order to study the long-term effects of syphilis. Almost every medical research facility now has a review board charged to ensure that its researchers do not harm or deceive the human subjects of their studies.

The story of the bodies of Qissuk and Ishi come from an earlier time, when the prerogatives of science were allowed to rule almost unchecked. Even now, though, the rights to dead bodies remain contested, involving issues of fairness, power, and poverty. Scientists want bones as much as ever, for teaching anatomy and for their own new research. Yet they do not seek these bones in any quantity from their own kind. And since American Indian remains can no longer be excavated or boiled down, the majority of the skulls and skeletons now come from China, India, and other poor parts of the world. At theboneroom.com or skullsunlimited.com, anybody at all can order online a skull with "spring-held jaw" for $509 or a whole skeleton in metal carrying case for $1,499. There is almost no regulation of this new international trade, and few questions are asked about just how the bones have been obtained. The same goes for the new traffic in organs for commercial sale in transplant surgery—a father in India selling one of his own kidneys to pay for his daughter's dowry, the eyes of a dead South African teenager in a township morgue cut out for transplantation to a moneyed patient at a private eye clinic. The trade in bones and organs is making the bodies of the world's poor into "spare parts" for the West's own needs, writes Nancy Scheper-Hughes, an anthropologist and the cofounder of a group called Organs Watch that is trying to stop the worst abuses.

Even so, a number of pathologists argue it would be wrong to imagine that the idea of an autopsy—a word derived from the Greek that means literally "seeing for oneself"—is somehow evil and objectionable by nature. Qissuk and Ishi were put under the scalpel without authorization and to satisfy the curiosity of researchers about "primitive man"; but today we may still need autopsies to investigate murders and catch killers. Dissecting cadavers is also vital for the training of new doctors, and the search to understand and to cure disease would also be impossible without the study of dead bodies (AIDS and Legionnaire's Disease, for example, were first identified through autopsies).

Unethical as his methods may now seem, even Aleš Hrdlička's collecting proved important and even pioneering in one way. Hrdlička's bone research advanced techniques for using a dead person's remains to decode age, gender, race, health history, and sometimes manner of death. In the 1930s, the Federal Bureau of Investigation sought Hrdlička's help with murder investigations and he became a founder of the new science of forensic anthropology, the skill of reading the stories that bones tell. Douglas Owsley, the ancient Americas specialist and a successor to Hrdlička in the Smithsonian's physical anthropology division, is also one of the world's leading forensic anthropologists; he has testified at the trials of mass murderers Ted Bundy and Jeffrey Dahmer, among others. Other investigators have adapted forensic anthropology to the identification of victims of genocide in Argentina, Bosnia, and Rwanda. Their work has led to the conviction of politicians and generals responsible for these crimes against humanity.

Yet nothing of lasting scientific value came from Hrdlička's brain collection. Lacking any tools of the new biology, the main legacy of Hrdlička's brain research is hundreds of pages of weights and other measurements of each specimen in the collection that are now of little or no interest to anyone. By the time of Ishi's death in 1916, even Hrdlička, who was already in his fifties, may have begun to realize that his brain collecting was not going to advance scientific knowledge. In contrast with his detailed measurements at Qissuk's dissection twenty years before, Hrdlička never recorded any information about Ishi's brain—and perhaps never even examined it. Ishi's brain was one of the last Hrdlička had troubled to collect, and his reply to Kroeber's offer of the organ had been perfunctory. "I hardly need to say that we shall be very glad to receive and take care of Ishi's brain," he'd said in just a single line. Much more on Hrdlička's mind were his negotiations with Kroeber for Egyptian bones donated to his museum by Phoebe Apperson Hearst, the wealthy heiress. "What have you decided to do with the Egyptian collection of bones?" Hrdlička pressed Kroeber, who agreed to ship the skeletons if the Smithsonian paid the freight.

Hrdlička's brains languished in their preserving solution for the rest of the twentieth century. Although his own enthusiasm had diminished for this project, the old Czech never lost his faith in having such collections available for present and future study. He would have been mortified to learn that his prized specimens had fallen into such neglect that no one ever bothered to top off the formalin in their jars every so often. As I'd learned from David Hunt, the collections manager and also a well-respected forensic anthropologist, not all of the Smithsonian's brains had even survived the century. By the early 1980s, as yet before Hunt assumed his post, a slow evaporation through imperfectly sealed jars had dried up a number of Hrdlička's specimens. Hunt's predecessors had to dispose of the shriveled ones before the subsequent transfer of the others to the tanks at the Smithsonian's new Maryland storage facility. It was pure chance that Ishi's brain had not also withered and been thrown into the incinerator—and that it was still there for Art Angle and his Maidu to recover now almost a century later.

But it's not exactly true to say that the collection served no purpose. The brain of the famed explorer John Wesley Powell, also later housed in Tank 6 with Ishi's brain, had one moment of usefulness, but in this case its function was ceremonial, not scientific. For the dedication of the Smithsonian's new John Wesley Powell Library in 1979, a museum staffer wheeled out the great man's brain as a kind of honorary presence. Powell, an early anthropologist and naturalist, might have enjoyed the half-amused, half-respectful attention from the two hundred guests there that afternoon. In contrast with Ishi, this hard-driving Victorian man of science had wanted his body preserved for posterity. Powell's unlikely wager with his colleague W. J. "Brownie" McGee about which of them had the larger brain was still a favorite bit of trivia in Smithsonian circles. As the posthumous measurements showed, Powell's brain did outweigh that of his fellow scientist by some seventy grams, although neither was unusually big. The pickled organ was kept out on display for the duration of the library dedication festivities and the duly carted back to join the other specimens on a backroom storage shelf.

# Twelve

# THE MAIDU GO TO

# WASHINGTON

After the *Oroville Opportunity Bulletin* reported the story, the news about the discovery of Ishi's brain spread fast. It even made NBC's *Tonight Show*. "Brain Found in Washington," deadpanned host Jay Leno in his nightly spoof of the latest headlines. Although the story was buried inside the *New York Times*, *Washington Post*, and other East Coast papers, it made the front pages of California's leading newspapers. "Academic Detectives Find the Long-Lost Brain of Ishi," led the *Los Angeles Times*. The article detailed the investigation of U.C. San Francisco's Nancy Rockafellar, then my find of the trove of letters leading to the Smithsonian and the missing brain. It was my few minutes in the spotlight. The phone rang for several days, with calls ranging from our local *Durham Herald-Sun* to the BBC and the Canadian Broadcasting Service.

Like Leno, some people saw humor in the idea of a mummified brain lost and found. If the search for the missing organ had a bit of a detective novel's twists and turns, the revelation that a leading anthropologist had mailed the excised body part of a famous person across the country seemed straight out of a bad horror movie. The hostess on NPR's *Weekend Edition* seemed bored when I spoke in our interview about Ishi and the devastation visited upon Native California in the nineteenth century—another droning, politically correct professor, I could almost hear her thinking. She perked up considerably, however, at the story of Hrdlička's "reference brain collection"—and the idea of the museum warehouse as a proverbial mad scientist's laboratory where pickled organs floated in tanks like tropical fish. "That's great," she chuckled.

Indians across the country began e-mailing me their reactions. Maurice Eben, a Nevada Paiute and the chairman of the National Congress of the American Indian, wrote to say how angry he was at Ishi's white friends in San Francisco. From his standpoint, Kroeber and the others were the "uncivilized" ones. "It is a sad fact that the U.S. government found a need to take the brains and skulls from the battlefield, but to have known Ishi and to have allowed the removal for their purpose is demeaning and uncivilized on their part." A San Diego woman thanked me for uncovering Ishi's "desecration" and hoped the revelation would speed repatriation. Unidentified Indian bones in museum collections should be honored "with a decent mass burial at a national holocaust memorial," she added. Aleš Hrdlička may have gathered bones to advance science, but these Indians considered his endeavor to be just more white arrogance and exploitation of Native America. They saw no humor at all in the fact that Ishi's brain had ended up in a steel tank.

I also heard from whites who were moved by Ishi's story. "I am almost 80 years old, 90% blind but somebody who has a 'hero,'" one Maryland woman wrote. She related having admired Ishi ever since first reading Theodora Kroeber's *Ishi in Two Worlds* back in 1964. A convict wrote from one of California's state prisons, authorizing in a neat hand the "Ishi repatriation lobby" to include his signature in absentia "on any document necessary in support of Ishi." Far more than in the mainstream media, the saga of Ishi and his tribe still stirred admiration and even reverence among people who were themselves at the margins of a too often complacent, self-congratulatory society.

Art Angle held a press conference in Oroville at the offices of his Enterprise Rancheria, just down from the Wal-Mart on Feather River Boulevard. He got a good turnout: reporters, a TV crew, local politicians, and the heads of Oroville's other two federally recognized Maidu groups, Berry Creek and Mooretown. Back in North Carolina, I read about the press conference in the newspapers. Art had referred to the brain as "the missing body part," I noticed. Maidu frowned upon mentioning the names of the dead anytime soon after their passing. I wondered whether Art's avoidance of the word "brain" reflected this traditional taboo or a more general feeling of protectiveness toward Ishi, whom he called "our red brother" in his statement. Art also announced that a delegation from the Butte County Native American Cultural Committee would travel to the Smithsonian. Repatriating Ishi was "the right thing to do," Art said. "We need this done soon."

After the press conference, Art told me one night on the phone that I would be invited to join the Maidu on their Smithsonian trip. As the date neared, I heard nothing more. That I had helped to locate Ishi's brain was an ice-breaker between Art and me, but I wondered if maybe Art or others in Oroville did not really want an outsider trespassing. My doubts were unfounded, however; just as I was staving off disappointment at being excluded, Art called from the Sacramento airport. They had missed their flight, Art shouted over the terminal's buzz. I should be at the Baltimore-Washington International Airport at 8:50 P.M, not 5:20. Art thought he had already arranged to meet me and the others there. In truth, in the last-minute scramble to get out of Oroville, he'd simply forgotten; among other distractions, the reporters had been calling so often that Art and his wife, Lindy, had to disconnect their phone when they wanted to sleep. I was thrilled in any event to be invited after all. I wanted to meet more of Art's people and to see if I could help in bringing Ishi back home. Canceling appointments, I rented a van to pick up Art and his delegation and once again ramped onto Interstate 85 for Washington.

One thought still bothered me: the possibility that the Smithsonian had incinerated Ishi's brain back in the 1980s. Was there any chance museum officials were lying about the missing organ? How could the Maidu verify the authenticity of whatever brain they were shown? Theoretically, any brain from Hrdlička's collection could be wheeled out. By now, though, I felt such a scenario was highly unlikely, if not completely impossible. I'd been impressed by the people at the Smithsonian's Native American Repatriation Office on my earlier trip to Washington. I very much doubted they were engaged in a cover-up. When I had asked for more information about the storage of Ishi's brain, the curator David Hunt had sent me a testy e-mail: "There is NO question to the identity of the specimen or its existence in the collections."

Frank Norick, the retired Berkeley curator, had originally told me that Ishi's brain had been destroyed, but he had backtracked when I checked with him again. The Smithsonian's JoAllyn Archambault may only have been talking about intentions, Norick now said. Norick had been right about the brain's being at the Smithsonian. It appeared he had been wrong about the organ being incinerated. Later, too, I asked Norick why he had shared the story with me in the first place. He liked JoAllyn Archambault, he said, and yet he did not like secrets to be "buried" and, in any event, thought Archambault could "take care of herself." Norick, I realized, prided himself on being a straight-shooter, an iconoclastic truth-teller who would not censor himself no matter what the consequences. But had Archambault ever spoken with the retired curator about Ishi's brain? And made some mention of planning to destroy it so that Indian activists would never learn the Smithsonian ever had it? Or was Norick making up the whole story, as Archambault had insisted to me? "It's her word against mine," Norick said. "And I don't care whether anyone believes me or not."

I had kept Art abreast of the latest claims and counterclaims. He was still unwilling to dismiss the possibility that the Smithsonian might be concealing the truth. During his own inquiry, the University of California had informed Art that Berkeley's anthropologists had cremated Ishi's brain in 1916 and placed it with the rest of the ashes at the Olivet cemetery. And the Smithsonian had in earlier times collected the severed head of Captain Jack and other ill-gotten Indian remains. Why should Art take the museum's word at face value now? So at Art's request, I had done some quick research into how to verify that the brain was genuine.

One option was a DNA test. A few strands of hair and eyebrow were encrusted in Ishi's death mask, stored at Berkeley's anthropology museum. Saxton Pope had made the mask just before the dissection, snipping hairs from the dead body and embedding them in the wet plaster of Paris to leave a more complete record. Although DNA could probably be extracted from a strand of this hair, the brain was another matter. We did not know exactly how Ishi's brain had been preserved in the three months before Alfred Kroeber sent it to the Smithsonian. Once there, however, Aleš Hrdlička kept it "fixed" in his favorite formalin, the same as his other jarred brains. Formalin both fragments and cross-links the strings of DNA in human tissue, making the tissue useless for genetic testing in most cases. Most laboratories now prefer ethyl alcohol because it does not have this reactive effect. Ishi's brain had been in ethyl alcohol since it was transferred to the Maryland storage facility in the 1980s, but the damage of more than a half century in the formalin would have already been done. In any case, the attempt to recover DNA from the brain for comparison with a death mask hair would require cutting off a bit of brain tissue. A piece about the size of a cherry pit would need to be removed and destroyed in the chemical tests performed in the laboratory.

That settled the matter for Art. In his view, scientists had already mutilated Ishi. He did not want any more cutting.

The other, simpler option was to go by weight. The 1916 autopsy report listed Ishi's brain at exactly 1,300 grams. As Aleš Hrdlička's own research into brain preservatives had shown, a "fresh" brain may gain as much as twenty or thirty grams as it soaks up the preserving solution. After that, the weight remains relatively stable, even over many decades. Therefore, if the Smithsonian brain belonged to Ishi, it should check out between about 1,300 and 1,340 grams. A figure that did not fall into this range would be cause for suspicion.

Art wanted to pursue this option. Could I arrange for a neuropathologist to accompany the Maidu to the Smithsonian and weigh the brain there? I had no luck recruiting anyone on short notice, not to mention for free. So Art decided that the Maidu would weigh the brain themselves at the Smithsonian. He asked me to tell the Repatriation Office to have a scale ready.


I reached the Baltimore-Washington International Airport just before Art's plane got in from Sacramento. At the gate, Jed Riffe was the first down the jetway. A Berkeley filmmaker who had made a well-received documentary about Ishi, Riffe had received permission from the Maidu to tape their Washington visit, making him the only other non-Indian besides myself on the trip. Then came Art and the rest of his Butte County Native American Cultural Committee. Three women and four men, all middle-aged or in their later years, they did not look Indian in any stereotypical way. Art had his mother's dark complexion, but the others were lighter-skinned. More than two centuries of intermixture means that being a California Indian is much more a matter of culture than biology, of inherited or revived traditions, not racial purity. The delegation's oldest member was Gus Martin, an eighty-year-old retired lumberjack. Dressed for the trip in a retiree's light blue polyester suit with a white straw cowboy hat, the light-complexioned Gus could easily pass for white. One of the world's last three fluent speakers of Oroville's Concow dialect of Maidu, he had learned about the old ways from his Indian mother. The strongest hint that the identity of the party was Native American was the women's understated beaded Indian jewelry and the black pony-tail on Joe Marine, who, in his late forties, was the youngest Maidu along on the trip.

Art needed a cigarette, but he introduced me to the others before ducking outside. Besides Gus and Joe, there was Sharon Guzman-Mix (a kindergarten teacher at a new Indian charter school), Lorraine Frazier (the cultural programs officer at Oroville's Mooretown Rancheria), Bruce Steidl (an Indian archaeologist also at Mooretown), and Art's sister, Rosalie Bertram, the vice-chair of Enterprise Rancheria. Everyone was friendly but tired. Oroville has no commercial airport, so they'd left before dawn to reach Sacramento. After getting everyone and their luggage loaded, I drove the van to a Holiday Inn in Alexandria's Crystal City. A few of us had a nightcap at the bar. Then we went to bed in anticipation of crossing the Potomac to see Ishi's brain.

I will not soon forget the emotions of that next day. We were to meet with the people at the Repatriation Office in the Smithsonian's National Museum of Natural History at 9:00 A.M. As I steered the van across the crowded 14th Street Bridge, the Washington Monument and the granite walls of so many federal buildings crowded up before us in the bright morning light. Only Lorraine Frazier had been to Washington before. Everyone was a bit nervous at the prospect of an intimidating formal meeting at the Smithsonian, and what the unhappy sight of Ishi's severed brain would be like. Still, my passengers were in high enough spirits to joke about Bill Clinton and his infamous cigar, the latest Washington scandal that still dominated the news. Jed Riffe was filming the entire scene inside the moving van with his handheld video camera. All of us laughed when the distracted Art accidentally put out his cigarette in Bruce Steidl's styrofoam cup of coffee. A tall, soft-spoken, older man in a stylish black leather Stetson, Bruce had studied archaeology at the California State University at Chico. He'd been hired by his Mooretown Rancheria to inventory Maidu baskets and bones in museums around the country, with an eye to the eventual return at least of the bones. Bruce and his wife, Leslie, also an archaeologist, lived in a beautiful wood-beamed adobe house they'd built themselves above Oroville in the same hills where Bruce's ancestors had lived for centuries. Bruce and Leslie were also amateur astronomers. They tried to make an annual expedition to Australia, Zimbabwe, or some other far-off place to view that rarest of celestial events, a full solar eclipse.

I dropped everyone off at the front entrance of Smithsonian's National Museum of Natural History. By the time I made it back from parking the van, the meeting had already begun, with coffee and doughnuts laid out. There were four representatives from the Smithsonian in the small, windowless conference room: Tom Killion, two of his staffers, and Randall Kremer, the museum's chief public affairs officer. I wasn't sure who made the decision, but the Smithsonian prohibited Jed Riffe from filming their meeting with the Maidu. I could only guess that they were worried the film might somehow later be used to cast the museum in a negative light. The revelation that Ishi's brain had been stored there was already bringing bad publicity. Editorials in several Bay Area newspapers had decried the "indignity" and "abuse" of the dead man's humanity.

The elderly Gus Martin had just begun a Maidu prayer when I slipped in at last. For a few moments, the powerful, unfamiliar sound of this non-Western tongue filled the little room. Yet Gus tired easily and was also going deaf, so Art had invited Joe Marine to take charge of the rest of the ceremonial duties. In jeans and a black leather jacket, the easygoing Joe was the grandson of the well-known Maidu activist and basketweaver Marie Potts. He'd been raised and still lived in Sacramento, but was also the lead dancer in a traditional Maidu Bear Dance held every June beyond Mount Lassen towards Nevada. Now we watched Joe light a small bundle of dried wormwood leaves. Then, with a few words of Maidu prayer, he blew the aromatic, almost sweet-smelling smoke in the four directions of the compass. Unlike Gus, Joe didn't speak Maidu, even though he knew a few simple blessings for occasions like this. Some version of prayer to the four directions is part of the repertoire of Indian medicine men—and sometimes white New Agers—all across the country. Joe himself wasn't sure where the ritual had originated, perhaps with the Navajo or some other southwestern tribe.

The ceremony over, Joe ended with a few words about "working together" with the Smithsonian to "get Ishi back home." The Maidu had reasons for mistrust and even anger toward the museum for having kept Ishi's brain as a specimen for so long, but Joe's words signaled that the Indians were not interested in finger-pointing. They did not seem to hold the museum's present-day authorities accountable for past sins, only wanting now to collaborate with the Smithsonian in the return of Ishi's remains to California.

Tom Killion was also conciliatory, even soothing. In an earlier era, the Smithsonian had become the single largest Indian necropolis in the world with its storage drawers full of bones. Now the law obligated the museum to help tribes with repatriation, an act of contrition and an uncanny reversal of policy that no one could have anticipated back in the days of Aleš Hrdlička. I suspected the old Bohemian scientist would have felt outraged and even betrayed to hear Killion tell the Maidu that the preservation of Ishi's brain had been "very wrong."

Killion explained that his office was required to repatriate remains to the closest living descendants and that the investigation into the possibility of any such survivors had to be pursued in this case. I knew the Maidu were assuming that no survivors would be found and that they would eventually receive the brain. Killion said nothing to suggest otherwise, though he mentioned he'd been in touch with a man in the northern Sacramento Valley who claimed to be part Yana, the larger language group to which Ishi's Yahi had belonged. He gave the Maidu the name and phone number of this man, Mickey Gemmill, in case they wanted to contact him.

I found Killion impressive, but he was also in damage control mode. He was trying hard to win over Art and his delegation to forestall any further criticism of the Smithsonian, and to move the repatriation of Ishi's brain to a smooth conclusion.

"I don't care what the media says," Killion told the Maidu. "All I care about is you guys."

Randall Kremer collared Art and Joe at a coffee break with a smile and friendly hand on the shoulder. A pale, thin man in pinstripes, Kremer resembled the actor Bud Cort from *Harold and Maude*, a classic seventies film. "Is everyone doing okay?" he asked Art and Joe, eyes blinking hopefully.

Yet trouble soon arose. After his welcome, Tom Killion turned the meeting over to Stuart Speaker, his deputy for California and the Great Basin. The slight, professorial Speaker, who had a Ph.D. in anthropology from the University of Oregon, told the Maidu that it had been arranged for them to see Ishi's brain that afternoon. The brain was already in the building, he added; it had been retrieved from its tank and brought over from the Maryland storage facility.

Art furrowed his thick black eyebrows at this unexpected news. He interrupted Speaker to have his say. A working-class man who did not want to come off poorly in this formal setting, Art was nervous as well as upset. He talked at first with odd eye blinks, throat clearings, and glances at the ceiling but then gathered steam as if remembering his sureness of purpose. Art said he was angry that the Smithsonian had brought the brain to the museum without any prior consultation. He'd wanted to see the tank and storage facility for himself in checking up on the matter of the brain's authenticity. Art also objected to Ishi's remains being carted around the nation's capital like a special express package. "There's been enough abuse of this body part," he said.

That no one asked his people about this latest shuttling of Ishi's brain suggested to Art that the Smithsonian did not respect Indians even now. "We need to have a short discussion about this with our people," he declared at last. Art gestured for Killion, Speaker, a third staffer, and the PR officer to leave the room.

After the four Smithsonian officials complied, Art ducked out to the restroom for a moment. "Why's Art so worried?" asked Sharon Guzman-Mix, the kindergarten teacher. "It's Indian suspicion," laughed Art's sister Rosalie Bertram, making a joke as well as a statement of fact.

The cheerful, gracious Rosalie loved country music, white zinfandel, and road trips to Reno. She'd once been a semiconductor assembly line inspector in the Bay Area. In the 1980s, she'd returned to her native Oroville and become a tribal council member at the Enterprise Rancheria, the smallest of Oroville's four small Maidu reservations. Apparently, Art had not shared the rumor of the brain's destruction even with Rosalie, so the others in the group did not understand his concern. When he returned, the others calmed Art down, and he agreed to go forward with the meeting. The people from the Repatriation Office were invited back in, and the talk turned to a timetable for repatriation. It would be no more than a few months, Tom Killion promised.

"That sounds wonderful," Rosalie exclaimed. "I'm a Virgo, and I like to get things done."

By mutual agreement, Smithsonian workers would bring Ishi's brain to the little conference room for viewing. Art wanted lunch first—he doubted he'd have the appetite afterward, he grimaced. We walked over to the nearby National Museum of American History for a sandwich.

A TV news crew was waiting when we came back. Tom Killion told the well-groomed blonde reporter that it had been a good morning with the Maidu and that everything was on course for Ishi's return to California. Art said a few guarded words, but Killion grasped his hand for a cordial handshake for the camera. In the course of all this it was clear that the young TV newswoman did not find the Maidu exotic enough. Except for his brown skin, Art looked like the rest of the middle-aged Washington tourists that we'd jostled among at our cafeteria lunch: short hair, comfortable walking shoes, light brown winter jacket. I saw the reporter looking around for more color. As a last resort, she pulled over Joe Marine for a walk-and-talk sequence with Art and Killion. His pony-tail was the best she could do for a bit of Indian flavor.

An Oroville elder, Virgil Logan, had told the Maidu before they left that they had nothing to fear from Ishi's brain. It was just inert matter, he'd explained, since the spirit had long ago departed the body for the Milky Way. Even so, we were all apprehensive for different reasons as Stuart Speaker unlocked the conference room door after lunch. None of us had ever seen a human brain before, much less a pickled one, so we had no idea what to expect. And this was the severed body part so long sought, the last fleshy remnant of suffering and survival that belonged to the Wild Man of Oroville, the lost brother, the legend.

A mound covered by a white cloth lay on the plastic wood conference table. Joe lit another plug of wormwood. He circled the room with a turkey feather wand and brushed smoke over each of us to purify and protect against any danger. He also smudged and shook a deer hoof over the brain itself, shrouded still in the middle of the table.

Joe instructed Art to remove the white cloth. He did so, revealing a glass jar about the size of a soup-pot. Something wrapped in a cheese-cloth sack was floating in a cloudy bath of ethyl alcohol inside the jar. We all stared at it. There was quiet in the room, broken only by the air-conditioner's low, metallic hiss.

When I raised my head to glance around, I found my companions distraught. Several were lifting at their glasses to wipe away tears. "It was just too much," Rosalie explained many months later back in Oroville. Like the other Maidu on the trip, Rosalie belonged to an older generation raised in the shadow of terror and carnage. Her people had been lynched, raped, and enslaved in the nineteenth century. Then in the twentieth century they'd suffered through the flooding of their land for Oroville Dam, the ravages of drink and drugs, and the loss of most of their traditional culture. It was a history no one wanted to remember—or to forget. The sight of the brain on the plastic conference table brought the emotions of violation and sadness welling to the surface. Historian Peter Brown speaks of the "inverse magnitude" between the tiny bone shard relics of martyred saints and the huge holy power ascribed to them by medieval Catholics. As small and forlorn as it looked in the jar in the middle of the large table, Ishi's brain possessed a similarly outsized symbolism for these modern-day Maidu, in this case embodying the destruction and suffering unleashed upon their people.

I felt the moment's power, too. Reading the letters and doing research was one thing; to be confronted with the thing itself was something else again. I believed that my disciplinary ancestor Alfred Kroeber was a decent man. By sending away Ishi's brain, however, he had violated a friend's trust. He'd breached the faith that Ishi, dependent on Kroeber, had placed in the professor's sense of decency and respect. That the severed organ had ended up in a jar a world away from home was one more outrage inflicted on a Native California that had already endured far too much.

Joe Marine broke the silence. He addressed the brain as if talking to Ishi himself, promising to return "you" to Mother Earth. But no one knew what to do next. Did anybody else want to say anything, Art asked? The neat, gray-haired Lorraine Frazier said a few quiet words about righting the past's wrongs and Americans "going forward as equals." By then, Tom Killion had left for a meeting in Chicago, but Stuart Speaker vowed again that the Smithsonian would work with the Indians for Ishi's repatriation. Silence fell once more. Finally, we filed out into a coffee room next door.

Art spoke now. Everyone was upset, he knew. Yet he thought they should return to the conference room and do what they could to certify the brain's authenticity. At this, Sharon Guzman-Mix shook her head, too dejected to confront Ishi's brain again. Gus Martin didn't want to go back, either. The old man had fallen and scraped his shoulder on the sidewalk on the way to lunch. We had found Gus a wheelchair, and he sat slumped in the seat, face sad and drawn under his white straw hat.

Nonetheless, we went back to the other room one last time. Art told Stuart Speaker we now wanted to see the brain itself. Speaker pulled on plastic gloves and put his hands in the jar. Gently lifting out the dripping cheesecloth sack, he put it on a white porcelain tray that Joe had sprinkled with more wormwood. Joe read out the accession number on the bag tie—60884. This was the number assigned to Ishi's brain when it was entered into the Smithsonian catalogue on January 12, 1917. Then Speaker peeled the sack back to reveal the contents. The brain looked solid and heavy, not mushy—as if its furrows and clefts were modeled from a thick grayish clay. Threaded through one of the cerebellum's convolutions was a second tag. Joe read this number aloud. It was also 60884. After a moment, Stuart Speaker pulled the cheesecloth back over the brain.

There was nothing more any of the Maidu wanted in the room. We departed, leaving Speaker to put the brain back in the jar until it could be officially returned to California.

Of course, the accession numbers proved nothing. If someone had destroyed Ishi's brain and then substituted another in its place, new accession tags could have been fabricated. The next day, Art told me that he should have pressed to weigh the brain. "We lost our nerve," he said.

The others had no doubts about the brain's authenticity. Joe, Lorraine, Gus, and Rosalie each remarked that they had felt something out of the ordinary from the moment they had walked into the museum. "I got chills," Lorraine said. She attributed her feeling to the brain, which none of us had known was in the building when we first came in.

These feelings—and especially the opinion of his elder, Gus—persuaded Art in the end. Art told the *San Jose Mercury News* a few months later that his people had "known it was really Ishi right when we walked into the museum."

This resolution of the authenticity issue suited everyone. The Smithsonian was glad to be done with allegations about its secret destruction of the brain of a legendary Indian. Art and the Maidu were relieved, too. It was a feeling of duty and obligation that brought the Indians to Washington in the first place. As unsettling as the sight had been for all of us, it eased their minds to think they had found Ishi's real brain at last and could bring it back home. Joe had decided that for symmetry's sake they should take the brain back by railroad. "That's how they must've sent it from San Francisco back then in the first place," he said.

We had dinner in Georgetown. The Maidu had been careful enough with their money to splurge at a pricey Italian restaurant with track lighting, polished brass, and a special that night of lobster agnolotti. A drained, exhausted Art stayed back at the Holiday Inn, but everyone else welcomed the meal as a release from the day's tensions. A glass of red wine put the blood back in Gus's cheeks. Rosalie told jokes, and Jed Riffe, although still disappointed at having been prevented from filming at the Smithsonian, recounted tales from his Texas childhood. Everyone had jobs and families back home and no time for sightseeing the next day. On the way back to the hotel, I cruised back past the brilliantly lit White House and Jefferson Memorial so that the Maidu could have at least a quick tour of the capital.

The next morning I drove back to North Carolina in time to teach my evening seminar. The Maidu flew back to California. They'd been in good spirits when we said goodbye, promising to stay in touch. Art expected that by the start of summer Ishi's brain would be in his possession and Olivet cemetery would release the ashes of the body. Then his people would lay Ishi's reunited remains to rest somewhere by Deer Creek just as the wild grass began to turn the color of gold in the broken foothills.

Only after cruising the Internet back in Durham did I realize that the story might not end so neatly. Art believed that the brain would come back to the Oroville Maidu because his people had launched the quest for Ishi's repatriation in the first place. The declarations made by the Smithsonian officials to the newspapers sounded more ambiguous, however. The museum would return the brain, said Randall Kremer, the public affairs officer, in the *Washington Post*. "When and to whom is the question," he added, leaving that part of the matter in doubt. Meanwhile, Art had told the *Los Angeles Times* that he understood the Smithsonian's Repatriation Office had to "work within the law," but that the delay was also "a little bit frustrating."

The newspapers played the Maidu's Washington visit as if it had been some kind of angry stand-off. "INDIANS ON WARPATH OVER WILD MAN'S BRAIN," reported London's *Daily Telegraph*. The *Los Angeles Times* headlined, "MUSEUM REFUSES TO GIVE ISHI'S BRAIN TO INDIANS." "SMITHSONIAN REJECTS ISHI CLAIM," added the *Sacramento Bee*. And neither Art nor the Smithsonian officials were going to be pleased to read what the other side had said in the meeting's aftermath. As far as further cooperation between the Maidu and the museum went, this was not a good omen.

# LINES OF DESCENT

That the Smithsonian had not handed Ishi's brain over to the Maidu during their visit to Washington had made the nation's biggest museum an instant target of criticism, even derision, in California. An editorial cartoon in the *Sacramento Bee* depicted a pea-sized brain in a bell jar. "BRAIN OF SMITHSONIAN OFFICIAL WHO REFUSES TO RETURN ISHI'S BRAIN TO INDIANS," read the caption. "I am both amazed and outraged that the federal government still doesn't get it," wrote Cruz M. Bustamante, California's lieutenant governor and a rising political star, in an op-ed for the *San Francisco Chronicle*.

The call for Ishi's repatriation did not surprise me. It was easy for the editorialists and state politicians to cast this as a story of insensitive Washington bureaucrats disregarding Native American concerns. In fact, the criticism of the Smithsonian was for the most part both unfair and uninformed. This was not some new episode in the trail of broken treaties, at least so far. Tom Killion and his staff had never "refused" to return Ishi's brain; to the contrary, they had made it a top priority. It was understandable that the Repatriation Office would need to take a few weeks to ensure that the brain went to the right people, and an investigation was mandated by their regulations.

But what would the decision be? As Killion had explained to Art and the other Maidu, family members always had first rights. Rarely could the Repatriation Office determine such clear-cut lines of kinship, however, since more than ninety percent of the Smithsonian's bone collection was unidentified except by tribe and place of excavation. When no blood relatives could be traced, then the remains could be repatriated to a "culturally affiliated group," according to the guidelines of the Repatriation Office. If Ishi had no living blood relatives, then which surviving group of California's Indians had the strongest link to the Yahi—and to Ishi's dissected body? It was up to Killion and his staff to make this determination.

The very idea that Ishi might have descendants of any kind was something of a novelty. He was supposed to be not just the last Yahi, but also the last "wild" Indian in North America. Many Americans tend to assume that you can only find Indians speaking native tongues and following their traditions somewhere in the Black Hills, the Painted Desert, or some other vaguely mythical place. As a college student, I'd driven off in my beat-up VW Bug to volunteer in Navajoland, that archetypal Indian country of John Wayne and Monument Valley. It never occurred to me that California had tribes to whom I could have offered my services.

Determining to whom, among the living, the remains of Ishi "belonged" cut to the vexed question of ethnic, and specifically Native American, identity in America today. From the very start, I'd puzzled about blood and culture—and the very definition of "Indian"—in the search for Ishi. "We are all mixed bloods now," the cultural critic Gerald Vizenor has said. And with reason. Over the last century, the rates of exogamy for Native Americans have been higher than for any other ethnic group—and Vizenor is surely correct about the United States as a "postnative" society at the level of biology. In the Eastern Band of the Cherokee in Oklahoma, for example, you can become an enrolled member with as little as 1/2,048 Indian blood. The government does not require any blood quantum of the tribes, allowing each to establish its own criteria for enrolling membership. The Cherokee chose loose standards to build up tribal numbers and influence (although as late as the 1960s the tribe, while encouraging those of European and Indian ancestry to enroll, discouraged those with African-American blood from becoming members).

A total of 2.1 million Americans checked the box for "American Indian/Alaska Native" in 2000, a jump of more than 200 percent from just thirty years before. Although part of the explanation lies in better health care and increased efforts by the census-takers to reach isolated areas, the increase cannot be explained by these factors alone. It has also to do with the changing winds of politics and identity, and, in particular, a new willingness and even eagerness of Americans to embrace their Indian ancestry—a "migration from whiteness to redness," in the words of the anthropologist Circe Sturm. Almost all of today's "racial shifters" also have white and sometimes African-American blood, but the census allows you to identify yourself as you please. The contrast is striking between the United States and what I'd seen in Peru. By any "objective" criterion of blood and culture, at least a million brown-skinned, Quechua-speaking villagers are very "Indian." Yet Indian identity remains so stigmatized in the Andes that villagers prefer to be called "farmers," "Peruvians," or some other name. To call someone an *indio*, an Indian, in Peru is still a street insult.

What explains the new acceptability and even fashionability of identifying yourself as Indian in this country? There are sometimes obvious, instrumental reasons: money and social opportunity. The rates of poverty, victimization by violent crime, and other negative social welfare indexes for Native Americans all remain higher than the national average. Even so, it can be advantageous to be Indian in applying for admission to college and professional schools. You may also be eligible for special scholarship programs, free health care, and low-cost housing if you are Indian. And only Native Americans among all other ethnic groups have the right to start casinos, at least if they have managed to get onto the rolls of officially recognized, certified tribes maintained by the Bureau of Indian Affairs. For the first time in the history of the United States, it can now sometimes pay to be Indian.

In this context, some young people may even strategically adopt—and then drop—their "Indian" identity. The head of the Native American Student Coalition at Duke—a fluent Choctaw speaker who was also a psychology major—complained to me about the applicants who checked "Native American" on their applications, playing on the university's desire for a more diverse, inclusive student body. When she'd call to invite these students to the annual pow-wow and other coalition activities, many of them would say that, well, they did have an Indian grandmother or grandfather, but they weren't really Indian and didn't want to come to such cultural events.

For thousands of others, however, the reasons for wanting to be Indian have little or nothing to do with such financial opportunism. Many Americans choose now to claim their Cherokee, Creek, or other tribal roots for cultural and social reasons—a lessening of the fear and stigma attached to being an Indian, a view of whiteness as "empty" and "blank" in comparison to a more unusual, romantic-seeming Native American heritage. There can also be a kind of moral capital attached to belonging to a people most Americans can agree have suffered awful injustices. "It's Cool to Be Indian," a bumper sticker reads. To be Native American has more often become something to be embraced instead of hidden away in twenty-first-century America.

At the same time, the criteria for qualifying as an Indian in the eyes of others have remained a matter of doubt and debate. Is it blood? Old Gus Martin was by any measure a "real" Indian, one of the very last speakers of the Maidu tongue, yet a white mother and Indian father made him only a "half-breed" by a biological measure. And if bloodlines are everywhere mixed and crossed in the United States, then the same is also true at the level of culture, where nothing so simple as "pure" or "uncontaminated" native heritage has ever existed. Already before Columbus, tribes had intermarried, absorbed cultural influences from their neighbors, and sometimes dissolved into or incorporated into other groups. Today, the majority of Indians do not speak their aboriginal language and more make their homes in Los Angeles, Dallas, and other big cities than on reservations. A group of native Canadian artists called their recent exhibition "Reservation X." The "X" denotes the idea that modern-day Indian identity no longer entails a fixed address or cultural purity, and perhaps never did. If languages and traditions have survived, they have also changed with the times. Consider the day-glo beads added to the costume of a Lakota Hoop Dancer, or the invention by the Navajo of their own words for "seat belt"(*ach'ą́ą́h sis*, literally "a something is obstructed strap"), "scotch tape"(*bee i'diljeehí*, literally, "by means of it something is stuck together"), and, more ominously, "AIDS" (*ats'íís yichą́ą́h nabahii bąąh dah hoo'aahi*, literally, "the fighters who protect the body are sick"). The quintessential Native American specialty almost everywhere in the United States nowadays is fry-bread, yet the dough is made from wheat, a European import to the Americas. Ishi, that symbol of primordial Indianness, was a hybrid in his own way, of course. Hadn't he scavenged iron nails and copper wire to fashion his salmon harpoons at Grizzly Bear's Hiding Place? And known a few words of Spanish and neighboring Indian languages? And gone from being a "wild" to an urban Indian in his own lifetime?

The realities of mixture and in-betweenness leave choices and also provoke quandaries. I recalled an aside by Art Angle's sister Rosalie over a drink at The Sierra Club bar in Oroville. Rosalie was complaining, though with her accustomed good humor, about infighting within her Enterprise Rancheria—and the difficulty of ever getting anything done. "You know," she smiled, "sometimes I just wake up and think I'll just forget about this whole Indian thing." She and Art shared a white father, but Rosalie was much lighter than Art and could pass for Anglo. Rosalie understood that "this whole Indian thing" was provisional for her and that her own heritage was mixed. For her, at least, identity was a choice, not some preassigned and unalienable essence.

Of late, some mixed bloods have acknowledged and put a positive spin on their impure, entangled heritage. "Half-Indian/Half-Mexican" is the title of poem by James Luna, a member of the Luiseño tribe in southern California, where native and Spanish blood have commingled for centuries:

> I'm half Indian and half Mexican
> I'm half many things.
> I'm half compassionate/I'm half unfeeling.
> I'm half happy/I'm half angry.
> I'm half educated/I'm half ignorant.
> I'm half drunk/I'm half sober.
> I'm half giving/I'm half selfish
> A self made up of many things.
> I do not have to be anything for anybody but myself.
> I have survived long enough to find this out.
> I am 41 years old and am happy with my whole-self
> Don't let your children wait as long . . .

Writer Richard Rodriguez argues for the admission—even celebration—of America itself as a "mongrel nation." He terms the recognition of our intertwined histories and genealogies "the last discovery of America."

Bruce Steidl, the affable star-gazing archaeologist who'd gone with us to Washington, saw himself as both Indian and white at the same time. Like Rosalie, Bruce could pass for white if he chose. In Bruce's opinion, however, you shouldn't have to meet any blood quantum to qualify as an Indian. He described a man without Indian bloodlines in California's Pit River valley named Indian Mike: "But he was raised by Indian people. He didn't know any other people, culture, surroundings." Was this adopted white man an Indian? "It's a hard one, and some might not agree," Bruce replied, "but in my own heart I'd say he was." It was culture and upbringing rather than bloodlines that mattered or at least should matter most in Bruce's view of the world.

I asked Art once why he saw himself first and foremost as Indian, even though his father was white. Art had grown up near Oroville in the 1950s before the Red Power and civil rights movements, when there was no up side to having brown skin. He told me his primary identification as Indian was in part forced upon him from the outside: "The white community didn't see you as white, because of your dark-complected skin. They kind of alienated themselves from us." He'd gained acceptance through sports at all-white Paradise High School, but before then "it was pretty tough. We were looked down upon." In the caste system of the Sacramento Valley during that time, people of color were "niggers," "chinks," "greasers," and "Japs"; even poor white arrivals from the Dust Bowl were "Okies" and "Arkies" often subject to the hatred so famously described in John Steinbeck's *The Grapes of Wrath*. Then, too, Art's relatives on his mother's Maidu side of the family had been more present in his life: "You felt more aligned with your Indian side because they'd help you." Art's Maidu grandmother had been his comfort with his mother dying young and his father sometimes battling the bottle.

Unlike Bruce, however, Art refused to let go altogether of a physiological concept of racial identity. He felt that "learning the heritage" was part of being Indian, and yet he also mentioned a kind of parallel example to Indian Mike—his elderly white neighbor who had married a Maidu woman and learned to speak some Maidu. "But he'll never be Maidu," Art said. "You've got to have some dark pigmentation." By the same token, Art felt, even a Navajo, Apache, or Maidu baby adopted by a white family always had some "Indian inside," no matter how he or she was raised. Art's incremental calculus of identity parsed degrees of Indianness; to be fully Native American you had to have both the blood and the culture. He cited Ishi, and his grandmother, Sadie Foreman, too. They were "one hundred percent Indian," he said.

If Art insisted still on a link between biology and race, he had followed his heart in his own personal life. Once on the phone, he lamented the "thinning of the blood" in Native California by intermarriage, but then laughed that he was "a culprit myself," referring to his marriage to Lindy. Art's daughters Sadie and Shannon were only a quarter Maidu by blood. That didn't keep Art from taking his two girls to weekend gatherings at the roundhouse above Oroville so they could learn some of the old Maidu songs and socialize with others from the tribe. "But they're kind of split," Art said. "They're into horses. They want to be cowboys." Art hoped at least one of his daughters would follow in his footsteps as an advocate for Native American culture and community. "Somebody needs to carry it on. Otherwise it's all going to be lost."

By even the most relaxed standards for descent, then, was Ishi really the last Yahi? Was his tribe truly extinct? There have been efforts to rekindle parts of the Yahi way of life in recent decades after all. As a graduate student at Berkeley, Jean Perry had joined the team organized in the 1980s to complete the translations of Ishi's Yahi stories recorded and yet only partly translated by Edward Sapir in 1915. She spent several years studying Yahi grammar and vocabulary and listened for hours to the old museum recordings of Ishi's singing. This talented, thoughtful woman became the first person to translate Ishi's "Journey of the Dead" about Yahi death rituals, which Thomas Waterman had taken down phonetically without fully understanding the words. When I lunched with her one day in her hometown of Trinidad on California's north coast, Perry confessed that her Yahi was rusty by now, but that she believed it might still be good enough for her to converse with Ishi. "I used to dream in Yahi," she said. Now in her fifties, with some Cherokee ancestry herself, Perry did not regard Yahi as a dead language. It was still possible to master the rudiments of Ishi's tongue if you had linguistics training and put in the work.

The truth remains, of course, that the Yahi ceased to exist as a living society almost a century ago. No one will ever know the Yahi name for every shrub and rock by Deer Creek or what a Yahi felt at the sight of the moon and the stars. We have only fragments, the shards of a destroyed whole. Ishi's people held out in hiding for decades, but they ended among the hundreds of tribes in Native America swept away by the West's violent progress. Only a stray mention in some early letter or diary now testifies to the existence of many of this continent's long list of vanished peoples—at least twenty tribes in California alone. We know more about the Yahi than other lost cultures thanks only to Ishi's work with the anthropologists.

There was one other wild card in the deck of Ishi's possible descendants, however. Though Ishi's tribe was extinct as a culture, there might yet be living people with Yahi blood in their veins, constituting descent at the level of biology. After all, Yahi children had been seized by the nineteenth-century Indian hunters and adopted into white families. After massacring thirteen Indians in 1853, for instance, a band of pioneers divided up the little ones as the spoils of war. "Captain Rose took one child, Mr. Lattimer another, and the others were disposed of in the same charitable manner among the party," reported the *Tehama News and Record*. These children probably grew up learning little or nothing about their murdered parents or Yahi culture, but some of them probably married. Any modern-day descendant of those adopted Yahi would be Ishi's closest living kin, maybe even blood relatives, given the tribe's tiny size. That person would perhaps have better rights than anyone to Ishi's brain and the title of his rightful living heir.

Alfred Kroeber himself believed that other Yahi besides Ishi may have survived. One rainy day in the early 1880s, Kroeber knew from various accounts, a pair of cowboys came across two Indian girls, one about twelve and the other about eighteen, shivering with cold and fright in a cave near Mill Creek. The Speegle family, who owned land in Deer Creek's canyon, took in the girls and arranged for them to go to a boarding school at the reservation in Round Valley. The girls spoke no English when they were found, but the teacher at Round Valley wrote back to the Speegles that the girls were intelligent, popular with everyone, and already learning to play sports and read and write. According to the teacher, the older girl had told her roommate something of her life in the wild and the reason why she and her sister had taken refuge in the cave:

> *She was married, and had a baby about six months old, healthy and strong. Everyone in the camp loved the baby. She had gone out with her husband's sister, and some other young Indians to gather acorns. Their baskets were about full when it started to rain. They hurried back to camp. As they came in, they heard the baby scream. The Old Doctor was striking the baby with a heavy stick. Her husband ran to stop [him]. The Doctor killed him with one blow, and then turned and killed the baby. The sisters knew they were next. They ran to the creek [Mill Creek], [and] swam across. [They] followed a ravine where the rain water was running to wash their tracks out. The rain also made it impossible for the*

*Doctor to see them. They had reached the cave a few minutes before George and Frank [the cowboys] arrived. But they did not expect the luxury of a warm fire, a hot meal, and a dry bed.*

The remarkable account of the elder Mill Creek girl offers a rare glimpse into the world of Ishi and the other Indians still in hiding in the canyons. We have no way of knowing if the girl and her younger sister belonged to the same band as Ishi, but her story told of rage, fear, and violence at the interior of the reduced society of fugitives, perhaps unsurprising in the forced proximity of hiding. That the "Old Doctor" should have been pegged as the source of the trouble was not surprising, either. We tend nowadays to think of the traditional Native American medicine man as the purveyor of a benign, "holistic," and "spiritual" brand of healing. At least in California, however, the shamanism of the old days was also sometimes linked to fear, jealousy, and the uncertainty of hatred and poisoning. In many tribes, you'd consult a medicine man to find out who'd sent a malignant poison or tumor to harm you, have him extract it, and then send it back to your original persecutor or someone else. I would later meet several elderly Native Californians who told me that doctoring was one part of the past they were happy was gone.

Alfred Kroeber wondered if the Mill Creek girls were relatives of Ishi's, the other surviving Yahi. No one seemed to know what had happened to the sisters after they'd been sent to Round Valley. One account had it that the younger girl had fallen ill and died, and the other, nicknamed Red Wing, might have survived and moved elsewhere. Kroeber took the possibility seriously enough to write the superintendent of the Round Valley Reservation in 1914. He explained that he'd heard the tale of the two girls from local homesteaders, who believed they'd been found "in 1883, or not many years after":

*If true, it must have caused some interest and comment at the time, since the women must have been almost if not quite uncivilized, and moreover, their language must have been entirely different from that of any of the tribe settled on the Reservation. I am wondering whether your office has any record substantiating this story, or in the absence of any official record sufficiently detailed, whether there is anyone in the Valley remembering the occasion.*

No record exists of any reply to Kroeber's inquiry; it is likely he never learned anything more about Red Wing and her sister, since he never mentioned having done so in any of his own writings. Could Red Wing have been a sister of Ishi's? Or an aunt? And did she perhaps marry and now have living descendants, perhaps great-grandchildren? Here, again, lay at least the possibility of a bloodline straight back to Ishi and the Yahi—and the existence somewhere out there of a person or people who would have first rights to the stewardship of his body.

Around this time, I received a letter from Robert Martin. A retired real estate broker in Sacramento, Martin had seen my name in the newspapers in connection with Ishi's brain. In a furiously loopy hand, Martin informed me that he was happy that Ishi would be buried at last, yet also "very angry" about being excluded from the process. Why? Because he, Robert Martin, was of Yahi descent and therefore Ishi's closest living relative.

As Martin explained it, he was the grandson of a Yahi, a man named Snowflake. The legend of Snowflake and his peculiar name was first recorded by Stephen Powers, the nomadic nineteenth-century anthropologist. According to Powers, sometime around 1870 a pair of armed settlers had headed into the hills to hunt the Indians accused of murdering a white family near Chico. One of these men was Sandy Young, the head cowboy at the Bidwell Ranch and the man who later lynched Indian Ned for killing his close friend Hiram "Hi" Good, the so-called Boone of the Sierras. On their way into the wilderness, Young and his companion captured an Indian woman and her daughter, who promised to guide them to the murderers' camp. It was winter. By nightfall, a storm rose. It began to rain, then snow. Suddenly, the mother and daughter disappeared toward a nearby creek. An escape attempt, Sandy Young and his friend assumed. Instead, as Stephen Powers wrote:

> *there came floating out on the storm and the roaring [of the creek] a thin young squeal. The party had been reinforced by one. The hunters then grasped the situation, and, laughing, set about collecting some dry stuff and making a fire. They were benumbed and half-frozen themselves, and supposed of course the women would come in as soon as they observed the fire. . . . [but instead] the grandmother took the new-born babe, amid the almost palpable blackness of darkness, the sleeting, and the yelling winds,*

*and dipped it in the ice-cold creek. Again and again she dipped it, while now and then the hunters could hear its stout-lunged protest above the roaring. Not only did the infant survive this unparalleled treatment, but it grew excellently well. In memory of the extraordinary circumstances under which it was ushered into this world, Young named it "Snowflake," and it is living to this day, a wild-eyed lad in Tehama.*

A tall tale from frontier days? No record exists of the Yahi or any other Native Californians welcoming newborns with a dunking in a freezing stream. But Robert Martin insisted that the tale was true. By his account, Snowflake grew up to marry a white woman and together they owned the Pillchuck Mine west of the town of Redding. Martin insisted that he was this mixed couple's grandson, and thus a quarter Yahi. As the old man lamented in a letter to me, no one seemed to believe his claim. "My new nickname, is 'Wahtaurisi,' the Yana/Yahi word for the bastard that sits at the foot of the ladder—or a person of <u>No Moment</u>."

It was hard to know what to make of Martin. He sounded a bit obsessed and cranky in a way that did not inspire confidence. Even so, intrigued and wanting to learn more, I planned to accept Martin's invitation to visit on my next California trip. As it happened, this invitation was soon withdrawn. A Central Valley newspaper had been considering a feature on the old man. The reporter e-mailed me to check the truth of Martin's tale of Yahi ancestry. I replied that I had no way of knowing, but that Martin was worth interviewing in any event. Apparently expecting a more positive confirmation, the reporter canceled his interview with the old man, telling him that Duke University's Orin Starn doubted his Yahi ancestry. Martin was livid. He was certain that I had told the reporter he was a fraud. On learning what had happened, I wrote to explain, yet to no avail. Martin no longer wanted to speak with me.

I tried to repair relations one last time, although by then I'd spoken with a couple of other people who'd met Martin and doubted his claim. Martin had cooled off when I phoned him one evening, but he still refused to meet me. "You know," he said, "I learned in real estate that when a deal starts off bad, it always goes wrong in the end." Anyway, the U.S.A. was really the U.S.S., the U.S. of Selfishness, added the old man, and now suggested that I only wanted his story to make money from it somehow. Martin also now hinted that Snowflake, his putative grandfather, was Ishi's brother, making him a blood relative of the legendary

211 I Lines of Descent    211

Yahi; perhaps, he said, he'd someday share the proof his genealogy's details with his grandson, a student at Penn State. "Maybe then the truth will come out at last. I'm sure that Ishi knows God works in mysterious ways." I was forced to leave Martin's story without knowing whether it was true or not.

More than a month had passed since the Maidu trip to Washington. There was no announcement yet from the Smithsonian. I heard later that Robert Martin had contacted the Repatriation Office, apparently without convincing anyone there of his putative lineal relationship to Ishi. No real or self-declared descendant of any other adopted Yahi had stepped forward. Then what about Art Angle and his Oroville Maidu? Would the Smithsonian decide that they were more closely connected to Ishi's Yahi than any other surviving tribe? The evidence was sketchy and contradictory about the actual historical relationship between the Yahi and the Maidu. The tribes had been neighbors in the old times, but they spoke languages as different as French and Chinese. There were also those stories about bad blood between the Yahi and the Maidu in the nineteenth century. At the same time, however, Art's grandmother Sadie had her tale of aiding Ishi and perhaps other last Yahi survivors, a suggestion of friendlier ties. The Repatriation Office had to determine any rights of the Maidu to Ishi's brain from this spotty, conflicting information.

The possibility also remained that Ishi had Maidu blood. Even before it became relevant to Ishi's repatriation, the archaeologist Steven Shackley had proposed that Ishi's father or uncle could be Maidu or from some other neighboring tribe. Alternatively, the hypothetical Maidu relative might have been Ishi's mother. It has long been a mystery why Ishi chose to head toward Oroville at the end, despite the town's distance from Deer Creek. Art speculated it was because Ishi had relatives among the Oroville Maidu from whom he could expect help. I'd noticed Art's physical resemblance to Ishi from the start. What if Art happened to be related to Ishi? That would end the debate about the entitlement of Art and his people to Ishi's body.

In the meantime, the Smithsonian was feeling the heat. Not giving Ishi's brain to the Maidu was a "classic case of the insensitivity of government agencies and cultures towards the people we have abused," Phil Isenberg, a lobbyist for the Alliance of California Tribes, told the

*Los Angeles Times.* Art himself was upset that Ishi's brain was still in its glass jar back in Washington. It was also a lean time for Art's family. Only in the summer would logging begin, allowing Art to make good money again hauling logs off the mountains with his truck. On the phone with me Art wondered aloud about a lawsuit to force the Smithsonian's hand. A week later, he sounded depressed to the point of wanting to be rid of the entire affair. "I can't keep doing this," he said. "I've got to feed my family."

Only in April did the Smithsonian's intentions become clear at last. As the rains were greening the foothills of the Mother Lode, the California Legislature held a hearing in Sacramento, and I flew out to be there. The hearing took place in the domed white state capitol building, a miniature of the one in Washington. As the room filled with about a hundred people, I sat down next to Art's sister Rosalie, who had driven down from Oroville. The afternoon began with representatives from tribal groups—the Native American Heritage Commission and the Alliance of California Tribes, among others—calling for Ishi's repatriation. Art also pulled on his glasses to read a statement he'd prepared the night before. "We want to bring our brother home for a proper Native American burial in his homeland," he told the committee. Art was a bit awkward and uncomfortable in the limelight, yet he also seemed reenergized by the prospect of some kind of action by the legislature.

The Smithsonian's Tom Killion was also there. When his turn came to testify, Killion found himself under fire from committee chair Darrel Steinberg, a liberal Democrat who represented Sacramento. Why had the Smithsonian concealed its possession of Ishi's brain for so many long decades? Why didn't the museum just give the organ now to the Maidu for a proper Native American burial? The lawyerly, hard-driving Steinberg was concerned yet also grandstanding as Native America's brave advocate against Washington's insensitive bureaucrats. The normally collected Tom Killion stammered and flushed under the grilling, but he held his ground. He insisted that the Smithsonian had never concealed having Ishi's brain. The museum never knew anyone was searching for it, Killion said, and it was now working toward Ishi's repatriation with all due haste. A decision would be made soon about the rightful recipient of Ishi's brain. In response, Steinberg arched his eyebrows with theatrical skepticism.

Yet the higher drama did not unfold until the hearing was almost over. It came with the testimony of Mickey Gemmill, the man Tom

Killion had mentioned to the Maidu in Washington as being part Yana. Gemmill, in his fifties, was not tall, but he still looked tough and strong with a graying pony-tail under his black tractor cap and the air of someone you'd avoid in a barroom brawl. He explained that he was the Child Welfare Services Officer for the Redding Rancheria, a little reservation in the northern Sacramento Valley toward Mount Shasta. At that point, the hearing had already lasted more than four hours; one assemblyman, with a yawn, was checking his pager. Almost as soon as Gemmill began to talk, however, you could feel the hearing room wake up to attention. There was something about Gemmill's low, raspy voice, almost a whisper, that aroused an expectant curiosity about what he would have to say.

And, in fact, Gemmill had a riveting story to tell. Sometime in 1860s, he recounted, a party of Indians had killed a farm wife named Mrs. Dersch not far from the town of Redding. Whites blamed the Yana tribe, of which Ishi's Yahi were supposed to have been the southernmost subgroup. Most Yana had already been slaughtered, had perished from disease, or had been confined to reservations, but bands of settlers swore to lynch any found left in the valley. For many decades after, surviving Yana had concealed their exact ancestry. "It just wasn't a good thing to say," Gemmill explained. "You were inviting very bad things to happen to your people." His own grandmother was one-quarter Yana, Gemmill related, but only revealed this toward the end of her life. Formed in 1985, the Redding Rancheria was a composite of Wintu, Pit River, and Yana descendants, Gemmill said. Still more Yana descendants could be found in the Pit River Tribe, which had its offices sixty miles up Highway 299 from Redding in the town of Burney. Everyone in the hearing room could see it was not easy for Gemmill to relate this tale of fear, death, and concealed identity. He paused several times to gather his emotions along the way. That the story seemed so hard for this bear of a man to tell added much to its power and immediacy.

The hearing room was hushed at the end of Mickey Gemmill's testimony. There had been plenty of talk about Native California's destruction that afternoon. Unlike anybody else, however, Gemmill had traced a direct family link to the dark days of terror and hatred in the nineteenth century. His testimony also transformed the dynamics of Ishi's repatriation. If Ishi's Yahi belonged to a larger Yana tribe, then it appeared that Mickey Gemmill and others in the northern valley with some Yana blood could rightfully claim kinship to Ishi's people—and entitlement to his remains. When Darrel Steinberg gaveled the hearing closed, a couple of reporters angled over to buttonhole Gemmill, the afternoon's unexpected star.

I was also moved by Mickey Gemmill's compelling tale. And later, too, I found more information about the Dersch Massacre and its aftermath in old newspapers of that time. After a string of robberies and murders by roving Indians in the early 1860s, the mood of the settlers in the far northern valley had turned ugly, much as it had to the south in and around Chico and Oroville. The area east of Redding across the Sacramento River was once home to the northern band of the Yana people. Like Sam Batwi and his wife, the surviving remnants of the northern Yana had long since left the wild for jobs in the kitchens and fields of white ranchers and, according to the nineteenth-century folklorist Jeremiah Curtin, were "distinguished beyond others for readiness to earn money." Yet some settlers still suspected northern Yana of participating in the raids, and their rage at the murder of loved ones led them to want to be rid altogether of Indians no matter how "tame." A citizen's committee formed in the town of Millville on October 8, 1864. It gave the Indians east of the Sacramento ten days to leave. If any remained beyond that date, "it shall be the privilege of our company or citizens to exterminate or expel them."

The Indians had their defenders, especially among the ranchers who depended upon them in haymaking and the harvest. A counter-meeting was rapidly organized in nearby Churntown to pass a resolution that denounced the exterminationist intentions of the Millville committee "not only as inconsistent with humanity but directly in opposition to the best interests of the people of this portion of the country." A wholesale campaign of slaughter and removal was temporarily prevented. Two years later, however, about fifteen Indians raided the Dersch homestead; they shot down Annie Dersch as she was in the backyard mixing water and ash to make lye for soap, then made off with everything they could carry from the ranch house. A posse of "volunteers" rampaged in response from the little towns of Jelly's Ferry to Cottonwood and Millville, killing the Indians they found as they went. A few kind-hearted whites hid Indians in their haystacks and cellars, but as many as thirty were gunned down by the enraged settlers. It was now perilous to be an Indian of any kind in the Redding area. To be a northern Yana was especially dangerous, since vengeful settlers linked them to the Dersch killing, whether justly or not. It made sense that

Mickey Gemmill's grandmother and others would have concealed their Yana ancestry for years afterward.

As powerful as the story was, it was less clear to me that Mickey Gemmill and his people had any stronger right to Ishi's brain than did Art Angle and his Oroville Maidu. To be sure, the northern Yana ancestors of Gemmill and others in the Redding Rancheria and Pit River Tribe spoke their own dialect of the Yana language, and Ishi's Yahi was also a dialect of this same tongue. At least as far as I knew, there was nothing beyond that to show that northern Yana and the Yahi saw themselves as related in any way. The two groups lived more than fifty miles apart, and were not even neighbors, since the central Yana occupied the land between them. If anything, some evidence suggested that northern Yana and Yahi disliked one another. According to two early anthropologists, the northern Yana had looked down on the Yahi as a "wild, mean bunch." Archaeologist Jerald Johnson believes that northern Yana may have had closer relations with the Indians to their north—and even before contact were through intermarriage being absorbed into the Wintu and Pit River Tribes. For his part, Ishi disliked his translator Sam Batwi, the only northern Yana whom we know that he knew. They sometimes did not even understand each other, since the Yahi and northern Yana versions of Yana were not always mutually intelligible.

As treacherous as the question of Ishi's closest living relatives was becoming, the Smithsonian still had various options, perhaps even repatriating the brain to Mickey, Art, and their people together. Tom Killion had given no hint of the museum's intentions in his Sacramento testimony beyond promising that a decision would soon be announced. Less than two weeks later, the Smithsonian issued a statement at last. It recognized that "all California Native Americans feel a powerful connection with Ishi and a responsibility to see that his remains are united and given a proper burial." At the same time, the Smithsonian declared that it had decided to return "the human remains of Ishi" to "California's Redding Rancheria and Pit River Tribe, Ishi's closest living relatives." The transfer would "occur at the time and place, in the manner, of their choosing," the statement added. Art had been cut out of the repatriation. Killion and his staff had decided that Mickey Gemmill and his people were the rightful heirs of Ishi and his body.

The Repatriation Office released a longer report justifying the decision. As I read it over, I realized that the decision for the Redding Rancheria and the Pit River Tribe boiled down primarily to a single criterion, language. That Yahi was related to the northern Yana of Mickey Gemmill's ancestors was true enough, although neither Mickey nor anyone else spoke northern Yana any longer and Mickey was only one-sixteenth northern Yana in the first place. When two peoples speak dialects of the same tongue, they usually have common ancestors if you trace history far back enough. Yet it does not follow that those two peoples necessarily feel a kinship of any kind; they can sometimes even be enemies, like Belfast Protestants and Catholics. It was a stretch to conclude, as the Smithsonian did, that a "close common identity" existed between the Yahi and the other Yana groups on the basis of language alone. Under pressure for some sort of decision, the Repatriation Office had overlooked the evidence that the actual relations between the Yahi and northern Yana may not have been close or even good.

Importantly, however, the report carried the imprimatur of the Smithsonian, the largest and most distinguished scientific institution in the country. Museum officials, reported the *Washington Post,* "have identified living descendants of Ishi, the fabled Native American of Northern California, and are arranging to send his brain to those relatives." None of the many newspaper stories mentioned just how thin the line of descent was between Ishi and anyone at the Redding Rancheria or Pit River Tribe. Most reporters also neglected to say that the Redding Rancheria and Pit River Tribe were not the Indians who'd taken the initiative in repatriating Ishi in the first place. They'd only been drawn in when they were contacted by the Repatriation Office in its search for the rightful claimant to Ishi's brain. Art and the Oroville Maidu were the ones who had first cared enough to make a cause of Ishi's repatriation to Deer Creek canyon.

There remained an understandable rationale for the Smithsonian's decision, of course. The Redding Rancheria and Pit River Tribe had a real link to the Yahi, albeit based for certain only in language. And yet, it was also possible that Ishi had some connection to the Oroville Maidu. Both the northern Yana and the Oroville Maidu suffered through the same nineteenth-century terror as Ishi's people; and both now had latter-day descendents who felt a powerful kinship to Ishi and wanted to bring him back to California. Tom Killion and his staff struck me as fair-minded professionals. Even so, I thought they had made a mistake in this case. It was never quite clear to me why they'd felt compelled to choose between the Redding Rancheria and Pit River Tribe and the Oroville Maidu in the first place. I wished that the Smithsonian had pursued the option of a joint repatriation, which I later learned that the Repatriation Office's own guidelines allowed for and even encouraged. That was an arrangement that would have allowed a role in Ishi's repatriation to all of the Indians who felt a special stake in his legacy.

As it was, Mickey and his people had been entrusted to pick up the brain in Washington. They would also have to procure the ashes from the Olivet cemetery, and arrange at last a final funeral for Ishi's reunited body. "We're glad that the Smithsonian realized that they have no right to keep someone's brain in a jar full of formaldehyde," Mickey told Redding's *Record Searchlight*. "The California Indians have suffered greatly, but they are returning today—and working for survival in the new millennium."

I wondered how Art was taking the news. Art had invested so much of his own time and emotion in Ishi's repatriation that he'd developed a kind of proprietary sense of mission in the cause. I suspected that he was going to be very upset at having been left out in the cold by the Smithsonian. I called him several times over the next week. Nobody answered the phone.

# Fourteen

# ANCESTRAL GATHERINGS

It had been an eventful few months for me. In Peru a decade before, I had lived life intensely, sometimes dangerously. Even the capital city of Lima was a war zone in those days, with guerrilla bombings and army death squads in Jeep Cherokees dumping the mutilated bodies of kidnaped young leftists in the desert. We'd wake up past midnight in our downtown apartment to the echoing boom of the latest car bomb. On one expedition into the Andes, I almost walked into crossfire between police and guerrillas before cowering into a doorway, bullets whizzing down the cobblestoned street. As terrible as the times in Peru were, I felt I was doing some good in writing about the forgotten plight of villagers and in volunteer work with war refugees. I'd been more adrift since coming back to assume my professor's job at Duke University, and returned to Ishi without a fixed sense of purpose. Unexpectedly, however, I'd been drawn into the controversy over the brain of my childhood icon. The journey of Ishi's body back to California was not yet over. I wanted to see it through.

I finished my classes at Duke in May. After turning in grades, I flew back to California for the summer with our daughter, Frances, and our new baby, Raymond. Like everyone else, I'd been riveted by Mickey Gemmill's testimony just a few weeks before. I hoped to meet Mickey that summer, but I also knew he was being pestered by reporters and others about the plans for Ishi's funeral ceremony. Even so, I left a message at Mickey's office at the Redding Rancheria, which lay within the city limits of Redding, a far northern California town sprawled around Interstate 5 on the way up to Oregon. A few days later, Mickey returned my call. Why didn't I come up north that weekend? he said. Mickey was organizing an event called the Ancestral Gathering at Mount Lassen National Park. It would be a chance for me to meet people, he explained, and also to watch a Bear Dance planned for the occasion.

Leaving Frances and Raymond with my parents in Berkeley, I made the five-hour drive up to Mount Lassen National Park that Saturday. This high country park boasts emerald glacial lakes and wide green meadows crowned by the jagged volcanic peak of Mount Lassen itself. It was the high summer tourist season, and I joined the caravan of cars, minivans, and campers along the main park road past the steamy hot springs of Bumpus Hell and then Kings Creek Meadow, with a view far out across to Nevada and the Great Basin. The Ancestral Gathering was only for Indians and their guests. A little, hand-painted sign, "A. G.," pointed the way into the campground that Mickey and the other organizers had reserved for the weekend.

I found Mickey over in the pine trees chatting with a few other men. Although employed by the Redding Rancheria and with a bit of Yana and Wintu blood, Mickey traced his main ancestry to the Madeisi, a subgroup of the larger Pit River Tribe headquartered in a peeling trailer in the town of Burney in northeastern California. The Pit River Tribe was considerably less well-off than the Redding Rancheria, but both groups received some federal grant money and, more important, had their own casinos. The Redding Rancheria had the advantage of being located close to the heavily traveled Interstate 5 and in the more populated valley. Their Win-River Casino was profitable enough that plans were in the works with the Hilton Hotel Company for a tribally owned four-star hotel in Redding. The Redding Rancheria already owned a mini-mart and had also bought up prime land overlooking the Sacramento River.

The contrast between this new prosperity and older Indian destitution was striking indeed, and a sign of how much had changed in the past century. The visiting folklorist Jeremiah Curtin left a description of the pathetic condition of the Indians in Redding and the surrounding hills in the late 1880s following upon the Gold Rush. In search of any last surviving Yana, he struck out across the Sacramento Valley:

*the next morning I found the Yana camp, a few huts near the foot of pine-covered hills. There was no land for them to cultivate; all the land belonged to nearby farmers. The Indians were in a destitute condition, several were sick, and all were in rags. I began to work with Jack, the "chief." He told me a fine myth.*

Curtin complained later of other Indians demanding four dollars a story; yet he was also the good Eastern humanitarian, outraged by pioneer crimes. In the town of Yainax,

*a man from Lakeview came to the house where I was boarding. He was proud of having assisted in exterminating the Yana Indians. He told me that the white men, in the region where he was living at the time, formed a band and each man took an oath to spend fortune, and life, if necessary, in killing Indians. They killed as many Yana as they could.*

"The people of northern California despise the red race, root and branch," Curtin declared. "They know nothing whatever of their language, customs, or beliefs." Toward the end of his trip, Curtin was approached by a group of ragged Yana and Wintu who asked him to inform President Harrison "what homeless condition they were in, how white men drove them from place to place." Curtin later convinced the president to set aside a few small tracts of land for the Indians.

Even the Redding Rancheria's Win-River Casino was not so profitable as to make individual members wealthy, at least not yet. Mickey and others lived in low-end tract houses. The tribal office lay behind the Redding casino in a new, tasteful building with track lighting and earth tones. A friendly, thirty-something lawyer, the chair, Tracy Edwards, was the image of corporate competence and sat on the board of the Redding Chamber of Commerce and several local charities. In the halls at the Redding Rancheria, however, you'd also see big, more rough-cut, blue-collar men and women quick to kid one another and very much at home. There had been some reports of corruption and the mishandling of casino money elsewhere in the country, but I was impressed by the convivial, inclusive spirirt at the Redding Rancheria and the way it was putting its profits into a tribal health clinic, day-care program, and other social services.

The changing fortunes of Native California were visible in other ways, too. The California Nations Indian Gaming Association had become one of the most powerful lobbying organizations in the state capital. A number of tribes handed out hefty campaign donations—a total of more than ten million dollars to various local, state, and national candidates in 1998 alone—to gain political leverage for continued casino expansion and Indian interests in general. At the same time, the big money that Indians could hope to make from their video slot machines, blackjack tables, and other gambling-hall games were creating new tensions. Some tribes had closed their enrollment rolls to prevent others from joining and having to share profits; there were ugly fights that pitted Indian against Indian. The casinos also exacerbated the rift between the haves and have nots in Native California—namely, the 107 tribes that enjoyed federal recognition and the nearly equal number of other groups that had failed to persuade the Bureau of Indian Affairs that they really existed as functioning entities. Unrecognized tribes not only were frozen out of most federal aid but could not reap the benefits of the "new buffalo," as pundits called the casinos.

The casinos also reversed the roles of whites and Indians in some cases. Now tribes could be the moneyed, bullying heavyweights. The Rumsey Band of the Wintu west of Sacramento was pressing forward with a new hotel and casino complex over protests by local homeowners angry at the prospect of increased noise and traffic. Down near Palm Springs, the Agua Caliente Indians had used casino receipts to buy an off-reservation housing tract and shocked residents by jacking up their lease payments by as much as four hundred percent. A group called "Stand Up for California!" coordinated opposition to tribal gaming. The case against the casinos revolved around concerns about unregulated, runaway development and the negative social effects of expanded gambling operations statewide. Supporters countered that the U.S. Supreme Court had upheld the sovereign right of Indian tribes to gaming on their own land. They pointed to the tangible benefits of the casinos—the employment of whites and Indians alike in many backwater countries, the steep decline in Indian poverty and welfare dependency, and the rising charitable giving by more affluent, revitalized tribes to community causes. I knew that Orovilles' Mooretown Rancheria wrote sizable checks every so often to the Salvation Army, Special Olympics, YMCA, and several area schools.

A revision of official history and memory was also taking place. Although not offering a formal apology for the horrors inflicted upon the Indians of California during the first decades of statehood, Governor Gray Davis acknowledged in 1999 that his state's native peoples had "for too long been denied the respect they deserved." His administration supported some casino growth and inaugurated a memorial to

Native California, the first of its kind, in front of the capitol building in Sacramento. No doubt the desire to tap into the new tribal wealth factored into these common expressions of goodwill by politicians. Gray Davis, a Democrat, hoped to persuade tribes to turn over a percentage of new casino revenues to reduce the state's astronomical and politically explosive budget deficit. He had collected almost a million dollars in tribal campaign contributions when he first ran for governor and, early in his second term, would need to muster still more money to try to survive an unexpected recall election. I wondered if the zeal with which Cruz Bustamante, the lieutenant governor and one of the candidates to replace Davis in the governorship, and Darrel Steinberg, the state assemblyman, were championing Ishi's repatriation had anything to do with wanting to look good to Indian political donors. Even so, the eagerness of so many prominent elected officials to court Native California was a striking about-face from a century and a half before, when an earlier governor, Peter H. Burnett, declared that a "war of extermination" would have to be waged "until the Indian race becomes extinct."

Mickey Gemmill had witnessed these sea changes in the span of his own lifetime. He had devoted much of his life to the struggle for Indian rights in California and was a veteran of almost every landmark protest. After growing up in the tiny town of Big Bend forty miles east of Redding, he'd gone off to San Francisco State in the 1960s, become radicalized, and joined the occupation of Alcatraz Island, among the showiest and most publicized actions of the Red Power movement of that time. Mickey and his fellow Indian protesters—with TV cameras rolling and celebrity supporters on hand—had issued a funny, bitter proclamation of intent to "purchase said Alcatraz Island for twenty-four dollars (24) in glass beads and red cloth, a precedent set by the white man's purchase of a similar island about 300 years ago." The island was "more than suitable for an Indian reservation, as determined by the white man's own standards," because it had "no fresh running water" and "inadequate sanitation facilities," and its population had "always been held as prisoners and kept dependent on others."

In 1970, Mickey led another occupation, this time of land owned by the Pacific Gas and Electric Company in his native Pit River country. Outside supporters also joined this action, among them the Cree folksinger Buffy Sainte-Marie and a whole hippie commune from New

Mexico. "We are the rightful and legal owners of the land," the young Mickey told reporters. Skirmishes with sheriff's deputes, local police, and U.S. marshals armed with riot equipment and shotguns continued over the next year. Mickey also joined the takeover of an abandoned army base west of Sacramento for the Deganawidah-Quetzalcoatl University, the first Indian-run institution in the state. As controversial as the tactics were, these protests announced the resurrection of Indians as a force to be reckoned with in modern-day California.

Mickey's grandfather was white, and I asked him much later about his mixed ancestry and identity. Yes, he said, he had a "European" grandfather; but all his other relations were Indian and he'd grown up Indian in the hills near Big Bend: "I know where my people are buried," he said. "I know who I am." Unlike those seeking to embrace the fact of impurity and multiple identities, Mickey believed you had to make a choice. "You can't be two things at once," he insisted: "You got to be who you are." Being a mixed-blood had only caused trouble for his father, Jake, Mickey explained. As a schoolboy, Jake fought white kids who called him a "dirty, no-good Indian." Then back home he'd mix it up with Indian kids who called him "half-breed." That experience—the hazards of life in between the color line—led Jake to believe that future generations of Indians should stick together. "He told me never to marry a non-Indian," Mickey said. Jake became a professional boxer, and Mickey wasn't one to back down, either.

In his protest years, Mickey had fallen in love with and married an Eskimo woman, following her north. He worked on the oil pipeline while living in Alaska for most of the 1970s. When the marriage broke up, Mickey returned to northern California. He served as the chairman of the Pit River Tribe for a couple of years, then took his job at the Redding Rancheria, helping Indian kids from broken families. Mickey also got married again, this time to Valerie Wilson, a Wintu. Although still imposing, Mickey was by now in late middle age, with his gray pony-tail, bad back, and some extra pounds around the middle. His grandfather, Albert Thomas, was an old-time Indian doctor, and as a boy Mickey would go to the all-night sings in his family's roundhouse in Big Bend. Now Mickey led prayers at weddings, funerals, and other local events. He lived with Valerie in a working-class subdivision just north of Redding. They had four teen-aged children and Mickey drove down to work every morning at the tribal office.

•   •   •

I learned these details of Mickey's biography only when I got to know him better over the next few years. On the weekend of the Ancestral Gathering, Mickey was busy with other duties and didn't have time for much conversation. He shook my hand, then wandered off to greet some other new arrivals. Mickey's brother Arnold, a jeweler from the Lake Tahoe area, noticed that I was alone. Hospitably, he took me over to pitch my tent with the rest of the Gemmills. A high school basketball star until he blew out a knee, Arnold was still a fan. We sat down at a picnic table to chat about Duke's perennially powerful team. Arnold's wife, Janet, soon joined us. Janet was white, and at 6'3", as tall as I was. She had held a basketball scholarship at the University of Nevada–Las Vegas back in the 1980s and was even able to dunk. Too bad she and Arnold never had children, Janet said. "The kid would have been another Michael Jordan," she lamented.

Arnold told me he had been reading my fellow anthropologist Alfred Kroeber's *Handbook of the Indians of California* in his spare time. "The guy knew what he was talking about," he said. "Except," Arnold winked, "he only talked to the friendlies and not us hostiles." The Gemmill's Pit River Tribe up in the northeastern California badlands had a reputation for feistiness—and, in fact, Kroeber had never done any research there. A local Indian agent in 1878 described the tribe as "very numerous and very hostile," with "a great aversion" to confinement to a reservation. They were still by reputation a people with a mind of their own. What about Kroeber sending off Ishi's brain to the Smithsonian? I asked. The good-humored Arnold was philosophical. "Well, I don't really hold it against him personally. That's just what they did to us in those days."

I also asked Arnold about the Smithsonian's recent announcement that it would return Ishi's brain to the Redding Rancheria and Arnold's own Pit River Tribe. When I had finally reached Art Angle a few days before, he was upset and bitter about this latest turn of events, even mentioning the possibility of somehow challenging the Smithsonian in court. By contrast, Arnold was confident that the correct decision had been made. He related that he and Mickey had been talking one night about their grandmother and how her Yana blood made them Ishi's descendants. "They must have been tapping our phone," Arnold laughed. "Because the next day they announced that Ishi was coming back to us."

The climax of the Ancestral Gathering was that night's Bear Dance. After dinner, all of us there in the campground gathered in a wide circle around a stoked bonfire shooting sparks up toward the starlit sky. In a version still celebrated by the high country branch of Art Angle's Maidu, the Bear Dance takes place in early summer—a rite of world renewal symbolically connected to the emergence of the bears from hibernation with the winter's end. The Pit River version of the dance could be held at any time of the year; it sometimes took place outside, sometimes in a roundhouse, and was an occasion of communion between the animal, human, and spirit worlds. The dance began that night with a line of men and women ducking, stamping, and swaying into the clearing and around the fire in grass skirts, shell chokers, and other old-time regalia. Then came the Bear Dancers themselves, all eight of them rushing in at the same time making loud snorting noises. "They live with the bear skin; they fast with it; they sweat in it [in the sweat lodge]," Mickey said. "And when they dance, the spirit of the bear comes into them." The human forms of the dancers were almost completely concealed in the thick, hairy bear hides complete with claws and teeth. In the fire's shadows, it looked as if the animals really had come out of their dens that night.

I wasn't sure what Ishi would have made of this dancing, or of the Ancestral Gathering itself. By the time he was a man, the Yahi were too few to hold any Big Times, as such large and often intertribal gatherings later came to be called among California's Indians. At the same time, however, the young Ishi may have gone to such festivities right here on the shoulders of Mount Lassen, the traditional summer meeting place for area tribes. At the very least, Ishi knew that his own ancestors, decked in their finest regalia, had once come together to dance, flirt, trade news, gamble, and sing. Many Yahi villages had a roundhouse for these social occasions. In one story, Ishi related how Coyote's sister had readied herself by putting on a "string of white shell disk beads" and decorating her face with geometric designs of "red paint." Then the people and the animals had sung and danced, until the earth shook in every direction.

The Ancestral Gathering also celebrated the finish of a week-long run from Mount Shasta to Mount Lassen. Native America has produced its share of fine distance runners, most notably Billy Mills, a Lakota and the 1960 Olympic 10,000-meter champion. However, the marathon ending here at Mount Lassen was not a competition, but rather what Mickey called a "spiritual run" between northern California's two great volcanic peaks. The runners, mostly teenagers, had straggled into the campground earlier that afternoon. Some wore running attire, while others

were dressed in high-top sneakers, cut-off sweatpants, and baggy basketball jerseys. There was a gathering around the circle to congratulate
the runners, and each one introduced himself (only a couple of girls had
participated in the run). About a third of these young Indians were not
from the sponsoring Pit River Tribe or any local tribal group. One was
Pomo from Santa Rosa, north of the Bay Area; another was Paiute, a
Nevada tribe; there was also a Navajo (some twenty thousand Navajo
make their homes now in California, mostly in Los Angeles). One young
man said he was Aztec, a descendant of Mexico's pre-Columbian empire.

In their varied origins, the participants measured the rising phenomenon of pan-Indianism, the feeling of solidarity among the diverse
indigenous tribes of twentieth-century America. Everyone knows that the
very label "Indian" had been a European imposition at the start.
Lumping the native peoples of the New World into this generic category had originated with Columbus's improbable geographic mistake
(some "Indians" joke that it's a good thing that Columbus wasn't looking for "Turkey"). Eventually, however, the idea of being one people
was embraced by many Native Americans themselves. "We all belong to
one family," the Shawnee leader Tecumseh already proclaimed in rally-
ing other tribes to fight with the British in the War of 1812 to slow
American expansion. In the early twentieth century, the experience of
being thrown together in boarding schools further inculcated a sense of
commonality and connection among young Indians from diverse tribal
backgrounds. And the American Indian Movement, People of All
Tribes, and other protest groups of the 1960s and 1970s promoted a
vision of unity among Indians in the struggle for change.

Without exception, the men and women I'd met in the search for Ishi
felt a bond with other Indians. "We were the first people here. And we
suffered the same things," as Art once told me. Mickey believed in solidarity not only among Native Americans but among tribal peoples everywhere around the world. He was Native California's delegate to the
International Indian Treaty Council and had flown not long before to
New Zealand for the annual meeting of this global native rights coalition.
There Mickey had mingled with Lakota, Mayans, Miskitu, New
Caledonians, and Native Hawaiians; he'd run his fingers over the beautifully carved, sea-going canoes of the meeting's Maori hosts, and learned
how they'd lost their land when Captain Cook first seized the island for
the British. The Maori had been subjected to the domination of an
"empire-building group of people" just like his own Pit River Tribe, or so
Mickey summed up the link between the treaty council's varied groups.

Even so, some Native Californians were wary about imported, more generic brands of Indian culture and tradition. One concern was the spread of pow-wows like the ones sponsored by the Native American student organizations at U.C. Davis, Sacramento State, and other universities. A mix of show, dance contest, ceremony, family reunion, and crafts fair, these events have become ubiquitous in fairgrounds and school gyms almost everywhere across the United States. The pow-wow is a thriving twentieth-century invention that mixes and matches a variety of influences. The word comes from the Algonquin *pauau*, for "big meeting"; the style of the drumming and singing derives from Plains Indian culture; American patriotism crops up in the presentation of the Stars and Stripes during the Grand Entry of the costumed, and sometimes very skilled, dancers. You can order instructional videos of the latest dance and beadwork styles at powwow.com, fourwinds-trading company.com, and other web sites. A powwow is intertribal by definition and offers a chance to show off your talents, have a weekend of fun, and meet other Indians from around the country (the annual Lakota event in Pine Ridge, South Dakota, draws hundreds of dancers from as far away as Florida and New York).

Yet Mickey, Bruce, Rosalie, Art, and other older Native Californians seldom went to pow-wows. "It's fine for Indians from out-of-state," Rosalie explained. "But it's not really our California culture." By contrast to Eastern Indians like the Tuscarora and Cherokee who first encountered the British almost half a millennium ago, the Maidu and other northern California peoples have been in contact with outsiders for the far shorter span of a century and a half. For this reason, you can still find men and women in California who can speak the old languages and know something of the aboriginal way of life—connections to the past that also have grown slimmer with each elder's passing. Lorraine Frazier, the Maidu activist who'd been with us at the Smithsonian, worried that pow-wows were drawing a young generation of Native Californians away from their own heritage. "They like the noise, color, and flash of the pow-wow. They think the traditional dances are boring."

A loyalty to Pit River custom was clear at the Ancestral Gathering. The event was about preserving the "ways of our people," Mickey said when he invited me. At first, I was puzzled that somebody had brought along a big Plains drum. A group of men was circled around the taut buffalo skin, pounding out a deep rhythm in the late afternoon. And yet, as if everyone knew that this imported instrument was inappropriate in a traditional Pit River ceremony, the Plains drum fell silent for the Bear Dance. Here the dancers circled the fire to the structured cacophony of reed whistles and clapper sticks. It was the sound of northern California's native music, unlike anything familiar to most American ears. Mickey bristled later when I asked whether the Bear Dance had changed with outside influences over the last century. "It's the way the elders taught," he insisted, "and the way we've always done it."

That Mickey and others were so committed to preserving their tribal traditions was predictable enough in one sense. In recent decades, the yearning to reconnect to their real and imagined roots has grown powerful among Americans of every background, a celebration of multiculturalism and heritage jostling against the old ideal of the melting pot. In this vein, Mormons every year reenact the harrowing trek of their nineteenth-century forbears to the promised land of Utah. African-Americans fly to Ghana to visit the slave forts where their ancestors were held before the Middle Passage. The reading room at Washington's National Archives fills with people seeking information about genealogy and the history of their families. The upheaval of today's fast-paced, mixed-up world can sharpen the longing for the meaning and continuity that knowing your past can offer.

Among Indians in California, I found varied motivations for the interest in heritage. One of Mickey's grandmothers, he told me, was "bought—B-O-U-G-H-T—by a white family at the age of eight. My other grandmother was kidnapped at twelve. All by white people. They weren't nice things that happened." The near destruction of his people and culture had sharpened Mickey's commitment to saving the Bear Dance and other Pit River traditions from oblivion. "It's about preserving what was almost taken from us," Lorraine Frazier explained, "and making a way for young people to learn about what's still left." Along with the Maidu language classes, Lorraine had organized a basketweaving course in Oroville, with ten pupils. She and other activists hoped that learning to speak Maidu, spending time in the sweat lodge, or even going to a pow-wow could offer young Indians an alternative to drugs, alcohol, crime, and a life behind bars (more than two thousand Native Americans are in California's prisons, and they even have their own gang, the "Skins"). "Tradition, Not Drugs" was already a catchphrase of the earlier Red Power movement.

There was pleasure involved, too, even a palpable joy. The linguist Jean Perry recalls how much her elderly Yurok in-laws still enjoyed speaking the language and retelling the myths. "It's hard," Perry said, "for outsiders to understand just how much a lot of older Indians just love their traditions." You could feel that attachment in the spirited energy of the young Pit River Bear Dancers—or in the silent concentration of a master basketmaker like Myrtle McKay Chavez as she wove golden sedge grass between dyed black bulrush root into a stunning design. In my eyes, the traditions of Native California were human treasures as much as a Raphael Madonna or a Michelangelo marble. That pleasure should be taken in knowing something of these skills, languages, and ceremonies was only natural.

Yet no one seemed to be deceived about just how little survived of the old Indian way of life. Unlike his brother, Mickey had never read Kroeber, but he used the identical image of fragmentation that the famous anthropologist had employed in describing Native California after the Gold Rush. "No one knows the old way of life anymore," Mickey said: "It's bits and pieces." Still, Mickey tried to do things as much as possible the way he'd learned them as a boy in Big Bend. That meant, for example, using instruments only in their appropriate setting. "It should be just the clapstick in the sweathouse; the earthdrum [a hollowed log] in the roundhouse; and a rattle or clapstick for stories or dances." Unlike Lorraine, Mickey was not a Christian, and he was proud his family "never had anything to do with the missionaries." A streak of messianism ran through Mickey's loyalty to native tradition. "When this world ends," he once told me, "certain people will survive, and it'll be the ones who follow the original teachings."

Like it or not, Mickey also knew that flexibility was sometimes necessary in a changing world. He'd use sage from southern California deserts to smudge the sick with purifying smoke, for example, or make prayer offerings of corn even though the plant was not native to Pit River country. "You have to be practical," he said, and saw such sharing between Indians as "how things change." If his people were now recovering from the trauma of conquest, it was inevitable that "we're not going to come out looking just the same." Mickey knew his own children—a generation further away from the genocide of the nineteenth century and lodged squarely within the new world of videogames, computers, and trips to the mall—would make their own choices. Michael, Mickey's grown son from his first marriage, wasn't especially interested in his Pit River heritage. He had gone to Nevada and Canada for Plains Indian-style Sun Dances that demand fasting and flesh-piercing from their participants. Mickey and Valerie's four teenaged children were sometimes too busy with their social lives to go to tribal events. "You can't control your kids," Mickey admitted, sounding just like any other American father who has learned the lessons of parenthood.

I never felt as comfortable around Mickey as I did with Art, and yet in later years I'd stop by his house on my way up to our family cabin in the Siskiyou Mountains. Mickey would talk for hours over the din of the TV and the comings and goings of his children and their friends. My most lasting image of him, however, remains the night of the Bear Dance. As an organizer and the master of ceremonies, Mickey had stepped forward to say a few words just before the dancers made their dramatic entry. His face aglow in the bonfire's orange light, he raised his shaman's eagle wing above his head. Mickey still exuded the fire of his young Red Power days as well as a bit of that storied Pit River prickliness and pride. The firelight projected the aging man's big shadow into the pine trees as if he were a latter-day Indian prophet. "The United States Army tried to conquer our people," Mickey intoned. "But they never did. We're still here. We'll always be here."

I still wondered that weekend about Ishi's repatriation. There were already rumors about disagreements within the Pit River Tribe about just when and how to proceed. The tribe was a coalition of eleven bands lately divided by the contested election of a new chairman that had shut down the tribal office for several weeks. "Too many chiefs, not enough Indians," Art's sister Rosalie chuckled when we talked about this on the phone one night. "We have that problem down here in Oroville some-times, too." As the child welfare administrator for the Redding Rancheria as well as a member of the Pit River Tribe, Mickey was a bridge between the groups and the point man for Ishi's repatriation. I guessed that he'd find a way to accomplish the task in the end.

I rose at dawn on the morning after the Bear Dance. Except for a cou-ple of sparrows chattering and pecking at the potato chip and Oreo crumbs on the nearest picnic table, the campground lay still in the early mountain light. A drowsy teenager trudged to the portable toilet, but everyone else was still asleep, the dance having lasted far into the night. Some people slept in their tents, a few on sleeping bags out in the open. One family nested in a pile of blankets in the bed of their pickup. Feeling bleary-eyed myself and yet contented to have been there that weekend, I got on the road back to Berkeley.

# Fifteen

# GRIZZLY BEAR'S
# HIDING PLACE

W e were moving toward closure with Ishi, at least to his body's return to California. I was hopeful that Mickey and his people would soon proceed with the funeral. For me, however, there was still one major expedition yet to be made. It was a trip to *Wowunupo Mu Tetna*, or Grizzly Bear's Hiding Place, the hideout in Deer Creek canyon where Ishi and his little band of survivors had concealed themselves from the world for so many decades. Like so many others who had fallen under Ishi's spell, I had dreamed about making the journey to this very special place ever since my Berkeley childhood. I did not want to leave Ishi's story without a pilgrimage to this last refuge of his people, a spot that has always been cloaked in considerable mystery and secrecy.

My ancestor anthropologist Alfred Kroeber had also very much wanted to make the Deer Creek expedition. Kroeber's plan was to visit the area with Ishi to learn more *in situ* about what the Yahi's former "primitive" life had been like. Thomas Waterman and Saxton Pope Jr. were also enthusiastic about going. Yet Ishi had resisted the idea when Kroeber and the others first proposed it. Well settled in San Francisco by then, he feared being abandoned again to the wild, or so Kroeber believed. Surely, too, Ishi had mixed feelings about his former homeland. Deer Creek was his birthplace and had been his people's territory for thousands of years. It was also where they had been massacred and forced into hiding. Ishi, an urban Indian now, had made a new life in the old Victorian museum with its carved totem pole in front and view out to Golden Gate Park and the Pacific Ocean. To return to Deer Creek threatened to revive painful memories of his family and people's fate.

Somehow Kroeber and the others managed to persuade Ishi, apparently reassuring him that they would not leave him there. As the date neared, however, a snag arose. The provisions purchased for the trip had been stacked in a museum storeroom filled with old bones, among them the same Egyptian skeletons that Kroeber would later donate to the Smithsonian along with Ishi's brain. Ishi objected that such proximity to the remains of the dead would contaminate the food. According to Theodora Kroeber, Saxton Pope's assurances that the packages were too tightly sealed to be tainted calmed the dubious Ishi, who respected his doctor friend as a *kuwi*, or medicine man.

Albert Elsasser, Kroeber's former student and colleague, gave me a different version of the same incident. Elsasser said that Kroeber and the others appeased Ishi by telling him they had bought new food, but just took the old food on the trip. If so, the deception recalled the earlier conduct of Kroeber's mentor, Franz Boas, with the Eskimo boy Minik. Recall that Boas had his staff wrap a log in a blanket to trick the little child into thinking that his father was receiving a proper Eskimo burial when, in truth, the corpse was boiled down to bones for the museum collection. Boas, Kroeber, and others were sounding the call for respect of other cultures, but that respect had limits. The anthropologists were sometimes even willing to lie to their "uncivilized" wards to have their own way, or, if Elsasser had it right, to avoid the inconvenience and expense of ordering new provisions.

Kroeber, Ishi, Waterman, Pope, and Pope's young son trekked back into Deer Creek canyon in May 1914. Once back in his native haunts, Ishi appears to have enjoyed himself. During the day, he swam in the emerald waters of Deer Creek, with little Saxton Pope Jr. clinging to his strong shoulders. Starvation had been a constant threat in Ishi's former life, but on this trip the food was plentiful—tins of mock turtle and oxtail soup, almonds and ginger snaps, dried eggs and meat. After dinner around the campfire, Ishi entertained his companions from his vast repertoire of Yahi songs. Pope led choruses of *Gunga Din* and *Mandalay*, British colonial classics that for whatever reason were Ishi's favorite songs in English.

The trip allowed the anthropologists to learn a great deal from Ishi. After the flurry of notetaking and recording during Ishi's first few weeks in San Francisco, Kroeber had been drawn back to his administrative and teaching duties as well as research connected to Egypt, Peru, and the southwestern United States. Here in the hills, Ishi was once again the center of attention. He guided Kroeber and the others to old village sites, taught them the names for dozens of animals, plants, and places, and took them to a rock pile where he'd long ago concealed a big bear hide.

"Have a good camp, fine weather, and Ishi is holding back nothing," Kroeber reported to Edward Gifford in San Francisco. Language seemed to be the only remaining barrier. One morning, Ishi led Pope and the anthropologists up to Grizzly Bear's Hiding Place beneath the rust-red cliffs under Deer Creek Flat. "Had him to his old houses yesterday," Kroeber said of their climb to the secret Yahi encampment, "and he told us more than we could understand." One wonders just what Ishi wanted to tell the anthropologists about the last years of his people and their life at Grizzly Bear's Hiding Place.

Kroeber was pleased enough with the trip to issue a press release on returning to the Bay Area. The expedition had been "one of the most successful ever undertaken by the university, and will add much to the storehouse of anthropological information being accumulated by the institution." An additional pay-off was to squash the persistent Sacramento Valley rumors that Ishi was a fake cooked up by the big city professors. "ISHI, INDIAN, IS EDUCATING COLLEGE PROFESSORS IN HILLS," headlined the *Sacramento Leader*. "Pioneer white men . . . who have believed that Ishi was counterfeit since his capture in Butte county, now are satisfied he is what is claimed for him." Ishi had shown that he knew "the maze of rugged hills better than any living white man . . . knew it like a book, in fact." Other valley newspapers still had a bit of the old pioneer contempt for Indians. Ishi had been one of the "wild and bloodthirsty Mill Creek Indians," the *Oroville Daily Register* reminded its readers.

After two weeks in the wilderness, the party had come back down to Vina, a tiny town in the flatlands just beneath the Yahi foothills. There Ishi mingled with a friendly throng of curious townspeople, second- and third-generation descendants of the pioneers who had exterminated his people. Whatever his inner thoughts, Ishi was courteous and even offered his stock demonstration of Yahi archery before the Bay Area–bound train whistled into the station. Once aboard, Ishi stuck his head out the window and waved his hat to the crowd. In an English perfect except for a missing *t*, he shouted: "Ladies and genelman, good-bye."


At the start of the search for Ishi's brain, I never thought I would have a chance to go to Grizzly Bear's Hiding Place. Only a handful of people have ever been there. Alfred Kroeber had described what the camp looked like and even photographed Ishi there on their 1914 trip, but he left no detailed directions. Later in the twentieth century, many hikers and amateur historians would try to locate the remains of the secret village, with every failure only adding fuel to their obsession. (One searcher had gone so far as to begin a poem about his frustrated quest: "Bear's Den, Bear's Den, Holy Grail of Modern Men.") For many years, it looked as if the exact location of Ishi's last refuge might be lost forever like a tiny Yahi Atlantis.

Only some skillful detective work by two men, Brian Bibby and Jim Johnston, finally solved the mystery. Bibby was a well-respected activist and scholar of Native California; his old friend, Jim Johnston, the man who'd told me about Art Angle, was the chief archaeologist for the Forest Service in the area. Their first clue was a little-known 1914 photograph showing Ishi, dressed in shirt and pants, his long hair in a pony-tail, kneeling on a rock by Deer Creek. His hand pointed upward toward Grizzly Bear's Hiding Place. In 1989, Bibby and Johnston managed to locate this exact rock. Yet it took a wildcat fire two years later—a late summer blaze racing down Cohasset Ridge into Deer Creek canyon—to lead them to the site itself. With the brush burned away, Bibby and Johnston found Grizzly Bear's Hiding Place at last, on a shelf about an acre in size not far above the creek.

The Berkeley filmmaker Jed Riffe chronicled the search for Grizzly Bear's Hiding Place in *Ishi the Last Yahi*, skillfully editing his well-received documentary to hide all clues to its exact location. Those coordinates remained a secret known only to Riffe, Bibby, Johnston, and a few others involved in Riffe's film. They wanted to protect Grizzly Bear's Hiding Place from being trampled by the curious and from potential looters who might dig for arrowheads and other Indian artifacts. It was decided that anyone wanting to visit Grizzly Bear's Hiding Place would have to go through Jim Johnston, the supervising Forest Service archaeologist.

I'd become friends with Riffe when we were with the Maidu in Washington. Riffe offered to guide me to Grizzly Bear's Hiding Place, and we secured Jim Johnston's permission for our expedition. I thought the trip would also interest the parties involved in Ishi's repatriation. Art was still upset about the Smithsonian's decision to turn over Ishi's brain to Mickey Gemmill and his people, but he was curious anyway about Grizzly Bear's Hiding Place and agreed to go. Before leaving the Ancestral Gathering, I also asked Mickey along on the trip. I thought the week together might possibly be a chance for Mickey and Art to get to know each other, maybe even plan Ishi's funeral together if it was not too late. When I told Mickey the journey to Grizzly Bear's Hiding Place would be a slog through the brush, he chuckled that he'd rather fly in by helicopter, but that he'd go anyway. Jim Johnston also offered to accompany us. To avoid the summer heat, we set the date for October, a couple of months away.

I made arrangements for the trip between my classes back in North Carolina. We planned to enter the canyon from the trailhead upstream, but it was still almost twenty miles across very rough terrain in what was now the protected Ishi Wilderness area. We couldn't easily carry the necessary food and water for the week's expedition on our backs. So I arranged for a mulepacker to haul our supplies. Dan Wells, a native of the valley town of Corning, had run cattle and logged the hills since he was a teenager. He had also carried the supplies for Jed Riffe's crew during the filming of *Ishi the Last Yahi.*

One thing I failed to anticipate was the forest fires. It had been a hot summer with little rain. A rash of wildfires had killed eight people, choking northern California in ashy smoke. One night shortly before our scheduled departure, Mickey Gemmill called to cancel. He couldn't even see across the street in his subdivision, he said. Although sorry to lose Mickey, I realized later that it was for the best, when I saw how hard the walk was into the canyon. Mickey had a serious, degenerative back injury from a stint as a Bay Area construction worker. There was no way he could have made it to Grizzly Bear's Hiding Place, except perhaps by the helicopter he'd joked about.

Even though a fire was raging just a few miles from his house in Oroville, Art Angle still wanted to go. "Our people used to burn off the brush so the fires wouldn't be that bad," he grumbled. I also checked in with Dan Wells, the mulepacker. He had reports of still another fire somewhere near Mill Creek. He called back a few days later after a reconnaissance trip. The fire had not jumped into Deer Creek's canyon. We would meet on Monday at the trailhead. Art could not afford a full week away from his truck during this busy fall time in the logging season. He and his daughter Sadie planned to ride in on their own horses to meet us in the middle of the week.

I flew out from North Carolina to the Bay Area that weekend. In Berkeley, I met up with Jed Riffe and my father, who had decided to come along with us to Grizzly Bear's Hiding Place. I had feared that Jed would also cancel out of the trip, but he was too much the enthusiast to let a few wildfires interfere with his plans. With his long white hair and a Texas twang from his childhood on a cattle ranch, Jed looked a bit like Wild Bill Cody. He had turned hippie and anti-war activist in the sixties and soon abandoned the Bible Belt for the countercultural promised land of the Bay Area and an eventual career in filmmaking. Like most independent filmmakers, Jed struggled financially, but he had made a name for himself with his gregarious personality and several first-rate documentaries about Native Americans. For almost ten years he had worked on *Ishi the Last Yahi*. The film, his biggest success, had been shown on PBS and won several awards.

The Cohasset Highway winds out of Chico up toward Deer Creek. Jed was driving and he gunned his old SUV around the turns, barely slowing when the paved road gave way to a dusty red-dirt track rutted by pickup and logging trucks. A last plunge in the road took us down to our trailhead, by an old steel bridge across the swift-falling waters of Deer Creek. Dan Wells was waiting there with his mules out of their trailers and ready to go. We started out right away to cover as much ground as possible before dark.

It must be admitted that Jed, my father, and I were not the most athletic trio of outdoorsmen. I was in decent shape, but I'd just come down with the flu. The chills and hot flashes added to the almost hallucinogenic intensity of that week in Ishi country. As for Jed, he was in his fifties, with asthma, a bum knee from his high school football days, and a few extra pounds around the middle. Although he was too proud to complain, I heard him wheeze and noticed the color was draining from his face. My father had just turned sixty. He had hunted and fished in his youth in Modesto, but his only recent exercise was the short walk from home to the Berkeley campus. Yet he still proved more resilient that day than Jed or me, a slender, bearded figure in a black fisherman's hat pressing forward like a grizzled mountain man across the Overland Trail.

Our guide, Dan Wells, was a tough cowboy and Vietnam veteran straight from central casting. He had Agent Orange burns up his shins, packed a Colt 45 as if ready for action in some new range war, and shared the political views of his favorite talk show host, Rush Limbaugh. "Dan Wells, Diversified Services," his card read. These services included running sheep and cattle, fence and road-building, and guiding fishing and hunting expeditions. Loading his animals and other backcountry skills came as second nature to Dan, just as they had been to the Gold Rush buckskinners. Dan was a modern mulepacker, however. He carried a cell phone and other high-tech accoutrements. In an emergency, Dan said, eyeing Jed and me as if one or both of us might collapse at any moment, he could call in a helicopter from Redding. He soon boosted the failing Jed onto an extra mule as a preventive measure.

Our trail followed Deer Creek for a few miles and then ripped up a hot, sandy hogback without the amenity of switchbacks. Then the way descended a ridge between Deer Creek and Dye Creek, with the vast Sacramento Valley spread out in the hazy distance. We were in the classic foothill country of dry grass and stunted oaks. Black lava boulders dotted the land like meteors fallen from the sky, but they were actually a product of this country's violent terrestrial geology. More than a million years ago, immense sheets of lava mud encrusted with rocks of every size had oozed down from the high country volcanos. Then the rains of countless winters had melted away the mud to leave the rocks within it still perched across the hills. When Ishi's ancestors arrived about four thousand years ago, it had already been hundreds of thousands of years since the last lava flows. Even so, Yahi mythology described a world of fire and ash at the dawn of time. Grizzly Bear "rose up, floated upon the air," chanted Ishi in one of his stories about the ancient days of people and the animals: "He saw fire in the south, streaming up, blazing."

We set up camp that night on the north rim of Deer Creek canyon. A much smaller yet still impressive version of Arizona's Grand Canyon, it gaped before us a couple of miles wide. Jed took us out to a promontory a few hundred yards from our camp to point out the approximate location of Grizzly Bear's Hiding Place on the other side of the gorge. It was hard to see much of anything that far away through the day's last, smoky gray light.

Dan's dogs were barking with excitement when we got back to camp. They'd sniffed out a rattlesnake under the tent I was sharing with my father. It had slithered away into the rocks before Dan could get to it with a shovel. Although the weather was still warm, the rattlesnakes were already denning up in preparation for the cold winter, Dan explained. The tent must have looked like a promising place for hibernation to this reptile. In 1914, Alfred Kroeber and his companions had killed and roasted a rattlesnake with macho bravado, but Ishi had refused to break the Yahi taboo against *kemna*, as the rattlesnake was called. Even the would-be white adventurers admitted later that the meat was a little greasy and tough for their taste.

At least in some ways, these hills were a wild, forbidding corner of the world. We saw five more large rattlesnakes that week. Ropy and muscular, they had green and black skin that camouflaged them perfectly against the lichen-splotched lava rock. There were also still mountain lions, black bears, red-tailed hawks, and plenty of other wildlife in the hills. No cabin or road lay anywhere around for miles (although one rancher was rumored to be growing marijuana up a side canyon). The Yahi knew how to make the most of this rocky land, but the pioneers had much preferred the fertile valley below. A century after Ishi had left Grizzly Bear's Hiding Place, the area was a wilderness saved by its own inhospitability from the voracious sprawl of freeway, mall, and subdivision that has been my home state's modern curse.

I had never realized just how close Grizzly Bear's Hiding Place had been to the Sacramento Valley. The Yahi hideout was a mere ten miles as the crow flies from the town of Chico. It was less than five miles from Grizzly Bear's Hiding Place down to the mouth of the canyon where the rushing waters of Deer Creek slow into a languid little river that spills onto valley farmland. Craggy and forbidding though the canyon may have been, it was simply amazing that Ishi and his band escaped detection for so long in such close proximity to the white world. At least in the early twentieth century, the Yahi did not have the protection of hundreds of empty forest miles still then enjoyed by tribes in the Amazon like the Kayapo and Xavante.

Ishi and the others learned to avoid leaving the slightest trace of their presence. They kept their fires small, retrieved milkweed snares and arrows, and stayed off the sandbars on the creek so as not to leave footprints. In precontact times, the Yahi typically camped by creeks, close to water for drinking, cooking, and washing. As the name indicates, Grizzly Bear's Hiding Place was almost certainly not a spot that Ishi's people had ever before inhabited. Retreating to this abandoned bear den up away from the water was an emergency measure when the creekside became too exposed. Many whites must have come up or down Deer Creek chasing lost sheep, hunting, or fishing without knowing that a silent band of Indians was observing them from the brush just a long stone's throw above.

Only by chance was Grizzly Bear's Hiding Place detected at last. Late on the afternoon of November 5, 1908, three surveyors from the Oro Power and Light Company were picking their way back up the creek to their camp. By then, the population of California had swelled to more than two million. To meet the new demand for electricity, power companies were damming Mother Lode streams, including the Feather River, Pit River, Tuolomne, and Trinity. All in their twenties, the surveyors—Edward Duesning, Alfred Lafferty, and Robert Hackley—were there to gauge Deer Creek's hydroelectric potential.

Suddenly, Robert Hackley later recalled, the three men spied a "curious figure standing, half-naked, close to the water and only about fifty feet away." When this "strange-looking man had brandished a spear and muttered in a threatening manner," the surveyors fled in fright, recalling the stories of "wild and dangerous Indians" in these parts. The man the surveyors saw was almost certainly Ishi, probably fishing with his harpoon with the canyon already deep in purple shadow. He and the other Indian survivors were always most vulnerable creekside, since the noise of the rushing water made it hard to hear any approaching stranger. Ishi must not have noticed the three men approaching until it was too late to hide.

The surveyors made it back to camp with their story. Early the next morning, the men and their cowboy guides returned and picked up a faint trail. As they broke into Grizzly Bear's Hiding Place with guns drawn, the party of whites saw two Indians fleeing across a rockpile. There was an old man, Ishi's uncle, helped along by the middle-aged woman who was Ishi's wife, sister, or perhaps cousin. According to what Ishi told Saxton Pope, his uncle had a foot that was lame from being caught in a steel bear trap. It must only have been because they knew the terrain so well that he and the woman were able to get away.

The intruding whites had found Ishi's mother a bit above the little brush houses of the concealed camp. She was so small, wrapped in her old rags, that Harry Keefer, the cowboy guide who first found her, thought he had uncovered a child. "Here we are, papoose!" he later recalled exclaiming. When Keefer came closer, he saw his mistake. "Her face was dry and yellow," the *Chico Record* reported, "and the party judged that she must be over 100 years old." The men gave the old woman a drink of water and tried to reassure her that they meant her no harm, but they also scooped up three fur capes, arrows, mortars, and a number of other items they found in the camp as trophies of their discovery. When the men departed at last, they left Ishi's mother where she lay in the expectation that the other Indians would come back to care for her. She was gone when the surveyors and their guides returned the next day for a last look around.

The discovery of Grizzly Bear's Hiding Place made headlines in the local valley newspapers. "INDIANS LIVE IN WILD STATE ON DEER CREEK," reported the *Oroville Daily Register*. For Ishi and the others, however, the events of 1908 were a catastrophe. The surveyors and their guides had stolen the arrows, baskets, fishing nets, and other basic equipment that Ishi's band needed to survive. Although we do not know how much longer she lived, Ishi's mother must have been in constant pain, and unable to care for herself. That winter was coming made matters even worse. The last surviving Yahi had to make it through without even the fur capes that were their only protection against the bone-chilling cold.

In a strange twist, Ishi was to meet one of the men who looted his camp again, this time under very different circumstances. Jack Apperson, a local rancher and cowhand, had been one of the three guides hired by the surveyors in 1908. When the party ransacked Grizzly Bear's Hiding Place that year, Apperson had claimed a large raccoon and wildcat skin cape. This same old cowboy was also contracted as a guide by Alfred Kroeber for his 1914 Deer Creek expedition with Ishi and the others. We have no reliable record of Ishi's reaction upon meeting Apperson six years after the plundering of Grizzly Bear's Hiding Place, or even whether he recognized him. For his part, however, Apperson never volunteered to give Ishi back the goods he'd stolen. Alfred Kroeber had to haggle with Apperson to buy back the cape, an otter skin quiver, and a few other things. Harry Keefer, the guide who'd found Ishi's mother, never did relinquish the cape and six arrows he'd taken from Grizzly Bear's Hiding Place. They later became part of a private

family museum that included hundreds of Indian arrowheads and baskets from various tribes, the mounted trophy heads of a tiger and moose,
an umbrella stand made from an elephant's leg, and other "curios" from
around California and the world.

I slept little on the first night of our trip, too restless with fever and the
emotion of being in the heart of Ishi country. When I awoke the next
morning, Jim Johnston was just coming into view over a ridge. As an out-
doorsman of the old school, the Forest Service archaeologist traveled
without the pricey equipment hawked these days to weekend hikers.
He carried an army surplus canteen and an old aluminum-framed backpack. Jim was accompanied by two other men, Brian Bibby and Jerry
Johnson; the three of them were supposed to have met us at the trailhead the day before but had been delayed and not started until late
afternoon. They'd camped back up the trail and risen early to catch up
with us now at the rim of Deer Creek canyon.

I felt lucky to have Jerry, Jim, and Brian along; each was an expert
about Ishi in his own way. The bald, bearded Jerry Johnson was the
leading specialist in the archaeology of the Yahi. Almost sixty, he had
been slowed by a stroke a year before but was still full of life and energy.
Jim Johnston and Brian Bibby were the two friends who had rediscovered Grizzly Bear's Hiding Place. Brian, in his forties like Jim, was a
quiet, black-haired man who was part Indian himself. He spoke bits of
Miwok, Maidu, and Nomlaki and belonged to the secret dance society
at the Grindstone Rancheria, a tiny Nomlaki settlement in farmland
near Willows on Interstate 5.

Over the years, Brian had accumulated an encyclopedic, almost magical, traditional Indian knowledge of native plants. He knew how to
pinch a leaf of yerba buena between the gums to cure a headache and
how to strip a redbud for basketmaking. He could spot the thin stalks of
a soaproot, which could be mashed for a foamy shampoo substitute or
thrown into pools to stun trout for easy capture. Although happy to share
his knowledge, Brian would often disappear on his own in search of a
plant or just to be alone. My father said Brain reminded him of Ariel, the
wood sprite from Shakespeare's *Tempest* who could converse with the
trees, the birds, and the wind.

There was no trail for the last leg of the trip down to Deer Creek. It
was also too steep for Dan's mules, and he stayed behind with the ani-

mals. The rest of us picked our way down into the canyon. At several points, I grabbed onto the scraggly poison oak to keep from falling. There was much old Indian lore about how to protect yourself from this native plant's toxins. Supposedly, the Maidu put bracelets of poison oak on their babies to build resistance, while the Pomo fed their children the plant's berries. I would itch and scratch my way back to North Carolina when our expedition was over.

We were very close now to Grizzly Bear's Hiding Place, and camped that night by the creek just beneath it. Although its green moss, silver boulders, and clear water were lovely, the canyon was a gloomy place on this late afternoon. The tall cliffs blocked out the last sunlight and the smoke now seeping into the canyon flattened the flaming autumn red-buds into a slate gray. Here Ishi must have crept down from Grizzly Bear's Hiding Place to carry up water for his mother once she had become too frail to make it down the hill. This was also the section of Deer Creek where the surveyors had in 1908 spotted the "curious, half-naked" figure of Ishi with his harpoon, marking the beginning of the very end for the Yahi.

I was grimy and pulled off my clothes to jump into Deer Creek. When Ishi and his companions had made their 1914 trip, the newspapers had fun speculating about just who would or would not go naked in the secluded canyon. "Friends who know something of the circumstances," the *San Francisco Examiner* reported, "express the belief that Kroeber and Pope would not attempt to emulate Ishi in his primitive state in the matter of clothing." Actually, the modest Ishi never took off his loincloth before the others, even when he went swimming. It was the "civilized" whites who'd gone "primitive" by skinny-dipping every day in Deer Creek.

As I dried off on a boulder, I recalled Saxton Pope's reminiscence of his last visit to this canyon. Pope had stroked his dying friend's hand in the hospital yet also insisted on dissecting Ishi and preserving the brain for the greater good of science and human knowledge. In 1924, almost a decade after Ishi's death, Pope made a final pilgrimage alone back to Deer Creek, even scrambling once again up to Grizzly Bear's Hiding Place.

Pope had found this lonely gorge haunted still by the ghosts of those who walked here once. "The spirit of the past fills the canyon," he wrote. "In the prattle of the stream I hear the babble of many tongues." Although an optimist by nature, Pope grew bleak and melancholy at the memory of the departed Ishi—and the murdered Yahi silenced forever by his own pioneer ancestors just "as a thoughtless child stamps upon a mountain flower." At the day's end, Pope lay down next to his dog, Dick, and gazed up at the canopy of stars. He wanted still to find signs of redemption, however bittersweet. "In the jeweled heaven above is imperishable and impalpable beauty. A great peace rests upon us and I almost feel the touch of a vanished hand."

Seventy-five years later, we saw no stars at night in that same place; they had all been smudged out by the wildfire smoke. For the first time on our expedition, however, we had a campfire. It was safer to have one down here by the water than up on the dry, grassy canyon rim. My father had caught a mess of small rainbow trout downstream. The trip had let him get away from the routines of university life and even to indulge in a passion of his youth. He had fished with his own father for trout in the Sierra and striped bass in the steamy delta of the Sacramento River. We roasted my father's catch on sticks, traded stories with Jed, Jerry, Brian, and Jim, then fell into our sleeping bags just next to the creek.

Next morning we made the final ascent to Grizzly Bear's Hiding Place. The first part of the climb took place under the cover of shady oaks. The carpet of shiny, fallen leaves on the steeply angled slope made it like crawling up a glacier without ropes. Then came the notorious brush. As our plant expert, Brian, noted, it was a jumble of buckbrush, toyon, manzanita, wild azalea, and, of course, poison oak—a veritable botanical garden. It was hard even to see a few feet up ahead through undergrowth that seemed as alive as one of Tolkien's enchanted forests as it ripped at our hands and clothes. We took an hour to make our way only about a hundred yards up the hillside.

Suddenly we were there. In the midst of blanketing brush, the spot was flat and contained some larger trees. The smell of bay leaf was strong in the late morning heat. I noticed a large pile of mountain lion dung streaked with white fragments of undigested deer bone. Otherwise, Grizzly Bear's Hiding Place held little immediate drama—no caves, no scattered bones, no mysterious petroglyphs. Even the panorama over the canyon was blocked by vegetation. "Are you disappointed?" Brian asked, as we caught our breath under an oak tree's shade.

In fact, I was overwhelmed by emotion to be in the final Yahi refuge at last. The power of the place seemed somehow all the greater for its unspectacular anonymity. There was no visitor center, no bronze plaque.

Yet Grizzly Bear's Hiding Place was to my mind every bit as extraordinary a landmark as Plymouth Rock, Gettysburg, or Ellis Island. Countless thousands of Indians had perished and millions more been dispossessed in the long, relentless march of white conquest. At the very end, it all came down to this little patch of ground and the handful of Yahi who held out here. The rest of Native America's survivors had been forced to make their way within the world of the reservations and the missionaries, the BIA and the boarding schools, the lure and repulsion of the Western way of life. Ishi and his companions alone, however decimated and besieged they had been at the end, had somehow managed to survive into the twentieth century as the last unconquered band of Indians anywhere in North America.

We fanned out to have a look around. Jim and Brian showed me where the largest of the hideout's three huts had stood. All that remained was the housepit, a faint circular depression about ten feet across, where the Yahi had scooped out the floor of their dwellings for a bit of insulation. Somewhere within a few years of here, the surveyors and their cowboy guides had come upon Ishi's aged mother, weak and emaciated in her blankets. On his trip alone in 1924, Saxton Pope had surprised a doe nesting in one of the little Yahi houses. At that time the structures, though already half-collapsed, were still standing.

Much more tangible evidence of the Yahi occupation lay strewn throughout Grizzly Bear's Hiding Place—dirty old blown glass bottles, a corroded coffee pot, even a rusted tin of Log Cabin syrup wedged in the fork of a tree. These wares bespoke the dependence of Ishi's band on scavenging wagon trail discards and pilfering from local cabins, the nearest being the Speegle Place a couple of miles upstream. The surveyors and their cowboy guides in 1908 had found arrows and other archetypal Indian items at Grizzly Bear's Hiding Place, but that was not all. Strewn around the camp were knives, forks, a U.S. Mail bag, pieces of furniture, gunny sacks, bottles, cans, old clothes, rope, rawhide buttons, and a quilt. A rusted saw blade had been the very first thing Jim and Brian had found at Grizzly Bear's Hiding Place, Jim later told me. At first, they thought they had come upon some abandoned pioneer camp. Only a careful walk-through revealed the housepits, a metate made of river rock, and a few other features matching Alfred Kroeber's description, proving beyond doubt that this was Grizzly Bear's Hiding Place.

That the Yahi had scavenged and stolen was hardly surprising. They no longer had the liberty their ancestors had enjoyed to roam their tribal lands for acorn, roots, and game. A few cans of beans or a purloined sack of barley could be the margin of survival during a hungry winter at Grizzly Bear's Hiding Place. To gulp down a mouthful of maple syrup must have been a special treat. The Yahi had also put what they poached from the invading pioneers to new, unexpected uses—the iron nails for harpoon tips, the broken whiskey bottles to fashion arrowheads. So accustomed was Ishi to glass that later at the museum he sometimes refused to work with obsidian, the traditional Yahi material.

The full extent of Yahi scavenging shattered that popular, almost sacred myth about Ishi as the purest of primitives. Alfred Kroeber had chartered this myth back in 1911 by calling his new Yahi ward "uncontaminated" and "uncivilized." A half century later, Theodora Kroeber still insisted that Ishi lived "his whole life up to his capture without modification of his Stone Age culture." In *Ishi in Two Worlds*, Theodora took her accustomed writerly liberties to make Ishi's band seem more isolated than they really were. For example, she described a cap dropped in 1906 by a fleeing Yahi as homemade Indian headgear "patched with bits of hide and sewed with sinew." Recovered by a settler, this cap is now stored in Berkeley's anthropology museum. On a viewing, I discovered the cap had no "hide" or "sinew" at all. It was just an old denim hat sewn with manufactured cotton thread and probably stolen from some cabin. The "untouched," "uncontaminated" Ishi was a creature of Alfred and Theodora's invention.

That said, I was struck even at Grizzly Bear's Hiding Place by the evident adherence of the last Yahi survivors to many traditions of their tribe. Ishi's mother, while still healthy, ground her acorns on a metate here just like generations of Yahi women had before her. Aside from chipping his arrowheads from glass instead of obsidian, Ishi hunted in the manner of his forefathers. He fashioned his bows from juniper, strung them with deer sinew, straightened his arrows in the fire, and observed customary precautions before the hunt (which included fasting and bathing to wash off as much telltale human odor as possible). Then there were the many old tales that Ishi had learned from his parents and elders—and, for that matter, the language itself, intact except for the addition of *malo* and a few other old Spanish borrowings. Somehow, even with his people targeted for extermination, a bundle of ancestral tribal ways had been handed down to the young Ishi.

Ishi, then, made his way between the old and the new. The sound of the train whistle from down in the valley was as familiar as the cry of an owl or the screech of a wild turkey. Ishi stalked game with his handmade bow and arrow and yet also wielded a stolen steel saw to cut the beams for his family's huts at Grizzly Bear's Hiding Place. As masterful as he was as a traditional Yahi storyteller, Ishi was just as skilled at the arts of concealment and seeing without being seen until his luck ran out in 1908. His life had demanded the capacity to improvise, adapt, and endure at every step along the way.

What might it have been like at Grizzly Bear's Hiding Place a century ago—say, on some fall evening? As I wanted to picture it, Ishi, his mother, and the two other last survivors were gathered around the fire inside one of their huts. A chill was already in the air and the Indians were bundled in their furs and a couple of purloined pioneer quilts for extra warmth. This night, however, there was a special treat, a salmon that Ishi had speared in Deer Creek with his iron nail-tipped harpoon. Chunks of the strong, silver-skinned fish were threaded through sticks anchored in the ground by the fire. As the sizzling meat turned from red to pink, the Yahi chatted about their day's doings. Then it was time to eat and to sleep, with only a coyote's faraway howl to break the still of the dark ravine.

We had crackers and cheese ourselves, sitting on rocks just above Grizzly Bear's Hiding Place. Jerry noticed another fat rattlesnake asleep down in a crevice not that far away. By this time we had encountered so many rattlers already that none of us even bothered to move to another spot. It was still very warm, in the late afternoon, and the smoke was once again flowing up the canyon. A loud helicopter stamped "Department of Fish and Game" swooped by for a look at us. The wardens were on the lookout for anyone in the Ishi Wilderness Area hoping to poach a buck before the season opened the coming weekend.

By then, however, it was time for us to go. In the 1950s, the archaeologist Martin Baumhoff and his team had carried away everything they could find for their museum collections, bones included. No archaeologist in these new, more chastened times would want or dare to be so peremptory about taking anything at all from an Indian village site. In their several trips to Grizzly Bear's Hiding Place, Brian, Jim, and Jerry had always left the metate and the rusted tin cans just as they had found them. On our way up to the hideout, we had hung pieces of toilet paper on the brush to help us find the way back down to Deer

Creek. Going back down we removed the markers so as not to leave any trace of the way.

I do not remember much about the trip's last two days. It was a slog back up to the steel bridge, and especially hard on our party's elders, my father and Jerry. Back at the cars at last, I shook off my dusty boots to find an infected ingrown toenail oozing blood. Plunging the foot into Deer Creek's cold water was the perfect remedy for this complaint.

As lucky as I felt to have made it to Grizzly Bear's Hiding Place, my vague hope that the expedition would bring Art and Mickey together had certainly not panned out. It had been a stretch to think some grand reconciliation would occur anyway, but even Art had not made it along at all. He and his daughter Sadie had never rendezvoused with us in the canyon as we had arranged on the phone beforehand. Art had been enthusiastic about visiting Grizzly Bear's Hiding Place. I was puzzled that he had never shown up and could only guess that another obligation must have come up at the last minute.

I knew that this trip had been a last stop for me. From the Oroville slaughterhouse to Parnassus Heights and Grizzly Bear's Hiding Place, I'd traced Ishi's footsteps just about as far as I could. In a strange way, I understood more, and at the same time less, about Ishi than at the start. Could Ishi's mother or one of the others at Grizzly Bear's Hiding Place have been Maidu or from some other tribe? There was simply not enough hard information either to debunk or to prove this particular theory. We have even less to go on about Ishi's missing years between the ransacking of Grizzly Bear's Hiding Place and his capture in Oroville three years later. How long did Ishi's mother and his other relatives survive in Deer Creek canyon? Did Ishi head at last for Oroville alone, as Theodora had it? Or with others, as Art Angle and other Maidu believed—and as Ishi seems to have told reporters in his first days of captivity? So much about Ishi and his life appears destined to remain unresolved for lack of conclusive evidence. Just that aura of doubt and uncertainty, in fact, has always been one part of why Ishi's story has intrigued people.

We had better luck solving the smaller mystery of Art's no-show. Back at the trailhead, someone had scrawled a message in the red dust on Jed's SUV: WE'RE SORRY WE MISSED YOU. WE'RE NOT MIND READERS. It turned out that Art, wife Lindy, and Sadie had driven up from Chico towing their horse trailer. As Art explained when I called him a few days later, they'd gotten lost in the labyrinth of logging roads, run out of gas, and had to coast the last part of the way back down to the valley's nearest gas station. They came up again the next day to scout around and had finally found the trailhead and our cars, but by this time it was too late to start down the trail. A peeved Lindy had left the note in the dust together with the peace offering of a plastic bottle of scotch.

Art had also cooled down enough to joke with me on the phone about the failed rendezvous. "That was a good one," he laughed. "An Indian getting lost in the forest."

# Sixteen

# THE SACRED FIRE

I spent that fall in Durham. By year's end, I still had no news from California about the arrangements for Ishi's funeral. More than six months had passed since the Smithsonian's announcement that it would repatriate Ishi's brain to Mickey Gemmill's people, the Redding Rancheria and the Pit River Tribe. As yet, the Indians had still not retrieved the brain from Washington or Ishi's ashes from the Olivet cemetery near San Francisco. Mickey issued only vague, cryptic declarations. "The way we see it," he was quoted in one magazine story, "it will happen when it's supposed to happen."

I spoke to Art several times that fall. The continuing delay in returning Ishi's remains to his homeland had only fueled Art's belief that the Smithsonian had made a mistake. At the very least, Art thought the museum should have awarded joint custody of Ishi's brain to Mickey's people and his own Maidu. Now that they'd been designated as the sole trustees of what Art still more delicately called "the missing body part," however, the Redding Rancheria and Pit River Tribe held all the cards—and they did not want anyone, fellow Indians or not, telling them what to do. In a curt letter, the Pit River Tribal Chairman, Lawrence Cantrell, turned down Art's proposal for a funeral with representatives from all of California's tribes. Cantrell misspelled Art's last name as

"Angel" for good measure. It looked as if Art himself, the man who'd done the most work toward repatriation in the first place, was not even going to be invited to the ceremony.

Art was restrained with the reporters who still called him now and then. He didn't want to come across as selfish or to backstab another Indian in the newspapers. With me, Art let slip an occasional barb about Mickey, the repressed bitterness surfacing for a moment. And I knew Mickey felt Art had been unduly insistent that his Maidu and other tribes be full partners in Ishi's funeral. It was ironic that Mickey and Art were set against one another since they had so much in common—a couple of aging, tough, independent characters who had been devoted to Indian causes for much of their lives. I assumed that Tom Killion and his Repatriation Office had made their decision upon what they perceived to be the facts of the case, however much one agreed or not with their conclusion that the Redding Rancheria and Pit River Tribe were Ishi's closest living relatives. Art took a different view. He saw the decision to exclude him from the return of Ishi's brain as corroborating his negative opinion of federal Indian policy. "It's always the same," he said. "They do things to keep Indian people divided so we'll stay down."

Only after the New Year did I make it back out to the Bay Area. It was a short trip mostly to visit my three failing grandparents, but I also squeezed in a coda to our Grizzly Bear's Hiding Place expedition. This time the destination was a place called Ishi's Cave, improbably located in the middle of San Francisco. According to a vague urban legend, Ishi had maintained a secret cave on the hill above his home at the museum as a retreat from the city's bustle. I'd always assumed the story was pure fabrication, a spinoff from an ugly cartoonish view of Ishi back in the newspapers of the day—as a "cave man" of limited intellect who dressed in skins and carried a big wooden club. Whoever heard of caves in San Francisco, anyway? Apparently, though, Ishi's Cave really existed, or so I'd just heard from a former classmate of mine in graduate school, Philippe Bourgois, a well-known anthropologist who is now a professor at U.C. San Francisco. Philippe had a friend named Rich Mertes, a teacher's aide for disabled kids at San Francisco's Lakeshore Elementary School. Rich, he told me, was an Ishi aficionado—and some years before had found Ishi's Cave somewhere not far below Twin Peaks.

We arranged for a Sunday expedition with Rich, Philippe, his son

Emiliano, my father, and Nancy Rockafellar, with whom I'd remained friendly. Another member of the party was a friend of Nancy's, Larry Crooks, an engineer who'd made a fortune as an inventor of the MRI and was also interested in the story of Ishi. Crooks had helped the Maidu with the expenses for their trip to the Smithsonian to view Ishi's brain the year before.

It was wet and cold, a blustery winter day with a sharp wind off the Pacific Ocean. We met the others by the little clock tower at U.C. San Francisco's imposing medical complex. Kroeber's anthropology museum had once stood just across Parnassus Avenue, although Ishi's San Francisco home had long since been demolished to make room for hospital expansion. Rich Mertes led us down Parnassus and around the corner to Willard, one of San Francisco's famously clifflike streets. On a clear day, there would have been a postcard view out to the Golden Gate Bridge and Mount Tamalpais beyond, but it was too cloudy on this gray morning to see even as far down as Golden Gate Park at the base of the hill.

Rich Mertes was a wry, good-looking man about my age with a goatee, thick black hair, and wire glasses. On our way up the hill, he explained that he'd learned about Ishi's story in college and had been intrigued ever since. He and his friends even developed a private jargon, Rich laughed. "To pull an Ishi" meant unplugging from modern technology—to get rid of your television, use a typewriter instead of a computer, or maybe even to frame your own house without power tools.

In his spare time, Rich was a bird-watcher, backpacker, poet, environmentalist, and sometime practitioner of T'ai Chi and eastern meditation. He had no illusions about Native California as a lost utopia (and, for example, mentioned to me the slave trading of several northern tribes, among them the Modoc). A native of San Francisco, however, he'd watched his home state clog up with cars, subdivisions, and strip malls in America's peculiar version of progress. In his direct way of putting it, Rich wondered how the Indians had managed to "live here for thousands of years without fucking it up." What was life like in that ancient California before the state had ten million people and the world's seventh largest economy? Rich saw Ishi as a last bridge back to the world destroyed to make way for the California of our own day.

Yet Rich was not some flaky, self-absorbed Californian of crystals-and-vision quest variety. Like other admirers of Ishi, he was revolted by the monstrous brutality of the conquest of Native California—and sympathized with Ishi, the last of his people, a man stripped of everything.

At the same time, Rich found inspiration in Ishi's capacity to maintain a sense of himself and to connect with others even in the alien world of the city. He had spent his whole career working for a pittance with the neediest children in San Francisco's beleaguered public school system. We turned out to have a friend in common. She told me later that Rich had once given the jacket off his back to a freezing old wino who'd been found in the gutter outside the soup kitchen. This homeless man, as it turned out, was a Navajo, and Rich collected bus fare so he could get back to New Mexico.

At the top of Willard, Rich led us off onto a trail into Sutro Forest, a vacant urban hillside lot that for some reason has never been developed. For a long time, he explained, he'd heard the tales about Ishi's Cave without much believing them. Out of curiosity, however, Rich and some friends who were bike messengers in the Financial District had started exploring around this patch of wilderness just above Ishi's home at the museum. One day they'd come upon a hole in the rocks away from the nearest path and half-concealed by weeds. In front was a doorknob still wrapped in hardware-store packaging. Rich recalled that doorknobs were one of Ishi's favorite modern inventions, along with matches, glue, and indoor plumbing. "I think maybe someone left it there as an offering," he told me. "Maybe it was a symbol to guide us."

The hole led into a cave about the size of the interior of a VW Beetle. It was unlikely that Ishi or anyone else really ever lived in this tiny, dark cavern, Rich knew. If Ishi sometimes spent the night outside away from his comfortable bed in the museum, it was probably in the conical brush Yahi house that he constructed a bit farther down the hill. The hut was an extra daytime attraction for museum visitors labeled "Yana Hut Built by Ishi." One emeritus chancellor at U.C. San Francisco recalls that Ishi really did sleep there on occasion after everyone else had left. Still, Ishi must also have at least known about the cave, since he often roamed above the museum. Rich and his friends made the spot into their own special shrine, regularly leaving candles and acorn meal there as offerings. And Rich even spent the last night of 1999, the dawn of the new millennium, curled up inside in the cave listening to a tape of Ishi's chanting on a little cassette player.

Historian Philip Deloria notes how common it has been for whites to want to "play Indian." He recalls the American revolutionaries who stripped off their shirts and painted their faces to look like Mohawks for the Boston Tea Party; the hippies of the sixties and seventies going off to live Indian-like in tepees and commune with nature; and YMCA summer campers learning to sew moccasins and make smoke signals as I had as a boy in northern California. To go native allows whites a taste of the "savage freedom" that Indians have been made to symbolize, Deloria writes. As for Rich, he was an unembarrassed worshiper in the cult of Ishi, but he was not really trying to play at being Yahi. His millennial New Year's Eve in the cave was a pilgrim's act of devotion and identification at a shrine to his patron saint. "I felt pretty connected to Ishi," Rich recalled of that night alone in the darkness.

Rich told many of his disabled students about Ishi, then took them to the cave with their parents. It has long been the premise of Ishi's white admirers that children should learn the story of Ishi and its lessons about injustice, survival, and the ways of America's first peoples. Four children's books about Ishi are now in print, including Theodora's *Last of His Tribe* (most recently, Ishi is the "I" in the best-selling *G is for Golden: A California Alphabet*). "It doesn't matter if Ishi was never here," or so Rich explained his reasons for bringing his students to the cave. "It's a big adventure and starts them thinking about a lot of important things." Rich found out later that others had already known about the cave. In the early 1980s, the U.C. San Francisco campus magazine had even run a story called "Ishi's Cave—A Sutro Legend," complete with a photograph of the entrance.

We followed Rich through some wet brush to an outcropping of gray rock covered with moss and ivy. There was a hole at the base of the stone—a crack, really. It looked too small for an adult to fit into. Adroitly, however, Rich contorted himself through the face of the rock and was swallowed up into the earth. I'm tall and skinny, if not very limber, and I followed. Then came Emiliano, Philippe's eleven year-old son, a slender, beautiful boy who had cerebral palsy and could walk only a short way (he had been one of Rich's students at the Lakeshore Elementary School). Although Philippe had carried Emiliano up the hill on his shoulders, the boy had been in the cave before. He knew how to pull himself in with his surprisingly powerful arms. Larry Crooks, the MRI inventor, crawled in last. My father and Nancy Rockafellar had taken one look and declined the opportunity to join us. Philippe, who had been in before with Rich and Emiliano, also stayed outside.

It was pitch dark inside the cave. The floor was muddy from water dripping in from the rains, and the ceiling was so low that even Emiliano had to splay down on his side. We lay there in silence for a few moments.

I tried to focus my mind on higher, more meaningful things, without much success. My pants were soaked and an old soccer injury to my back was stiffening in the cramped cold. I'd also felt a rush of claustrophobia as I'd flattened through the stony slit of the passageway into the cave. As it happened, I'd recently read *Winnie-the-Pooh* to my daughter and wondered whether I'd become stuck on the way out like Pooh in Rabbit's Burrow. Would the Fire Department have to rescue me in the end? I was relieved to squeeze back out once again into the wet, gray forest.

I chatted a bit more with Rich on the way back down. He wanted to hear the story of how Nancy Rockafellar and I had tracked Ishi's brain to the Smithsonian. Rich had long been troubled by Theodora's mention in *Ishi in Two Worlds* that the brain had been "preserved," an indignity that for him symbolized the suffering inflicted upon Native America. Later, he mailed me a poem he'd written several years before, "Ishi's Brain," a meditation about the organ's confinement to a "formaldehyde reservation." Rich wanted now to know about the delay in Ishi's reburial. "I hope it's not much longer," he said. "We need to get him back in the earth."


Art thought so, too. With the help of his friend Don Blake, the lawyer and editor of the hometown *Oroville Opportunity Bulletin*, he took time away from his truck to organize a conference intended to keep Ishi's repatriation on the front burner. They staged the event in the dining hall at the Travelodge off Highway 99, a cavern of a room with worn carpeting and potted plastic plants. Art invited a mixed cast of characters. There was the mayor of Oroville and California's State Attorney General (who had become involved in preparing the case to recover Ishi's ashes from the Olivet cemetery); an assortment of academics specializing in Ishi and Native California; a variety of Indians from around the area; and representatives of the Redding Rancheria and Pit River Tribe as an olive branch to Mickey's people. A far cry from the incestuous, anthropologists-only professional conferences to which I was more accustomed, this gathering measured the diverse affiliations and backgrounds of all who felt a stake in Ishi and his legacy. Art and other latter-day Native Californians now pressed their agendas in a twenty-first century world defined for them at the interface of Indians and non-Indians, bureaucrats and lawyers, and even politicians and professors.

The day opened with a welcome from Art. Then the mayor of

Oroville and California's Attorney General said a few words before they slipped out for the next stops on their schedules. There was also a dance by some enthusiastic local Indian kids in beads and feathers, then a Maidu prayer from Gus Martin, the retired lumberjack. Gus had recovered enough from his fall in Washington to walk on his own, although he still looked very frail. Mickey and a few others were there, too, having accepted Art's invitation to come down from Redding. Could some kind of reconciliation between Mickey and Art now be in the offing?

Various scholars spoke about Ishi and his life that morning, among them me, Nancy Rockafellar, and Sacramento State's Jerry Johnson, the archaeologist who'd accompanied us to Grizzly Bear's Hiding Place. The Indians listened courteously enough to our presentations, although I overheard Art comment to another Maidu that he hadn't "heard anything I didn't already know." We were far now from that more colonial day of Alfred Kroeber and his colleagues; no longer could an anthropologist or any other white scholar expect to have the last or exclusive say about Native America. Art had reserved the afternoon for his fellow Indians to take to the microphone.

The conference turned more personal during this second half of the meeting. Among the first to the microphone was Mickey; his face was grim under a black baseball cap that said "Native." Voice rising with passion, he gave his own unvarnished, intense version of the brutal state history of Indian extermination and how little most Californians still know about it:

> *When you grow up in California, there's only a few things you read about in the educational system. One of them is Ishi, the so-called—I hate the term—"wild person" or "wild Indian." And they talk a little about the mission Indians. . . . And anyway, that's it. It's basically left out. It's omitted on purpose. And I think we need to think about why it was omitted. The history has not truly been told yet. Because it's too painful; it's too ugly. You know, when you hear about what they call the Holocaust of the Jewish: it happened here. It happened here. Entire groups of people were gone forever after thousands and thousands of years of existence.*

Jed Riffe, the filmmaker, was videotaping, but an emotional Mickey asked Jed to switch off the camera for a moment. Now Mickey lit a bundle of sage to smudge himself with smoke, eyes closed. Then he chanted a song to the hushed room. I couldn't tell whether the song was in a dialect of Pit River or some other tongue. In any event, Mickey looked calmer when he'd finished; the muscles in his determined jaw were more relaxed. Now Mickey promised that Ishi's burial would be carried out soon and "with dignity." He thanked the Butte County Maidu for having "brought attention to this issue," but I suspected the Redding Rancheria and Pit River Tribe still had no intention of inviting Art to Ishi's funeral. Only a "small group of our people" would be at the ceremony, Mickey said. I wondered just how Art was going to respond when his turn came to address the crowd of a hundred or so people at the Travelodge.

The other Indian speakers had strong, sometimes tearful reactions to Ishi's story, and especially to the removal and disposition of his brain against his own wishes. "How could a person do that to another person?" asked Claire LeCompte, a rail-thin, Maidu grandmother from the Honey Lake branch of the tribe in Susanville up Highway 36 toward Nevada. Like many other Indians (and for that matter, non-Indians like Rich Mertes), LeCompte connected the appropriation of Ishi's brain to other injustices committed against Native America, injustices that older Indians like herself had experienced personally. She recalled being sent during the 1950s to the Stewart Indian Boarding School in Carson City, Nevada. Gesturing toward the metal folding chair where she'd been sitting, LeCompte said she and her sister were beaten at the school "with iron pieces like this of a broken chair." LeCompte, trembling and angry, spoke also of the denial of the petitions of her Honey Lake Maidu for the benefits of federal recognition. "Why not accept us for what we are?" she asked. "On one hand, they abused us and treat us with prejudice—and on the other hand they say we won't recognize you as Indian. I think that's wrong and something needs to be changed."

There was nothing novel about what LeCompte or Mickey were saying about Indian suffering. In some cases, admittedly, the claim of Indians to victimhood has swerved into a kind of shakedown of mainstream America. Some Red Power activists used to joke sadly among themselves that variations on the line "My heart is heavy—and my wallet is empty" seemed to be the only way to raise money to fight reservation poverty and finance other causes for their people. The rhetoric of victimization can always be used to try to silence debate or solidify entitlements. As I'd felt at other times over the last year, however, the strong emotions expressed by LeCompte and other speakers that afternoon did not come across as formulaic or self-serving. I knew in the abstract how much Native Californians had lost, the tribes destroyed and the number dead. Yet I was still knocked off guard every time by the powerfully felt pain and anger among the survivors, especially those old enough to have suffered discrimination and sometimes worse in an era before it was "cool" to be Indian. The vulnerability and mistrust ran deep in this generation to which Art and Rosalie belonged.

At the end of the meeting Art took the cordless microphone. At one point in his talk, Mickey had insisted on the close relationship and intermarriage between the Yahi and the other Indians of far northern California. The Smithsonian was right to pick his Pit River Tribe and the Redding Rancheria as Ishi's closest living relatives, Mickey was saying. For his part, Art still believed that Ishi may have been part Maidu, and he brought up now his own theory that Ishi's mother was a Maidu who'd either been kidnapped by Yahi or chosen to go off with them. I hoped the meeting was not going to end in some fruitless contest between Art and Mickey over their rights to the dead body of Ishi.

It turned out that Art had other plans. Abruptly, he dropped the contentious question of the ownership of Ishi's remains and turned gracious and conciliatory toward the visitors from the Redding Rancheria and Pit River Tribe. He expressed his "complete confidence" that Mickey and his people would fulfill their obligation to complete Ishi's repatriation as soon as possible. Unlike Mickey, Art was never the most effective of public speakers, sometimes straining for the right words. But I'd never heard Art so eloquent as on this afternoon. He spoke with a new kind of serenity and self-assurance, secure in the knowledge he was doing the right thing to let go of his personal disappointment at being excluded from the last chapter in Ishi's repatriation. Art could sometimes be bitter and brooding about real and perceived slights, especially about the suffering inflicted upon his Maidu and the rest of indigenous California. Even so—and perhaps also influenced somehow by the talk about trauma and healing so much a part of America's zeitgeist at the turn of the century—he was a forgiving and hopeful man by nature. "When the repatriation comes to a closure," Art said now before laying down the microphone, "that will mean that a part of the healing process is begun."

Art had a well-deserved moment of glory the next morning. It was the day of the parade for Oroville's Feather Fiesta Days, the town's annual town fair. For his efforts toward the repatriation of Ishi, still an Oroville icon, the organizers had named Art the Grand Marshal of this event. Art was resplendent for the occasion in a Western shirt with an

Indian-looking pattern, a beaded headband, and even a peace pipe that he had turned up somewhere. The parade featured various high school marching bands, baton twirlers, an African-American cowboy, a caravan of restored antique military jeeps, a Noah's Ark float sponsored by the Assembly of God, and a flatbed truck carrying a local rock band belting out the B-52s' *Love Shack* at full volume. Art rode at the parade's head in the lead car, a snazzy red Camaro. He was pleased and waved his peace pipe to the happy crowd along Main Street.


Art had planned one last event, this one private and unannounced to the public. It was a bonfire in Ishi's honor—a "sacred fire," as Art explained it to me—out on Table Mountain, the mesa just above Oroville. Like all the land in these parts, Table Mountain had once belonged to the Maidu, but the land was now owned mostly by white ranchers and a few backcountry recluses. Art had asked one rancher to allow the bonfire on his property just beyond the big, white "O" for Oroville painted on a bluff visible from the town. The rancher had said no ("He'll get his," Art's sister Rosalie said with a cheerful smile). Art then asked the California's Department of Fish and Game to use their preserve on another part of Table Mountain. The wardens gave permission as well as the key to a locked gate so the Maidu could drive in their pickups with firewood and other supplies

The idea for a fire came from old Maidu tradition. Although the custom died out early in the twentieth century, the annual bonfire for the dead had once been the area's biggest ceremony. There the living wept for their departed loved ones—and honored them by setting ablaze tall poles strung with blankets, clothes, and baskets with brilliant geometric designs. Art knew only stories about the burnings from his grandmother, but he wanted to revive a version of the tradition to "assist Ishi's spirit into the next world," as he put it. Art and the others planned to start their bonfire with the traditional fire drill, the friction of stick against stick. Unfortunately, the day was cold and wet, and their best efforts at producing a spark failed. Perhaps appropriately enough, the Indians had to resort to newspaper and a match. Although Ishi had been happy to make fire in the laborious traditional manner for museum visitors, it was not his preferred method. He regarded matches "with evident delight" for their convenient simplicity, his friend Saxton Pope would recall.

Art had invited my father and me to join him on Table Mountain the afternoon after the parade. The fire had already been burning for a week by then, and this would be the last day. We took the winding little highway out of Oroville to Table Mountain, then bumped off onto a dirt track running west for several miles, with the grass so lush and high on either side that the way was barely visible. It was cold, and there were only a few brief moments of sunshine between the rushing gray clouds of yet another storm blowing down from the northwest. On this early spring day, the mesa was a carpet of green dotted with purple lupine, golden poppies, red owl's clover, and dozens of other wildflowers in fragrant bloom. The Indians had made the fire at the edge of the mesa just above the great valley. You could look across the many miles of orchard, farms, and rice fields spread out below to the Marysville Buttes. To those strange little peaks in the middle of the Sacramento Valley, according to Maidu myth, the dead had to journey in order to climb up into the Milky Way.

Art wasn't there yet. A couple of Maidu I didn't know, two men and a woman, stood wrapped in blankets by the fire. They had spent the previous night camped out in a tent to tend the fire and looked tired and dirty from the smoke. Just a few minutes after my father and I arrived, another car came down the road, this one bringing Rosalie, Nancy Rockafellar, Nancy Scheper-Hughes and her husband, Michael. Nancy Scheper-Hughes, a former chair of the Berkeley anthropology department, was the co-founder of "Organs Watch," the group monitoring abuses in the new black market for transplanted organs around the world. When the truth about Alfred Kroeber mailing Ishi's brain to the Smithsonian had been revealed, Scheper-Hughes had convinced her colleagues to apologize on the department's behalf for the actions of its founder (a more radical proposal to rename Kroeber Hall as Ishi Hall was rejected). She and Michael had come up to Oroville for the conference and had become friends of Art and Rosalie.

I'd noticed that one of the Indians tending the fire looked uncomfortable and less than pleased to see us. Quite suddenly, he addressed Rosalie as if we were not there. "They told us," he said, "no white people were allowed." After so many decades of intermarriage with whites and sometimes Latinos, there were no pure-blooded Maidu anymore, but the lines of ethnic identity and belonging remained strong in this corner of California. The gambling tournaments and other ceremonies up at the roundhouse at Feather Falls were Maidu only, with exceptions sometimes made for spouses or other special cases. It had also been decided to close the fire to outsiders, a private ceremony. Rosalie knew that Art, the organizer, wanted to make an exception for the six of us, however. She had just taken the two Nancys and Michael for a drink at the Sierra Club bar down in Oroville, her favorite hangout with its country jukebox and pool table. Yet Rosalie was also a woman of formidable will and determination. "No," she replied now to the doubtful man. "It's okay. They're with me. And Art knows they're here." Rosalie had camped out herself in the cold one night earlier that week to tend the fire, and the man who questioned her appeared satisfied.

I went off to look out over the valley. It was a sheer drop down to the floor of the plain. The face of the gray-black lava cliff was pocked by the nests of hundreds of swallows now swooping out after bugs with the approaching dusk. When I turned back around to rejoin my father, Rosalie, and the others, I could see them silhouetted against the flat sea of grass and the sparking red glow of the bonfire. A century and a half before, the U.S. Army had marched hundreds of Maidu and other Indians away to the Round Valley reservation. Maidu legend still has it that those evading the round-up had also lit fires here on the cliffs, a beacon for their friends and relatives to escape back home. The idea of fire as a guidepost figured in Yahi mythology, too. According to one of Ishi's songs, a large blaze burned near the hole in the sky, a marker for the spirits of the dead to find the rope into the upper world. The concept of such a grand pyre must have seemed almost exotic to Ishi and the others in hiding, who had had to keep their own fires small to escape the outside world's detection.

Art and a number of other people were arriving now, negotiating their vehicles over the bumpy terrain and parking in the grass away from the fire. Among them was Gus Martin, helped across the field by his daughter, Daisy. When Gus and the other last two Concow Maidu speakers died, the language would go with them to the grave, a unique human treasure lost forever except for the ghostly recordings and transcriptions made by a few linguists. What can it be like to be a last speaker of your language in the whole wide world? First Ishi and now Gus found themselves in that same lonely position in the last years of their lives. Bruce Steidl, the Indian archaeologist who'd gone with us to Washington, had told me about Jack Johnson, in his fifties the youngest of the last trio of Concow Maidu speakers. Johnson would sometimes speak Maidu to baffled grocery store clerks or security guards at the casino; it was the only way he could make sure he didn't forget the language himself, he said. Bruce and his wife, Leslie, were taking a class at the Mooretown Rancheria from the other last speaker, an old man named Virgil Logan. Yet they knew that no one else would really ever again speak the language. A more realistic hope, Leslie believed, was that a few words and phrases would continue to be passed on down the generations. "It might be a bit like Jewish kids learning some Hebrew for their bar mitzvah without really knowing how to speak it," she said, "a kind of way to commemorate their past and their identity."

Gus was unsteady with his cane and somebody found him a lawn chair. As the rest of us also circled around the fire, the old man's standard Maidu blessing was little more than a whisper. Then Art and Rosalie's brother Marx began to sing in Maidu. It was Lizard's Song, Rosalie told me later, rather than a chant intended specifically for a funeral. Not even Gus still knew any of the many more special chants for the dead. "What else, Gus?" Art said, looking for guidance. "I don't know," Gus answered. It had drained the old man's little energy to be at the conference the day before. He couldn't recall any other bits of ritual for performance in Ishi's honor and Art asked us for a moment of silence. As wrenching as the sight of Ishi's brain had been a few months before, I had managed to keep my emotions under control, and yet now I wiped away tears at the thought of what the man and his people had gone through. Only the faint peeping of the swallows out beyond the cliffs broke the stillness.

The moment was powerful for everyone, but especially for Art. The burial of Ishi's body was out of his hands now, and Art realized his part in Ishi's repatriation was over. Later in the evening, the fire would be allowed to burn down to embers and then to cold ash, the end of this tribute to Ishi and a measure of closure for Art himself. Although Art had enjoyed being at the center of things, the responsibility of doing right by Ishi had also weighed heavily upon him. He looked sad, relieved, and exhausted now that the task, or at least his part in it, was done. We shook hands and my father and I said goodbye to drive back to Berkeley. Art was going to stay up at the fire for a few hours more, he said. Then, he grimaced with the slightest of smiles, he'd need to get back to town for a stiff drink.


It was up to Mickey Gemmill and his people now to finish the job. A few weeks after the conference in Oroville, I talked to Mickey on the phone. He was upbeat and, without explaining the reason for the delay, told me that he and others were making arrangements at last for the trip to bring the brain back from Washington. Mickey added that the Attorney General had already won the release of Ishi's ashes from the Olivet cemetery. Bill Lockyer, a well-respected liberal lawyer who'd embraced the chance to help the Indians, had brought the case to the San Mateo County Court, the county just south of San Francisco where Olivet was located. The superintendent of the cemetery had no objection to giving up Ishi's ashes (he was part Hopi himself, as it happened). Still, the law requires a court order for any transfer of human remains. A judge had mandated that the ashes be turned over to Mickey and Floyd Buckskin. Buckskin was the man the Pit River Tribe had picked as its main representative for the repatriation (although he was a member of the Pit River Tribe, too, Mickey was acting as the representative for the Redding Rancheria, his employer). The superintendent at Olivet had removed the shiny black Pueblo pot containing Ishi's ashes to a locked storage vault until the Indians came to take it away.

I was just about sure that Ishi himself would have wished his divided remains reunited. We humans have variously cremated, mummified, and buried the bodies of our dead—and have also invented every manner of accompanying ritual to mark life's ending, whether placing coins over a dead man's eyes to pay the boatman's toll for crossing the River Styx, as in ancient Greece, or lowering the flag when a famous American dies. Nomadic Woodland Tribes of ancient New York State hauled the bones of their dead with them to each new camp as if they could not bear to be separated from their ancestors. Yet with only a few exceptions—such as the Egyptians, who sometimes kept the hearts of their pharaohs in special jars—a belief that the corpse should be laid to rest whole has been almost universal. Only the new secular religion of science allowed for the organs of the dead to be pickled for the purposes of study, or, more recently, to be transplanted into the bodies of the living. The high percentage of Americans refusing to sign organ donor forms expresses an enduring uneasiness about the cutting apart of our own dead bodies, even to save another. It was certainly always the Yahi custom to bury their dead whole, usually with just a few shelldisk beads or other ornaments. Dismembering Ishi's body had violated the principle of wholeness in no uncertain terms.

But what about Ishi's final place of rest? Art had intended it to be somewhere by Deer Creek, and the Redding Rancheria and the Pit River Tribe had also decided on the canyon. It was a matter of "bringing Ishi back home," as Art and then Mickey had so often said. For my own part, I wondered if Ishi himself in his last years still regarded the canyon as his home. After all, Ishi was reluctant in 1914 to return even for a few days to Deer Creek, the homeland and yet also the killing fields of his people. He had little choice about being brought to San Francisco in the first place, but according to Theodora Kroeber, he developed such positive feelings for the museum that he'd declare, *"Wo-wi! Wo-wi!"* (My house! My home!) when he approached the building after some excursion to Ocean Beach in the city or south to Santa Cruz. Theodora may have exaggerated Ishi's emotions to forestall any criticism of her late husband, Alfred, for keeping Ishi in so peculiar a place. All the same, at least as far as I knew, Art, Mickey, and the other Indians never considered the possibility that Ishi might have felt a real attachment to the museum and perhaps might even have preferred to rest in some spot on Parnassus Heights. A belief that Ishi was a prisoner in the white man's city led the Indians to assume he'd want to be buried back in the foothills.

I knew that I wasn't going to be invited to the ceremony, and I didn't think any other whites would. It had been just the opposite at Ishi's first funeral at Olivet cemetery back in 1916, when no Indians had come. Besides himself, only "Professor Watterman [*sic*], Mr. Gifford, and two members of the Anthropology Museum" had been there, Saxton Pope wrote. Somehow, Pope had convinced himself that his friend was receiving a proper traditional burial, even though the brain was pickled back up the peninsula in San Francisco. Just before Ishi's embalmed, sewn-together body went into the crematorium's oven, Pope and the others placed with it acorn meal, tobacco, sticks for making fire, and other supplies to provision Ishi for his journey to the land of the dead. "We were his friends and nearest of kin," Pope explained. He believed his own friendship with Ishi had thickened into a kind of blood bond. "I learned to love Ishi as a brother," he insisted, "and he looked upon me as one of his people." The claim was extravagant, and yet Ishi had admired his dashing friend, with his magic tricks, ready laugh, and world-class skills in the operating room.

That Indians were in charge this time symbolized the recovery of Native California from virtual extinction. So close to being destroyed altogether in the nineteenth century, they had reclaimed the body of California's most famous Indian. Not wanting to intrude or appear somehow to be angling for an invitation, I didn't call Mickey in the last weeks. Only in the newspapers did I read that he, Floyd Buckskin, and ten others had flown out to the Smithsonian at last. It was early August and the story appeared beneath the coverage of the Republican Convention and the nomination of George W. Bush as the party's candidate for president. "Indians from California are scheduled to take possession of the jar containing Ishi's brain in a private ceremony Tuesday at the Smithsonian in Washington, D.C.," explained the Associated Press story. "They will reunite it with Ishi's cremated remains, which have spent decades in a cemetery south of San Francisco, and bury both in a secret ceremony in the foothills of majestic Mount Lassen in northern California." A few days later it was all over, or so I also learned. "The final remains of an Indian icon go home," reported *U.S. News and World Report*. The story gave few other details except that Ishi's remains had been laid in the ground earlier that week.

I was never told or asked much about the last ceremony. Yet Mickey and I would remain on good terms, and he could be observant and sensitive behind his intimidating boxer's exterior. One day much later, as if understanding that I'd want to know a bit about the end of the story, Mickey shared a few details about Ishi's funeral. He and the others had arrived on a Tuesday at the Smithsonian's National Museum of Natural History to find that Tom Killion and the Repatriation Office had readied everything for them in a private back room. Mickey's people had said prayers, then prepared to take the brain from its jar to wrap it in the pelt of a silver fox, a symbol of the Pit River Tribe. Mickey himself lifted the organ, still dripping in ethyl alcohol, out of its jar. Even for tough, fearless Mickey that moment was too hard to put into words. "To hold that man's brain in your hands like that after everything . . ." His voice trailed off.

It's illegal to transport body parts across state lines without authorization, so Tom Killion had accompanied the Indians to Dulles International Airport to show his credentials if necessary. Packed into a carrying bag, the pelt with the brain passed undetected through the X-ray machine in those days preceding the attacks of September 11, 2001, and the subsequent heightened airport security. Mickey and the others boarded United Airlines Flight 757 for San Francisco with Ishi's brain as carry-on luggage. They connected to a commuter flight up to Redding's little airport, met a few others waiting with cars and pickups, and then caravaned eastward across the baking-hot valley toward the mountains. By now, the Indians had also picked up the pot with Ishi's ashes from Olivet. The sealed black Pueblo pot and the brain bumped together toward their destination.

It was a couple of hours into the hills and then off the highway onto one of the dirt roads winding down into Deer Creek's canyon. The party had parked there, then walked into a forested spot not far from the water. All were sworn never to divulge the exact location of this place, out of respect for Ishi and for fear of someone digging up the grave someday. It had also been decided that the group should be mixed so as better to represent the tribes. There were a number of women, children, and old people, one of whom, Willard Rhoades, had just turned eighty. A few Indians who were not from the Pit River Tribe and the Redding Rancheria were also invited, among them Mike Bejorquez, whom I met later. A short, thin man with wire-rimmed glasses and a black pony-tail, Bejorquez was a friend of several Pit River men and a self-described "half-breed" of mixed Mayan and Spanish descent.

It was never reported in the newspapers, but one white man was also present: Tom Killion. According to Mickey, it had been a last-minute decision to invite Tom to fly back with them for the ceremony. He and the others appreciated Tom's work to facilitate Ishi's repatriation and liked him personally. Although I felt a pang of envy, I appreciated the symbolism of inviting Tom to Deer Creek. That the ceremony was closed measured the new Indian possessiveness about Ishi—and, in particular, the feeling among the Pit River Tribe and the Redding Rancheria of being the rightful stewards of his legacy. Yet inviting Tom was also a gesture of forgiveness and reconciliation toward the Smithsonian. To have at least one white there was also to reject or at least avoid any new absolutist politics of ethnic purity and separatism, and, in particular, to acknowledge that Ishi ought not to be the property of any single group in the final account.

A big, beautiful old Pit River basket had been found to hold Ishi's remains. When they discovered that the top of the shiny black pot was sealed with cement, Mickey and the others had no choice but to crack the vessel open with a rock. Inside were the ashes as well as shards of calcified bone and a few melted pieces of obsidian—the arrowheads that the anthropologists and Saxton Pope had placed with the autopsied body before it was cremated along with tobacco, shell money, and other goods for Ishi's journey to the next world. There was one other thing, Mickey told me: a handwritten note on yellowing early twentieth-century paper, a message of some sort sealed inside along with the ashes.

Here was a last bit of mystery. But when Mickey had looked over at Floyd Buckskin, a well-liked young tribal leader and the other man in charge of the ceremony, neither wanted to read it. They were ready to move ahead with no more doubt, no more intrusion, no more unnecessary return to what for them was the painful tale of Ishi's life. It would be for others to speculate what the note might have said. It couldn't, in any event, have been from Ishi, since he only knew how to write his name. I guessed it might have been some special last message from Pope. He'd wanted to cut out Ishi's brain and yet he had also been closer to the last Yahi than anyone else in San Francisco.

No prescribed "traditional" ceremony existed for reuniting a dismembered body. How could such a contingency ever have been anticipated in Native California? Still, it was agreed not to cremate the brain; this particular decision was in line with Yahi tradition whether Mickey and Floyd realized it or not. Alfred Kroeber and his Berkeley anthropologists had believed that the Yahi had always cremated their dead. If they'd been able to better understand Ishi's Yahi language, they would have known that this was not the case. One of Ishi's stories, for example—only translated in the early 1990s by the linguist Jean Perry—describes cadavers as "flexed, stiff and cold." In the last decades, too, the archaeologist Jerald Johnson has confirmed in his excavations that Yahi bodies were buried intact, usually on their side with knees folded to the chest. That Ishi's brain went whole into the basket was thus true to his people's customs in a small way. I never did ask Mickey whether he, Floyd, or anyone else knew this somehow or chose for some other reason to proceed as they did.

A hole had been dug a few feet deep for Ishi's grave. With care and reverence, Mickey and Floyd put everything into the basket: Ishi's remains, the melted obsidian, the pieces of the broken pot, and even the unread note. They sprinkled purifying wormwood and tobacco over everything. Then the basket was lowered into the hole, and the hole was covered with dirt. The Indians scattered twigs and leaves over the spot to leave no trace of what lay beneath. It was growing dark by then. On such summer nights, the smell of pine hangs in the air and the black lava rock is warm to the touch from the day's fierce sun. I pictured a sliver of moon rising above the stone walls of the canyon that had been home to Ishi's people for more than four thousand years. It was done, but nobody had wanted to leave, Mickey told me. So they stayed at Deer Creek, and they sang and wept late into the night.

# Seventeen

# DERSCH MEADOW

The funeral by Deer Creek was not the last chapter in the story of Ishi's brain, however. As another fall semester began at Duke, a fax from Mickey Gemmill appeared in my box announcing a final memorial—a "joyous day of tribal ceremony, food, and music to celebrate Ishi's successful repatriation"—under the auspices of the Redding Rancheria and Pit River Tribe. In contrast to the secret canyon ceremony a few weeks before, this would be a public event in Ishi's honor to be held that weekend at Mount Lassen National Park. "This is your official <u>Indian Invitation</u>!" Mickey scrawled across the cover sheet. He wanted me to speak at the memorial along with others who'd participated in the reuniting of Ishi's remains.

I canceled my Friday classes and flew to California. My parents decided to go with me to Mount Lassen, and we were joined by Jim Clifford, a professor at U.C. Santa Cruz who was writing about Ishi and the mythologies created around him. We stopped for dinner in Chico. This early Anglo outpost with the Spanish name has grown into a spreading town of almost seventy thousand people. Although the local state university may be best known as one of America's top ten party schools, a visitor to Chico can also tour the award-winning Sierra Nevada Brewing Company and the restored Victorian mansion of founding father John Bidwell, with an adjacent museum. There are also other, unmarked landmarks, like the big valley oak where one story has it that vigilantes hanged two Indians in 1863 to avenge the Lewis children's murders by Mill Creek raiders. The tree stands today near the busy intersection of Eighth and Salem Streets close by a pizza parlor and the postal employees credit union.

After dinner, we packed ourselves back into the car for another few hours of driving up Highway 32 above Deer Creek. The sunset was lovely, as it always is in the Yahi foothills on clear days. The broken land glowed in the red-gold light, which separately illuminated each tree and rock. I recalled how as a boy, thirty years before, I'd come up this same road in my friend's station wagon with the excited idea that lost Yahi might yet roam the hills. My mother steered the old Toyota Corolla around the meadow at Mill Creek's headwaters and then up through the shadowed pine forest to Mount Lassen.

We reached the park just after dark and set up our tents by flashlight. Late into the night, cars, pickups, motorcycles, and more RVs were still pulling in for the next day's memorial. The sound of ice chests, folding chairs, and sleeping bags being unloaded kept me awake until just before dawn. In the stillness that fell after the arrival of the last campers, I thought once more about two other departed souls—Alfred and Theodora Kroeber.

Native California's mythology had inspired the final passage of Theodora's biography of Alfred, her own last book. After a twilight stroll along Paris's Left Bank, she related, Alfred suffered a massive heart attack in their hotel room. The doctor arrived too late. With her husband's corpse on the bed, Theodora asked to be alone with Alfred until daybreak. "Through those shadowed hours between life and death when, as the California Indians put it, the Spirit lingers, reluctant to depart, concerned for the living, I relived the memory of our story," she recalled. "Paris was quiet for those hours. A soft persisting rain caused buildings and river to shimmer in a gray unreality. The world was contained in our single room. With daylight and morning sounds, Alfred was wholly gone from me into the abstractness of death. His Spirit had taken leave of the body, of the world of the living, to find its way to the Trail down which it must journey, to the Land of the Dead."

In anticipating her own death, Theodora turned to Native California once again. Beliefs about the afterlife varied much more across this land's diverse cultures than she allowed in her generalizations about the "California Indians." Even so, no tribe in the state had sacrificed prisoners, erected pyramids, or decked the body in golden ornaments as, say, the Aztecs did to commemorate a ruler's death. Typically in Native California's more egalitarian societies, your relatives buried you without ostentatious material display. They grieved and cried by your grave, then moved on with the hope that your spirit would travel to the next world and would not return to haunt them. Theodora admonished her own family to follow this example in a poem she wrote a few years before her own 1979 passing:

> *When I am dead*
> *cry for me a little.*
> *Think of me sometimes*
> *But not too much.*
> *It is not good for you*
> *Or your wife or your husband*
> *Or your children*
> *To allow your thoughts to dwell*
> *Too long on the dead.*
> *Think of me now and again*
> *As I was in life*
> *At some moment which is pleasant to recall—*
> *But not for long.*
> *Leave me, in peace*
> *As I shall leave you, too, in peace*
> *While you live let your thoughts be with the living.*

"Howsoever one touches Ishi, the touch rewards," the elderly Theodora had also written near the end, ever attached to her view of Ishi the healer and redeemer. Afflicted with leukemia, she died in her Arch Street house with its view across the bay to the Golden Gate Bridge and the Pacific Ocean beyond.


The dawn came clear and cold at 7,000 feet with a half-moon still hanging over Mount Lassen's jagged peak. Tom Killion had arrived during the night, and he came over to share a cup of our camp coffee. Caution and mutual suspicion had marked my interaction with Tom from time to time during the controversy about who would receive Ishi's brain. I'd tried to be circumspect in my comments to the press, but Tom believed I'd been too eager to bask in the limelight. "I don't think you deserve the Nobel Prize for finding the brain," he said when I'd last seen him. Most of that tension had dissipated by now, and our relations were more relaxed. We chatted for a bit, then strolled with my parents and Jim Clifford over to Dersch Meadow for the day's festivities.

Ringed by pines and mountains, the meadow was big and beautiful, covered with grass that had turned classically California golden-brown at the dry summer's end. Mickey and his people from the Redding Rancheria and the Pit River Tribe had already set up a large ring of black plastic chairs and a portable sound system. They'd worked hard to pull off the day, and they were paying for the rented equipment and the U-Haul out of their own pockets. Because it was casino money, however, the expense was minor for the tribes at this point. That video poker proceeds were financing Ishi's memorial seemed highly appropriate, since gambling was so popular in traditional Native California. Ishi had been an aficionado himself, even teaching students at the dental school to play his stick games so that he could have company. The anthropologists recorded many of Ishi's favorite gambling songs, among them two he'd somehow learned in Atsugewi, a language still spoken by one of the old men at the memorial at Dersch Meadow, Willard Rhoades. You sang for the fun of it—and to confuse your opponent as he tried to guess which hand you'd concealed a piece of bone in. Guess wrong, and your opponent got one of your colored sticks; you lost when you didn't have any more sticks. It's not known just what was wagered in older times, but in the nineteenth century gambling games could be high stakes—for money, gold, horses, hats, or anything of value.

If the Redding Rancheria and the Pit River Tribe assumed the basic expenses, the National Park Service contributed a half-dozen sturdy rangers. These federal overseers were a delegation of goodwill, and the traffic cops directing cars to the nearest parking lot. Trouble was brewing elsewhere between tribes and the Department of Interior over the ownership of old bones found on federal lands. Here at Mount Lassen relations were cordial between the park authorities and the Redding Rancheria and the Pit River Tribe. The park waived entrance fees in recognition of the Indians' prior claim to these lands, which had once been a meeting place for the area's tribes. The chief ranger, a woman in full dress uniform, was chatting with Mickey, who appeared relaxed and in good spirits. He'd arrived the night before in his minivan with his wife, Valerie, as slim as Mickey was solid, and their three daughters, Brandy, Honor, and Shasta.

About two hundred people had gathered in Dersch Meadow by midmorning. There was a TV news crew from the Sacramento Valley, but no other press. By this time media interest in Ishi's brain had waned, and Mount Lassen was too long a drive for the San Francisco or Los Angeles newspapers. Those present, however, included many of the familiar cast of characters, together one last time: Nancy Rockafellar and her daughter; the Forest Service's Jim Johnston and his daughter; Jed Riffe and his film crew; Tom Killion; Mickey and his family; Berkeley's Nancy Scheper-Hughes and her husband Michael; and many other faces both Anglo and Indian I recognized from other events along the way.

It would have been nice also to have present Karl Kroeber, Ursula K. Le Guin, or one of the other aging Kroeber children. They'd been upset, however, by the posthumous bad press heaped upon their father for having shipped Ishi's brain to the Smithsonian. There had been an outpouring of opprobrium against Alfred Kroeber and the "predations of anthropologists" against native peoples, in the words of journalist Alexander Cockburn. A first draft of the U.C. Berkeley anthropology department's official apology also decried the role of its founding father in "the exploitation and betrayal of Ishi." The final statement was softened after an emeritus professor, George Foster, objected that it was "untrue and unfair" to Kroeber and the other anthropologists.

In a newspaper interview, Karl Kroeber, an emeritus English professor at Columbia University, had fired back at his father's critics. They overlooked the real generosity and friendship that Alfred offered Ishi, Karl said, and the considerable good Alfred had done for Native California. I later met Karl and his brother Clifton in Berkeley. They were funny, smart, and delightful men, both in their seventies. Karl had his father's handsome gray beard; Clifton, who was Theodora's son by her first marriage, was a genial retired historian who called me "Brother Starn" even though we had just met. Their filial loyalty was understandable, but the Kroeber brothers and their famous sister, Ursula K. Le Guin, seemed reluctant to admit the less heroic aspects of the record. At least in public, they said nothing about Alfred's unwillingness to speak out about the crimes committed against Native California, or that cool distancing that once led him to describe Ishi as a "strange living survival of an aboriginal pre-civilization." Karl and Clifton were at a loss to explain just how it was that Ishi's brain had been sent to the Smithsonian in the first place. By his own admission without any evidence, Karl speculated to me that some sort of legal obstacle had kept his father from rejoining Ishi's brain to the ashes at the Olivet Cemetery. As much as I admired her fiction, Ursula had no better explanation. In a lecture for the one hundredth anniversary of the Berkeley anthropology department, she noted that having an organ jarred was a privilege reserved for the pharaohs in ancient Egypt, as if it had somehow also been an honor for Ishi.

Yet the Kroebers were not present at Dersch Meadow, either by choice or because they had not been informed of the ceremony. I'd made sure myself to call Art Angle the week before to tell him in case he hadn't heard. Lindy, his wife, said he was somewhere on the road in Oregon for a new part-time job as a express delivery driver, but that he'd be back before the weekend and she'd tell him about the memorial. Art never did show up, however. He'd made his own peace at Table Mountain and, I suspected, was still unhappy enough about having been excluded from Ishi's repatriation that he did not want to be present at any memorial staged by Mickey and his people.

The circle in Dersch Meadow had been decorated with tall wood poles at each of the four directions. Each pole displayed with what one older Pit River man, Vern Johnson, later explained was a special tribal symbol—a few flicker feathers ("strictly California Indian medicine"); a silver fox pelt ("our Pit River flag"); an eagle feather ("he flies the highest of any other bird. He takes our messages to the great spirit-God upstairs"); and a wood staff carved with a stern face ("that's the Grandfather, the spirit. No one can catch him. He can duplicate himself and go all over but nobody can catch him. That's what white people call God"). The entryway to the circle was an arch of branches that looked a bit like the chuppah at a Jewish wedding. Everyone who entered was supposed to twist a full turn around, pass under the branches, and then walk around the wood fire in the center of the circle before taking a seat. The seats of honor near the archway entrance gate were taken by the important Indians, among them the tribal officers from the Redding Rancheria and the Pit River Tribe, along with a few elders from these and other tribes. An exception was made for Tom Killion—"our good friend Tom," as the young master of ceremonies called him—who was invited to sit with the Indian leaders and wise men. Other Indians occupied most of the chairs in the circle, while the rest of the Anglos, myself included, stood or lay on the grass at the periphery of the circle. We were welcome at the event, and yet Indians had now claimed the role of first and best custodians of Ishi and his memory.

It was a lovely warm autumn day. The blue mountain sky was spotted with lazy white clouds, and you could smell the vanilla scent of the Ponderosa pines. Slowly, Mickey went around smudging each person with smoke from a plug of sunflower root blown with his eagle wing. Then he closed his eyes and offered a prayer:

> *We need to acknowledge and pay respects to those ancestors and those spirits of this place because they're here, those old ones. . . . I call them the unseen Grandmothers and Grandfathers because they're always with us—all you have to do is ask. At this time, Grandfather, our people are living in a world that has a lot of confusion for some of us and this is because some of those laws and rules or ways are not being honored or respected and that we've forgotten what we need in order to take care of ourselves in order to be happy and take care of the others around us. So, Grandfather, have pity on us. Be with us today. Let everyone's heart be free.*

When I'd last seen him, at the Oroville Travelodge conference, Mickey had been edgy and irritable, at least until he'd sung and smudged himself back to calm. Here, in contrast, his relief, even pleasure, at the completed repatriation was palpable. It was as if the burial at Deer Creek had not only freed Ishi from his uncertain, liminal, not-quite-dead existence, it had also liberated Mickey and the Redding Rancheria and the Pit River Tribe. A bad death had been made good. "This day has been a long time in the coming," Mickey said. "It's a beautiful occasion."

Greetings followed from the leaders of the two tribes. Tommy George, the Pit River tribal chairman, wore jeans and a cowboy hat and had a broad cowboy twang. He offered a few words of welcome in his Pit River tongue before continuing in English. George was soon to be booted out of his post in the latest fractious turn of the byzantine internal politics of the Pit River Tribe, whose tribal office in the town of Burney would shut down for several weeks as a result. "I'm here to make you welcome," said the affable George, with tribal politics set aside for the day. He wanted to think that Ishi's return to Deer Creek was a good omen, and the familiar image of Ishi as a touchstone of healing and renewal was also present in his words. "I believe my tribe is going to be healed in the months to come," George said. "But we ask your prayers, too."

Barbara Murphy, a big woman in dark glasses who was a leader at the Redding Rancheria, came next. Unlike George, Murphy did not speak any native tongue, but the first thing she said after taking the microphone was in Wintu: *heztum*. "That's a Wintu word," Murphy explained, "that my father spoke many times when he would greet somebody, so I can only assume that it's 'Hello' or 'Welcome.'" I was struck by the frankness of Murphy's admission that she was not even sure what this elementary word meant. Nor did Murphy pretend to any real knowledge of the original clan system of her people (these exogamous descent groups were typically linked to a totemic animal and still found among some of California's tribes as late as the early twentieth century). "I'm of the Grizzly Bear clan," Murphy said, but then added: "I don't understand what that means, but my mother has told us that we were of the Grizzly Bear clan."

Murphy's wistful words made me think of a useful catchphrase coined by the anthropologist Elizabeth Povinelli, the "cunning of recognition." In these new times, as Povinelli recognizes, a new symbolic and moral capital can now attach to being Indian, the ideal of multiculturalism now embraced. The catch, however—the "cunning," in this new recognition—is that a "real" Native American is expected to have "copper-colored" skin, speak a native language, and be able to tap a fount of tribal wisdom and mythology at the drop of a feathered bonnet. This standard of authenticity is one that the vast majority of Indians—so many of them urban, of mixed blood, and retaining only the slim connections to the traditional past—cannot possibly meet. The result may be to prompt a feeling of anxiety and even inadequacy, or at least so Povinelli worries in the parallel case of aborigines in Australia.

I was sure that Barbara Murphy wished she'd been taught Wintu, or even just a bit about the clan system. And yet, she was also the strongwilled former chair of the Redding Rancheria, and confident in her sense of purpose and leadership. Although her voice cracked with emotion several times, Murphy explained that she and her people took comfort in having been able to bury "our relative" Ishi at last. She thanked everyone at Dersch Meadow for "coming this far to join us in this great celebration."

The mood at the memorial was of an overwhelming, almost vulnerable sincerity. Mickey and the others had decorated the poles with the flicker feathers and the rest in allegiance to their own Pit River symbols and customs. Also on display in the ceremony, however, were the more generic, pan-Indian traditions that emerged in the twentieth century. "Ho!" everyone would chorus when a speaker made a powerful point. This exclamation of approval isn't indigenous to any Native California tribes, but is a commonplace at pow-wows and other intertribal gatherings. At one point, too, a black-haired teenager in a blue t-shirt and Reebok sweatpants performed a "Flag Song" to the memory of Ishi (this is a kind of unofficial Indian national anthem sung at the start of pow-wows and rodeos). The girl, Amby Stone, who'd driven up with her grandfather from the Hot Springs Rancheria in southern California, sang beautifully, with a touch of MTV teen diva style. An enthusiastic "Ho" from the circle greeted her when she finished.

There were also moments of humor, as much a trademark of modern Indian culture as anything else. "We laugh a lot because it's been the only way to make it through," Art's sister Rosalie had explained to me. Vern Johnson, the old man who also explained the symbolism of the decorated poles, related a story about his recent trip to Medicine Lake. Many local Indians believe that this gorgeous glacial lake east of Mount Shasta is a holy spot. Over the last decade, Vern and others have fought the plans of the Pacific Gas and Electric Company to drill for natural gas in the area. Vern asked the circle to pray for the protection of Medicine Lake—and also noted that his own last trip there had confirmed his conviction that it was a "power place": in Reno the following week, he'd won $400 dollars on a slot machine at Harrah's Club. "I knew," Vern grinned, that "the spirits were helping me."

Among the diverse people gathered at Dersch Meadow, a feeling of general satisfaction now prevailed, thanks to the apparent righting of history's wrongs that the repatriation of Ishi had brought. I was also glad to be at Dersch Meadow, yet I felt a nagging doubt about the way our obligations to Ishi had been fulfilled. The premise of the memorial was that the saga of Ishi's brain had ended in the fulfillment of Ishi's own wishes. But had it? I recalled the possibility that Ishi would have preferred to be buried in his second home, San Francisco. And what would he have thought about his funeral being conducted by the Redding

Rancheria and Pit River Tribe? Or Art's Maidu, if that had been the out-come? Isn't it possible he might have viewed these non-Yahi people as members of "foreign" tribes with no right to take charge of his remains? Group distinctions, after all, could be finely drawn, powerfully felt, and sometimes tense, in the old Native California. We know very little about Ishi's feelings toward the other Yana peoples, the various Pit River bands, the Maidu, or other area tribes. In San Francisco, at least, Ishi had been mourned by people he knew and liked, white though they may have been. Like so much else about Ishi, the real truth of the matter would never be known. I knew that Mickey and the others sincerely believed that they'd done what Ishi would have wanted, but it wasn't altogether clear to me that this was so.

Many of the younger Indians there did not know or pretend to know much about Ishi, except in the barest detail. They were members of a Generation X who'd grown up facing the new challenges of drugs and gangs and I sensed that they were searching for some kind of bond with the man they wanted now to claim as an ancestor, however tenuous that link might be. With his adorable toddler daughter at his side, Mark LeBeaux, the soft-spoken pony-tailed master of ceremonies, told us that he felt especially close to Ishi because his mother—a student at Shasta College in Redding—had once played Ishi's mother in a play, and then in the HBO movie *Last of His Tribe*. "So in one sense, in one small way," LeBeaux said, "I consider Ishi my brother." A young man in a red Adidas t-shirt also made his connection through the play at Shasta College and through seeing photographs of Ishi making bows and arrowheads. "I thought that was pretty awesome," Louis Gustafson smiled. Turning more serious, he said he believed that Ishi went to San Francisco "to teach those people how to live off the land." Gustafson described his reaction to looters who still dig for artifacts in ancient Indian graves and village sites:

> *I've asked some elders about how do I get along with these other people when they do things that are very upsetting? Well, you've got to teach them. But how can I teach them if this fire in my heart is very angry? How do I show compassion to the other people? And the word is the body and spirit—they've lost the spirit. I guess they're still searching.*

"Thank you," Gustafson concluded, "for coming to honor a relative in this way."

That these young Indians had limited knowledge of Ishi did not keep them from wanting to feel close to him. The new assertion of members of the Redding Rancheria and Pit River Tribe to primary kinship with Ishi was echoed in a poster the tribes had printed to commemorate the day that featured a line drawing of Ishi based on an old photograph. Big letters across the top of the poster read: "WELCOME HOME OUR RELATIVE ISHI," and at the bottom: "MAY WE NEVER FORGET OUR ANCESTORS." The poster artist, Jim Clifford noticed, added a Plains-style eagle feather to Ishi's hair. No Yahi ever wore feathers like this; they belonged to the very familiar pan-Indian iconography of the strong male "brave" out on the warpath or riding bareback in pursuit of the buffalo. If the Redding Rancheria and Pit River Tribe saw themselves as Ishi's closest relatives, the poster converted Ishi into a broader, more generic and univeral Indian hero and symbol, a beloved grandfather to every Native American.

In 1909, just before Ishi's capture in Oroville, the young doctor William Carlos Williams published his first book of poetry. Williams, in his own quirky way, subscribed to the familiar white American doctrine that the "Indian"—in the abstract, of course—was humanity's noblest and most authentic touchstone. The "average American" is an Indian, he wrote, "but an Indian robbed of his world." Williams declared his own wish "to go out and lift dead Indians tenderly from their graves, to steal from them, as if it must be clinging even to their corpses—some authenticity." This was the familiar nostalgia of alienated Euro-American moderns wanting to recharge themselves through contact with the power of ancient Native America. Here in Dersch Meadow I sensed a similar nostalgia in operation: the Indians also wanted to lift up the dead Ishi and "hug him tenderly." That impulse reflected the decline of the assimilation model of leaving behind the old Indian ways and embracing a brave new American future. Now it was a matter of duty to remember the ancestors, to hold onto the heritage, and to insist on a distinctive apartness from the American mainstream. To claim Ishi as a grandfather—and to lay his desecrated body to rest—was to fulfill one's obligation to the past. It was also to use Ishi to shore up, if not to "steal," an Indian identity by positioning oneself as a descendant from a nineteenth-century icon of native survival.

I understood better now just how much Ishi's repatriation was tied to twenty-first-century identity politics. Why had I, the anthropologist, ever thought it could be otherwise? After all, as every under-graduate major is supposed to know, funerary rituals are inevitably as much for the living—for ourselves—as for those vanished souls being remembered and mourned. Even today in parts of China, for exam-ple, the eldest son buries the corpse of his deceased father or mother—and then a year or so later digs it up, polishes the bones, and places them carefully in a jar in the family temple. To do any less is not only to fail the ancestors but also to jeopardize the well-being of one's lin-eage. A death improperly mourned threatens the social order, in other words. A "good death," in contrast, promises the renewal of the world of the living. To provide one's dead with a satisfactory funeral is at once an altruistic and a selfish act. Tommy George and several other Indians acknowledged that they had gained by Ishi's repatriation, the "healing" of their tribes.

For all the complications, it was still an extraordinary, even joyous day there in the high country. That so many Indians—waitresses, loggers, teachers, social workers—were gathered was an affirmation of the real-ity of Native Californian survival and renewal through it all. Even if the exact lines of kinship from Ishi to any single modern-day group were uncertain, it was understandable that any Indian might see him as a rela-tive in a larger sense. All the way from Ishi's band of Yahi beneath Mount Lassen to the seafaring, totem-pole carving Kwiakutl of the Northwest and the pyramid-building Mayan kingdoms far to the south in Guatemala, the native peoples of the Americas could hardly have been more different in precontact times. Yet each of these groups suf-fered the devastation of their lives and cultures to the invading Europeans. "The Indians left in the world are all part of each other," Mickey explained to me. As survivors and descendants of this conti-nent's first peoples, he and any other Indians had the right to call Ishi their "red brother," as Art put it.

Ishi himself, it seemed to me, remained elusive. In a Berkeley lecture a few months later, Karl Kroeber would offer still another view. Alfred and Theodora's youngest child compared Ishi to a pair of figures from the Western literary canon: Oedipus and King Lear. Although they were not of his own making, Ishi had also lived through extremes of violence, loss, and physical suffering. Having lost everything, however, both Oedipus and King Lear find a strange kind of peace and even serenity in their lonely last days. Likewise, Karl said, Ishi in San Francisco became a man "beyond tragedy, beyond fear and pity." Karl supported Ishi's repatriation and yet was skeptical of any latter-day claims to proprietorship of his legacy. "The dead are not ownable," he insisted. Karl's Ishi transcended the limits of ethnicity or any other more particular form of identity.

For my own part, I recalled other images of Ishi in the old newspapers, the ones that were never claimed or reprinted—a barefoot Ishi in his suit, for instance, squatting and smoking a cigarette. From a first cigar he was offered in Oroville, Ishi loved to smoke, but the pictures were never reproduced in later years because they didn't fit the idealized image of an "uncontaminated" native man. I thought, too, of the other odd bits of information we have about Ishi, little tidbits that don't fit any of the expected narratives. In 1915, Alfred Kroeber had been moved to write the following curious note to the laboratory administrator at the veterinary school next to the museum:

*Dear Mrs. Newell:*
*I should be greatly obliged if you would speak to the gentleman in charge of your Dog Laboratory requesting him to give orders not to permit Ishi in that building. I shall be obliged to you for continuing Mrs. Wisner's policy of not allowing Ishi in the hospital after 5 o'clock, unless he is wanted by the staff for a demonstration. In this case we should like to have previous notice and would also ask you to send for him and bring him back. As there is generally only one man in the building after 5 o'clock and he is under instructions not to leave it.*

Was Ishi straying from his duties? Was Kroeber enforcing curfew on an errant employee, or was there something about the Dog Laboratory that made Kroeber decide it should be off limits to Ishi? No one wanted to claim this more complex, unpredictable, mysterious, and ordinary Ishi, the one who couldn't be pigeonholed. And all the more so because we have so little direct information from the man himself—"Ishi Obscura" as writer Gerald Vizenor has called him—it has always been possible to make up our own and usually singular Ishi, the one we want to see. A man steeped in the traditions of his tribe? A wild man? An urban Indian? A healer? A teacher? A relative? An Oedipus or King Lear? An everyman? In varying degrees, each of these images is at once true and fails to tell the whole story.

. . .

The microphone was open until the late afternoon. Lorraine Frazier was the sole representation from Oroville and Art's Butte County Native American Cultural Committee. Lorraine, the cultural affairs officer at the Mooretown Rancheria, had lupus and wore a broad-brimmed straw hat to protect herself from the sun. Although passionate about preserving the Maidu language and other traditions, Lorraine worshiped every Sunday at Oroville's Temple of Praise, an evangelical church. She saw no contradiction between her Christianity and native heritage ("He placed Native Americans and everyone else on this earth because he wanted a multicultural world," she had told me). Now Lorraine spoke about the importance of intertribal gatherings and the intricate blood ties that linked all the tribes there that day:

> *I'm classified as Concow Maidu, but my grandmother was from Geneseee Valley and one of our family histories says that her mother was Mary Adkins from Pit River. . . . There's a man who is researching the multicultural population of Fort Ross—which did include Maidu. They took the healthy strong men and boys, put them on boats and sent them down the Feather River to the Sacramento, out the Golden Gate and up along the coast. They sold some of them, some they gave away—and many of them sailed up to Fort Ross and married into the Pomo people and coast Miwok.*

More broadly, Lorraine concluded, all the world's population was one. "There's a lot of scientific things coming out now about the differences between the races," she said, and the discovery was that "there aren't any. We're the human race."

Of course, we non-Indians had views of our own. When Tom Killion took the microphone, he was emotional and eloquent, generous with his thanks and also thoughtful. In acknowledging all who helped make it possible, he included Art Angle and his committee, "who came to the museum and really got the ball rolling in terms of the return—the procedure, the process of getting this individual home." Killion reserved his greatest thanks for Mickey Gemmill and Floyd Buckskin, saying that he was "just very impressed and humbled to see how they came to the museum and took care of Ishi's remains in a ceremonial way and a very strong way." Mickey and Floyd, he said, "told Ishi that they love him and they want him to come home—they told him not to look back. I consider it a great honor to have seen them demonstrate that strength and knowledge, to be able to take care of him in such a good way." "I feel strong emotion right now talking to you about him," Killion added. "And it changes the way you look at things—the way you understand things.

Nancy Rockafellar and I took our turns late in the afternoon. We both had our own reasons to be thankful for Ishi's repatriation and the feeling of purpose and even accomplishment it had allowed us. I wanted to say something honest and wise about my childhood hero and his legend, about the pain and beauty of life, about my questions and doubts, and about my happiness at being there at Dersch Meadow. All that came out were a few words of admiration for Ishi and thanks to the Redding Rancheria and Pit River Tribe, which were genuine enough but little more that clichés. That the loudspeaker's feedback made it hard to hear myself talk did not help. I was a bit ashamed later at having failed to rise to the occasion.

Tom Killion had said that the repatriation of Ishi's remains was "an affirmation of his connectedness to the communities here—to the relatives here—to his friends here." And yet, if the Redding Rancheria and Pit River Tribe were Ishi's relatives, as I agreed was true in an important way, they were distant ones by any conventional blood reckoning, and it was still a possibility that Ishi would not have chosen to be buried either by Deer Creek or by Indians from neighboring tribes. I guessed that Tom and perhaps Nancy also understood this, but none of us voiced our thoughts out loud. It was not the time or the place to stir up controversy or to get in the way of the implicit transaction that was taking place. We were mutually acknowledging that Ishi's reburial was something to be celebrated. Indians could feel that they had fulfilled their duty to the man they all wanted to embrace as an ancestor. Tom, Nancy, and I could feel that we were "good" whites who had played a part in expiating the sins of our forefathers, won a little trust from Native America, and earned a place at the celebratory picnic afterward. Everyone at Dersch Meadow, it must be said, had his or her own investment in assuming we had done right by Ishi.

Were we wrong, or just presumptuous, to feel good about what had been accomplished with Ishi's return to Deer Creek? It was not an easy question, and I did not have the answer. I wished that all of us at Dersch Meadow had somehow been able to speak about the paradoxes, complexities and tensions that figured in the story of Ishi's repatriation. In wondering what Ishi would have wanted, I thought it was quite possible that he would have been pleased to have Mickey and other Indians lay his remains to rest in the canyon he knew so well. At the very least, reuniting Ishi's brain with his ashes—the body of the last Yahi made whole again—was almost indisputably in accordance with his wishes. Many good, sometimes beautiful things had happened along the way to that final, private burial ceremony not far upstream from Grizzly Bear's Hiding Place. I had seen many people trying to learn and understand, to reach out and find it in themselves to forgive and to seek reconciliation. I wanted to think that Ishi would have approved.

There were a few flashes of unexpected and jagged emotion before the day was over. One came when an attractive, husky-voiced woman in jeans and turquoise earrings stepped forward. She said her name was Netta Burgeray, that she lived in Sacramento and her nickname was the Painted Pony Woman, after the paintings she sold of Indians and their horses out on the plains. Whether Burgeray was Indian or not wasn't clear, and she didn't say. I'd noticed her earlier, smiling wanly with her Yorkshire terrier for Jed's camera crew, but she was heartbreaking at the microphone as a blue jay squawked off in the trees. She'd just learned from the doctors that her husband, a trucker, had cancer. Out on the road on this day, also the first anniversary of his mother's death, he hadn't yet heard the news. "I'd like all of you to please pray for this wonderful French-Canadian Indian man," the Painted Pony Woman said, fighting back tears.

Others spoke in more predictable ways, if also from the heart. One athletic-looking white woman with pigtails, for example, expressed her unreconstructed romantic faith about Ishi and his Yahi tribe as a paragon of communal values and harmony with the land. It was again the modern-day fairytale about Native America as a beacon of everything lost in the West. Now that Ishi's spirit was brought back to the land that "was so sacred to him," the woman said, "the spirit is whole." A Pit River man, a self-declared poet and children's book writer who lived in San Francisco, read almost an hour of his poems. "Stay on the red road, my brothers and sisters," he advised. "I/you/we are the only ones left that do pray to the rocks, that do still pray to the rivers and streams, and yes we do still pray to the mountains."

Bored by so much serious talk, a group of small boys had wandered off to play tag and wrestle at the edge of the meadow. One brandished a small bow and arrow. A number of adults, white and Indian, had also gotten up and slipped away during the Indian poet's hour-long reading, and several grimaced as if they'd reached the limits of patience. The chairs in the circle were half-empty by the end of the day when the final speaker, Floyd Buckskin, rose to speak. Buckskin lived outside the town of Fall River Mills north of Mount Lassen, and he'd presided along with Mickey at the Deer Creek burial. He was a private man with no telephone who had worked with the California Department of State Parks to preserve ancient village sites in the area and in other local Indian causes. About my age, forty or so, with short black hair and a movie star's two-day growth of beard, Floyd exuded a charisma in his plaid shirt and jeans that was almost messianic. His sense of the moment was as strong as his sturdy lumberman's body.

"Ishi has gone back to where he was supposed to go," Floyd said. "He's at peace and whole with the Creator." I recalled that Wovoka, the Paiute prophet of the nineteenth-century Ghost Dance Movement, came from Nevada, not so far from the high deserts of Pit River country, and found many followers among the Pit Rivers. More recently, the Jehovah's Witnesses and Assembly of God had brought their own visions of apocalypse and redemption to this wildest, most forgotten corner of California. It was Floyd who now assumed the duties of prophecy, delivering his message rapid-fire as if there could be no room for doubt. "One day the Creator will look down and raise up the people into a beautiful world that he proposes to make. No sickness. No sadness. That's what we have to look forward to. For now, we've all got the tests of this life."

And with that, we ambled back over to the picnic glade. Very often in the United States funeral services—Indian or not—have become a two-part drama of resurrection. The first act, taking place at graveside, allows for the expression of trauma, grief, and unrestrained emotion—everything that I imagined happening at the burial of Ishi at Deer Creek. In the second act, a memorial held at another place, there's the opportunity to recall and even celebrate the life of the deceased, and in the process the opportunity for the living to come out of the space of grief back into the world. Some sort of shared meal very often marks the reentry of the community of grievers into the world of the living, the world of sustenance and the physical body, of life yet to be lived.

A team of women had readied a celebratory final dinner in the picnic area at the meadow's edge. I'd attended many wakes in the Andes, where there were no hospitals and so many died in poverty before their time. Though the dead were sometimes buried only in an old canvas tarp, even the poorest families invited everyone who'd been at the funeral to their farmhouse for a plate of goat stew afterward. Here the Redding Rancheria and the Pit River Tribe, assuming the duties of Ishi's relatives, provided the dinner for the ritual of closure. They'd brought up the food, drink, cooking stove, folding tables, and the utensils in their rented U-Haul.

And it was quite a spread. A couple of Yuroks from the north coast had slow-roasted several huge salmon in strips over hot coals. There was boiled deer meat, too, and a pot of acorn stew, albeit made in an aluminum pot and not a basket heated with red-hot rocks as in the old manner. Of late, many Indian activists have urged a return to more aboriginal fare, insisting that Krispy Kremes, McDonald's burgers, and other greasy junk food were "poisoning our people," as it is often put. Poor diet has contributed to the devastating high rates of heart disease and especially diabetes in Indian country. On this evening, however, nobody wanted to worry about such matters. There were platters of fried chicken, coleslaw, tuna casserole, macaroni and cheese, and a tub of I-Can't-Believe-It's-Not-Butter, all by now traditional Indian foods in their own right. As at many tribal events these days, liquor was banned; the price of alcoholism for Indians and their families was still too high to be ignored.

The atmosphere was relaxed around the picnic tables in the twilight, and there was plenty of joking among the chaos of paper plates laden with food, old acquaintances meeting again and new ones made. I fell into conversation with a matronly woman from the Redding Rancheria about the art of dealing with one's small and willful children. The mysterious Floyd Buckskin, nowhere to be seen, had headed off for parts unknown.

"While you still live," Theodora had advised, inspired by Native California, "let your thoughts be with the living." Theodora hadn't meant to say that you should forget your past. With so many Indians concerned with recovering their roots and still haunted by their hard history, there was no longer much danger of that. New controversies, new worries, and new obsessions doubtless awaited Mickey, Floyd, Art, Rosalie, and the others. With the speeches over, the last songs sung, and the TV news crew long since departed, this much was certain: they could move forward without worrying any longer about Ishi. Their "red brother," the last Yahi and the most famous of California's Indians, was back in the earth at last.

I needed to fly back to North Carolina the next morning for a seminar. Jim and my parents had their own obligations to fulfill. We walked back to Summit Lake to pack the Toyota for our return to the Bay Area. Ishi could rest now, I hoped. And Theodora, Alfred, Saxton Pope, Sam Batwi, and all those other "old ones," too. The rest of us had to get on with our own lives.

# VERA'S PARTY

Almost two years had passed since Ishi was laid in the ground. I am not the speediest of writers and still hadn't finished this book. My wife Robin's eyes glazed over whenever I shared some new fact I'd learned about Ishi at the dinner table. In the first months of writing, Frances, our elementary school-age daughter, often asked enthusiastically if I'd be done soon. On one family vacation, she and a cousin made a brush hideout in the woods. It was their Bear's Hiding Place, she explained, happy in the fun of fort-making and pleasing her father with an interest in his passions. After awhile, however, Ishi's novelty wore off even for Frances. And she stopped asking about the book, although she would still companionably come into my office to read her Nancy Drews while I tapped away at the computer.

In the spring of 2002, I went to Mill Creek in search of some last inspiration. According to what Alfred Kroeber and the other anthropologists believed, this canyon was Ishi's birthplace and a center of Yahi society before the tightening circle of white settlement forced the last survivors into the narrower, more inaccessible watershed of Deer Creek. In the early years of the Gold Rush, exhausted pioneers struggled above Mill Creek on the last stretch of the famous Lassen Trail to the New Arcadia of California. The trail was "well-marked with tracks of oxen, cows, horses, mules, naked Indian feet, coarse shoes of a man; bears, deer, wolves, rabbits &c," reported J. Goldsborough Bruff, the first white man to record his impressions. There were bleached oxen bones along the way and abandoned "boxes & trunks of dry-goods, &c, broken open, & contents strewn along the muddy road." Loggers called the "Shingle Men" had a camp on the brow of one hill. They were suspected by valley whites of providing weapons to renegade Mill Creeks for a share of the spoils of their raids.

Bruff observed signs everywhere of Indian camps. He kept his distance, but at one point saw "blue smoke curling up" from one Indian village not far from the strange towering lava pyramid of Black Rock, the major landmark in the canyon. As the half-starved and stranded Bruff tried to make it down to Peter Lassen's ranch, he came across a "low, square-built indian, very dark . . . he was nude, except a kind of fig-leaf, had a knife, a quiver full of arrows on his back, and a bow in his band." Ishi had not yet been born in this first year of the Gold Rush, but the man Bruff saw may have been Yahi. This tribesman spoke no English or Spanish, and Bruff could not make him understand his desperate request for directions out of the hills to the valley. Although so hungry that he "thought of eating" the Indian, Bruff could not bring himself to pull the trigger as the man headed off in the opposite direction. "I could not shoot the poor wretch in the back," he recalled. Only a bit farther along the path did Bruff run into another party of Indians, this time ones who spoke some Spanish and pointed him to the valley.

Once again I recruited my father for the expedition to Mill Creek, and also brought along Frances and her favorite cousin, Gabriel. We stopped on the way up in the little old farm town of Tehama, population 401. Hi Good was buried here at the foot of the hills where he'd hunted down so many Indians—and then been shot down himself by his own hired hand, Indian Ned. The cemetery lay out in the orchards across the train tracks. Good was a war criminal, as far as Mickey Gemmill and other Indian activists were concerned. Although he had had no family, someone had seen to a proper granite marker for the legendary Indian killer. The tombstone stood by the fence near the entrance of the cemetery: "H. A. GOOD, DIED MAY 4, 1870 AGED 34 YRS."

I noticed the trailer of a farmworker family by the quiet country road on the way back to town. The kids playing in front looked Mexican, or maybe Central American with plenty of Indian blood, to judge by their brown skin and black hair. Good and his companions couldn't have guessed that California would fill up over the next century with hundreds of thousands of new "Hispanic" arrivals who looked like Ishi and were descended from the Mixtec, Zapotec, Yaqui and other tribes, in a kind of re-Indianization of the United States. You can hear Maya and Nahuatl, the language of the Aztecs, spoken in Central Valley migrant camps today up and down the state. By now, too, there were plenty of another kind of Indian, those from South Asia, making their homes in the polyglot valley—like the turbaned Sikh owners of some of the largest rice farms not far south of Hi Good's Tehama grave. If precontact Native California was a land of many tribes, it is even more so today with the changing mix of Afghanis and Hmong, Koreans and Peruvians, Samoans and Filipinos, as well as the descendants of the Anglo pioneers and the survivors of the Maidu, Achumawi, and other native peoples. The first Spanish explorers believed they'd happened upon the "island of California," and, indeed, this "terrestrial paradise" had been cut off from the rest of the world longer than almost any other part of the hemisphere. In the short span of a century and a half after the Gold Rush, however, California has been transformed into one of the world's busiest, most varied crossroads.

We rendezvoused with Brian Bibby in Tehama. Brian had hiked and camped in Mill Creek for more than thirty years and had agreed to guide us into the canyon for an overnight. At the last minute, Bruce and Leslie Steidl had decided to come along, too. The Weather Channel had forecast a storm for that weekend, but we decided to chance it anyway. It was a couple of hours' drive into the hills and across the muddy Ponderosa Highway to the little campground at Black Rock, the most popular jumping-off point for hikers into the Ishi Wilderness Area.

Brian led us down the trail to a special spot for the kids—a big rock some believe was Yahi play equipment, a natural stone slide polished by many centuries of use. After Frances and Gabriel took a few turns zipping down, Brian took us across a meadow to another Yahi stone landmark, a smaller rock pocked with human-made depressions. Various theories exist about these so-called pitted boulders. According to Leslie, an archaeologist with the state park system, elders in the Achumawi band of the Pit River Tribe believe that these boulders possess magical powers as a natural decongestant—you rub your chest against the depressions to get rid of a cold. The pitted boulders were apparently used in fertility rites by the Pomo in present-day Mendocino County, though the exact connection is nonetheless unclear. One early-twentieth-century ethnographer was told that women would eat a bit of the ground stone dust to encourage pregnancy.

And yet, the ever-increasing remoteness of the native past struck me most powerfully at Mill Creek. As arbitrary as such signposts may be, a new century had just begun—and this made it three centuries now back to the time when Ishi's people had roamed this canyon, and the precontact history of Native California was fading into the shadows of the past. Although the canyon still looks wild enough on the face of it, the ecology has been transformed over the decades. Whole flats by Mill Creek have been colonized by the prickly yellow star thistle—"Saddam's Revenge," as mulepacker Dan Wells called it—an import from the Middle East that now infests millions of acres in California. Among the canyon's other many non-native plants are foxgloves, sweet white clover, wooly mullein, spotted knapweed, and goat's beard. We didn't see any, but feral pigs now forage in the Yahi hills; these pigs are the descendants of the domesticated animals of Old World origin that escaped the farmyards of early homesteaders. As "wild" game, they are now prized targets for well-heeled hunters who sometimes helicopter in from Los Angeles and the Bay Area.

More so than other, less-visited stretches of the foothills like Deer Creek, Mill Creek has also been stripped bare by souvenir hunters, who have made off with thousands of stone choppers, metates, projectile points, and shell beads from the ancient Yahi village sites that dot the canyon. It's only because they were too large to carry off that the rock slide and the pitted boulder were still here. By now, the detritus of more recent white occupations is more notable than any signs of the Yahi. The rusted skeleton of what looked to be a World War II–vintage Dodge DeSoto lay at the bottom of one dry creek bed. There was also the tumbledown compound of a cinder-block cabin and a couple of weather-beaten trailers that belonged to an old woman named Lorena. She was something of an area legend for letting her cattle loose across the hills despite the threats of the Forest Service and other private landowners, angry about fouled springs and trampled meadows.

We made our way down at last to a flat by Mill Creek, a strip of meadow about the length of a football field edged by ponderosa, black oak, and bay tree. Although it remains a matter of speculation among the most committed history buffs, new research by Chico journalist Steve Schoonover suggests that this was the site of the village of Three Knolls, the spot where Hi Good had led one of the last and most brutal massacres of the Yahi. That was the retaliatory raid in 1865 set off by the murder of two white sisters and their hired hand down the mountains in the town of Concow.

It was easy enough to imagine the gunshots and the cries of pain by the creek back in that nineteenth-century dawn. Even in this place, however, the signs of the past were also growing fainter, the history more distant and undecipherable. When he'd first come in 1970 or 1971, Brian said, the scooped-out, circular depressions of Yahi housepits had still been clearly visible. There were still uneven places, but Brian couldn't tell any longer whether they were housepits or simply earth shifted around by burrowing gophers, grazing cows, and booted visitors like us. Boy Scout Troops and wilderness lovers come in pilgrimage and for a taste of Ishi country; and the area had just been featured in *Backpacker* magazine. In a cluster of bay trees, campers had left a stone fire ring. Brian squatted down and turned over one flattish river rock in the makeshift fireplace, showing me the almost imperceptible yet telltale wear of ancient Yahi grinding. It was a metate, scorched and sooty from use by modern campers oblivious to the rock's older history.

It began to rain at last just as we made it back from the trailhead, slowly at first and then harder with night falling. The children had been good sports up to now, but they were already complaining about the cold, so we decided to drive out instead of camping for the night. On the slippery, muddy Ponderosa Highway out of Mill Creek, the rain turned to sleet and then snow. The spring mountain snowstorm blew horizontal as it caught the headlights like some fierce Alaskan blizzard; even Interstate 80 across to Nevada would be closed that night at the higher elevations. As I looked back down at Mill Creek canyon one last time, I recalled the names of old-time Yahi villages that Ishi had listed in a map he'd made with Kroeber—*Tuliyani, Kandjau-ha, Yish'inna, Puhiya, Mahmapa.* You couldn't see anything through the dim, driving snow that was covering the land in a thin crust of white.

I wasn't finished with Mill Creek, however. The last disappearing physical signs of the Yahi told a kind of truth—about endings, decline, and the limited span of civilizations, whether as large as Rome or as small as the Yahi. Even so, as much as the words had also sometimes proved to conceal about the tenuousness of real connections to the past, the saga of Ishi's brain had turned out to be just as much about renewal and survival. There was the exuberant, unflagging afterlife of Ishi and his Yahi as a symbol and myth—and also the twenty-first-century reincarnation of Native California with its casinos and Plains Drums, pickup trucks and RVs, paradoxes and pride. It was this part of the story, the motif of life over death, that was always lost in the once dominant and now contested story of Ishi as the last of his kind, the sad termination point of Manifest Destiny.

Of the many people I'd met in the journey, none seemed more alive to me than a woman who was also the oldest: Vera Clark McKeen. I'd first met the legendary Maidu matriarch of Yankee Hill three years earlier, when she was just ninety-seven. Now Vera was about to celebrate her hundredth birthday, and I'd timed the expedition to Mill Creek to be there. Yankee Hill is a backcountry scatter of little ranches, trailers, and houses, not even really a town, a bit north of Table Mountain about halfway between Oroville and Chico. It happens to overlook the little Concow Valley, home of the men who'd pursued the Mill Creeks to Three Knolls to avenge the murders of their women and now underwater as a small reservoir. I'd heard about Vera, Yankee Hill's oldest resident, from Chico State professor Michele Shover, who had co-authored a short book about Vera's adventures: growing up a backcountry Indian girl in the early twentieth century, going away to work in Oakland as a maid for the wealthy Ghirardelli chocolate heirs, and touring New York and the East Coast with her sister. I wanted to meet Vera because one of her stories involved a close encounter with Ishi back in 1911.

With Michele's blessing, I'd called Vera and she invited me over to see her that afternoon. She lived alone in a house down a dirt driveway with a sunny flower garden decorated with rusted farm implements and a couple of old bathtubs as planters for petunias and marigolds. When I knocked, Vera shouted out from her easy chair in the living room, "The door's open. Come on in!" The house was packed like a mouse's burrow with the memorabilia of her long life—framed pictures of her family, an acrylic of Elvis, a papoose of the kind they sell in souvenir stores in the Black Hills, and colorful kitsch prints of noble war-bonneted Indian warriors and slim, buckskin-clad Indian princesses. Vera switched off her soap opera and greeted me with a smile. Though her hands were knobby with arthritis and her brown skin leathery from age and a lifetime outdoors, she had a sparkle in her eyes, an easy laugh, and an aura of positive energy. She was the kind of person who always made you leave feeling better about the world and yourself than when you arrived.

Vera, a born raconteur, was happy to share her Ishi tale. In 1911, when she was nine, her family was working in the family garden, a place they called "The Potato Patch." Suddenly her uncle, John Adams, spotted a thin plume of spoke farther down the hill, and went off to investigate. There Adams saw an Indian, clad only in a "little skin thing," as Vera put it. The man darted off into the woods. The alarmed Adams rushed back up the hill. He shouted to his sister-in-law Annie, Vera's mother, to get the children back into the house because there was "a wild man or a crazy man out there." Later, Vera's family found evidence—hay hollowed into a sleeping place—that the man had been living in their barn. Both John Adams and Vera's mother Annie were half-Indian, and Vera's Maidu grandmother Yohema Clark, or Little Flower, would sometimes grind acorns to make a traditional Indian flatbread for the family. By that time, however, the family had long since become regular farmers and loggers intermarried with Scotch and English settlers. They were just as frightened by the idea of a "wild," "mean" Indian as any other homesteader in 1911. Many local people remembered old stories about the ferocious raids of the Mill Creeks. Shortly afterward, Vera's family heard the news of Ishi's capture in Oroville. They'd always assumed that their wild man must have been Ishi.

That identification of the man in the "skin thing" was credible enough. Yankee Hill is about halfway between Deer Creek and Oroville, and it was very possible that Ishi came through, whether alone or with some other Yahi that the McKeens never saw that morning, on his way south. An archaeologist at Butte College, John Furry, has found a cave in the bluffs less than a mile from Yankee Hill. He assumed it was some kind of a pioneer garbage dump at first, since he found medicine and whiskey bottles and rusted buckets there. But Furry also turned up glass trade beads and six stone arrowheads among the detritus—and the points are side-notched and beautifully crafted just like ones that Ishi made at the museum. Did Ishi hide for a while in this cave? Or had there been, as local lore has it, other holdout "wild" Indians in this wilderness? Furry wants to believe that Ishi made the points, and, like Art and also Vera, he thinks that Ishi may have been part Maidu, coming down this way from Deer Creek because it was part of his home turf. He points out that it was only about twenty miles from Grizzly Bear's Hiding Place to Oroville if one followed the natural breaks in the lava across the intervening canyons. There could have been much more back-and-forthing between the adjoining Yahi and Maidu than allowed for in any simpler view of the two "tribes" planted in discrete, unconnected "territories."

Vera and I hit it off, and after my visit we exchanged phone calls, notes, and Christmas cards. Even though she herself had not seen him in the flesh, she was a last living link to Ishi. What amazed me most about Vera, however, was her zest for life, in particular her capacity to reconcile and even embrace the seeming contradictions of the past and the present. On my journey to Ishi I'd encountered so many people who were trapped in one way or another into a search for a certainty and wholeness that would always elude them. I recalled those poor Ishi buffs tramping through the poison oak in a vain search for Grizzly Bear's Hiding Place. Robert Martin, the retired real estate agent, wanted and failed to convince the world of his Yahi blood. And, more broadly, there were the many people who've enshrined Ishi as a lodestar of primitive purity, regardless of the precarious, scrambled realities of his life in Deer Creek canyon. In these ranks of unfulfilled strivers and wannabes I counted myself—a white man who likes Indian company, a Californian stranded in North Carolina, a writer who hates to write.

Vera's own life was a study in the happy refusal to be boxed in by society's expectations. A beauty who loved to dance—she must have driven mountain men wild in the juke joints—Vera had also grown up learning to handle a gun, and hunted deer on her own in the mountains. She was proud of her Maidu heritage, and her grandmother Yohema's heavy pestle for grinding acorns was one of her most treasured heirlooms. At the same time, Vera recalled how her farm family had also followed her father's English custom of an afternoon teatime. Vera loved to talk about the old days but never pretended to know more than she did. It was one of her few regrets that her mother had never taught her to "talk Indian." Near the end of her life, Vera lived very much in the here and now, seizing the day's pleasures as they came. Late one Sunday morning, I called her from North Carolina to say hello. She sounded upbeat and full of energy, as always. She reported she'd made a road trip to Reno the day before with her daughter-in-law. They'd gone to a show and played the slots late into the night, Vera laughed, and she'd returned to Yankee Hill at two in the morning.

Vera's one hundredth birthday party was so big that it had to be held in the gym of the local elementary school. The weather was still wet and overcast from a storm, and dozens of cars and pickups were parked in the muddy fields around the school, as if for a rock concert. The gym had been decorated with balloons and streamers; Vera sat in state with a plastic diamond tiara on her head, and her well-wishers packed in around her. Brian, Bruce, and Leslie had already left us by then, leaving me with my father, Frances, and Gabriel. When we walked in the door, a trio of Maidu dancers from Sacramento—big men stripped to the waist, decorated with feathers and shell-bead headdresses, and swaying and stamping to the sound of their whistles and clackers—was performing in Vera's honor in the middle of the basketball court. The tradition of Maidu dancing had altogether disappeared by the mid-twentieth century, but in the 1960s the painter and activist Frank Day had recruited young men to form a new society to bring the dances back from extinction. When the Sacramento Maidu dancers finished, a blonde, suburban-looking in-law of Vera's read a framed proclamation from the mayor of her Michigan suburb—where she was a town councilwoman—congratulating Vera on reaching the milestone of one hundred years. Somebody else took the microphone and asked everyone in the gym related to Vera to raise their hand. More than a hundred people did, everyone from blue-eyed toddlers to tough-looking tattooed white working men and Maidu matrons with brown skin and black hair.

Among those raising their hands was Sharon Guzman-Mix, the kindergarten teacher whom I'd met on the trip to Washington. One of Vera's dozens of nieces, she was now working for the Feather River Indian Health Service in Oroville. Sharon was partly descended from the mountain Maidu, the branch of the tribe high back up in the mountains. She said she'd just been up to Chester with a cousin, who'd become carsick on the winding highway into high country. "You're a heckuva mountain Maidu," Sharon recalled teasing her relative, and smiled now as she took a bite of a chocolate chip cookie.

For a moment, however, Sharon turned more serious. "Everything's okay," she almost whispered with the buzz of Vera's party around us in the school gym. I was puzzled. What was okay, I asked? "Ishi," Sharon said. She knew a couple of the people who had been at the Deer Creek burial almost two years before. They'd been back to the spot recently, Sharon said, and it was undisturbed. Sharon sounded surprised as well as happy that Ishi was still resting in peace. So ingrained were the idea and the reality of her people's graves being dug up and the artifacts looted that her worry did not come across as paranoid.

I recalled being down by Lake Oroville with Bruce and Leslie a few months before. The water had dropped so low that it exposed an ancient Maidu graveyard. A scruffy young white couple in an old Plymouth drove up and began scouring the ground for arrowheads, until Leslie informed them she worked for the Park Service and told them they could be fined and even sent to jail. Bruce added, pleasantly enough, that he was Native American, and the graves here were of his people. The woman was addict-skinny, empty-eyed, and seemed to be on methamphetamines, "crank," the drug of choice among poor whites; said she made dream-catchers that she sold in turn to the Feather Falls Casino. A drug-addled white woman who was arrowhead-hunting in an Indian burial and made "Indian" artifacts for Indians to sell in their casino? Somehow it seemed emblematic of the strange, mixed-up condition of life and culture I'd encountered along the way in the search for Ishi. As we drove off, the couple casually resumed their search for arrowheads, oblivious to Leslie's threats.

Now at Vera's party the toasts and the speechmaking came to a close. I went up to Vera to congratulate her and introduce her to Frances. When I bent over to kiss her on the cheek, Vera grabbed me for a hug that was almost a lover's embrace with the strength of a woman a third her age. Everything else seemed to dissolve in the surprising power of Vera's grip. It was life itself that Vera was hugging to her breast.

That night, we drove to Oroville for dinner with Art and a few others at The Depot, a steakhouse that occupies a converted train station—the same station where the shoeless Ishi had waited for the train to San Francisco back in 1911. Along with his wife Gladys, Gus Martin was there, weak after a stroke and quiet as usual, but happy to be out. Art had brought his two daughters Shannon and Sadie. A skinny little girl when I'd met her and Art five years before, Sadie was a long-legged teenager now, big into horse shows. She still looked at Art when he talked with the same mixture of love and indulgence I remembered from the Cornucopia.

One person was missing from our reunion. A month before, Rosalie Bertram, Art's sister, had died suddenly of a seizure on a plane back from Washington, D.C.. She was returning from a meeting of the National Congress of American Indians, an umbrella advocacy group she'd joined as the vice-chair of the Enterprise Rancheria. The pilot made an emergency landing in Denver, but they couldn't save Rosalie. Along with Vera, Rosalie was one of the people I'd met through my Ishi work that I liked the very best—a model of good humor and intelligence, a person who loved life the same way Vera did, and a stalwart activist whose most recent cause had been to steer her Enterprise Rancheria toward the construction of a nursing home for elderly, family-less Indians in the area. The last time I'd seen her, when we'd had a drink with Art at the Sierra Club, Rosalie told me that I was one of her "favorite people." She was the kind of person who told everyone that to make them feel good, but she did it with such good humor that you believed her anyway.

There'd been a memorial for Rosalie in an Oroville funeral home—with Christian hymns, and a Maidu song performed by one of her sons with an elderberry clapper. It was an old song, Leslie said, one she'd never heard before. Then Art and other family members took her body for burial in a private little Indian cemetery down a dirt road above the flooded-over Enterprise Rancheria. No one brought up Rosalie's death during our dinner at The Depot; they were observing the Maidu custom that made it dangerous or at least bad manners to utter the names of the recently dead, however greatly they were missed. Art did say that he and his girls had gone up to Bald Rock to do "our own thing," a ceremony of their own, in Rosalie's honor.

For the first time in his life, Art wasn't making his living hauling logs, chopping brush, or some kind of manual labor. He'd been hired with money from California's Department of Water Resources as a liaison between local tribes and government officials in the complicated relicensing of Lake Oroville by the Federal Energy Regulatory Commission. The three rancherias were among the interested local parties who had to sign off on the relicensing—and to ensure access to the vast supply of water and electricity for the rest of California that the dam provided. As tireless a campaigner as ever, Art was pressing for major concessions in exchange for tribal approval, among them government money for an Oroville museum of Maidu culture. He also wanted land for burial of the Maidu skeletons he still intended to bring back from Sacramento. Lingering unease about the malevolence of the spirits of the dead meant that none of the rancherias wanted the bones buried too close on their own small, existing plots of land. He hoped to make an annual event of the fire in Ishi's honor at Table Mountain, and, deep down, he was still curious about whether or not Ishi had had a Maidu mother, or at least Maidu relatives of some sort. To this end, Art had met with the Berkeley museum director to explore the possibility now of a DNA analysis on the hairs encrusted in Ishi's death mask. If a match could be made with the blood of any Maidu around Oroville, it would be the best evidence yet for Art's theory that Ishi had been coming home when he left Deer Creek for Oroville and Maidu country. Art told me that he himself had not long before recreated Ishi's trek to Oroville by making the week-long journey on foot from Deer Creek. The trip was something of a spiritual pilgrimage for Art and not easy for a man who'd just turned sixty. Art's own journey to Ishi, clearly, hadn't ended with the discovery of the truth about his brain or his repatriation; his eyes lit up as he recalled his long hike from Deer Creek, slipping through barbed wire fences and around barking dogs. He wasn't about to let Ishi go anytime soon.

My father, Frances, and Gabriel returned to the Bay Area the next day, but I had one more stop to make. Ira Jacknis, the Berkeley museum specialist, had noted that eight of the more than two hundred songs Ishi performed for the anthropologists were listed as being in languages other than Yahi. Four were Atsugewi songs, and four more were Maidu; that Ishi knew these songs again suggested a more fluid, hybrid, and uncertain history of his band than allowed for by the fixed idea of the Yahi as a tribe unto itself cut off from any contact with other Indians or the modern world. The museum made cassettes for me of the eight non-Yahi songs, dubbed from the reel-to-reel tapes that had been dubbed in turn from the original wax cylinders. I'd played the four Maidu songs for Virgil Logan, an old man about Gus Martin's age and one of the last three surviving speakers of the dialect of Maidu spoken around Oroville. The recording was faint and scratchy and Virgil hard of hearing, but he made out enough to think that the song was not in his dialect of Maidu. He thought it was in the mountain Maidu of the high country.

I phoned a cousin of Bruce Steidl's, young mountain Maidu named Farrell Cunningham, to tell him about Ishi singing in mountain Maidu and to ask if there were still living speakers of the language who might be able to understand the words. Cunningham, who worked for a small social welfare agency in the tiny town of Taylorsville, said he'd get together a few local elders and we could listen to the songs together.

It was a spectacular drive up the gorge of the Feather River. Snow blanketed the high peaks, and the run-off was still pouring down over the cliffs above the highways in a cascade of loud, large waterfalls. The twisting, two-lane highway itself had been blasted through the rock in a brutal, superhuman feat of engineering with a long, Middle Earth–like tunnel somehow cut through the sheer granite at Grizzly Bear

Slide. Several old-fashioned industrial steel suspension bridges spanned the violent white waters of the swollen Feather River, and a railroad track ran next to the highway. This was the track for the line over to Nevada that was completed in 1911 a few months before Ishi appeared in Oroville.

All of a sudden, the highway emerged out of the gorge into a green mountain valley ringed by snow-capped peaks. This place, Indian Valley, was one of those out-of-the-way sites with a sparse population of ranchers, loggers, and impoverished retirees. As the name suggested, it also had a mountain Maidu reservation, the Greenville Rancheria, with eighty members. At the head of the valley, there was a cow pasture of a golf course with "GOLF" spelled in uneven white letters on the roof of the barn-like clubhouse; high-country alfalfa fields and meadow stretched out beyond the course. I took the fork down to Taylorsville, a town so small, at just over a hundred people, it didn't even have a gas station. The eerie quiet of the land and the big mountains was full of beauty.

Farrell Cunningham, a quiet young man, was waiting for me in his office with three older Indians, two women and a man. The man, Frank Mullin, wore a cap that said "Native Marine Veteran"; one of the women, Wilhelmina Ives, used a cane to support herself. After we exchanged greetings and some small talk, I asked if there had been stories about Ishi among the mountain Maidu. Not really, Frank replied, chuckling with an edge of derision at the idea of so many other Indians rushing to claim Ishi as a relative. "Our story was just that he was a wild Indian," Frank said. Of course, Frank added, leaving open the possibility that even his mountain Maidu had some sort of relationship to Ishi, and returning to the theme of Indians as all related in one way or another, "We're all cousins."

In the meantime, as Farrell's sister Trina went out to find a boom box, Tommy Merino, another short-haired older Indian man in a tractor cap, happened by. There wasn't much else to do on a weekday morning in Taylorsville, I suspected. "What's this pow-wow?" Merino joked, then stuck around to listen when Farrell explained that I'd brought a recording of Ishi singing in mountain Maidu.

When everything was ready, I snapped the cassette into the boom box. Although Ishi's voice was almost ghostlike through the heavy static and other background noise, you could still imagine him singing into the trumpet of the record player almost a century before. I looked around at the broad, brown, lined faces of Wilhelmina, John, Frank, Tommy, and

Hallie. Since the mountain Maidu language was a private code now that only they and a few others in the world could decipher any longer, I'd expected that they might take pleasure in hearing and perhaps being able to understand Ishi's songs across the decades. Yet as they listened the five elders were looking impassive, even a little grim, as if they were disturbed by what they were hearing.

There was a long silence once I turned off the tape. At last, Wilhelmina, the one with the cane, said: "He shouldn't have sung those songs." It turned out that she and the others had no objection to the two gambling songs, which they recognized as ones they'd heard as children. These were songs made up of vocables instead of real words, a kind of Indian scatting intended for the raucous fun of a gambling tournament. What bothered the five elders were the other two songs, which were doctoring songs. "He shouldn't have sung those songs," Wilhelmina repeated. "They were given by the spirit to the medicine man." Could they have been Ishi's own songs? If Ishi was a healer, as some believe, then he would have had his own songs. Wilhelmina didn't reply. It was as if she knew that the songs belonged not to Ishi but to some mountain Maidu doctor, and yet was reluctant to say so straight out. As I had already learned, contrary to the more benign New Age view of "Indian healing," the secret casting of jealous deadly spells was part of the doctoring of the old days. I could only guess that Wilhelmina didn't want to enter into the tense, even dangerous subject of the medicine men and their power for good and evil, especially with an outsider.

So much of the modern mythology about Ishi had cast him as a saintly healer bringing peace and wisdom. But these old mountain Maidu in this little mountain town conjured up another picture entirely—of an Ishi involved in matters he shouldn't have been, a betrayer of secrets. I recalled now a brief story about Ishi as a malevolent shaman expelled by his tribe. It had been told in 1997 to researcher Richard Burrill by a middle-aged Indian woman from an unidentified tribe:

*Ishi fishy. Ishi is a dead issue. All the people who really know the truth about Ishi are now dead. I have notes from what [an older woman] told me about Ishi; that Ishi stole food from his own people during hard times. He got chased out by his own people. Too bad. You could have interviewed Ishi's sister but she died just a couple years ago.*

There was also the tale of Red Wing and her sister, the two Indian girls found next to Mill Creek in the early 1880s, who'd described an evil old medicine man in the tribe, one who'd beaten Red Wing's baby to death with a stick. Even if that story were true, that malevolent shaman was too old to be Ishi, who would have been a young man at the time of the story. The tale of Ishi's expulsion from his tribe, however, presented once again a more dystopic picture of the Yahi and life among the last survivors, not to mention a considerably more negative image of Ishi himself. I had heard myself that some older Native Californians had resented the fuss made over Ishi. One woman I'd spoken with after the Dersch Meadow memorial told me that her elderly Karok grandmother used to call Ishi "the Last Retarded Indian in North America." As her grandmother saw it, the woman explained, Ishi was a reminder of the "primitive" and "backward" ways that she and her generation had been obliged and had sometimes chosen to leave behind.

None of the mountain Maidu seemed to be saying that Ishi was an evil figure. But they were curious about his motivation for singing the doctoring songs, with their dangerous power. "How long after that did he die?" Wilhelmina asked. It had been two years after singing the song that Ishi had passed away of tuberculosis, I said. Wilhelmina nodded as if she'd expected that answer. She said something in mountain Maidu to Farrell. "You know what that means?" she asked. Farrell paused and then replied, "Hunting for his own death." By Wilhelmina's guess, Ishi had sung a doctor's song on purpose, as a kind of suicide by a man weary of life.

Yet, as always with Ishi, one theory only gave rise to another. "Maybe," said Hallie, the other elderly woman, "he figured it didn't matter what he sang because everything was over, there wasn't anyone else left." When I asked Brian Bibby later about this, he related a story. An aging Pomo medicine man had sold his cocoon rattle to a museum. "But doesn't it have a lot of power?" a surprised anthropologist and friend of the man had asked. "Only if you know how to use it," he replied. A cocoon rattle is fashioned from the sacks of moth cocoons, filled with little pebbles, and then tied to a stick with deer sinew. It has long been used by Pomo shamans to cure the sick and sometimes to bewitch an enemy. As the old man indicated to the anthropologist, however, the rattle was an inanimate, ordinary object once it was "unplugged" from the culture and knowledge that went along with it—and thus could be shared or even sold. Hallie Mullin was suggesting that Ishi may likewise have felt that the doctor's songs he had heard in some roundhouse were no longer dangerous or powerful in San Francisco, so distant from their original context, and sung by Ishi alone and in another world.

I asked the others what they thought, but the conversation had petered out. Was there more to the story? Unshared secrets about the meaning of the songs? It would have been rude to press further. I stayed only a bit longer before heading back down the highway.

It was fitting that my search for Ishi should end without closing. I'd fantasized earlier that the songs in mountain Maidu might be some kind of message in a bottle from Ishi to the twenty-first century. Would some final truth at last be revealed? I should have known it wouldn't work that way at all. Even in remote Indian Valley among the last mountain Maidu who spoke their own language, there were still more mysteries, more theories, more guesswork. As much as we can know about the Wild Man of Oroville, no one will ever pin down his story for good. In this sense, at least, Ishi never has and never will quite be captured after all.

It was time for me to give up the chase. I didn't want to turn into a crazy old man muttering about Ishi trivia and the latest theories as I had sometimes almost believed might be my eventual fate. I knew that I would be drawn back to see Art, Bruce, Leslie, Brian, and other friends and to hike in Yahi country, but I was not going to bring my anthropologist's notebook to take down and think through every detail. It would be for other scholars and seekers to make their own discoveries about Ishi's life and, I hoped, learn as much as I had in the journey.

It was impossible to predict whether the legend of America's last "wild" Indian would be told and retold for yet another full century. Will the story of Ishi, his people, and other vanished tribes some day fade from memory like the canyon dusk yielding to moonless night? Another old Native Californian, the Kiliwa wise man and prophet Rufino Ochurte, refused to worry about that possibility:

> *The deeds of the people,*
> *the way they were,*
> *the people who spoke those things are heard no longer.*

*This will surely be the end of all that.*
*Those things that were said are no longer heard.*
*None have lasted beyond.*

*Those who continue beyond into the future*
*will surely say the same about me,*
*when I have gone off wearing my crest of stars.*

*Nevertheless,*
*what I've said and the way I have been*
*will remain in this land.*

# NOTES

PROLOGUE: TRAILS TO ISHI

12 One leaflet: the leaflet is reproduced in Philip J. Deloria, *Playing Indian* (New Haven: Yale University Press, 1988), p. 162.

14 Marvin Whitehorn: this is a pseudonym.

16 "There has been all the time": D. H. Lawrence, *Studies in Classic American Literature* (London: Martin Secker, 1924), p. 40.

16 less than one-fifth: there were 561 federally recognized tribes as of 2002, and 196 had casinos; there were approximately 300 unrecognized tribes, which have no legal status and thus cannot have casinos. The most up-to-date statistics are available from the Bureau of Indian Affairs.

18 "readier to make friends": Thomas Waterman, "The Yana Indians," *University of California Publications in American Archaeology and Ethnology* 13 (1918): 65.

18 *What Wild Indian?*: A photograph of the painting with a commentary by Tuttle is in Clifton Kroeber and Karl Kroeber, eds., *Ishi in Three Centuries* (Lincoln: University of Nebraska Press), pp. 394–395.

19 "It brought chills to me": Liz Dominguez, *News from Native California* 12 (1998): 17.

19 population of 242,000: this figure comes from the 1990 U.S. Census.

21 Grizzly Bear's Hiding Place: the Yahi hideout has also sometimes been referred to as "Bear's Hiding Place"; but the more precise translation is

"Grizzly Bear's Hiding Place," according to the linguist Leanne Hinton, personal communication, February 20, 2003. See also Richard Burrill, *Ishi Rediscovered* (Sacramento: The Anthro Company, 2001), p. 50.

## CHAPTER ONE: A "COMPROMISE BETWEEN SCIENCE AND SENTIMENT"

23 "Considerably emaciated Indian": the autopsy record is reproduced in full in Saxton T. Pope, "The Medical History of Ishi," *University of California Publications in American Archaeology and Ethnology* 13 (1920): 209.

23 for embalming: Pope, "The Medical History," p. 213.

24 "uncontaminated and uncivilized": Philip H. Kinsley, "Untainted Life Revealed by Aborigine," *San Francisco Examiner*, September 6, 1911.

24 "ISHI, LAST OF STONE AGE INDIANS": *San Francisco Chronicle*, March 26, 1916.

24 "like the dissipating mist": James J. Rawls, *Indians of California* (Norman: University of Oklahoma Press, 1984), an invaluable source about the treatment of California's Indians.

24 an estimated 150,000: Alberto L. Hurtado, *Indian Survival on the California Frontier* (New Haven and London: Yale University Press, 1988), p. 1.

24 as many as five hundred groups: William S. Simmons, "Indian Peoples of California," in Ramón Gutiérrez and Richard J. Orsi, eds., *Contested Eden: California Before the Gold* (Berkeley: University of California Press, 1998), p. 49.

24 Approximately ninety distinct languages: Herbert W. Luthin, "Notes on Native California Languages," in Herbert W. Luthin, ed., *Surviving Through the Days: A California Indian Reader* (Berkeley: University of California Press, 2002), p. 545. This great anthology is indispensable for anyone interested in Native California.

25 only about 20,000: Simmons, "Indian Peoples of California," p. 48.

25 "My grandpa say": Young in Malcolm Margolin, ed., *The Way We Lived: California Indian Stories, Songs, and Reminiscences* (Berkeley: Heyday Books, 1993), p. 159.

26 the "only man in America": this was the title of an article by Kroeber about Ishi, *San Francisco Call*, December 17, 1911

26 107 small Indian reservations: the number is for federally recognized Indian groups; the figure is still in flux and has grown in the last few years, with the government accepting the petitions for official status of several previously unrecognized groups.

26 50 different native languages: this is the approximate estimate of linguist Leanne Hinton in her superb book *Flutes of Fire* (Berkeley: Heyday Books, 1994), p. 27. Hinton also point out that there are speakers of Arapaho, Hopi, and more than twenty other Native American languages in California, migrants from other areas of the country.

26  "We're the landlords": Paul Chaat Smith and Robert Allen Warrior, *Like a Hurricane: The Indian Movement from Alcatraz to Wounded Knee* (New York: The New Press, 1996), p. 136.

26  occupation of Alcatraz Island: Chaat Smith and Allen Warrior, *Like a Hurricane*, is a valuable history of the occupation and the Indian movement of the 1960s and 1970s.

27  a healthy $1.5 billion dollars: John Stearns, "Gaming Referendum New Beginning for Indian Tribes," *Reno Gazette-Journal*, December 10, 2000. This article was the first in a well-researched special report about California's Indian casinos.

27  "We need to look": Mary Curtius, "Group Tries to Rebury Tribe's Last Survivor," *Los Angeles Times*, June 8, 1997.

28  "unclean": Alfred Kroeber, *Handbook of the Indians of California* (Washington: Government Printing Office, 1925), p. 300. Among the tribes that Kroeber noted viewed contact with a dead body as "unclean" were the Yurok and Shasta, both in northern California.

28  "Please shut down on it": the letter is reproduced in Robert F. Heizer and Theodora Kroeber, eds., *Ishi the Last Yahi: A Documentary History* (Berkeley: University of California Press, 1979), p. 240. This key source book has many primary materials related to Ishi and his life.

29  "compromise between science and sentiment": Theodora Kroeber, *Ishi in Two Worlds: A Biography of the Last Wild Indian in North America* (Berkeley: University of California Press, 1961), p. 235.

29  at least five million Indians: the question of the precontact population of the Americas—and just how many then perished in the course of European conquest—is notoriously controversial; the figure of five million for the decline of North America's native population from the landing of Columbus to about 1,800 is a very conservative estimate.

30  $5 apiece: Shasta City offered this price in 1855, Rawls, *Indians of California*, p. 185.

30  "war of extermination": Rawls, *Indians of California*, p. 180.

30  "human hunt": Laurence Hauptman, *Tribes and Tribulations: Misconceptions about American Indians and Their Histories* (Albuquerque: University of New Mexico Press), p. 10.

30  a good deal about him: the two most up-to-date works about Ishi's life are Clifton Kroeber and Karl Kroeber, eds., *Ishi in Three Centuries* and Burrill, *Ishi Rediscovered*.

30  "industrious, kindly, obliging": Heizer and Kroeber, *Ishi the Last Yahi*, p. 166.

30  "He liked everybody": Thomas Waterman, "The Yana Indians," p. 68.

30  "I loved the old Indian": Waterman to Herbert Moffit, Dean of the Medical School, March 29, 1916, Department of Anthropology Papers, Bancroft Library.

31 "You stay, I go": Saxton T. Pope, *Hunting with the Bow and Arrow* (London: G. P. Putnam's Sons, 1925), p. 13.

31 a pair of TV movies: The most interesting of the two TV movies is the 1992 HBO version, *Last of His Tribe*; Jed Riffe's *1992 Ishi the Last Yahi* is the best and most widely available documentary; among the plays are Henry Beissel, *Under Coyote's Eye* (Dunvegan, Ontario: Quadrant Editions, 1978) and Gerald Vizenor's provocative "Ishi and the Wood Ducks," in Gerald Vizenor, ed., *Native American Literature: A Brief Introduction* (New York: HarperCollins College Publishers, 1995).

## CHAPTER TWO: THE WILD MAN OF DEER CREEK

32 exactly 100 degrees: thanks to Jim Ashby of the Western Regional Climate Center for this information.

33 "Ad! There's a man": there are at least two different recorded versions of Adolph Kessler's reminiscence of that evening. One was taped by park ranger Steve Morehouse on July 18, 1973; the tape and a transcript are on file at Bancroft Library. Kessler also recounted the incident for a fourth grade class in Oroville sometime in 1974; a transcript of this tape appears in Burrill, *Ishi Rediscovered*. The two versions do not contradict one another but are slightly different; I draw from both in my quotations from Kessler here and below.

35 He'd just published his memoirs: Robert A. Anderson, *Fighting the Mill Creeks: Being a Personal Account of Campaigns Against Indians of the Northern Sierras* (Chico: Chico Record Press, 1909). This short book is reprinted in Heizer and Kroeber, *Ishi the Last Yahi*, pp. 32–59.

35 "I think it is extremely probable": *Chico Record*, September 13, 1911.

35 a second butcher, Bill Kroeger: this version of events appears in Burrill, *Ishi Rediscovered*, p. 219.

36 "He is a savage": *San Francisco Examiner*, August 31, 1911.

36 "Indians in Overalls": the title of a book by de Angulo (San Francisco: Turtle Island Foundation, 1973).

36 "rich mine to the ethnologist": Alfred Kroeber, "The Elusive Mill Creeks" (1911), in Heizer and Kroeber, *Ishi the Last Yahi*, pp. 45, 87.

36 Kroeber had hired Waterman: Alfred Kroeber, "Thomas Talbot Waterman," *American Anthropologist* 39 (1937): 527.

37 *si'win'i*: Waterman, "The Yana Indians," p. 64.

37 "It was a picnic": Kroeber, *Ishi in Two Worlds*, p. 8.

38 "very friendly terms": *Chico Daily Enterprise*, September 4, 1911.

38 "from where he had come": *Oroville Daily Register*, August 30, 1911.

38 "He has a yarn to tell": Kroeber, *Ishi in Two Worlds*, p. 8.

39 "He has committed no crime": *Chico Record*, August 30, 1911.

39    "the person of an elderly Yana Indian": the receipt is reproduced in Burrill, *Ishi Rediscovered*, p. 154.

39    they gave him a banana one afternoon: Raymond S. Richmond to Theodora Kroeber, March 1, 1962, Theodora Kroeber Papers, Bancroft Library. Richmond was a cub reporter for the *Oroville Daily Register* at the time of Ishi's capture.

40    "We can't just go on calling him": Heizer and Kroeber, *Ishi the Last Yahi*, p. 99.

40    "Is he": Kessler offered this explanation for Ishi's name in his 1973 interview with Steve Morehouse on file at the Bancroft Library, p. 12.

40    a "great chief" of his tribe: papers of John Peabody Harrington, microfilm on file with the Department of Linguistics, University of California at Berkeley, Part 2, frame 0559.

41    "*Hansi saltu*": Kroeber, *Ishi in Two Worlds*, p. 139.

41    "bewildered": Heizer and Kroeber, *Ishi the Last Yahi*, p. 111.

41    post-traumatic stress disorder: Nancy Scheper-Hughes, "Ishi's Brain, Ishi's Ashes: Anthropology and Genocide," *Anthropology Today* 17 (2001): 17.

41    "A poor old squaw": Robert E. Hackley, "An Encounter with the Deer Creek Indians in 1908," unpublished, undated manuscript on file in the Theodora Kroeber Papers, Bancroft Library.

42    *Rattlesnake will bite*: Brian Bibby, "The Meaning of Ishi: Reflections by a Native American Scholar," *The Museum of California*, Winter 1994, p. 14.

42    "[He] jumped to his feet": "Ishi Tells Tale of Wood Duck for Six Hours," *San Francisco Examiner*, September 7, 1911.

43    "White man up there?": Waterman, "The Yana Indians," p. 67.

43    incongruities like a gardener pulling weeds: *San Francisco Examiner*, September 6, 1911

43    "A certain member of my family": Waterman, "The Yana Indians," p. 67.

43    three hundred words: Pope, "The Medical History of Ishi," p. 188.

44    preferred cure for a cold: Pope, "The Medical History of Ishi," p. 181.

44    kept their hair long: Edward Sapir and Leslie Spier, "Notes on the Culture of the Yana," *Anthropological Records* 3 (1943): 254.

44    carving wood dolls: Marcella Healey to Theodora Kroeber, May 20, 1962, Theodora Kroeber Papers, Bancroft Library. Healey recalls how Ishi made the dolls for her and her friend Bess, and sometimes gave them piggyback rides down the street.

44    "in a fit of depression": Waterman, "The Yana Indians," p. 69.

45    "crude jargon": Edward Sapir, "Terms of Relationship and the Levirate," *American Anthropologist* 18 (1916): 329.

45    By later accounts: Kroeber, *Ishi in Two Worlds*, p. 152.

45    week-long tour down the coast: Carolyn Swift, "Ishi's Doctor Friend Began as PV Physician," *Santa Cruz Sentinel*, August 13, 2000.

45   "He quietly helped the nurses": Pope, "The Medical History of Ishi," p. 178.

46   "famous redskin": this line and the column with "survival of the fattest" come from a collection of unidentified, undated newspaper clips about Ishi, which I would be happy to send to any reader upon request (henceforth, author's collection).

46   "It's our responsibility": Alfred Kroeber to Edward Gifford, July 7, 1915, reproduced in Heizer and Kroeber, *Ishi the Last Yahi*, p. 237.

46   Kroeber and Pope corresponded: Saxton Pope to Alfred Kroeber, January 11, 1915, Alfred Kroeber Papers, Bancroft Library.

46   "I was with him at the time": Pope, *Hunting With the Bow and Arrow*, p. 12.

46   "He wants to make a cast": Edward Gifford to Alfred Kroeber, March 18, 1916, Department of Anthropology Papers, Bancroft Library.

46   remove a man's diseased kidney: Pope, "The Medical History of Ishi," p. 180.

47   "a revolting and a terrifying experience": Kroeber, *Ishi in Two Worlds*, p. 176.

47   "URGE COMPLETE ADHERENCE": Alfred Kroeber to Edward Gifford, March 24, 1916, Department of Anthropology Papers, Bancroft Library.

48   "We cremated": Saxton T. Pope, "Ishi, The Indian Archer," *Forest and Stream* 86 (May 5, 1916): p. 963.

48   "disposed of according to the customs": "Ishi's Funeral Held from U.C.," *San Francisco Examiner*, March 28, 1916.

48   "Modern Life": the story is one in a collection of unidentified, undated newspaper clips in the possession of the author, with copies available on request.

48   *"You did not fit"*: Ernest J. Hopkins, "To the Late Mr. Ishi," *The Bulletin*, April 1, 1916.


CHAPTER THREE: ISHI, ALFRED, AND THEODORA

49   I learn more about Alfred: the two most useful sources about Kroeber's life are Theodora Kroeber, *Alfred Kroeber: A Personal Configuration* (Berkeley: University of California Press, 1970), and Julian Steward, *Alfred Kroeber* (New York: Columbia University Press, 1973).

50   "sharp knife for dissecting": Kroeber, *Alfred Kroeber*, p. 15.

50   "guru": Alfred Kroeber, *The Nature of Culture* (Chicago: University of Chicago Press, 1952), p. 57.

50   Franz Boas: for more about Boas and his life, see George W. Stocking, *Race, Culture, and Evolution: Essays in the History of Anthropology* (New York: Free Press, 1968), and Lee D. Baker, *From Savage to Negro: Anthropology and the*

*Construction of Race, 1896–1954* (Berkeley: University of California Press, 1998).

51  front ranks of great reformers: I am grateful to Lee D. Baker on this point.

51  "handmaiden of colonialism": Lévi-Strauss offers his view of anthropology's relationship to colonialism in "Anthropology: Its achievements and future," *Current Anthropology* (1966): 124–127.

51  "the differences between the races": Franz Boas, *Anthropology and Modern Life* (New York: W. W. Norton and Company, 1928), p. 41.

52  "complacent yielding to prejudice": Franz Boas, *Race and Democratic Society* (New York: J. J. Augustin, 1945), p. 2.

52  His books were burned: "Environmentalist," *Time*, May 11, 1936, p. 42.

52  "Our ideas and conceptions": Boas, *Anthropology and Modern Life*, pp. 204, 205.

53  "Would like": Seton Heiatt to Alfred Kroeber, October 4, 1913, Department of Anthropology Papers, Bancroft Library.

53  "nearly a thousand": Alfred Kroeber to Seton Heiatt, October 7, 1913, Department of Anthropology Papers, Bancroft Library.

53  "anthropologist's anthropologist": Interview with Albert Elsasser, Berkeley, California, August 18, 1999. Elsasser recalled Julian Steward—Kroeber's student and later fellow anthropologist and biographer—using this phrase.

53  "I thought he was a genius": Interview with Elsasser, who later became Kroeber's colleague.

54  "absolute equality and identity": Alfred Kroeber, "Eighteen Professions," *American Anthropologist* 17 (1915): 285.

54  "Anthropologists now agree": Alfred Kroeber, *The Nature of Culture* (Chicago: University of Chicago Press), p. 139.

55  a famous 1917 essay: Alfred Kroeber, "The Superorganic," *American Anthropologist* 19 (1917): 162–213.

55  "no historical value": Kroeber, "Eighteen Professions," p. 284.

55  "shrinking to insignificance": Alfred Kroeber and Clyde Kluckhohn, "Culture: A critical review of concepts and definitions," *Papers of the Peabody Museum of Archaeology and Ethnology* (Cambridge: Harvard University Press, 1952), p. 9.

55  "no people" in it: Eric Wolf, "A. L. Kroeber," in Sydel Silverman, ed., *Totems and Teachers: Perspectives on the History of Anthropology* (New York: Columbia University Press, 1981), p. 57.

56  "My brothers and I": this appears in the author's note to Theodora Kroeber, *Ishi Last of His Tribe* (New York: Bantam Books, 1973), pp. 199, 200.

56  Theodora's family moved to Sacramento: the most useful sources about Theodora's life are her own *Alfred Kroeber*, especially pp. 121–142, and an

oral history, Theodora Kroeber, *Timeless Woman: Writer and Interpreter of the California Indian World* (Berkeley: Regional Oral History Office, Bancroft Library, 1982).

57   "of the fragility": Kroeber, *Alfred Kroeber*, p. 132.

57   "smoothly brushed back hair": Kroeber, *Alfred Kroeber*, p. 132.

57   "unboreability": Kroeber, *Timeless Woman*, p. 151.

57   "You ask me": Kroeber, *Alfred Kroeber*, p. 132.

58   "old enough to know better": this and the following quotation come from an interview with Theodora in *The Berkeley Review* 3 (1961): 18.

58   "hand-to-hand struggle": Theodora Kroeber, "About History," *Pacific Historical Review* 22 (1963): p. 1.

58   another version: Interview with Elsasser.

59   "I've read an average of 700": William Wallace Stahler Jr. to Theodora Kroeber, August 17, 1967, Theodora Kroeber Papers, Bancroft Library.

59   "I am a worse uh-uh-uher than most": Theodora Kroeber, "Retrospective, Oral History," July 16, 1977. This unpublished piece can be found with the transcript of Theodora Kroeber's oral history, *Timeless Woman*, on file at the Bancroft Library.

59   "to whom Ishi was Rousseau's unspoiled savage": Kroeber, *Ishi in Two Worlds*, p. 171.

59   "affectionate and uncorrupt": Kroeber, *Ishi in Two Worlds*, p. 230.

60   "intimate friends": Kroeber, *Ishi in Two Worlds*, p. 160.

60   "Dear Mrs. Kroeber": Constatine [*sic*] Panunzio to Theodora Kroeber, November 26, 1961, Theodora Kroeber Papers, Bancroft Library.

60   "We both feel deeply about the Indian": Gwen A. Jacobs to Theodora Kroeber, undated letter, Theodora Kroeber Papers, Bancroft Library.

61   "The peace of the bay tree": Gabriele S. Brown, *Ishi Country: The Shadows and the Light* (self-published, 1995).

61   "I hope I can get across": this letter of June 8, 1962 was sent by Barbara J. Daniel to the staff of what is today Berkeley's Phoebe Apperson Hearst Museum of Anthropology, and is on file in a small collection of clippings and letters related to Ishi at the museum.

61   "was too interested in the present:" Ursula K. Le Guin, lecture for the Centennial Lecture Series sponsored by the Department of Anthropology, University of California at Berkeley, November 16, 2001.

62   "I am grateful": Mel "Buddy" Smith to Richard Burrill, undated letter.

62   as historian James Clifford has noted: James Clifford, "Ishi's Story: History, Anthropology, and the Future of Native California," 35th Annual Faculty Research Lecture, University of California, Santa Cruz, October 26, 2000.

62   "torn, disordered, without design": Kroeber, *Alfred Kroeber*, p. 80.

63   "he felt Ishi trying to comfort him": Kroeber, *Alfred Kroeber*, p. 90.

63  "Anthropology is my religion": Kroeber, *Alfred Kroeber*, p. x.

63  "bone beads": from the frontispiece of Kroeber, *Ishi in Two Worlds*.


CHAPTER FOUR: ISHI'S ANCESTORS

65  "Praxitelean marble": Kroeber, *Alfred Kroeber*, p. 51.

65  the work of the archaeologists: Martin Baumhoff, "An Introduction to Yana Archaeology," *University of California Archaeological Survey* 40 (1957); Jerald Johnson, "Yana," in Robert Heizer, ed., *Handbook of North American Indians*, 8 (Washington: Smithsonian Institution Press, 1978), pp. 361–369); Jerald Johnson, "Ishi's Ancestors," unpublished manuscript, Department of Anthropology, California State University, Sacramento.

65  thirty Yahi skeletons, nine children among them: Martin Baumhoff, "Excavation of Teh-1 (Kingsley Cave)," *University of California Archaeological Survey* 30 (1955): 62–64.

66  "Indians of California may be compared to a species of monkey": Rawls, *Indians of California*, p. 26.

66  "moderate and equitable climate": Rawls, *Indians of California*, pp. 31–32.

66  managed the land in their own ways: M. Kat Anderson et al., " A World of Balance and Plenty: Land, Plants, Animals, and Humans in Pre-European California," in Gutiérrez and Orsi, *Contested Eden*, pp. 12–47.

66  "all the beauty of an English park": M. Kat Anderson et al., "A World of Balance and Plenty," p. 14.

67  average man about 5'4": Johnson, "Ishi's Ancestors," p. 25.

67  tribal creation story: Jeremiah Curtin, *Creation Myths of Primitive America in Relation to the Religious History and Mental Development of Mankind* (Boston: Little, Brown, 1898).

67  about 1,900 people: Johnson, "Yana," p. 363.

67  could watch the sky fill with geese: Johnson, "Ishi's Ancestors," p. 19.

68  a few hundred people at any one time: Johnson, "Yana," p. 362.

68  less than one person per square mile: Johnson, "Ishi's Ancestors," p. 11.

68  "ecological Indian": Shepherd Krech, *The Ecological Indian: Myth and History* (New York: W. W. Norton and Company, 1999).

68  broke off whole branches: Fergus Bordewich, *Killing the White Man's Indian: Reinventing Native Americans at the End of the Twentieth Century* (New York: Anchor Books, 1996), p. 212.

68  "blitzkrieg" hunters: Bordewich, *Killing the White Man's Indian*, p. 212. For the counter-case, Vine Deloria Jr., *Red Earth, Whites Lies: Native Americans and the Myth of Scientific Fact* (Golden, Colo.: Fulcrum, 1997).

68  the ancient Anasazi: Douglas Preston, "Cannibals of the Canyon," *New Yorker* 74 (November 30, 1998): 76–89.

68   "It's our land": Bordewich, *Killing the White Man's Indian*, p. 130.

69   *hanmawi madu*: this and the other places names appear in Baumhoff, "An Introduction to Yana Archaeology," pp. 49–54.

70   standard Yahi village feature: Jerald Johnson, personal communication, October 14, 2000.

71   bleached white clam shell beads: Baumhoff, "The Excavation of Teh-1 (Kingsley Cave)," p. 54.

71   Runners sometimes carried news: Stephen Powers, *California Indian Characteristics* (Berkeley: Friends of the Bancroft Library, 1975), p. 21.

71   of Maidu, Wintu, and Atsugewi: Alfred Kroeber, *Handbook of the Indians of California*, p. 345.

71   Relatively little modification: Johnson, "Ishi's Ancestors," p. 1.

71   "Towering reef of the human dawn": Pablo Neruda, *Canto General*, translated by Jack Schmitt (Berkeley: University of California Press, 1991), p. 34.

72   more than three hundred camps: Jerald Johnson, personal communication, October 14, 2000.

72   three of Ishi's stories: Herbert Luthin and Leanne Hinton have published their translation of "A Story of Lizard in Kroeber and Kroeber, *Ishi in Three Centuries*, pp. 293–317. Excerpts from their other translation work appear in their wonderful essay "The Days of a Life: What Ishi's Stories Can Tell Us About Ishi," in Kroeber and Kroeber, *Ishi in Three Centuries*, pp. 318–354.

72   a fourth story: Perry has published her translation of an excerpt from the Yahi creation myth in "When the World Was New: Ishi's Stories," Kroeber and Kroeber, *Ishi in Three Centuries*, pp. 275–292. She made this translation on her own after leaving Berkeley's Yahi Translation Project in the late 1980s.

72   traveled underground: I am indebted to Jean Perry for this information.

73   *Coyotes came up to meet them*: Perry, "When the World Was New," p. 286.

73   *Rabbit took the sun on his back*: Perry, p. 281.

74   more than one hundred Juaneños: Lisbeth Haas, *Conquest and Historical Identities in California, 1796–1936* (Berkeley: University of California Press, 1995).

75   as early as 1815: Dottie Smith, *The History of the Indians of Shasta County* (Redding, Calif.: CT Publishing Company, 1995), p. 1.

75   *saltu*: Sapir and Spier, "Notes on the Culture of the Yana," p. 243.

75   the folklore of today's living descendants of the Yurok: Jean Perry, personal communication, July 9, 2001.

76   joined by Peter Lassen: Gerald Richard Lathrop, "The Life of Peter Lassen," Master's Thesis, Department of History, California State University, Long Beach, 1974, p. 42.

76   "beautiful and clear": Lathrop, "The Life of Peter Lassen," p. 43.

77 "as wild as a deer": Rockwell D. Hunt, *John Bidwell: Prince of California Pioneers* (Caldwell, Idaho: The Caxton Printers, 1942), p. 140.

77 a prospector's diary: J. Goldsborough Bruff, *Gold Rush: The Journals, Drawings, and Other Papers of J. Goldsborough Bruff* (New York: Columbia University Press, 1949), p. 342.

77 *Malo, malo*: *Oroville Daily Register*, November 11, 1908. Waterman, "The Yana Indians," reported that the old woman spoke "a few words of broken Spanish," p. 6.

77 knew several Spanish words: Pope, "The Medical History of Ishi," p. 188.

77 linguists have discovered: William Bright, "Spanish Words in Patwin," *Romance Philology* 13 (1959): 164.

78 "from fifteen to twenty Mexicans and Indians:" Charles Lott, "As It Was in the Days of '49," *The Diggins* 43 (1999): 30.

79 nearly ten to one: Hurtado, *Indian Survival on the California Frontier*, p. 100.

## CHAPTER FIVE: OROVILLE

81 "some rain": Vine Deloria Jr., *Custer Died For Your Sins: An Indian Manifesto* (London: Macmillan, 1969), p. 78. For a discussion of Deloria's criticism and the larger relationship of anthropology and Native America, see Thomas Biolsi and Larry Zimmerman, eds., *Indians and Anthropologists: Vine Deloria Jr. and the Critique of Anthropology* (Tucson: University of Arizona Press, 1997).

81 "spyglass of anthropology": Zora Neale Hurston, *Mules and Men* (New York: HarperPerennial, 1990), p. 1.

82 Angle's Maidu: for more on the Concow Maidu, see Roland B. Dixon, "The Northern Maidu," *Bulletin of the American Museum of Natural History* 17 (1905): 119–346; Alfred Kroeber, *Handbook of the Indians of California*, chapters 27–29; Francis A. Riddell, "Maidu and Konkow," in Heizer, ed., *Handbook of North American Indians*.

82 In Maidu myth: Roland Dixon, "Maidu Myths," *Bulletin of the American Museum of Natural History* 17 (1902): 33–118.

83 "Little things precede great changes": Coyote Man, *The Destruction of the People* (Berkeley: Brother William Press, 1973), p. 42.

83 the single largest movement of people since the Crusades: the figures below come from Malcolm J. Rohbrough, *Days of Gold: The California Gold Rush and the American Nation* (Berkeley: University of California Press, 1997), p. 25.

83 "populous and swarming": Smith, *The History of the Indians of Shasta County*, p. 4.

84 "a naked, filthy, degraded set": Rawls, *Indians of California*, p. 198.

84  According to one Sacramento Valley newspaper: Rawls, *Indians of California*, p. 99.

84  one pioneer: Rawls, *Indians of California*, p. 98.

84  "succeeded in sending Master Indian": Smith, *The History of the Indians of Shasta County*, p. 51.

84  rounding up 461 Maidu Indians: Michele Shover, "John Bidwell's Role in the 1863 Indian Removal from Chico, Part 2, and Through 1866," *Dogtown Territorial Quarterly* 50 (2002): 46.

88  or "repatriation": two excellent overviews of this issue are David Hurst-Thomas, *Skull Wars: Kennewick Man, Archaeology, and the Battle for Native American Identity* (New York: Basic Books, 2000), and Devon A. Mihesuah, ed., *Repatriation Reader: Who Owns American Indian Remains?* (Lincoln: University of Nebraska Press, 2000).

88  Thomas Jefferson, an amateur archaeologist: Hurst-Thomas, *Skull Wars*, p. 33.

88  Harvard biologist Stephen Jay Gould: Stephen Jay Gould, *The Mismeasure of Man* (New York: W. W. Norton and Company, 1981).

88  "the American savage": Samuel Morton, *Crania Americana; or a Comparative View of the Skulls of Various Aboriginal Nations of North and South American* (Philadelphia: J. Dobson, 1839), p. 6.

89  "diligently collect": Hurst-Thomas, *Skull Wars*, p. 57.

89  corpses of six Pawnee Indians: Hurst-Thomas, *Skull Wars*, pp. 57–58.

89  about 18,000 Indian skeletons: Thomas Killion, personal communication, January 27, 1999.

89  "if the body is disturbed": James Riding In, "Repatriation: A Pawnee Perspective," in Devon Mihesuah, ed., *Repatriation Reader*, p. 109.

89  "grave robbers with a Ph.D.": "Walter Echo-Hawk Fights for His People's Right to Rest in Peace—Not in Museums," *People*, September 4, 1989, p. 43.

89  Archaeologists countered: James C. Chatters, *Ancient Encounters: Kennewick Man and the First Americans* (New York: Simon and Schuster, 2001).

91  "our Ishi": *Chico Daily Enterprise*, September 12, 1911, p. 3.

91  "They would sneak in our camps": Marie Potts, *The Northern Maidu* (Happy Camp, Calif.: Naturegraph Publishers, 1977), p. 7.

92  "sure onward march": Rawls, *Indians of California*, p. 173.

93  self-taught Oroville artist Frank Day: for more on Day, see Rebecca J. Dobkins, *Memory and Imagination: The Legacy of Maidu Indian Artist Frank Day* (Oakland, Calif.: Oakland Museum of California, 1997).

93  "abulia induced by starvation and grief": Kroeber, *Ishi in Two Worlds*, p. 117.

94  Saartije Bartman: Bernth Lindfors, ed., *Africans on Stage: Studies in Ethnological Show Business* (Bloomington: Indiana University Press, 1998). Bartman's remains were returned for reburial in her native South Africa in January 2000.

94 "El Negro": Rachel L. Swarns, "Africa Rejoices as a Wandering Soul Finds Rest," *The New York Times*, October 6, 2000, p. 4. The remains of "El Negro" were returned to Botswana in October 2000.

94 Joaquin Murieta: Richard Rodriguez has a wonderful essay about the myth of Murieta and his head in *Days of Obligation: An Argument with My Mexican Father* (New York: Viking, 1992), chapter 6.

94 Captain Jack: for more on Captain Jack and the Modoc rebellion, see Jeff C. Riddle, *The Indian History of the Modoc War* (San Jose, Calif.: Urion Press, 1988), and Arthur Quinn, *Hell with the Fire Out: A History of the Modoc War* (Boston: Faber and Faber, 1997).

95 cut off the heads from each corpse: Francis S. Landrum, *Guardhouse, Gallows, and Graves: The Trial and Execution of Indian Prisoners of the Modoc Indian War by the U.S. Army* (Klamath Falls, Ore.: Klamath County Museum, 1988), p. 78.

96 "would under no circumstances": this quotation comes from the report prepared by the Phoebe Apperson Hearst Museum of Anthropology, on file with the Butte County Native American Cultural Committee, September 1997.

96 "The brain of Ishi": Jay Stowsky to Arthur Angle, October 27, 1997. Reprinted in *Oroville Opportunity Bulletin* 2 (1999): 5.

## CHAPTER SIX: THE DESTRUCTION OF THE YAHI

99 "would eat and drink nothing": Kroeber, *Ishi in Two Worlds*, p. 4. Among many newspaper stories at the time describing the hungry Ishi as, in fact, eating heartily from the start after his capture, were the *Chico Record*, August 29, 1911.

99 "Dirsch": all of the many newspapers accounts of the murder reprinted in Smith, *History of the Indians of Shasta County*, record the proper spelling as "Dersch."

99 "packed full of snow": Kroeber, *Ishi in Two Worlds*, p. 107.

100 these revisionists: a good place to start with this literature is Patricia Nelson Limerick, *Something in the Soil: Legacies and Reckonings in the New West* (New York: W. W. Norton and Company, 2000).

100 "full vocabulary of terror": Nelson, *Something in the Soil*, p. 44.

100 though probably with a ghostwriter: Michele Shover, personal communication, October 21, 1999.

100 "like a lone, but trusty sentinel": Heizer and Kroeber, *Ishi the Last Yahi*, p. 20.

101 "dodging and ducking": Heizer and Kroeber, *Ishi the Last Yahi*, p. 51.

101 "We . . . [sent] a good many Indians": Heizer and Kroeber, *Ishi the Last Yahi*, p. 67.

101 "first act of injustice": Heizer and Kroeber, *Ishi the Last Yahi*, p. 59.

101    state militiamen: Steve Schoonover, "Kibbe's Campaign," *Dogtown Territorial Quarterly* 20 (1994): 10–49.

101    "It was decided": Heizer and Kroeber, *Ishi the Last Yahi*, p. 33.

101    "The Indians lived like Swine": Rawls, *Indians of California*, p. 193.

101    "like orang-outangs than human beings": Rawls, *Indians of California*, p. 198.

102    "ready and eager": Rawls, *Indians of California*, p. 70.

102    "very foot in the scale of humanity": Rawls, *Indians of California*, p. 186.

102    "miserable people": Rawls, *Indians of California*, p. 63.

102    "unbounded happiness and prosperity": Rawls, *Indians of California*, p. 79.

102    "filthy lot": Sim Moak, *The Last of the Mill Creeks and Early Life in Northern California* (Chico: self-published, 1923), reprinted in *The Mill Creeks, Volumes 1 and 2*, mimeo, on file in Northeastern California Collection, Merriam Library, California State University at Chico, p. 8.

102    "The squaws": Heizer and Kroeber, *Ishi the Last Yahi*, p. 40.

102    questions the large casualty numbers: Steve Schoonover, "The Three Knolls Massacre," *Dogtown Territorial Quarterly* 15 (1993): 15.

103    "some fun with the bears": Heizer and Kroeber, *Ishi the Last Yahi*, p. 51.

103    multiplied in Mexico's California: William Preston, *Serpent in the Garden: Environmental Change in Colonial California,"* in Gutiérrez and Orsi, *Contested Eden*, p. 279.

104    "general clean-up": Heizer and Kroeber, *Ishi the Last Yahi*, p. 50.

104    "procured arms and ammunition": Heizer and Kroeber, *Ishi the Last Yahi*, p. 39.

105    biography of Mary Hoag: Burrill, *Ishi Rediscovered*, pp. 16–17.

105    eventual murder of Hi Good: Bill Anderson, "The Murder of Hi Good," *Dogtown Territorial Quarterly* 12 (1992): 28–29.

106    "Goddam you American sonsabitches": Sim Moak, "Moak Letters Tell of Local Indian 'Troubles' in 1860," *Dogtown Territorial Quarterly* 23 (1995): 8–11.

106    "composed of renegades": U.S. Department of War, *The War of the Rebellion: A Compilation of the Official Records of the Union and Confederate Armies*, Series 1, Volume 50, Part 2 (Washington: U.S. Government Printing Office, 1897), p. 942.

106    a theory posed by Steven Shackley: M. Steven Shackley, "Ishi was Not Necessarily the Last Full-Blooded Yahi: Some Inferences for Hunter-Gatherer Style and Ethnicity," *Berkeley Archaeology* 3 (1996): 1–3. Shackley has published an expanded, revised version of this article as "The Stone Tool Technology of Ishi and the Yana of North Central California: Inferences for Hunter-Gatherer Cultural Identity in Historic California," *American Anthropologist* 102 (2001): 693–712.

107    taller and more thick-boned: Jerald Johnson, "Was Ishi Yahi?," unpub-

lished paper, Department of Anthropology, California State University at Sacramento.

108 no "justification": Rawls, *Indians of California*, p. 124.

108 single wealthiest and most powerful man: my information below about John Bidwell comes from a series of articles by Michele Shover, all published in the *Dogtown Territorial Quarterly*: "John Bidwell: Reluctant Indian Fighter," 36 (1998): 32–54; "John Bidwell and the Rancho Chico Indian Treaty of 1852," 42 (2000): 4–37; "John Bidwell: Civil War Politics and the Indian Crisis of 1862," 46 (2001): 4–38; "John Bidwell's Role in the 1863 Indian Removal from Chico," 49 (2002): 4–24; "John Bidwell's Role in the 1863 Indian Removal from Chico, Part 2," 50 (2002): 34–59.

108 "intuitive insight": Shover, "John Bidwell: Reluctant Indian Fighter, 1852–1856," p. 33.

108 "malicious and brutal vagabonds: Hurtado, *Indian Survival on the California Frontier*, p. 193.

109 "infuriated drunken men": Shover, "John Bidwell: Civil War Politics and the Indian Crisis of 1862," p. 11.

110 "It is becoming evident": Rawls, *Indians of California*, p. 181.

110 "*As soon as the sky*": the August 20, 1865, letter of Daniel Klauberg to the *Butte Union Record* is reprinted in Schoonover, "The Three Knolls Massacre," pp. 54–55.

111 "Ishi," Theodora wrote: Kroeber, *Ishi in Two Worlds*, p. 81.

111 "I saw one": Moak, "The Last of the Mill Creeks and Early Life in Northern California," in Heizer and Kroeber, *Ishi the Last Yahi*, p. 66.

112 "could not bear": Waterman, "The Yana Indians," p. 66.

112 Historian Sherburne Cook, *The Conflict Between the California Indian and White Civilization* (Berkeley: University of California Press), p. 352.

113 "It is a mercy": Rawls, *Indians of California*, p. 183.

113 25 cents for Indian scalps: Rawls, *Indians of California*, p. 185.

113 One resident of Shasta City: Rawls, *Indians of California*, p. 185.

113 state of California reimbursed Indian hunters: Rawls, *Indians of California*, p. 185.

114 "no more sickness": Jack Wilson in William S. E. Coleman, *Voices of Wounded Knee* (Lincoln: University of Nebraska Press, 2000), p. 9.

114 left out a bottle of poisoned whiskey: Burrill, *Ishi Rediscovered*, p. 119.

114 came upon four ragged Indians: Thomas Waterman, "The Yana Indians," p. 59.

114 wishful family legend: Burrill, *Ishi Rediscovered*, p. 109.

114 from various accounts: Dorothy Hill, "A Trip to Ishi's Cave," *Dogtown Territorial Quarterly* 12 (1992): 24–45.

115 "*No human eye ever beholds them*": Heizer and Kroeber, *Ishi the Last Yahi*, p. 74.

115 tried to surrender: Waterman, "The Yana Indians," p. 58.

116 *She took up her acorn mush*: Luthin and Hinton, "The Days of a Life," p. 338.

116 "clear reverence and love": Luthin and Hinton, "The Days of a Life," p. 351.

116 a few freed blacks: Michele Shover, *Blacks in Chico, 1860–1935: Climbing the Slippery Slope* (Chico: Association for Northern California Records and Research, 1991).

CHAPTER SEVEN: NICHE 601

120 "cemetery urn": Kroeber, *Ishi in Two Worlds*, p. 234.

121 "This is the sunniest room": Edward Gifford to Alfred Kroeber, September 30, 1915. Department of Anthropology Papers, Bancroft Library.

122 "All a same monkey-tee": Kroeber, *Ishi in Two Worlds*, p. 232. For more on Ishi's pidgin, see Victor Golla, "Ishi's Language," in Kroeber and Kroeber, *Ishi in Three Centuries*, pp. 208–225.

122 an editor from one of Chinatown's several newspapers: Kroeber, *Ishi in Two Worlds*, pp. 137–138.

122 "likeable old Indian": Heizer and Kroeber, *Ishi the Last Yahi*, p. 98.

122 a survey showed: Aleš Hrdlička, "Contribution to the Knowledge of Tuberculosis in the Indian," *Southern Workman* 37 (1908): 628.

123 "a museum is a hell of a place": Thomas Waterman to Alfred Kroeber, November 7, 1915, Alfred Kroeber Papers, Bancroft Library.

123 "killing Ishi": Thomas Waterman to Alfred Kroeber, March 25, 1916, Alfred Kroeber Papers, Bancroft Library.

123 food must have been the infection's source: Pope, "The Medical History of Ishi," p. 213.

123 "dropped somewhat in weight": Edward Gifford to Alfred Kroeber, July 16, 1915, Department of Anthropology Papers, Bancroft Library.

123 "How about his temperature?": Alfred Kroeber to Edward Gifford, August 10, 1915, Department of Anthropology Papers, Bancroft Library.

126 "He was energetic": Alfred Kroeber, "Saxton Temple Pope," *American Anthropologist* 29 (1927): 342.

126 "yellow in color": Pope, *Hunting with the Bow and Arrow*, p. 4.

126 "glory and romance": Pope, *Hunting with the Bow and Arrow*, p. 3.

126 in the Pacheco Pass: Swift, "Ishi's Doctor Friend Began as PV Physician."

126 "all savages": Saxton T. Pope, "Yahi Archery," *University of California Publications in American Archaeology and Ethnology* 13 (1918): 125.

127 "perfect": Pope, "Yahi Archery," p. 105.

127 "left us the heritage": Pope, *Hunting with the Bow and Arrow*, p. 13.

127 a recent feature: Mike Lapinski, "A Stone Age Dream," *Bowhunter*, October/November 1998, pp. 65–67.

127 "wonderful companion": Pope, "Anthropologic Regrets," unpublished, undated ms., 1925 or 1926, p. 2.

127 "loved to joke": Pope, "The Medical History of Ishi," p. 188.

127 real Indian name: Pope, "Anthropologic Regrets," p. 4.

127 "rare find": Pope, *Hunting with the Bow and Arrow*, p. 9.

128 "long journey to the land of the shadows": Pope, *Hunting with the Bow and Arrow*, p. 13.

129 "I assume": Robert Fishman to Nancy Rockafellar, March 19, 1998.

131 hundreds of the Bay Area's Ohlone Indians: Robert H. Jackson and Edward Castillo, *Indians, Franciscans, and Spanish Colonization: The Impact of the Mission System on California Indians* (Albuquerque: University of New Mexico Press, 1995), p. 41.

132 "representatives of all the tribes": Robert Heizer, ed., *"They Were Only Diggers": A Collection of Articles from California Newspapers, 1851–1866, on Indian and White Relations* (Ramona, Calif.: Ballena Press, 1974), p. 120.

132 "Hat Creek Liz": for more on this fascinating figure and a rare photograph of "Shavehead," see Michele Shover, "John Bidwell's Role in the 1863 Indian Removal from Chico," *Dogtown Territorial Quarterly* 49 (2002): 4–24.

133 Shavehead escaped: Smith, *The History of the Indians of Shasta County*, pp. 100, 136.

133 "who has doubtless murdered": Smith, *The History of the Indians of Shasta County*, pp. 135–36.


CHAPTER EIGHT: "DR. KROEBER'S PET BUFFALO"

135 "indolence" and "mental weakness": this and the following quotations come from Powers, *California Indian Characteristics*, pp. 1, 6, 8.

136 "a band of human monsters": *New Era* (Redding, California), March 9, 1991, p. 1.

136 "to pieces": Robert Spott and Alfred Kroeber, "Yurok Narratives," *University of California Publications American Archaeology and Ethnology* 35 (1942): v.

136 as the linguist John Peabody Harrington put it: Herbert Luthin, "A Brief History of Collection," in Luthin, *Surviving Through the Days*, p. 497.

137 "stone blind": Kroeber's description of his encounter with Inyo-kutavere is reprinted in Luthin, *Surviving Through the Days*, pp. 437–452.

137 "Jew Kroeber": for this and much more about Harrington, see Carobeth Laird, *Encounter with an Angry God* (Banning, Calif.: Malki Museum, 1975).

137 "DO YOU SUPPOSE": Jane McLaren Walsh, *John Peabody Harrington: The Man and His California Indian Fieldnotes* (Ramona, Calif.: Ballena Press, 1976).

138   Victor Golla recalls: personal communication, February 8, 2003.

138   Stonewall Jackson: Victor Golla, ed. *The Sapir-Kroeber Correspondence.* Survey of California and Other Indian Languages, University of California, Berkeley, Report 6, p. 71.

138   "take up one group by itself": Thomas Buckley, "'The Little History of Pitiful Events': The Epistemological and Moral Contexts of Kroeber's Californian Ethnology" in George W. Stocking, ed, *Volkgeist as Method and Ethic* (Madison: University of Wisconsin Press, 1996) p. 271.

139   "had never come among the survivors": Buckley, " 'The Little History of Pitiful Events,' " p. 284.

139   "heartless forces": Buckley, " 'The Little History of Pitiful Events,' " p. 275.

139   "bastard cultures": Buckley, " 'The Little History of Pitiful Events,' " p. 259.

139   "I have omitted": Kroeber, *Handbook of the Indians of California*, p. vi.

139   "the little history": Buckley, " 'The Little History of Pitiful Events,' " p. 257.

139   "barbarity and inhumanity": Buckley, " 'The Little History of Pitiful Events,' " p. 285.

140   "could not stand all of the tears": Buckley, " 'The Little History of Pitiful Events,' " p. 277.

140   "ice cold flame of the passion": Buckley, " 'The Little History of Pitiful Events,' " p. 261.

141   "taxidermy": Fatimah Tobing Rony, *The Third Eye: Race, Cinema, and Ethnographic Spectacle* (Durham: Duke University Press, 1996), p. 99.

141   "As to posterity:" Kroeber, *Alfred Kroeber*, p. 258.

142   "Even in the interior of Africa": "Lone Survivor of Southern Yahis Strange Man," *San Francisco Chronicle*, September 6, 1911.

142   "the greatest anthropological treasure": Heizer and Kroeber, *Ishi the Last Yahi*, p. 101.

143   "We have become": Alfred Kroeber to Phoebe A. Hearst, April 2, 1912, Department of Anthropology Papers, Bancroft Library.

143   "Dr. Kroeber's Pet Buffalo": undated, untitled newspaper clip, author's collection.

143   "In the wild, he was slender": untitled, unidentified newspaper clip, author's collection.

143   The Chamber of Commerce: unidentified newspaper clip, November 22, 1911, on file at the Phoebe Apperson Hearst Museum of anthropology.

144   "Ess he wild?": December 26, 1913, unidentified newspaper, author's collection.

144   "Slowly Ishi rose to his feet": Heizer and Kroeber, *Ishi the Last Yahi*, p. 110.

144   "not very comfortable": Esther Watson to Theodora Kroeber, undated, Theodora Kroeber Papers, Bancroft Library.

144   "did not even seem conscious of the stage or the players": Heizer and Kroeber, *Ishi the Last Yahi*, p. 111.

145   "I have knit a scarf": E. D. Van Denburgh to Alfred Kroeber, December 29, 1912, Department of Anthropology Papers, Bancroft Library.

145   "Whiskey-tee . . . die man": Pope, "The Medical History of Ishi," p. 186.

145   "redwoods and redskins": Robert Louis Stevenson, *The Silverado Squatters* (London: J. N. Dent, 1893), p. 229.

145   "imperialist nostalgia": Renato Rosaldo, *Culture and Truth: The Remaking of Social Analysis* (Boston: Beacon Press, 1989), p. 68.

146   "remnant of a Vanished": Louis Stellman, "Ishi, the Lonely," *Sunset*, January 1912, p. 107.

146   "You could hear a pin drop": *Daily Californian*, March 1, 1962.

146   "weaving/baskets": Christopher Shea, "The Return of Ishi's Brain," *Lingua Franca*, February 2000, p. 55.

146   a kind of mother lode: Heizer and Kroeber, *Ishi the Last Yahi*, pp. 87–103.

146   "intellectual property": Leanne Hinton, "Ishi's Brain," *News from Native California* 13 (1999): 5.

147   "The affair was more or less": Edward Gifford to Alfred Kroeber, June 25, 1915, Department of Anthropology Papers, Bancroft Library.

147   "Can you pick up": Alfred Kroeber to Edward Gifford, January 15, 1915, Department of Anthropology papers, Bancroft Library.

147   "He has been free": Alfred Kroeber to E. B. Merritt, June 4, 1914, Department of Anthropology Papers, Bancroft Library.

147   as Berkeley Native American Studies professor Gerald Vizenor: Vizenor led a successful campaign that led to the 1993 renaming of the courtyard at U. C. Berkeley's Dwinelle Hall after Ishi. See Gerald Vizenor and Gary Strankman, "The Power of Names," *News from Native California* 7 (1993): 38–41.

148   "I can recall him": Laura M. Schumacher to Theodora Kroeber, February 25, 1962, Theodora Kroeber Papers, Bancroft Library.

148   "knew a great deal": Jeremiah Curtin, *Memoirs of Jeremiah Curtin* (Evansville, Wisc.: The Antes Press, 1940), p. 339.

148   "phony white man": Kroeber, *Ishi in Two Worlds*, p. 149.

148   "on slight provocation": Heizer and Kroeber, *Ishi the Last Yahi*, p. 232.

149   "a very high grade of Indian": Pope, "The Medical History of Ishi," p. 189.

149   A gift to the oldest Blackfoot: Interview with Elsasser. Elsasser recalled having heard that Ishi was making a present of the bow and arrows in this picture—reproduced with the rest of the photographs in this book. This seems likely, since Ishi often made presents of his bows and arrows, including to the visiting U.S. Secretary of the Interior in 1913.

150   "The pygmy was not much taller": Phillips Verner Bradford and Harvey Blume, *Ota Benga: The Pygmy in the Zoo* (New York: Delta, 1992), p. 181.

150   "Occasionally," remembered Nels Nelson: Nels Nelson to Theodora Kroeber, November 1, 1962, Theodora Kroeber Papers, Bancroft Library.

150 "puny native civilization": Heizer and Kroeber, *Ishi the Last Yahi*, p. 123.

150 infuriated Kroeber: Heizer and Kroeber, *Ishi the Last Yahi*, p. 111.

151 No, Ishi said: Herzer and Kroeber, *Ishi the Last Yahi*, p. 99.

151 "interminable droning": "Ishi in Concert Attracts Crowds," *San Francisco Chronicle*, November 12, 1911.

152 "lengthy harangue": Heizer and Kroeber, *Ishi the Last Yahi*, p. 104.

152 "may have motivated": Ira Jacknis, "Yahi Culture in the Wax Museum: Ishi's Sound Recordings" in Kroeber and Kroeber, *Ishi in Three Centuries*, p. 243.

152 "You know he always": Juan Dolores to Alfred Kroeber, October 23, 1912, Department of Anthropology Papers, Bancroft Library.

## CHAPTER NINE: THE PAPER TRAIL

160 "white" with "good": Kroeber, *Ishi in Two Worlds*, p. 234. The original of the letter with "white" is Alfred Kroeber to Edward Gifford, March 24, 1916, Department of Anthropology Papers, Bancroft Library. Leanne Hinton deserves credit for pointing out Alfred Kroeber's original wording in her "Ishi's Brain," *News from Native California* 13 (1999): 5.

160 "I feel like congratulating": Thomas Waterman to Alfred Kroeber, March 25, 1916, Alfred Kroeber Papers, Bancroft Library.

160 "The most important New York news": Pliny Goddard to Alfred Kroeber, April 1, 1916, Department of Anthropology Papers, Bancroft Library.

161 "was too much the stuff of human agony": Kroeber, *Alfred Kroeber*, p. 93.

161 "Ishi and His Fellow Aborigines": notices of the 1917 lecture appear in two unidentified newspaper clippings, author's collection.

161 "Nothing gives me greater pleasure": a transcript of the interview is on file at the Phoebe A. Heart Museum of Anthropology.

161 "Indian-like reserve": Theodora Kroeber, "About History," p. 4.

161 "old sense of pain and hurt": Kroeber, *Alfred Kroeber*, p. 93.

161 "Traces of the storyteller": Walter Benjamin, *Illuminations* (New York: Schocken Books, 1969), p. 92.

162 Lakota Ghost Dance shirts: these shirts have by now been returned to the Lakota. Thomas Killion, personal conversation, November 15, 2002.

163 would insist to *Science News*: Bruce Bower, "Ishi's Long Road Home," *Science News* 157 (2000): 25.

## CHAPTER TEN: THE WET COLLECTION

167 "If a pattern": Andrew L. Slayman, "A Battle Over Bones," *Archaeology*, On-Line Edition 50 (1997): 4.

167 "the story of America": "Claims for Remains," *Nova Online*, November 2000.

167 "sold down the pike": Geoffrey Clark, NAGPRA, Science, and the Demon-Haunted World," *Skeptical Inquirer*, May/June 1999, pp. 44–46.

168 "I feel like an Indian [today]": "Return of Chief Big Foot's Lock of Hair to his People," *Weekend Edition*, National Public Radio, September 20, 2000.

168 "age of apology": Elazar Barkan, *The Guilt of Nations: Restitution and Negotiating Historical Injustices* (Baltimore: The Johns Hopkins University Press, 2000).

171 1,300 animal brains: for a complete inventory, see Aleš Hrdlička, "The Brain Collection of the U.S. National Museum of Science," 154 (1916): 739.

173 "quest to find the truth": "It's Time to Bring All of Ishi Home," *Oroville Opportunity Bulletin*, February 18, 1999.

CHAPTER ELEVEN: ALEŠ HRDLIČKA AND THE GREAT BRAIN HUNT

175 Hrdlička's biography: Frank Spencer, *Aleš Hrdlička, M.D., 1869–1943*, Ph.D. Dissertation, Department of Philosophy, University of Michigan, 1979; Ashley Montagu, "Aleš Hrdlička, 1869–1943," *American Anthropologist* 46 (1944): 113–117.

175 giggled "like a little boy": Montagu, "Aleš Hrdlička, 1869–1943," p. 116.

175 "first-class human and comparative brain collection": Aleš Hrdlička to Dr. Abbot, November 25, 1903, National Anthropological Archives.

178 brains of the dead leaders: Mark Lander, "German Radical's Daughter Seeks Brain Kept After Suicide," *The New York Times*, November 12, 2002.

178 Matthew Hale: *Weekend Edition*, National Public Radio, July 7, 1999.

178 "Eskimos, Lapps, Malays, Tartars": Gould, *The Mismeasure of Man*, p. 87.

179 "differentiate between the brain of a Swede and a Negro": Boas, *Anthropology and Modern Life*, p. 20.

179 Hrdlička sniffed: Spencer, *Aleš Hrdlička, M.D.*, p. 258.

179 "No definite relation between any": Barkan, "Mobilizing Scientists Against Nazi Racism," p. 188.

179 "assiduous excavation and collecting": Aleš Hrdlička, "Physical Anthropology: Its Scope and Aims; Its History and Present Status in America," *American Journal of Physical Anthropology* 1 (1903): 10.

179 the "reality of the human condition": Frank Spencer, *Aleš Hrdlička, M.D.*, p. 49.

179 "indescribable flush": Spencer, *Aleš Hrdlička, M.D.*, p. 27.

180 published a whole treatise: Aleš Hrdlička, "Brains and Brain Preservatives," *Proceedings of the U.S. National Museum* 30 (1906): 243–320.

180 His 1906 checklist: Aleš Hrdlička, "Brains and Brain Preservatives," p. 304.

180 "the dead man's daddy:" Stephen Loring and Miroslav Prokopec, "A Most

Peculiar Man: The Life and Times of Aleš Hrdlička," in Tamara L. Bray and Thomas W. Killion, eds, *Reckoning with the Dead: The Larsen Bay Repatriation and the Smithsonian Institution* (Washington: Smithsonian Institution Press, 1994), p. 26–40.

180 "Religious beliefs": Hrdlička, "Physical Anthropology," p. 11.

181 "child of the forest": Patricia Wickman, *Osceola's Legacy* (Tuscaloosa: University of Alabama Press, 1991), p. 151.

181 purchased skulls for five dollars: Hurst-Thomas, *Skull Wars*, p. 59.

181 direct and disturbing antecedent: Kenn Harper, *Give Me My Father's Body: The Life of Minik, The New York Eskimo* (Royalton, Vt.: Steerforth Press, 2000).

182 "appease" Minik: Harper, *Give Me My Father's Body*, p. 88.

182 "An Eskimo Brain": Aleš Hrdlička, "An Eskimo Brain," *American Anthropologist* 3 (1901): 454–500.

184 "spare parts": Nancy Scheper-Hughes, "Truth and Rumor on the Organ Trail," *Natural History*, October 1998, p. 56.

185 "What have you decided": Aleš Hrdlička to Alfred Kroeber, December 20, 1916, Department of Anthropology Papers, Bancroft Library.

185 the subsequent transfer of the others: these surviving brains were rehoused in 1981 and kept in tanks at the downtown Washington's National Museum of History before their final transfer in 1994 or 1995 to the Smithsonian's new facility in Suitland, Maryland.

185 a museum staffer wheeled out the great man's brain: I thank David Hunt and Margaret Dittemore, branch librarian at the John Wesley Powell Library of Anthropology, for helping to confirm the story of Powell's honorary "appearance" at the library dedication. Another researcher recalls that one Smithsonian physical anthropologist stored Powell's brain in his office around this time. If so, the brain may have been returned to that office following the dedication ceremony, and not back with the rest of Hrdlička's collection. Hrdlička's colleague Edward Spitzka conducted an examination of Powell's brain, sadly using it to advance the familiar spurious argument about the intelligence of men of the "advanced races." Spitzka's "A Study of the Brain of the late Major J. W. Powell" was published in *American Anthropologist* 5 (1903): 585–643. A photograph of Powell's brain in its specimen jar appears in Peter Miller's "John Wesley Powell: A Vision for the West," *National Geographic* 185 (1994): 86–115.

## CHAPTER TWELVE: THE MAIDU GO TO WASHINGTON

187 "Academic Detectives Find the Long-Lost Brain of Ishi": Mary Curtius, *Los Angeles Times*, February 20, 1999.

189 "There is NO": David Hunt to author, March 2, 1999.

193 "indignity": "Bring Ishi Back Home," *Contra Costa Times*, March 26, 1999.

197 "inverse magnitude": Peter Brown, *The Cult of Saints: Its Rise and Function in Late Christianity* (Chicago: University of Chicago Press, 1981), p. 70.

198 "known it was really Ishi": Julia Prodis Sulek, "Ishi's Final Journey," *San Jose Mercury News*, August 6, 2000.

199 "When and to whom": Jacqueline Trescott, "Museum, Tribe at Odds Over Brain," *Washington Post*, March 29, 1999.

199 "work within the law": Mary Curtius, "Museum Refuses to Give Ishi's Brain to Indians," *Los Angeles Times*, March 25, 1999.

199 "INDIANS ON WARPATH": *The Daily Telegraph*, March 30, 1999.

199 "SMITHSONIAN REJECTS ISHI CLAIM": *Sacramento Bee*, March 25, 1999.


CHAPTER THIRTEEN: LINES OF DESCENT

200 "I am both amazed and outraged": Cruz M. Bustamante, "Ishi's Proper Burial Overdue," *San Francisco Chronicle*, April 20, 1999.

201 "We are all mixed bloods now": Gerald Vizenor, personal communication, April 20, 1999.

201 1/2048 Indian: Circe Sturm, *Blood Politics: Race, Culture, and Identity in the Cherokee Nation of Oklahoma* (Berkeley: University of California Press, 2002), p. 88.

202 "migration from whiteness to redness": Circe Sturm, "Claiming Redness: The Racial and Cultural Politics of Becoming Cherokee," Fellowship Application to the National Humanities Center, Research Triangle Park, North Carolina, 2002, p. 2. Sturm is working on a new book that takes up the question of "race-shifting" in the Cherokee context.

203 "Reservation X": Gerald McMaster ed., *Reservation X: The Power of Place in Aboriginal Contemporary Art* (Seattle: University of Washington Press, 1992).

204 *"I'm half Indian"*: Margolin, *The Way We Lived*, p. 205.

204 "the last discovery of America": Richard Rodriguez, *Brown: The Last Discovery of the Americas* (New York: Viking, 2002).

206 Ishi's "Journey of the Dead": the translation appears in Perry, "When the World Was New," pp. 278–280.

207 "Captain Rose took": Robert Heizer, ed., *The Destruction of California Indians* (Santa Barbara, Calif.: Peregrine Smith, 1974), p. 252.

207 a pair of cowboys: Burrill, *Ishi Rediscovered*, p. 96.

207 *"She was married"*: Burrill, *Ishi Rediscovered*, p. 98.

208 "in 1883, or not many years after": Burrill, *Ishi Rediscovered*, p. 102.

209 *"there came floating"*: Heizer and Kroeber, *Ishi the Last Yahi*, p. 76.

210 "My new nickname": Robert Martin to the author, May 19, 1999.

211 Ishi had relatives among the Oroville Maidu: I found various conflicting bits of other information as to whether Ishi mentioned or felt a connection to the Oroville Maidu. On his trip back to Deer Creek in 1914, Ishi apparently explained to Mel Speegle, one of the Speegle boys who had a cabin

upstream from Grizzly Bear's Hiding Place, that his mother had sometimes taken him south in Maidu country, even stopping at a store with a kind white owner. "He indicated," Speegle recalled to an interviewer in 1971, "that when he was a papoose on his mother's back [on these trips], there was a good white man that would give him candy." According to Speegle, Ishi even drew a map in the sand to show their route across the creeks into the backcountry just north of Oroville. If this story hints at Ishi's close, possibly familial ties to the Oroville Maidu, Alfred Kroeber believed that Ishi had no connection at all to the area. "The Indians of Oroville he does not know," Kroeber wrote, adding that Ishi only described Oroville as *"p'ansasa,"* or "far." Speegle's story appears in Hill, "A Trip to Ishi's Cave," 44; the information from Kroeber comes from his notes from May 5, 1913, Alfred Kroeber Papers, Bancroft Library.

211   a "classic case": Mary Curtius, "Museum Refuses to Give Ishi's Brain to Indians," *Los Angeles Times*, March 25, 1999.

214   "distinguished beyond others": Heizer and Kroeber, *Ishi the Last Yahi*, p. 72.

214   "it shall be the privilege": Smith, *The History of the Indians of Shasta County*, p. 109.

214   "not only as inconsistent": Smith, *The History of the Indians of Shasta County*, p. 109.

215   "wild, mean bunch": Sapir and Spier, "Notes on the Culture of the Yana," p. 245.

215   closer relations with the Indians to their north: Jerald Johnson, personal communication, October 14, 2000.

215   "all California Native Americans": "Remains of Ishi Coming Home to California," press release, National Museum of Natural History, Smithsonian Institution, May 7, 1999.

215   longer report: "The Human Remains of Ishi, a Yahi-Yana Indian, in the National Museum of Natural History, Smithsonian Institution" prepared by Stuart Speaker, Repatriation Office, Department of Anthropology, National Museum of Natural History, April 21, 1999.

216   "close common identity: "Remains of Ishi Coming Home to California," press release, Smithsonian Institution.

216   "have identified living descendants": Jacqueline Trescott, "Tribe to Receive Brain," *Washington Post*, May 8, 1999.

217   "The California Indians have suffered greatly": Kimberly Bolander, "Ishi's Remains Return from the Smithsonian," *Record Searchlight*, May 11, 2000.


CHAPTER FOURTEEN: ANCESTRAL GATHERINGS

220   *"the next morning"*: Curtin, *Memoirs of Jeremiah Curtin*, p. 343.

220   *"a man from Lakeview"*: Curtin, *Memoirs of Jeremiah Curtin*, p. 368.

220  "The people of northern California": Curtin, *Memoirs of Jeremiah Curtin*, p. 373.

220  "what homeless condition": Curtin, *Memoirs of Jeremiah Curtin*, p. 415.

221  "a new hotel and casino complex: happily, an agreement was reached in 2003 between Rumsey leaders and the county government in which the Wintu agreed to scale back their building plans and made other concessions.

221  "for too long": James P. Sweeney, "Tribes, Governor Sign Compacts," Copley News Service, September 11, 1999, Lexis-Nexus Academic.

222  "war of extermination": Hurtado, *Indian Survival on the California Frontier*, p. 135.

222  "purchase said Alcatraz Island": Chaat and Warrior, *Like a Hurricane*, p. 28.

223  "We are the rightful": Troy R. Johnson, *The Occupation of Alcatraz Island: Indian Self-Determination and the Rise of Indian Activism* (Urbana: University of Illinois Press, 1996), p. 226.

224  "very numerous and very hostile": E. Steele to H. B. Sheldon, February 14, 1878, Bureau of Indian Affairs, Round Valley Agency Papers, National Archives, Pacific Region.

225  Many Yahi villages had a roundhouse: Jerald Johnson, personal communication, October 14, 2000.

225  "string of white shell disk beads": Luthin and Hinton, "The Days of Life," p. 341.

226  "We all belong to one family": Hazel W. Hertzberg, *The Search for an American Indian Identity: Modern Pan-Indian Movements* (Syracuse: Syracuse University Press, 1971), p. 7.

227  intertribal by definition: one useful study of the pow-wow phenomenon is Gloria Young's *Powwow Power: Perspectives on Historic and Contemporary Intertribalism*, Ph.D. dissertation, Department of Anthropology, Indiana University.

## CHAPTER FIFTEEN: GRIZZLY BEAR'S HIDING PLACE

232  According to Theodora Kroeber: Kroeber, *Ishi in Two Worlds*, p. 206.

232  a different version: Interview with Elsasser.

232  *Gunga Din* and *Mandalay*: Kroeber, *Ishi in Two Worlds*, p. 214.

233  "Have a good camp": Alfred Kroeber to Edward Gifford, May 19, 1914, Department of Anthropology Papers, Bancroft Library.

233  "Had him to his old houses": Alfred Kroeber to Edward Gifford, May 19, 1914, Department of Anthropology Papers, Bancroft Library.

233  "one of the most successful": Alfred Kroeber to C. M. Torrey, June 3, 1914, Department of Anthropology Papers, Bancroft Library. This letter has attached a press release Kroeber prepared for distribution about the expedition with Ishi.

233   "ISHI, INDIAN, IS EDUCATING COLLEGE PROFESSORS": *Sacramento Leader*, May 31, 1914.

233   "wild and bloodthirsty Mill Creek Indians": *Oroville Daily Register*, May 31, 1914, author's collection.

234   "Ladies and genelman": Alfred Kroeber to C. M. Torrey, June 3, 1914, Department of Anthropology Papers, Bancroft Library.

234   chronicled the search: Riffe has also produced a shorter film called *Bear's Hiding Place: Ishi's Last Refuge.*

237   Grizzly Bear "rose up": Perry, "When the World Was New," p. 282.

238   killed and roasted a rattlesnake: Saxton Pope Jr., untitled, undated recollection, Theodora Kroeber Papers, Bancroft Library.

239   "curious figure": these and the following quotations come from Hackley, "An Encounter with the Deer Creek Indians in 1908."

239   an old man, Ishi's uncle, helped along: Waterman, "The Yana Indians," p. 61. One story, probably apocryphal, has it that Ishi let fly an arrow from his hiding place in the brush in an effort to turn back the intruders. Yet no mention is made of any the newspaper accounts of the time of an arrow being shot. And Robert Hackley, the surveyor, also wrote that he "was not aware that the Indians shot any arrows at any of us at any time."

239   Ishi told Saxton Pope: Pope, "Anthropologic Regrets," p. 4.

240   "Here we are papoose": Burrill, *Ishi Rediscovered*, p. 72.

240   "Her face was dry and yellow": "Camp of Wild Indians Reported Found in Deer Creek Canyon," *Chico Record*, November 10, 1908.

240   "INDIANS LIVE IN WILD STATE": Burrill, *Ishi Rediscovered*, p. 71.

240   We have no reliable record: There is an account of a supposedly friendly interaction between Ishi and Jack Apperson in a book by Apperson's daughter-in-law Eve Marie Apperson, *"We Knew Ishi"* (Red Bluff, Calif.: Walker Lithograph, 1971). Yet Eve Marie-Apperson wanted to show her family's role in the Ishi story in the most favorable light possible, and she herself only knew the story of Ishi's reencounter with her father-in-law from him and other relatives.

242   "Friends who know something": undated, untitled clip, author's collection.

242   "The spirit of the past": This and the following quotations from Pope, "Anthropologic Regrets."

244   knives, forks, a U.S. Mail bag: Burrill, *Ishi Rediscovered*, p. 46.

245   "his whole life": Heizer and Kroeber, *Ishi the Last Yahi*, p. 2.

245   "patched with bits of hide": Kroeber, *Ishi in Two Worlds*, p. 109.

CHAPTER SIXTEEN: THE SACRED FIRE

249   "The way we see it": Bower, "Ishi's Long Road Home," p. 25.

252   One emeritus chancellor: "Ishi's Cave—A Sutro Legend," *UCSF Journal* 7 (1983): 1.

252 Historian Philip Deloria: Philip J. Deloria, *Playing Indian* (New Haven: Yale University Press, 1998).

253 "savage freedom": Deloria, *Playing Indian*, p. 3.

258 the annual bonfire: for more on the custom, see Dixon, *The Northern Maidu*, although Dixon never actually witnessed one himself.

258 "with evident delight": Pope, "The Medical History of Ishi," p. 185.

260 Maidu legend still has it: Bruce Steidl, personal communication, November 5, 2000.

260 According to one of Ishi's songs: Perry, "When the World Was New," p. 275–276.

263 according to Theodora Kroeber: Kroeber, *Ishi in Two Worlds*, p. 139.

263 "Professor Watterman [*sic*]": Pope, "Ishi, the Indian Archer," p. 86.

264 "Indians from California": "84 Years After Death, 'Ishi' Awaits Soul's Release," *Chicago Tribune*, August 8, 2000.

264 "The final remains": Andrew Curry, "The Last of the Yahi," *U.S. News and World Report*, August 21, 2000, p. 56.

266 "flexed, stiff, and cold": Perry, "When the World Was New," p. 278.

266 archaeologist Jerald Johnson: Johnson, "Ishi's Ancestors," p. 28.

## CHAPTER SEVENTEEN: DERSCH MEADOW

268 one story has it: John Furry, personal communication, February 29, 2000. Various sources suggest that two Indians were indeed lynched in 1863 near the location of the Salem Street School House, among them Thankful Carson; see Heizer and Kroeber, *Ishi the Last Yahi*, p. 32. The identification of the present-day tree on Salem Street as the spot where the killings took place is far less certain. Chris Boza, a city forester, believes the valley oaks around Salem Street are no more than 150 years old, and thus in 1863 would have been far too small, if even planted, for any one of them to have been the lynching tree.

268 "Through those shadowed": Kroeber, *Alfred Kroeber*, p. 286.

269 in a poem she wrote: the poem is titled "A Poem for the Living" and is reproduced here by permission of Jed Riffe and Associates on behalf of the John H. Quinn Trust of 1992.

269 "Howsoever one touches": Heizer and Kroeber, *Ishi the Last Yahi*, frontispiece.

271 "predations of anthropologists": Alexander Cockburn, "What Happens When Genocide Poses as Science," *Los Angeles Times*, October 8, 2000. For one critical view of Kroeber for his handling of Ishi's remains, see Jonathan Marks, "They Found Ishi's Brain!," *Anthropology Newsletter*, April 1999, p. 22.

271 "exploitation and betrayal": Nancy Scheper-Hughes, Laurie Wilkie, and Kent Lightfoot, Memo, March 2, Department of Anthropology, University of California at Berkeley.

271 "untrue and unfair": George Foster, "Re: March 17, 1999 'Statement on Ishi's Brain,'" March 24, 1999.

271 "strange living survival": Heizer and Kroeber, *Ishi the Last Yahi*, p. 116.

273 uncertain, liminal: I am borrowing from Iztván Rév, "Parallel Autopsies," *Representations* 49 (1995): 30.

274 "cunning of recognition": Elizabeth Povinelli, *The Cunning of Recognition: Indigenous Alterities and the Making of Australian Multiculturalism* (Durham: Duke University Press, 2000).

277 "average American": William Carlos Williams, *In the American Grain* (New York: New Directions, 1956), p. 128.

277 "to go out and lift": Williams, *In the American Grain*, p. 74.

279 "beyond tragedy": Karl Kroeber, "The Humanity of Ishi," paper presented at "Who Owns the Body?: An International Conference," September 22, 2000, University of California at Berkeley. A revised version of this presentation appears in Kroeber and Kroeber, *Ishi in Three Centuries*, pp. 132–145.

279 *"Dear Mrs. Newell"*: Alfred Kroeber to Mrs. Newell, November 9, 1912, Department of Anthropology Papers, Bancroft Library.

279 "Ishi Obscura": this is the title of an essay by Vizenor in his *Manifest Manners: Postindian Warriors of Survivance* (Hanover: Wesleyan University Press).

## EPILOGUE: VERA'S PARTY

287 "well-marked with tracks of oxen": Bruff, *Gold Rush*, p. 218.

288 "low, square-built Indian": Bruff, *Gold Rush*, p. 312.

289 "island of California": Garcí Rodriguez Ordóñez de Montalvo, "The Queen of California," in James Hicks et al., eds., *The Literature of California: Writings from the Golden State* (Berkeley: University of California Press, 2000), p. 76.

289 one early-twentieth-century ethnographer: Edwin Meyer Loeb, *Pomo Folkways* (Berkeley: University of California Press, 1926).

290 millions of acres: Kenneth Howe, "State Plague of Thistles," *San Francisco Chronicle*, January 19, 1999.

290 the site of the village of Three Knolls: Steve Schoonover, "The Three Knolls Massacre."

292 a short book about Vera's adventures: Michele Shover and Antone Grieco, *Vera Clark McKeen of Yankee Hill: Memoir of a Maidu Matriarch* (Chico, Calif.: self-published, 1998).

293 found a cave: John Furry, personal communication, February 29, 2000.

300 told in 1997 to researcher Richard Burrill: Burrill, *Ishi Rediscovered*, p. 126. Burrill is leading an initiative for a U.S. postage stamp in Ishi's honor. He

also runs an annual seminar about Ishi, with visits to Oroville and various sites in Yahi country; Burrill can be contacted at P.O. Box 524, Chester, CA 96020.

302   *The deeds of the people:* Luthin, *Surviving Through the Days*, p. 494. Mauricio Mixco recorded and translated Ochurte's words.

# ACKNOWLEDGMENTS

I would never have completed this book without the help of many people along the way. My gratitude goes to the Butte County Native American Cultural Committee, Redding Rancheria, and Pit River Tribe. I want to express special thanks to Lorraine Frazier, Arnold Gemmill, Sharon Guzman-Mix, Joe Marine, Gus Martin, Bruce Steidl, and Willard Rhoades. And of course, I owe a special debt to Art Angle and Mickey Gemmill, a pair of men I admire very much.

I am very grateful to Nancy Rockafellar and Frank Norick for sharing valuable information with me. Also generous with their assistance were Alan Archuleta, Philippe Bourgois, Chris Boza, Grace Buzaljko, Suzanne Calpestri, Farrell Cunningham, Nancy Distefanis, Rebecca Dobkins, Michael Dugas, John Furry, Ron Grunwald, Merel Harmel, Ira Jacknis, John Jackson Jr., William Jones, Rosemary Joyce, Daniel Kaplan, Sara Kashing, David Keightley, Valerie Lambert, Kent Lightfoot, Herbert Luthin, Malcolm Margolin, Vera Clark McKeen, Rich Mertes, Karen Mudar, Douglas Owsley, Kathy Rudy, Steve Schoonover, Jill Shiflett, William Shipley, William Simmons, Clay Slate, Stuart Speaker, Leslie Steidl, Greg Wray, Sylvia Yanagisako, and the late Albert Elsasser.

I was lucky to have the guidance of Lauren Lassleben at Berkeley's Bancroft Library. Thomas Killion and David Hunt were a huge help at the Smithsonian Institution. Lee Baker, George Stocking, and Alan Goodman counseled me expertly about the history of anthropology. Nancy Scheper-Hughes and Michael Hughes have inspired me with their intelligence and commitment to social justice. Gerald Vizenor, a key thinker about Native American politics and culture, took time to share his astute insights about Ishi and his meaning. I am not sure if Clifton Kroeber and Karl Kroeber will agree with everything I have written in this book, but I thank these two fine men and distinguished scholars for sharing some of their family lore with me. I cannot begin to express my gratitude to Brian Libby, Leanne Hinton, and Jean Perry for teaching us so much about Native California in their pathbreaking work. They went far beyond the call of duty in answering my questions about the life of Ishi and his people. Jerry Johnson and Jim Johnston, who have led the way in Yahi archaeology, were also enormously generous with their expertise. It has been a special privilege to have enjoyed the advice and support of Jed Riffe, the extraordinary filmmaker. Donald Moore, a great friend and anthropologist, has always been there for me.

Several other West Coast friends offered comments about the manuscript. I had precious encouragement from James Clifford, a dazzling and humane scholar whose writings have deeply influenced me ever since my graduate school years. Michele Shover was also a trusted reader and advisor. Her scholarship sets the standard for the nineteenth-century history of northern California. Richard Burrill, the author of an important recent study on Ishi, and Victor Golla, a leading expert in Native Californian languages, generously reviewed the entire manuscript. I am very grateful for the many valuable corrections and suggestions they provided. All final responsibility for *Ishi's Brain* lies with me, of course, and not with any of those who read the manuscript in any earlier version.

Gail Ross was a delightful, gung-ho agent. Both Gail and her wonderful assistant, Jenna Land, gave me precious feedback about the project. So did my editor at Norton, Angela von der Lippe, who gave superb suggestions for improving the book. Alessandra Bastagli was also a pleasure to work with at Norton. Howard Yoon helped me to sharpen my plans at an early stage. Michele Morgan tracked down missing photographs and references. And Victoria Nelson, a magnificent author and critic, rescued me from the despair of writer's block with her masterful editing. Thank you, Vicki!

A Duke Endowment Fellowship from the National Humanities

Center enabled me to complete a draft of the manuscript. Jean Houston and Eliza Robertson, the librarians, were always efficient and helpful. Tista Bagchi, Winifred Brennis, Deborah Cohen, Sean McCann, and Gunther Peck took time to read chapters, or provided suggestions and bibiliography. My great friends Ralph Litzinger and Catherine Lutz were also early readers of the manuscript, and stalwart enthusiasts.

I am blessed beyond measure to count Anne Allison and Charles Piot as friends and colleagues. My gratitude and love for my parents, Frances and Randolph Starn, is also boundless. My children, Frances and Raymond, pulled me through with their beautiful and rambunctious love of life. And without Robin, of course, I'd be nothing at all.

# INDEX